To my dear friend, Nancy Schumacher. I hope that she will find book of interest.
Love
Bill Fields

To and Through the
Texas Medical Center

A Personal Odyssey

By William S. Fields, M.D.

EAKIN PRESS   Austin, Texas

FIRST EDITION

Copyright © 1995
By William S. Fields, M.D.

Published in the United States of America
By Eakin Press
An Imprint of Sunbelt Media, Inc.
P.O. Drawer 90159   ★   Austin, TX 78709-0159

ALL RIGHTS RESERVED. No part of this book may be reproduced in any form without written permission from the publisher, except for brief passages included in a review appearing in a newspaper or magazine.

2   3   4   5   6   7   8   9

ISBN 1-57168-052-7

Library of Congress Cataloging-in-Publication Data

Fields, William S. (William Straus), 1913–
  To and through the Texas Medical Center: A Personal Odyssey / by William S. Fields.
    p.   cm.
  ISBN 1-57168-052-7
  1. Fields, William S. (William Straus), 1913–. 2. Neurologists — Texas — Houston — Biography. 3. Texas Medical Center. 4. Fields, William S. (William Straus), 1913–. 5. Texas Medical Center. I. Title.
  [DNLM: 1. Physicians — United States — personal narratives. 2. Neurology — personal narratives. 3. Academic Medical Centers — history — Texas — personal narratives. WZ 100 F463 1995]
  RC339.52.F54A3   1995
  616.8'092--dc20
  [B]
  DNLM/DLC
  for Library of Congress   95-31786
                                                                      CIP

*To my dear wife, Alma,
for her support in this
and many other ventures.*

Contents

Preface		vii
1	The Early Years	1
2	Medical Education and Training	21
3	The War Years (1941–1946)	44
4	Neurology Training and First Full-time Job	72
5	Baylor College of Medicine: My Early Days (1949–1957)	86
6	Establishing a Neurology Department (1958–1965)	106
7	Texas Medical Center: The Beginning	122
8	Texas Medical Center: Growing Pains	142
9	Harris County Medical Society and Houston Academy of Medicine	173
10	Houston Neurological Society and Neurological Symposia	194
11	Participation in Community Affairs	208
12	To Dallas and Back	224
13	The University of Texas Medical School at Houston: Early Development	246
14	The University of Texas Medical School at Houston: Toward Maturity	265
15	Travel to the Soviet Union (1971–1972)	281
16	Medico-legal Matters	309
17	M. D. Anderson Cancer Center and Retirement (Perhaps)	320
Index		345

Preface

The reason I have committed to paper the thoughts and reminiscences which follow is that I have had the great and good fortune to have seen the growth of the Texas Medical Center in Houston from a somewhat unusual perspective almost from its inception. It has been my privilege to have served in a senior capacity in each of the major teaching institutions in the center and on the staffs of virtually all of the health care facilities.

It was never my objective to produce an autobiography which would be solely a justification of what and where I am today. I am neither trying to settle old scores or to create new ones. I have tried to the best of my ability to provide some perspective of what has molded my career in medicine and me as a person, as well as what led to my connection with the Texas Medical Center.

Medicine has been and still is my vocation. I will be forever grateful for the opportunity which has come my way to contribute my small measure to progress in neurology, my chosen field.

My career in medicine has been the product of the advice and assistance which I have received along the way from innumerable persons in many walks of life. Many of them are mentioned in this book, others are not, but they all have played an important role and I would be remiss if I did not recognize their contributions. It is fair to say that what I may have achieved could not have been accomplished without them.

Chapter 1

The Early Years

I ENTERED THIS WORLD on August 18, 1913, at the Union Memorial Hospital in Baltimore, Maryland. My mother, Lenore Gutmann Straus, was a native Baltimorean whose maternal ancestors had lived in that city for nearly two centuries.

My father, Arthur Mortimer Fields, was born in Springfield, Massachusetts, but I know little about his family. Although I came to know his father, Henry Fields, quite well, I have no idea where he was born, but I do recall that he had lived for many years in Buffalo, New York. Pauline was my paternal grandmother's first name, but her maiden name is unknown to me. I was about ten years old when I saw them for the first time in their home in Belmont, Massachusetts, a suburb of Boston. My parents had sent my younger brother Arthur and me to spend a week with them.

One memorable event of that week occurred when a boy in the neighborhood brought over a crystal radio, the first I had ever seen. We played with the galena crystal until we got a clear signal and then stayed glued to the set, listening to the world championship prize fight between the champion, Jack Dempsey, and the French challenger, Georges Carpentier. As far as I know, that was the first heavyweight championship fight to be broadcast. Dempsey retained his title with a victory over the surprisingly durable "Gentleman Georges."

My father had three younger sisters and a brother. The eldest sister, Janet, was director of social work at Hull House in Chicago before her marriage and for a while thereafter. His second sister, Anna, married Col. Luke Peck, who served in the army during World War I. In 1926 he went to work for the Veterans Administration; his last job before retiring was as director of the Veterans Administration Hospital in Brockton, Massachusetts. The third sister, Esther, married a man named Franklin Gould but later divorced him. She remained in Boston as part owner of an automobile finance company, and I visited her there while I was at Harvard College and during my four years in medical school. She died in 1976, in her eighties. My father's brother Ben was only six years older than I; consequently we shared many activities and interests. He taught me to drive in his Model-A Ford. In those days a learner's license was superfluous on the country roads west of Boston. Ben died of a malignant brain tumor in 1965, at age fifty-eight.

My father, the eldest child, born January 24, 1890, graduated from Rindge Technical High School in Cambridge, Massachusetts, entered Harvard College at seventeen, and graduated with a degree in industrial engineering in 1911. In those days industrial engineering was a new field, whose practitioners served principally as consultants to large companies for time and motion studies. My father did this kind of work until the early 1930s. He was one of the people in this field who became known as "efficiency experts."

My paternal grandfather, who graduated from high school but never attended college, had established his own small and successful business, I was told. I have no idea where it was; by the time I got to know him, he had retired. Both my paternal grandparents died soon after I entered Harvard Medical School in 1934. My grandfather, otherwise a reasonable man, at least in my opinion, was a great fan of Gerald L. K. Smith, who, along with Father Coughlin, was one of the far right-wing zealots of the 1930s. Grandpa used to hang on to every word they uttered over the radio. Those hatemongers made a big splash during the Great Depression and then disappeared along with the leaders of the America First movement.

I know much more about my mother's family because they lived in my hometown, Baltimore. My mother was the eldest of her generation and seven years older than my father. All but one of her seven brothers and sisters, and many of her cousins, continued to live in the city and its environs.

The Early Years

The name of my great, great-grandmother, Caroline Elder Kayton, was adapted from Käthen, the family name of her husband before he left Prussia in 1780. His brother, who also immigrated to America, changed the name to Caton. He and his family were the original settlers of Catonsville, Maryland.

Caroline Elder's mother was a Robinson. William, the first of the Robinsons, came to Maryland in 1697. I have the original charter for the land grant William received on the Patapsco River just southeast of Baltimore. Signed by Charles Calvert, Lord and Proprietor of the Province of Maryland and Avalon (Lord Baltimore), it reads:

> Charles, Absolute Lord and Propy of the province of Maryland and Avalon, Lord Baron of Baltimore. To all yee and to whom these presents shall come Greeting in our Lord God Everlasting know yee that for and in consideration that William Robinson of Baltimore County in our said Province of Maryland hath due unto him Ten acres of Land within our said Province by Virtue of a warrant for the quantity granted him the 28th day of April Anno Domini 1724 as appears in our Land Office and upon such Conditions and Termes as are Specified in our Conditions of Plantations of our said Province bearing date of the fifth day of April Sixteen Hundred and Eighty-four and remaining upon record in our said Province Together with such altorations as in them is made by our instructions bearing Date at Land on the twelfth day of September Seventeen hundred and Twelve and registred in our Land Office of our said province.
>
> We doe therefore hereby Grant unto him the said William Robinson all that Tract or field of Land called Robinson Addition Lying in the County aforesaid on the South side of Patapsco River . . .

My maternal great-grandmother was Bertha Kayton, Caroline's daughter. I have a lovely daguerreotype of her, taken on the occasion of her engagement in February 1851 to Joel Gutmann. My maternal grandmother, Pauline Gutmann Straus, was one of their seven children, five of whom survived to adulthood.

My maternal great-grandfather, Joel Gutmann, came to Maryland as a young man in 1848 at the time of revolution in Western Europe when many Germans immigrated to other parts of the world, principally to the United States. He started out in the new country as a peddler with a pushcart and later a wagon, but quickly built that into a flourishing dry goods business. Soon after the Civil War started, he became a major supplier of uniforms to the Union army, accumulating enough money to build up his own business as Joel Gutmann and Company in Baltimore. He became well known as a philanthropist, with an interest in the arts. When he died in 1893, his obituary in the *Baltimore Sun* was quite long. It ended with, "He died of a heart seizure, and his personal physicians, Dr. Charles Baden and Dr. William Osler, remained at his bedside until he breathed his last."

One of the original "Big Four" of the Johns Hopkins Medical School, Osler was my grandfather's family physician as well, and my mother told me stories about Osler's house calls. Once, when she was at home recovering from scarlet fever and sitting on the living room floor playing jacks with her brothers, Osler, with his top hat and frock coat, came downstairs after having seen my grandmother, who was ill. He laid his coat on the chair, put his hat on top of it, and got down on the floor to play with the children. Another time, Osler had come to see my mother's oldest brother, Joel, also ill with scarlet fever. Mother was downstairs eating her breakfast porridge when Osler, who, she said, was a great practical joker, took the salt shaker and poured a little more salt on her cereal. "Now, Lenore," he said, "see if that doesn't taste better."

My mother planned to go to college in 1901, expecting to go on to medical school. Few women in those days would undertake a career in medicine. Unfortunately, she suffered a bout with diphtheria, which kept her at home for about five or six months and diverted her from going to college. Instead she entered nursing school at Johns Hopkins Hospital, but, again, after completing one year, she became ill and dropped out. Upon return to her studies, she decided nursing was no longer her desire and chose to enter a class in medical art. This was a new venture by Max Brödel, who only a short time earlier had been invited to the United States to establish a department of medical illustration at Johns Hopkins. Mother was one of his first students. Some of her drawings illustrated the medical reports of the world-renowned neurosurgeon Harvey Cushing. After her marriage in 1912, she decided that continuing a career in medical art would be too difficult and she began to work at home designing jewelry. Several family members, including myself, treasure some of her designs.

During the height of the influenza pandemic in 1919, my mother became severely ill with the disease. One complication of her illness was an abscess involving the soft tissue on the left side of her face over the lower jaw. As was the custom in those days, this was widely incised, leaving her with a jagged scar. I don't know why she was never offered plastic surgical repair. It was clear to me later on that this unsightly scar produced a serious psychological barrier for her for the rest of her life.

Mother's tales about Dr. Osler's house calls stimulated my interest in him, perhaps in part because I was already determined that my future would be in medicine. I cannot recall exactly why I chose that path since there had never been a medical doctor in my family. Perhaps it was because my mother had been frustrated in her attempt at building a career in medicine. The closest to a medical career was that of her youngest brother, William L. Straus, Jr. He had gone to Harvard at age sixteen but was so young and so homesick that he dropped out after a year and returned home to Baltimore to obtain his bachelor's degree and later a Ph.D. from Johns Hopkins University. About twenty years later, he became professor of anatomy at Johns Hopkins Medical School, where, in addition to teaching human anatomy, he became intensely interested in research in physical anthropology. He was well known in this latter field as one of the first, if not *the* first, to expose as a hoax the "discovery of the prehistoric Piltdown Man" in England. His work was recognized internationally, and he received the Axel Wennergren Prize, a highly esteemed award in his chosen field. William Straus was only thirteen years my senior, and by the time of my graduation from Harvard, in 1934, that gap seemed much smaller. Tragically, he died in 1978 after having been in a nursing home for several years suffering from Alzheimer's disease. We had always maintained close communication, and his mental deterioration saddened me very much. Perhaps my distress was amplified by the fact that I was by that time a practicing neurologist.

My maternal grandfather, William Levi Straus, was born in Baltimore. His father also had emigrated from Germany in 1848 at the time of great turmoil in Western Europe. He had several brothers and sisters, both older and younger than he, but he was the first of his family to be born in the United States. I have the diary he kept when he accompanied his oldest brother, Louis, to Europe in 1870 to see the sights and visit relatives. Their journey took place only five years after the end of the Civil War, when William was seventeen years old. The two sailed by steamship from New York to

Southampton and on to Hamburg. William's diary is a fascinating account of travel in that era as experienced by a homesick teenager.

Grandfather Straus founded the Monumental Brewing Company, which eventually became the largest brewery south of the Mason-Dixon Line. It closed when Prohibition arrived in 1920, after passage of the 18th amendment to the U.S. Constitution. Grandpa could not tolerate the idea of selling 3.2% beer. In addition, he was a founder of the Crown Cork and Seal Corporation, the first to manufacture and market crimped metal caps for bottles. These caps very quickly replaced the conventional corks used up until that time.

When I was a teenager, Grandpa Straus told me about a pharmacist named Isaac Emerson, who had a drugstore near his brewery. Emerson approached him one day with a business proposition concerning a concoction he had developed and found to be effective in relieving the next-morning hangovers of some of his customers patronizing the neighborhood bars. Emerson believed he could undertake large-scale production of the compound, which he called Bromo-Seltzer, and could market it as a patent medicine. Grandpa loaned him $3,000, which in those days was a considerable sum of money, to get this project off the ground. Unfortunately, Emerson was unable to get it organized on the first attempt. When he came back for more support and with an offer of partnership, Grandpa declined and Emerson went elsewhere for funding. His second effort was a resounding success. The manufacture of Bromo-Seltzer took off like a skyrocket, and the Emersons became multi-millionaires. The Bromo-Seltzer clock tower, still a local landmark in downtown Baltimore, has been declared a national monument. And so it goes.

I spent my first seven years in Baltimore. I had two siblings — Arthur, Jr., two years younger, and Lenore, five years younger. For children, five years is really a large gap. Art and I, however, were very close as youngsters up through grade school and high school. We shared a bedroom, played games, and were both fascinated by geography and history.

In our school work, my father, who prided himself on his own academic record, was a severe taskmaster. My mother was concerned, too, but not to the same extreme. I started kindergarten and then first grade at the Friends School, a Quaker institution. When we moved to a suburban area west of the Pimlico racetrack, I changed to the nearby public school. I did not return to my child-

The Early Years

hood neighborhood until 1972, and by then, except for a few scattered landmarks, it was virtually unrecognizable. The demographics of the neighborhood had changed drastically, but I did finally locate my old home at 2 Taney Road.

The memories of my early years at the end of World War I are still surprisingly vivid. Two of my uncles, my mother's second brother, Philip, and another younger brother, Louis, went into the navy. Philip spent most of his service time at the Brooklyn Navy Yard as a lieutenant in naval communications. Louis started out as an ordinary seaman and became a petty officer. My father, declared essential to the war effort, remained a civilian. He ordered some khaki overcoats and military caps for Art and me, which made us look military and feel patriotic. We wore our uniforms in the winter months, even after the war ended on November 11, 1918.

My father bought his first car, a Hupmobile, early in 1918, when few people in our Baltimore neighborhood had automobiles. Most people today have never heard of a Hupmobile because that company was swallowed up by one of the big three automakers and went out of independent business in the 1920s.

Uncle Philip, who was four years younger than my mother, collected all sorts of memorabilia. One of his hobbies was numismatics, and he eventually put together one of the world's great collections of United States gold and silver coins. He also had a treasure trove of autographs he had started as a boy. In fact, he had accumulated so many different items that he never had enough room to store his collections in a safe place. Among his possessions was some of the original correspondence between John and Mary Surratt of Baltimore, which revealed, in part, their participation in the assassination of President Lincoln. He had one of three existing signed copies of Gen. Robert E. Lee's surrender at Appomattox. He had letters signed by every signatory of the Declaration of Independence and every American president up until the time of his (Philip's) death. A lifelong bachelor, he became somewhat reclusive in his later years. One night a small fire broke out in his bedroom and before it could be extinguished, the Surratt correspondence and the surrender document were destroyed along with some other irreplaceable artifacts.

When Uncle Philip died, one of the choice objects in his estate was Abraham Lincoln's appointment book for his first one hundred days in office. The handwriting was mostly that of John Nicolay, the president's appointments secretary, with a few notations by Lincoln himself. The book was sold at auction in 1961 by Sotheby Parke Burnet as part of my uncle's estate, along with some autographs and other items. The buyer of the appointment book, the Carnegie book shop in New York, sold it soon thereafter to a Texas gentleman, Lyndon Baines Johnson, then vice-president of the United States. When Johnson became president, he placed Lincoln's appointment book in the National Archives.

I have a photograph of my uncle holding the book in his lap, and I also remember reading it myself. Much later, when my Aunt Ada reached her late seventies, she told me about correspondence which related to Uncle Phil's purchase of the little volume. She said, "Nobody else in the family is interested in those letters regarding Lincoln's appointment book, why don't you take them?" I later retrieved them from a box in the attic of her 1790 "row house" on Hamilton Street in Baltimore. She and her older sister, Edith, had lived there for many years across the street from their gift shop, The Artisans. The house is now under the protection of the National Preservation Society.

In 1902 President Theodore Roosevelt had presented William Crook with the appointment book and said, "You knew him (Abraham Lincoln), so I think you ought to have this." Crook was one of the security guards assigned in 1864 to protect President Lincoln. As Carl Sandburg wrote in his biography of Lincoln and as Jim Bishop said in *The Day Lincoln Was Shot*, Crook was with the president on that fateful evening. Crook's usual habit had been to walk with the president until the night man came on duty. Crook recalled later that on that particular evening, when the president left him, he said, "Goodbye, Crook." He thought that peculiar because Lincoln had habitually said, "Goodnight, Crook." The night man arrived late and was drunk. What followed is history.

The four letters which I had found in the attic had been written by Crook in his own handwriting on White House stationery between November 6 and December 5, 1913, and addressed to my uncle. In one of them Crook had written, "I will be willing to sell you some autographed letters and the appointment book as long as I know that you are making this a personal matter. I surely would not part with it for speculation." In another letter he described how to find his home at 1362 Columbia Road, Washington, DC. My uncle obtained the autographed letters for $30 and the Lincoln appoint-

The Early Years

ment book for $40. Vice-president Johnson paid $10,000 for it in 1960.

Crook was still employed by the White House in 1912, and he remained there through Woodrow Wilson's first term. By the time I came into possession of the correspondence, the book was already in the National Archives. My friend, Dr. Charles LeMaistre, then chancellor of The University of Texas, arranged for me to meet with Harry Middleton, curator of the Lyndon B. Johnson Library in Austin, and Lady Bird Johnson. My wife, Alma, and I drove to Austin to take this historical material and a long explanatory letter which I had addressed to Mrs. Johnson. We also presented her with a handsome engraved ticket that my grandfather had used to attend the Democratic National Convention in Baltimore in 1912, when Woodrow Wilson was nominated. My father was a page at that convention. Alma and I enjoyed a delightful visit and morning coffee with Mrs. Johnson in her penthouse apartment in the library building — one of those fortuitous circumstances that occur in one's life.

My Uncle Philip's intense interest in collectibles has had a lifelong influence on me. It encouraged me to keep relics related to family and friends, as well as some which were connected to people whom I was fortunate enough to meet. The main difference between my uncle and me is that he never married, whereas both my wives have been impatient with me at times because of the storage problems these treasures created. Just the same, at least in my opinion, my closets have been organized better than those of the famous 1940s radio character, Fibber McGee.

When I was seven years old, my family moved to Woodmere, Long Island, because my father's consulting business took him so frequently to New York City. My parents sent me to public school for two years and then to a private one, Woodmere Academy, along with my brother and, a few years later, my sister. Southwest Nassau County on Long Island seemed far out in the country in those days, but now it is well within the metropolitan area of New York.

We lived in a large three-story house on Yale Avenue in Woodmere, just behind the lower school of Woodmere Academy. Directly behind us for at least three-quarters of a mile were no landmarks but only vacant fields. On the east side of our house was a large piece of land, the home of Devereux Milburn, a well-known international polo player, with whose daughters, Grace and Charlotte, I played occasionally. Milburn stabled some horses at the back of his property. These buildings have long since been torn down and the fields behind our former home have been completely filled with houses. When we lived there, the paved street on the west side of the lower school ended at Yale Avenue, with sawhorses marked "Not a Road" blocking the unpaved portion beyond. When I returned many years later, I found that the street had been extended and named Knotta Road.

In 1923 my mother's eldest sister, Bessie, who was married to Mack Gordon, my father's college classmate, died unexpectedly. Since Uncle Mack traveled most of the time, their two children, Mack, Jr. and Paula, came to live with us. Paula went with us to Woodmere Academy and Mack, Jr., to boarding school at Lawrenceville in northern New Jersey. Five years later, in France, Uncle Mack married a Parisian woman named Thérése, whom we called "Thesy." They stayed with us for a few weeks, then moved with the two children to Cleveland, Ohio.

This was during the era of Prohibition. Uncle Mack, who was always full of schemes for making an instant fortune, proposed to bring some fine French wine into the United States in casks topped off with olive oil. Someone had told him that the two liquids would not mix in transit. He arranged such a shipment and the casks arrived at a pier in New York harbor at the appointed time. My father had some of the casks delivered to our home. When they were opened in order to siphon off the olive oil, he discovered that they contained a fine emulsion of oil and wine. My father was furious because the shipment had been very expensive, and he stated bitterly that there was no way we could use so much salad dressing.

At about that same time, my father and Mack Gordon learned from Mack's brother Albert, a reporter for *The New York Times*, that a large insurance company, Globe Insurance, had been placed in receivership and the bottom had dropped out of the value of its stock on Wall Street. The probate judge in whose court the matter was placed was a friend of Al Gordon, and he had promised to let Al know in advance how he would rule on the company's solvency. Al was then supposed to pass this information along to my father and Mack, who were prepared to buy a large block of stock, which at the time was available for a few pennies a share. Unfortunately, just then Mack and Al's mother became ill and was admitted to a Boston hospital. Al took off to visit her and was out of town when the judge was about to issue his ruling and, consequently, my father and Uncle Mack never got the word. The day after the judge declared the company solvent, the stock went up to $35 a share. Mack and my father never forgave Uncle Al for this missed opportunity.

Uncle Mack died in an accident at the age of fifty, right after he was married for a third time. He and his wife, Lynne, had left New York for Cleveland on a United Airlines flight from LaGuardia Airport. The plane crashed soon after takeoff, and he was fatally injured. Lynne suffered only minor injuries.

My first year in high school, 1927, was a time of rapid advances in aviation. Our house in Woodmere was not too far from Mineola, the site of Roosevelt Field (named after Theodore Roosevelt). This was the takeoff point for the early trans-Atlantic flights.

In May of that year the New York newspapers reported that a young man, Charles Lindbergh, had just flown in from San Diego after making one stop in St. Louis. My brother Arthur and I persuaded Dad to take us to Mineola to see Lindbergh's plane and also that of Commander (later Rear Admiral) Richard Byrd, who was preparing a Ford trimotor plane for an overseas flight. There was also a third plane owned by Charles Levine and piloted by Clarence Chamberlin. A heated race was in progress for the Raymond Ortieg Prize of $25,000 (1927 dollars), which was to be awarded to the first person to fly nonstop from New York to Paris. On the evening after Lindbergh's unheralded arrival, we went over to the airfield and soon noticed that almost everyone else who had come was there to look at Byrd's and Chamberlin's planes. Lindbergh had arrived in his Ryan monoplane from San Diego by way of St. Louis so unexpectedly that virtually no one was paying attention to him. As we entered the hangar where his plane was parked, we saw him standing nearby talking with a mechanic. He was quiet and reserved but stopped long enough to speak to us. He asked my brother, "How would you like to sit in the cockpit?" Arthur climbed up into the cockpit of the *Spirit of St. Louis* and looked through the periscope, which was the only means of forward vision. I missed my chance because, while this was going on, I found a silver thread hanging from the tail assembly, and when no one was looking, I cut the thread off with my Scout knife. I kept that little thread for many years. Later that evening we visited the other hangars to see the planes of Byrd and Chamberlin, who flew to Europe only a few weeks after Lindbergh's pioneering adventure.

Lindbergh took off the next day. I stayed home from school and listened all day long to our Atwater Kent radio, one with three dials and exposed vacuum tubes. I recall being somewhat concerned that during the flight the tail assembly might unravel because of the loose thread which I had cut off without first asking someone. Lindbergh landed at Le Bourget Field near Paris during the night and was welcomed by a crowd holding big torches to direct him to the runway. He was practically mobbed by the elated Frenchmen. I remember that after hearing the news bulletin, I went running out of the house, almost breathless, to the tennis courts two blocks away to tell some of my friends that my idol had completed his flight successfully.

When Lindbergh returned to New York, Art and I were able to watch his ticker-tape parade up Fifth Avenue from the third-floor office of one of Dad's clients, which was located between 40th and 42nd streets across from the New York Public Library. I still cherish the picture I took from the office window, a black and white photograph showing Lindbergh with Mayor Jimmy Walker and Grover Whalen, the city's official greeter, sitting in the back of a big open touring car rolling up Fifth Avenue. Across the street, the steps of the library were crowded with children, most of them in school uniforms, a custom long since abandoned by New York public schools.

I also treasure the photographs signed by Lindbergh and Byrd, which Al Gordon obtained for me. The picture of Lindbergh was a copy of one which had originally appeared on the front page of *The New York Times* the day after he landed in Paris. Lindbergh's vertical signature along the left margin, I have been told, was in the characteristic manner by which he autographed his pictures. The photograph of Byrd shows him standing alongside his plane, the *America,* with Floyd Bennett, his pilot on an earlier pioneering flight over the North Pole. In the picture Bennett has one leg in a large cast and is on crutches because of an injury that prevented him from making the trans-Atlantic flight as originally planned. Byrd and Bert Acosta, the pilot who took Bennett's place, flew in the *America* to France but, after reaching Paris, could not locate the airport. They eventually were forced to ditch the plane off the coast of Brittany.

All through high school I was active in athletics and played football on the Woodmere Academy team. Our coach was the mathematics teacher, Lester Babcock, who had come to our school from Riverdale School in the Bronx. We traveled around the New York area playing other private schools. I was also a pitcher for our high school baseball team in the spring of my senior year.

Each summer in the late 1920s my father arranged for me to go to summer camp. In 1927 I was at Camp Moosilauke in New Hampshire, a camp affiliated with the Horace Mann School in the Bronx. This was my first summer away from home, and I was appropriately homesick. In 1929 I went to Camp Zakelo in Harrison, Maine. During both that summer and the next, my parents leased a house at 260 College Avenue, Poughkeepsie, New York, from Miss Violet Barbour, a Vassar College professor.

During the fall of 1929, Dad decided to sell the big house on Long Island and move into an apartment in Tarrytown, Westchester County, New York. My brother Arthur, who had two more years in high school, transferred from Woodmere Academy to the Hackley School at Tarrytown. Since I, however, was in my last year of high school, the family decided that I should remain behind and not change schools, and arrangements were made for me to live in the home of David Harrower, my science teacher. From that time on, I never spent a full year at home. During the summer I was away either at camp or working at some temporary job, while in the winter I was at first in college and later in medical school.

As a teenager I developed an active interest in natural science, which was encouraged by my close contact with Harrower. Each year I kept a list of birds I had identified and the dates on which I had first spotted them. I held on to those lists for many years. Looking back, I am sure that I chose to major in biology at college because I had been exposed to natural science at an early age. In addition, probably because of my mother's influence, I wanted to develop my artistic skills. Although I never took a formal lesson, I learned to draw animals and other creatures, and this innate talent has remained with me. During the period between 1950 and 1980, I always carried a sketch pad on my travels and did charcoal-pencil drawings of landscapes and buildings that had caught my eye. Although many of these sketches lay in a drawer for years, my present wife, Alma, thought that some deserved to be framed and exhibited on the walls of our apartment. My younger daughter, Anne, has become a much more skillful and talented artist than I.

In March 1930, while I lived with the Harrower family in Woodmere, my mother took my sister Lenore, then eleven years old, to Baltimore to see a surgeon about her frequent attacks of abdominal pain. The doctor decided that these were caused by recurrent appendicitis, and he admitted her to the South Baltimore General Hospital for an "interval" appendectomy. In those days, patients were hospitalized much longer than they are today. On the third postoperative day, Lenore suddenly went into a coma, and in a few hours she died. I went immediately to Baltimore to join my parents. My mother was devastated by Lenore's death and she felt guilty about consenting to the operation. I had never attended a funeral and could not bring myself to do so this time. I stayed at home with my grandfather, who was so grief-stricken by Lenore's untimely death that he became ill and died within a month.

Why would someone in good health, someone recovering uneventfully from what should have been a straightforward and simple surgical procedure, have died so suddenly? Not until four or five years later did I learn what had actually happened. Apparently, the nurse on Lenore's hospital floor had given her both the oral and intramuscular medications that had been ordered for a cardiac patient in an adjacent room. This horrible mistake had undoubtedly resulted in Lenore's cardiac arrest. For years I could not bear to tell my mother what I knew about the circumstances of Lenore's death. Today an error of this kind would undoubtedly trigger a malpractice suit, but that was unheard of in those days.

Soon after my graduation from high school in 1930, I was offered a job as a junior counselor at Camp Zakelo, where I had been a camper a year earlier. The camp was then owned and directed by Isadore "Izzy" Zarakov, who during the early 1920s had been a star athlete at Harvard in three major sports — football, ice hockey, and baseball. For the summer of 1930, he had invited some well-known college athletes to come to Maine as counselors at his boys' camp. One was Al Lassman, who had been an All-American at New York University, which was a great football power in those days. Lassman had an imposing physical presence; he was about 6'8 and weighed 265 pounds. In addition to his football prowess, he was the National Collegiate Athletic Association heavyweight boxing champion and was being groomed to fight for the world heavyweight crown, held at that time by Gene Tunney. His death, during the latter part of July, when he went out in a canoe after dark and drowned in the lake which bordered the camp, put a pall of gloom over all of us campers for the remainder of the summer. The circumstances of his death were never determined.

The Early Years

Another counselor was Clarence DeMar, probably then in his late thirties or early forties and undoubtedly the most famous marathoner of that era. He had won the Boston Marathon several times, and it may have been his influence that inspired me to train and run twice in the Boston Marathon. More about that later.

Since my father had graduated in engineering from Harvard in 1911, it had never occurred to me to attend college elsewhere. I was accepted for entrance there in September 1930, just after my seventeenth birthday.

During my freshman year, Dad provided me with an allowance every month and paid for my books, board and room, and my tuition ($400 a year). Even though the stock market had crashed in 1929, everything in my life was still tranquil and comfortable. As a consulting industrial engineer during the 1920s, my father had always earned what in those days was a substantial income, and we had almost everything we could dream of at home. In fact, at the time I left home for college, my mother and father were traveling in Europe.

My living quarters were in McKinlock Hall on the Charles River front. The following year that dormitory became part of the newly constructed Leverett House. In the past, all upper classmen had lived in the Harvard Yard, but in 1931, when the Houses were established, the freshmen moved into the Yard and the upper classmen lived in the new Houses. The members of our Class of 1934 had the unique distinction of living in freshman dormitories which became parts of Houses the next year, and we never had the opportunity to do something that every previous and subsequent Harvard resident undergraduate remembers—living in the Yard. I do not recall much about our life in the dormitory except that Prohibition was still in effect and some of us experimented with making home brew. It wasn't the most enjoyable drink I have ever sipped, but we made a valiant effort to make it palatable.

After my first year in college, it became evident that my personal affairs would not continue to be as easy as they had been. As the Depression deepened, my father found that consulting engineers were no longer in demand and that most businesses considered them excess baggage. Just before I entered my sophomore year, Dad said, "Bill, if you are going to remain in college, you will have to obtain a scholarship." He had become unemployed and could not afford to keep me in college while Arthur was attending a private secondary school in Westchester County. Fortunately, by having earned a grade-point average sufficient to place me on the Dean's List, I was awarded a scholarship. I also needed to go to Cambridge a week before the second school year started and find a job. I found two: waiting on tables in a restaurant off Harvard Square on weekends and working at the Peabody Museum, Harvard's natural science museum, three afternoons a week.

My first year in the museum job was devoted to reassembling pot shards and other Indian artifacts excavated in southeastern Utah by a Harvard archeological expedition and brought back for study of the life and utensils of the pre-Columbian Indians of that area. My supervisor was Dr. Joseph Brew, a cultural anthropologist, who later became director of the museum. An authority on American Indian civilization in the Southwest, he took students and faculty members each summer to excavation sites in Arizona, New Mexico, or northern Mexico. My job was to take pot shards from "a dig" and rebuild the pots. One can see on display in many museums reconstructed pottery in which pieces with no design have been used to fill in gaps here and there. This project gave me some very useful experience in working with three-dimensional concepts. After gluing the pieces, I had to balance them in a box of sand. Then I filled in the missing portions and smoothed them out. The task resembled completing a three-dimensional jigsaw puzzle, and for me it was a fascinating challenge. In any case, it helped pay for board and room and part of my tuition that year.

My museum job changed the following year when I transferred to the department directed by Dr. Ernest A. Hooten, a world-renowned physical anthropologist, best known as the author of a volume entitled *Up from the Ape*. He taught me much about paleontology as well as human physical anthropology. This work was more in line with my major in biology. Fitting skull fragments together in his laboratory was an even more challenging three-dimensional task than reassembling pot shards.

Despite the extra work, I had managed to stay on the Dean's List during my sophomore year and won another scholarship. I had very little time for social activities. The scholarship and the money I earned enabled me to continue at Harvard College. My brother Arthur joined me at Harvard at the beginning of my junior year, and his arrival there added to my father's financial burden.

In the summer of 1932, when I urgently needed another job, one turned up in New York City in the department of comparative anatomy at the American Museum of Natural History. My parents had moved to an apartment on 96th Street just west of Central Park. From there I could walk to work or ride the subway for a nickel in rainy weather.

My job at the American Museum allowed me to meet Dr. Harry Raven, a well-known anthropologist and anatomist, who had been an associate of my uncle, William Straus (my mother's youngest brother), on the anatomy department faculty roster of Johns Hopkins Medical School. On an expedition to the Belgian Congo (now Zaire), Raven and Dr. William King Gregory, professor of comparative anatomy at Columbia University, had obtained a gorilla for study. The one they brought back had been embalmed and placed in a lead-lined casket. I was recruited to assist Raven with the dissections. This was my first attempt at this kind of work, except for elementary animal work required in college biology courses, and it served as a tremendous stimulus for my interest in studying human anatomy. My first assignment was a detailed dissection of the hand and foot, from which I prepared anatomical drawings. Raven subsequently published a definitive atlas on the anatomy of the gorilla. My contribution was the portion devoted to hand and foot, in which my rough drawings were refined by a professional artist.

In 1959, when my nine-year-old daughter, Anne, and I visited the museum in New York, we found one of my exhibits in the Hall of Comparative Anatomy marked with a small engraved plaque: "Prepared by William S. Fields." It made our day.

Raven had also brought back an orphaned baby gorilla he and his wife planned to raise in their home. He was one of the first persons, I believe, to attempt to keep a gorilla under such circumstances. His effort to do so was reported in *The New York Times* Sunday supplement and in several magazines. I first met this young ape, named "Meshie," quite unexpectedly one morning when I turned the corner of a corridor on the top floor of the museum. He came scooting along on a tricycle and nearly knocked me down. Unfortunately, as time passed Harry Raven learned, like all others before and since, that an ape very soon is no longer a baby and must leave his human family to live in a zoo.

That summer at the museum I also became acquainted with Bob Snedeker, the man in charge of caring for live reptiles in the department of herpetology. One evening Bob invited my friend Joe Guerry, an artist in the preparation department, and me to play bridge at his apartment in Hoboken, across the Hudson River from Manhattan. Our foursome was completed by Bob's young neighbor. The game and conversation were going along well when suddenly Bob's friend screamed and fainted. The six-foot pet python Snedeker always left coiled around the chandelier while he was at work had slithered down and wound itself around the young man's forearm. Our host had not told us that he had a snake in the apartment — for Bob this was apparently like having a cat or a dog. The appearance of the snake, however, ended our bridge game.

One day at the American Museum one of my supervisors told me that Col. Charles Lindbergh was coming the next day and would discuss the assembly of a temporary exhibit of artifacts which he and his wife had brought back from a recent flight to the Amazon. I was asked if I would like to assist him and quickly responded that I would. When I was reintroduced to Lindbergh, I mentioned how my father, brother, and I had spoken to him at Roosevelt Field before his takeoff for Paris. He was cordial but always reserved. He and Mrs. Lindbergh had moved to England for several years to escape the publicity surrounding the kidnapping and death of their firstborn child, Charles, Jr. During those few weeks, I got to know him and Anne Morrow Lindbergh fairly well. She lived in Darien, Connecticut, during the summer and spent winters on the island of Maui in Hawaii, where her husband is buried.

Unfortunately, a year or two later, Colonel Lindbergh got involved with America First, an organization determined to keep the United States out of World War II. While Lindbergh was visiting Germany at the request of President Franklin Roosevelt, Hitler actually conned him into believing that the Nazis had built a substantial air force. As everyone learned later, the Germans accomplished this by moving planes during the night from the airfield which Lindbergh had just visited to the one he was to tour the next day. Lindbergh's report to the president that Hitler had built a tremendous fleet of military aircraft was in direct contradiction to our government's intelligence information. We all learned some years later that Hitler had achieved his purpose by using the aforementioned ruse.

Since I had been a football player in high school, I tried to fit intercollegiate sports into my schedule. While playing football during my sophomore year, however, I partially dislocated my right hip. That is the reason, no doubt, I wound up many years later with a total hip prosthesis. An orthopedic surgeon at the Massachusetts General

Hospital told me in 1931 that I would never be able to play contact sports again. Closing my ears to his advice, I played lacrosse and ran on the track team. This was the time, in fact, that I trained intently and ran twice in the Boston Marathon. The first time I was forced to quit after eighteen miles because of blistered and bloody feet. In those days running shoes were not as well designed as they are today. The next year I competed again, finishing the marathon in two hours and fifty-nine minutes. I had been determined to finish the course in less than three hours, and obviously made it, but barely. I could not train for a third marathon and gave up competitive running because I needed to concentrate on my medical school studies.

I managed to stay out of trouble during my college years, although just narrowly on one or two occasions. In the spring of 1933, as the weather improved, we students staged a couple of our own brands of riots, throwing bags of water out of dormitory windows and rocking cars that drove through the neighboring city streets. I was more often a spectator than a participant.

This was the time of the Great Depression, when everyone was talking about hard times and the need to maintain world peace. Harvard had an active "peace movement," which, in retrospect, seemed to me to have been fostered by people with left-wing sympathies. A picture in the *Boston Globe* showed me in a group of students standing at the top of the steps of the Widener Library, haranguing the crowd down below. This picture prompted my father to tell a friend that if his son was a socialist at age twenty, he might disown him, but if he was still a socialist at age thirty, he would kill him. He had to do neither.

That same year, about five of my classmates and I went to the downtown theater in Boston where Rudy Vallee and his orchestra were playing. Vallee was a Yale graduate, which inspired us Johnny Harvards to go and heckle him. I was unaware that several of my companions had brought along fruit which they planned to throw at Vallee when he sang through his megaphone. Fortunately, only one missile, a grapefruit, was launched, and it barely missed the singer. Nevertheless, the owners of the theater called the police and had us removed bodily. Several of my buddies who were suspected of having launched the missile were taken to the police station for questioning. Why I was exempted, I no longer recall. The incident made headlines in the Boston newspapers the next morning.

The passage of time has made it increasingly difficult for me to believe that I was in college (Class of 1934) before the appearance of ballpoint pens, computers, radar, frozen foods, and credit cards. My children, and especially my grandchildren, cannot visualize such a world. In those days time-sharing signified togetherness, a chip was a piece of wood, hardware meant hammer and nails, and software was what one slept in during hot summer nights.

There were no ice makers, dishwashers, clothes dryers, or electric blankets. Pizza, frozen orange juice, and instant coffee were unheard of. Grass was mowed, smoking was fashionable, pot was something one cooked in, and fast food was something one ate during Lent.

There were five-and-ten cent stores where things could be bought for five and ten cents. For a nickel one could ride the streetcar or bus, make a phone call, or buy a Coke. One could also buy enough stamps to mail a first class letter and two postcards. Interest rates were at a steady three percent and farmers or businessmen took risks without requesting government assistance. One could buy a new Ford coupe for $680 — but who among us could afford that, even though gasoline was eleven cents a gallon?

We made do with what we had — if it worked, we would not dream of fixing it. We were probably the last generation to think that a girl needed a husband to have a baby. We also believed in daily worship, and a liberal education meant lots of history and English.

Chapter 2

Medical Education and Training

AFTER GRADUATING *CUM LAUDE* from Harvard College in 1934, it seemed reasonable to pass up the commencement exercises because they were held late in June. Moreover, it was imperative that I earn some money to be applied to next year's tuition at Harvard Medical School, and a job had been offered me to go to Canada as tutor and companion for two teenage boys. This was my first excursion outside of the United States. I drove with my new employers from New York City to Bobcaygeon, Ontario, a small town on the Rideau Lakes just north of Peterborough, where I would spend July and August.

    The day before the fishing season opened on July 1 (Dominion Day, now Canada Day), the boys and I visited the canal locks between Sturgeon and Pidgeon lakes. Swimming in the locks was the biggest muskellunge I had ever seen or have seen since. Unfortunately, the fishing season did not open officially until the next day. One week later, when we were fishing in the lake near our house, the younger boy hooked a muskie which he insisted on bringing in by himself. At forty pounds, it turned out to be the largest fish caught in Ontario that summer, and the youngster was so thrilled that he begged, and finally persuaded, his father to have it mounted. We were certain, of course, that it was the same fish we had seen earlier in the locks.

Returning to Boston in September, I entered Harvard Medical School. This career decision was made during the heart of the Great Depression, when I knew that it would be very difficult for me to meet the cost of tuition. Though tuition was only $400 a year, that was a lot of money in 1934. I had been accepted by both Harvard and Johns Hopkins, which allowed me to make a choice. I valued admission to Harvard Medical School highly because, to maintain a geographic balance, it accepted only a limited number of Harvard College graduates, and that was where I really wanted to go. There were 125 men in each first-year class at Harvard and, in those days, no women in the entire medical school.

Once again I had to seek financial assistance. The medical school did not grant scholarships to incoming first-year students because, as the school explained it, they came from so many diverse institutions with widely varying grading systems. The awarding of scholarships, therefore, was deferred until the second semester. Fortunately, I found a job as a waiter in the dining room of the medical school dormitory, Vanderbilt Hall. The classmates with whom I shared this work provided me with some pleasant memories, and all subsequently had distinguished careers.

A scholarship eventually enabled me to close out my career as a waiter. Although the money provided me with board and room, I knew that still more financial support would be required. I decided to contact Dr. Alexander Hamilton Rice, a physician whose course in geography I had taken during my senior year at Harvard College. This decision was probably the result of a combination of juvenile audacity and wisdom. He was the richest man I knew.

Rice, who graduated from both Harvard College and Medical School, had a grandfather who was mayor of Boston and later governor of Massachusetts. From his late teens, Alexander Rice was an explorer from inside the Arctic Circle and south to the Amazon. He never practiced medicine except in service during World War I. His specialty was rivers, and his familiarity with headwaters was similar to what other society folk know about head waiters. The expedition which led him to the Harvard Chair of Geographical Exploration was not the one to the equatorial rain forest but to the dedication of the Widener Library at Harvard in 1915. It was there that he met the donor, Eleanor Elkins Widener, widow of Harry Widener, who had been lost when the luxury liner *Titanic* struck an iceberg in the

North Atlantic in 1912. This wealthy woman, whom Dr. Rice later married, had given the Widener Library to the university.

Dr. and Mrs. Rice set up housekeeping in her sixty-five-room Newport residence, Miramar, and her Fifth Avenue mansion in New York City. With his wife's largess, Rice established Harvard's Institute of Geographical Exploration in 1930–31. His professorial title was a condition of the gift, and Rice lectured imposingly on how to mount an expedition. When Mrs. Rice died in 1937, she left him $60 million, at that time a tremendous fortune. In the 1950s, offended by the lack of interest in geography at Harvard, Rice withdrew his support of the institute, and it was closed. When Rice died in 1956, his biography was one of the longest in *Who's Who*.

When Dr. Rice met me at his New York home, I told him that I needed $400 for my medical school tuition next year. He said, "Fields, I don't give out such things often, but I will speak with my wife — I suspect that she knows you are asking for something. You received an A in my geography course and I think you can do a good job in medicine." Then, after speaking with Mrs. Rice, he gave me his check for $400. I know he never expected to see the $400 again, but within eighteen months, I had repaid the loan.

During my first medical school year, my younger brother, Arthur, was still in Harvard College. He realized that our father's difficult financial situation would make it almost impossible for both of us to remain in private school. Arthur discussed the problem with his close friend, Franklin Delano Roosevelt, Jr., who urged him to stay at Harvard. Despite the fact that he was a junior Phi Beta Kappa, Art decided to drop out of Harvard and enter the U.S. Naval Academy at Annapolis. The following weekend, he went to Washington with Franklin, Jr., and had dinner with the president and his family at the Executive Mansion. He told President Roosevelt of his desire to enter a service academy, and an appointment to Annapolis was arranged for him by Congressman Sol Bloom of New York. Only then did Arthur tell our father that he was leaving Harvard. Dad was visibly shaken and unhappy. He had counted on Arthur's graduation with the Class of 1936, which would have coincided with Dad's twenty-fifth reunion year and the tercentenary celebration of the founding of Harvard College.

During the late spring of 1935, I was hunting a job to keep me gainfully employed from mid-June to mid-September. Like a lot of others, I went to Washington hoping to find temporary employment with the federal government. By chance I was referred to the personnel director of the Resettlement Administration, who, much to my surprise, turned out to be none other than Winston B. Stephens, the former headmaster of Woodmere Academy, from which I had graduated in 1930. He was equally surprised to see me and to learn that I had already entered medical school. He promised to help me find work for the summer. When I returned to his office the next day, he offered me a job in his division, where I would carry out liaison functions between his office and field operations across the country.

I had no place to live, so one of the young women in the office suggested a large house at 1620 Massachusetts Avenue, N.W., where one of her friends had found a room. Occupied in winter by the Fairmont School for young women, this house turned out to be a lovely old mansion (long since replaced by a high-rise apartment building) that had been the home of Col. Henry DuPont. Mrs. Earickson, a Fairmont School faculty member, who remained there for the summer, rented out rooms, mainly to recently hired government workers. The house was a museum-like place full of antique furniture. The reception room on the second floor was filled with Louis XV furniture. On the third floor, reached by an ornate marble staircase, I was shown a room that apparently served as a dormitory for four girls during the school year. The walls were covered by maroon tapestry embroidered with a *fleur-de-lis* design. The adjacent large bathroom was outfitted with rather old-fashioned fixtures. "If you wish," the manager said, "you can have this room alone for now, but eventually I must rent it to two persons. I will give you a week to find yourself a roommate." The rent was $7.50 per week until I had a roommate, then it would cost us $5 each. Luckily, I found a roommate in Harold Salmon, who was working in another government department. He had lost his job as personnel director for Childs Restaurants in New York because they were not hiring new employees during the depth of the Depression. He, too, had come to Washington looking for work.

Before Salmon arrived, I was the only male in the house, a fine arrangement from my point of view. I traveled for a day or two every week, however, and met interesting people all across the country. Until that time I had never been west of Cleveland, Ohio.

A few days after moving into the DuPont mansion, I was startled late one evening to hear screams from across the hall. I was not acquainted with the occupants of that room, but I rushed over in my pajamas and found two young women, both in their nightgowns, huddled in one corner. A bat was flying around, and the girls were terrified. With a broom which I found in the hall closet, I climbed on one of the beds and swatted at the bat until I finally knocked it to the floor, picked it up, and threw it out the window.

This unexpected event resulted in my first encounter with an attractive young woman from Indiana, Florence Dunnington, whom I dated frequently during those summer months. Together, Florence and I explored Washington and the surrounding countryside. One evening we attended a dinner dance at the nearby Shoreham Hotel. While we were dancing, a stocky man, moderately drunk, came up to us, grabbed my arm, and tried to cut in on my date. I fended him off, and when he began to curse and threaten me, two men appeared from the sidelines, grabbed him and took him away. I had no idea at that moment who he was. About ten days later, from the visitors' gallery of the U.S. Senate, to which I had been given a ticket, I saw the same man, Senator Huey P. Long of Louisiana, making a speech. He had acquired a reputation of being a hard drinker who made a nuisance of himself after consuming too much liquor.

I must have done a good job for the Resettlement Administration that summer because I was offered an opportunity to stay on. My mind was set, however, on getting back to my medical education. The money earned in Washington was applied to my tuition for the following year.

In the summer of 1936, between my second and third years in medical school, I went with five friends on an eight-week canoe trip to Canada. I was invited to be the doctor for the group and made certain that I had some basic medical supplies. Among my companions was Colin Irving, who later became the headmaster of Exeter Academy in New Hampshire. His son John is the author of several bestsellers including *The World According to Garp*.

Our group went by train to Rouse's Point, New York, at the north end of Lake Champlain, where we leased three canoes and purchased some supplies. Then we started down the Richelieu River, which flows north out of the lake, and into the St. Lawrence River at Sorel, Quebec. From there we went by truck to the Victoria Pier in Montreal, boarded a passenger ship of the Canada Steamship Lines, and then sailed downriver to Quebec City, where we camped on the steamship pier overnight. The following morning two of us went into town to obtain an entry permit from Price Brothers Lumber Company, owners of the large tract of land through which we planned to travel. Our next stop was at Murray Bay (La Malbaie), where Guy Lombardo and his famous band, The Royal Canadians, were playing at the Manoir Richelieu. In the winter they played at the Roosevelt Hotel in midtown New York City, where I had taken my date to dance on several occasions.

We stayed at Murray Bay overnight and late the next morning another steamer took us to Tadoussac at the mouth of the Saguenay River. There we had time to visit the provincial fish hatchery. When we arrived at Chicoutimi two hours later, we went by truck to a nearby stream. The following morning we paddled from there down a long, narrow lake into Lac St. Jean. The latter is about thirty miles across and appeared relatively calm when we arrived. That body of water, however, is notorious for sudden storms. We were paddling along serenely about 200 yards from shore when, virtually without warning, a strong wind started to stir up four- to five-foot waves, and it began to rain very hard. It took all the strength we could muster to get the canoes onto the nearest bank without foundering. As soon as the weather quieted down, we went on, staying closer to the shore. At a prearranged location up ahead we were met by a truck dispatched by Price Brothers to convey us over a logging road to their base camp. This road, which we learned to our dismay was little more than two ruts cut out of the forest, led to a lumber camp thirty miles away, bypassing the unnavigable rapids of the Peribonka River.

When we arrived at the camp, it had just stopped raining. Clouds of mosquitoes immediately covered all of our exposed skin, even though we had used insect repellant. This persuaded us to promptly load our canoes and start upstream. Fortunately, the pests were far less bothersome when we got away from the camp. Nevertheless, we were never without them, particularly late in the day and at night. Mosquito netting kept out both mosquitoes and black flies, but gnats, known to the local Indians as "no see 'ems," had no difficulty penetrating the mesh. I had grown a beard at the time and recall several nights when I ducked into the river in order to get some relief from the tiny insects.

Lac des Deux Montagnes, our final destination, was reached by poling upstream along the river bank for about ten days. The day after our arrival there, we planned to go fishing at a spot where some Indians had told us we might find land-locked salmon. However, the night before this excursion, one of our group, whom I shall call Alan, cut the index finger on his left hand down into the knuckle, and I had to suture and splint it. This prevented him from paddling a canoe, so he and I stayed in camp while our other colleagues went upriver.

Later that morning, the two of us—with me paddling and Alan sitting in the bow—canoed to a stream at the lake's north end. Suddenly Alan told me he felt strange. I asked him to lie down in the bottom of the canoe and, as soon as he did I jumped out into waist-deep water, while trying to keep the canoe from capsizing. I turned it around and onto a sandbar. After dragging Alan out of the canoe, I found a piece of driftwood nearby which I forced between his back teeth so that he wouldn't chew up his tongue. He turned blue and became comatose, then fell into a deep sleep. When I noticed that two of his front teeth were missing, I remembered that he had a dental bridge and was terrified by the thought that I might have knocked it out with the stick and that it was now lodged in his throat. Fortunately, I found it lying in the sand.

I finally lifted Alan back into the canoe and, wading near shore, pulled the canoe over to a forest ranger's cabin at the top of a high embankment at the head of the lake. The cabin was unoccupied, so we stayed there until our friends returned from fishing a few hours later. I could see and hear them across the lake, and they eventually heard my shouts and came to get us.

I did not know at the time that Alan's mother and his father, a prominent Boston surgeon, were ashamed of their son's epilepsy. He had had seizures since his high school years and was required to take phenobarbital regularly (Phenytoin, or Dilantin, now the most commonly used anti-epileptic drug, did not become available until the following year). Neither he nor his family had warned us that he had a medical problem.

For Alan's sake, we decided to abort the trip and return to Chicoutimi. All the way back, Alan paddled from the bow of my canoe, which made me exceedingly apprehensive. I made sure that he took his medicine faithfully, and when we reached Quebec City, I telephoned his mother to express my concern. Three days later she met us at North Station in Boston with a chauffeur-driven car. I was delivered to my medical school dormitory and dismissed without further word. I was disappointed never to hear from Alan or his parents again, but I should not have been surprised because in the 1930s the prevailing attitude toward epilepsy was still one of shame and humiliation. This experience probably had some influence on pushing me later into neurology.

Back in Boston, I learned that my next outpatient clinical rotation was to be in obstetrics. In the 1930s all Harvard medical students had to reside for a month in one of the so-called "District Houses" where each was responsible for delivering, at home, the babies of patients who had received prenatal care in a nearby maternity clinic. With two classmates, I was assigned to the house on Chambers Street in the heart of downtown Boston, and we took calls in rotation.

One of these classmates still looked like a young high school student, which on occasion was for him a distinct disadvantage. Once, when responding to a call from a clinic patient in labor, he was greeted at the door by, as he later described it, an imposing-looking fellow who took one look at him and with a heavy middle European accent asked, "Iss you de doc?" When he answered "yes," the prospective father said, "You better go den 'cause it took a man to put it dere and it will take a man to get it out." Intimidated, my classmate hastily retreated to the District House and asked me to substitute for him. I must have looked old enough, being 6'5, and the husband allowed me to do what was required. After an uncomplicated delivery and the birth of a healthy baby, I got a big hug and a kiss on each cheek from the father. I saw this man several times again when I went for postpartum home visits and he was really no more ferocious than a big teddy bear.

Another time, on a call to Charlestown, across the harbor, I was startled by the disarray of the patient's home. After examining the woman, an Irish immigrant, it was obvious that she would not be ready to deliver the baby for several hours. I was very tired and it was already quite late so I decided to lie down on the living room couch while waiting. After just a few minutes, I realized that there were fleas jumping all over me. Knowing that I could not leave, however, I spread newspaper over the couch and slept soundly until I was needed. The place was such a mess that even my home visits later on were very unpleasant.

One of the more pleasurable experiences during this rotation was in marked contrast to the preceding one. I was dispatched to the home of a young Italian-American couple where the wife was having her first child. This home was in shining order and everything was absolutely squeaky clean. After the baby's birth, the maternal grandfather, who had been born in the "old country," insisted that I share with them some cakes and red wine. On each visit thereafter, they insisted that I share some food and wine, or homemade anisette. That family stayed in touch with me until I graduated from medical school.

While at the District House, I thought nothing of walking around at night or in the early morning hours alone in Boston close to North Station. The situation there changed dramatically during World War II, as it did in most large cities. Today I would not even dream of being out at night alone in that part of the city.

During the fall of my senior year, I was assigned to a rotation in surgery at the Massachusetts General Hospital. I was working in the emergency ward one afternoon when a skinny man, about fifty years of age, was brought in. Extremely short of breath, he had trouble describing his problem. He told us he was a deep-sea diver who had been working on a project in Boston harbor. He was stripped to the waist and just below his breast bone, we observed a fluttering movement of his upper abdomen. I noted that he had an eagle tattooed on his left forearm. All I could get out of him was an almost breathless statement, "Doctor William Porter, Richmond, Virginia. JAMA (*Journal of the American Medical Association*) 1937." In all the ensuing years, when taking histories from patients, I never encountered anyone else who cited a reference to a medical journal when I was obtaining a history of the present complaints. A fluoroscopic examination of the patient's chest and upper abdomen showed a flutter of his diaphragm. We admitted this fellow to the hospital and, although I lost track of him then, he turned up twice later in my career.

In 1946, in the waiting room at the Mallinckrodt Institute of Radiology at Barnes Hospital in St. Louis, I came across my friend, Dr. Louis Gottschalk, then a uniformed officer in the U.S. Public Health Service. He had with him a thin, little man who was extremely short of breath and very pale. I did not recognize this fellow until I saw the eagle tattoo. This time the man claimed to be a Spanish-American war veteran who had been working on a job in South St. Louis when he suddenly developed shortness of breath and chest pain. I told Gottschalk of my previous encounter with this person but, again, I do not know how he was treated.

Four years later, when I was a consultant at the Veterans Administration Hospital in Houston, I was asked to see a patient who had a peculiar diaphragmatic flutter. Once again I found the same scrawny individual, this time in bed and having obvious difficulty breathing. Surgical scars on each side of his neck above the collarbone indicated that he had had both phrenic nerves cut in order to paralyze his diaphragm and prevent the flutter. Even this drastic treatment had failed to cure him. Apparently he could induce the abnormal movement but could not stop it. His physicians were astonished to learn that I had seen this fellow twice before. When they looked up diaphragmatic flutter in the literature, they found the same patient already described several times. He had been admitted to other hospitals under different names and declared a variety of previous occupations. The patient was a classic example of Münchausen syndrome, a condition characterized by repeated presentation at a hospital for treatment of an apparent acute illness, the patient giving on each occasion a plausible and dramatic story, all of it untrue.

During my final year in medical school, I was able to arrange a three-month rotation in internal medicine at Johns Hopkins Hospital, along with a classmate, Phil Giddings, while two seniors from Johns Hopkins replaced us in Boston. I found a room in a row house on Broadway, directly across from the hospital, where several Hopkins students were also renting rooms.

The Johns Hopkins house staff in medicine included W. Barry Wood, whom I had known as an undergraduate at Harvard College, and Palmer Futcher, whom I encountered several years later in St. Louis, where he was a junior member of the staff in the department of internal medicine. He later became full-time director of the American College of Physicians. The chief resident was Halsey Barker, son of Dr. Lewellys Barker, one of the early members of the Johns Hopkins faculty. I learned a great deal from all of them. I was told that this was the first time anyone had been so bold as to ask to participate in a reciprocal Harvard-Johns Hopkins arrangement. Later, by strange coincidence, when I served a residency in pediatrics at Children's Memorial Hospital in Montreal, I met the doctor from Johns Hopkins, Lewis Meyers, who had taken my place at Harvard during those same three months.

The American College of Surgeons met in Baltimore while I was studying there. This provided me with the opportunity to observe a brain operation by Dr. Walter Dandy, a pioneer American neurosurgeon. Seated in the gallery next to me was Dr. Frank Leahy, whom I knew only as the founder of the famous surgical clinic in

Boston that carries his name. During the procedure, a student nurse dropped some instruments from a tray, making enough noise to distract Dandy. He shouted some profanity, turned around and threw a surgical clamp in her direction. Leahy looked at me and said, "That's enough for me, young man, I am leaving." I got up and walked out with him. This was a first for me, but I encountered some equally temperamental surgeons in later years. Each seemed to have a dual personality—tantrums in the operating room, politeness and good nature elsewhere.

I went to Baltimore, as I think of it now, primarily to find out whether or not I had missed anything by electing to stay at Harvard. My three months in Baltimore were enjoyable and worthwhile, but I concluded that for my medical education, Harvard had been the right choice.

In our senior year, many of my classmates and I wanted to be surgeons, the specialty we thought of as glamorous and lucrative. I applied for a residency position at Columbia-Presbyterian Medical Center in New York and at the Massachusetts General Hospital in Boston. In those days there was no matching plan; it was sort of catch-as-catch-can. When I went to New York to take an examination, I was not even asked to remain for an interview.

Dr. Edward (Pete) Churchill, chief of surgery at the Massachusetts General, and other staff surgeons had encouraged me to apply there. Surgical services A and B had sixteen residency positions open, and Churchill assured me I would have a job. The first hurdle was to take a written test along with about 200 other candidates. When that examination was graded, thirty of us, including several of my classmates, were asked to stay for interviews. I had one interview in the morning, after which I was told to have lunch and return so that several of the staff surgeons could talk with me in the afternoon. That marked the second round, for which nineteen or twenty applicants remained. The results were to be posted on the bulletin board at the medical school's Vanderbilt Hall the following Monday. My classmate, Garrett Allen, and I felt confident that our names would be on the final list. When the day arrived, neither he nor I found our names posted.

We were distressed because both of us had been promised appointments, and little time remained to find another place. It was already March 1938 and I was to graduate in June. Fortunately, a telephone call landed me a job in general pathology at Vanderbilt

University Medical School in Nashville, Tennessee, in Dr. William Goodpasture's department. Garrett Allen stayed on to complete a fellowship in surgery with Dr. Champ Lyons, who was working in the experimental surgery laboratory at the "Mass General." Champ subsequently returned home to Birmingham and the University of Alabama, where he eventually chaired the Department of Surgery. Our paths crossed more than twenty years later and we became close friends. He and I served together on the executive committee of the Joint Study of Extracranial Arterial Occlusion, a study of stroke, supported by the National Heart Institute. He died prematurely of a malignant brain tumor.

After my final examinations I took a three-week vacation, the longest I had had in several years, and on July 1, 1938, started my residency training at Vanderbilt. My graduation present from my father was a one-way plane ticket to Nashville. This was my first trip by air — a turbulent flight in a DC-3 and a miserable experience. I have logged many air miles since then and have never been airsick again.

The year I spent in Nashville was one of the most valuable of my career. I worked at Vanderbilt Hospital for the first week, then was invited to accompany Dr. William DeMonbreun, an associate professor who was moving across town to establish a pathology department at Nashville General Hospital. DeMonbreun was a very patient man and knowledgeable teacher. During that year, another intern, Campbell Haynie, and I each performed more than one hundred autopsies. I kept my records for all these autopsies until 1982, when Elizabeth White at the Houston Academy of Medicine-Texas Medical Center Library in Houston asked for these detailed autopsy records to be placed in the historical archive. I was pleased that she considered them worthy.

Some of the cases are still unforgettable. One, a black male in his late thirties, had been found dead in the Davidson County jail after having been incarcerated for nearly four months and sick for less than twenty-four hours. The court ordered a complete autopsy. I could find nothing on gross inspection of the internal organs, but microscopic examination of the brain revealed inclusions (Negri bodies) in the nerve cells of the cerebellum (hind brain). These findings proved conclusively that the man had died of rabies either from a dog bite before his arrest or a rodent bite later while in jail. The case was investigated at length.

I also performed an autopsy on another individual who had died in the city jail. Neither I nor DeMonbreun, my boss, could find an explanation for the man's death except that he was emaciated. Later, I learned from his teenage son that the man before his death had told his family he was "hexed," by what or whom I never learned. Except for the son, the whole family believed this explanation. The young man had sought me out at the time of the postmortem examination to see if I had found anything else to explain his father's death. Unfortunately for him, I had not.

On weekends when there was not much to do in the laboratory, I worked in the hospital emergency room — an exceedingly busy place, particularly at night. One Saturday night, at about 9:00, an intoxicated, belligerent white man was brought in, bleeding profusely from a slash across his back. He was wearing blue denim overalls, black socks, and nothing else. In the main emergency room doctors were busy treating two persons seriously injured in an automobile accident. The bleeding drunk was placed in a small adjoining room that had a door to the corridor and another to the main emergency room. The policemen who had accompanied him told him to lie on the examination table so that I could suture his wound, and then they left to take care of their paperwork.

The man's wound evidently had been inflicted by a straight razor. It ran across his back from the left shoulder to his right buttock. Instead of trying to suture such a long laceration, I decided to close it by using metal clips. I told the patient to lie down on the table so that I could get on with the job, but he was surly and refused. As I turned to a nearby cart to get some antiseptic and instruments, he slid off the side of the table and, still bleeding profusely, drew a switchblade knife from his pocket, opened it and started toward me. I grabbed the nearest object I could find, which turned out to be a bottle of spirits of ammonia. As he staggered toward me, I swung the bottle, cutting a large gash over his right temple. He stumbled, hit his head on the floor, and was knocked unconscious.

The noise alerted everyone in the next room and several people rushed in to find a disorderly scene and a room reeking of ammonia. The first words from the head nurse were, "Please get him back on the table, doctor, and finish suturing that wound." To which I responded, "I don't care whether the sonofabitch lives or dies — I'm not going to take care of him." After scolding me for my unsympathetic attitude, the head nurse assigned a student nurse to assist me, and we closed the wound. I was certain that the clamor in that room had been heard in the corridor where this man's friends were waiting, and that they would be very angry when they discovered that their friend, who had come in for treatment of a long, but superficial, wound on his back, now had a gash on his head as well and was unconscious. I did not want any more encounters with intoxicated citizens that night and very quietly retired to my room upstairs.

About six weeks later, again in the emergency room on a Saturday, an eighteen-year-old black male was brought in with a switchblade knife stuck firmly between his ribs at the front of his chest next to the breastbone. The handle of the knife was pulsing with every heartbeat. Fortunately, the blade was wedged in so securely that no one had been able to withdraw it — he would have died instantly if anyone had done so. The chief resident suggested calling Dr. Theo Davis, a chest surgeon, and asking him to come as quickly as possible. Dr. Davis arrived in about thirty minutes, and since no one else was immediately available he asked me to assist him at the operating table. Beginning at the midline of the chest above the knife, Davis made a semicircular incision, going left to the armpit and back again below the knife, leaving about one and a half to two inches on all sides of the blade. Then he opened down to the chest wall, quickly cut through the exposed ribs, and asked me to be alert when he turned back the flap to visualize the hole in the heart. He told me to be ready to put my gloved finger into the hole, which turned out to be in the left auricle. As the knife blade was pulled out, blood spurted clear across the operating room. I put my index finger into the hole and held it while Davis sutured around it. The operation was an unqualified success. The event was reported in the press and later mentioned in *TIME* magazine as the first case of open-heart surgery in which the patient survived after removal of a foreign body. This, of course, antedated by about six years the great era of open-heart surgery, which began at the end of World War II.

During that year in Nashville, I met some senior members of the police department and had occasion to ride in their patrol cars on emergency calls. This latter experience was quite an enlightening excursion into a world very different from anything that I had known previously.

On April 29, 1939, shortly before midnight, Detective R. L. (Bob) Tarkington, a homicide officer from the district attorney's office, asked me to accompany him to the Old River Road, where the bullet-riddled body of someone named George Johnson had been discovered. This man had been the proprietor of Palace Hatters, a downtown cleaning establishment. We found the body supine with a pool of partially dried blood under the head. There was an inch-long scalp laceration in the midline at the back of the head. Because the dried blood and matted hair made it difficult to examine him at the scene, the body was transferred to the General Hospital for an autopsy. This examination, witnessed by Tarkington and Inspector Burgess (who later became Nashville's chief of police), showed not only the wound previously noted but also a small bullet entry hole behind the right ear. The missile turned out to be a .38 caliber lead bullet that had gone inward and downward, striking the base of Johnson's skull and then deflecting upward into the brain. It was my opinion that the bullet had caused Johnson's death.

Two days after this postmortem examination, the police brought additional evidence to the pathology laboratory — two pockets cut from the trousers of the prime suspect, Bill Frazier, and samples of upholstery from the implicated automobile. These tested positive for blood. Luckily, the trousers had been found at another dry cleaner's establishment before they had been cleaned.

In late June, when I left Nashville to go to my next postgraduate job at the Children's Memorial Hospital in Montreal, I agreed to return to testify in court if my presence was required. In October the district attorney-general of Davidson County wrote to tell me that the Johnson murder trial involving Bill Frazier and three others was set for November 13 and asked me to come on twenty-four hours' notice. I appeared in court on November 18 to describe the scene where the body had been found and the details of the autopsy. I stated that the gunshot wound would have caused instant death, that I had found blood on the car seat and on the pocket lining of the trousers taken to the cleaners by Bill Frazier. A month later, the DA-general told me in a telegram that two of the defendants had been given life terms and two others had been found not guilty. This was my first venture into medicolegal testimony.

Not many interns and residents were married in those days. With only board and room, plus $25 a month, we could not afford matrimony. Before leaving Boston, I had a steady girlfriend, a head nurse at the Children's Hospital, and we continued to correspond. She may have influenced my next career decision because after the year in pathology, I decided to go into pediatrics rather than surgery as previously planned.

In Nashville, I had met another resident, Robert Elder, who had spent one year in Montreal, Canada. Since I thought I wanted to work in pediatrics, I followed his recommendation and accepted an appointment at the Children's Memorial Hospital in Montreal beginning July 1, 1939.

My brother, Arthur, was scheduled to graduate from the U.S. Naval Academy at Annapolis in 1939 and to participate in the commencement exercises on June 2 at Thompson Stadium, the academy's football field. A few days before the dress parade, however, Arthur was admitted to the academy hospital with what was diagnosed as bronchitis. Although his doctors thought that he would not be able to receive his diploma at the graduation exercises, he recovered sufficiently to be present at the dress parade. He did not march, and he was unfortunately too ill to attend the commencement exercise where he, fifth in his class, was to be among the thirty-three midshipmen graduating with star rank. Star rank has great significance with respect to assignments and promotion throughout one's naval career. Arthur had been assigned to duty on a cruiser, the USS *Concord,* based at San Diego, which was sunk in 1942 in the Battle of the Java Sea.

At the presentation of prizes, the most important event of June Week, he received three prizes for highest standing in mathematics, English, and history, and a fourth for the best showing in practical ordnance and gunnery. On behalf of the Third Battalion, which he commanded, he accepted a cup for winning the interbattalion competition in athletics. In addition, Arthur was awarded a life membership in the United States Naval Institute, a prize given by the Colonial Daughters of the 17th Century to the graduate excelling in history.

On the day after the dress parade, Arthur was too ill to leave the hospital, and he was soon transferred to the U.S. Naval Hospital in Brooklyn, New York, for more definitive treatment. A lymph node biopsy revealed a malignant growth. I was still in Nashville completing my year of training in general pathology. My distraught father called me to tell me about Arthur's diagnosis. I asked him to have the hospital send me slides made from the tissue which had been removed. I was heartbroken when my chief and I studied the slides under the microscope. I had already lost my sister and now I knew that my only brother would not survive this illness.

The doctors at the Naval Hospital decided the only treatment available for Arthur's malignant lymphoma was radiation to the chest, the site of the primary tumor. The therapy made Arthur extremely ill, and it was a particularly difficult period for both him and my parents.

On my way from Nashville to Montreal on June 27, I had a chance to see Arthur once more. His terminal illness was brief and he died quietly on July 19. At the insistence of some of his classmates and the commandant of midshipmen, my father agreed to have Arthur buried at Arlington National Cemetery. I attended the funeral with my parents. By a special bill introduced in the United States Congress by Senator Walsh, Arthur was awarded his diploma posthumously — small solace for my grieving parents. For me, Arthur's death was a low point in my life because it left me without siblings and my parents devastated by their loss. I was twenty-five years old at the time but I was determined to try to fill for them, as best I could, the void left by my brother's untimely demise.

My first two months in Montreal were spent in Pointe St. Charles at the Alexandra Hospital, a contagious disease institution, which has long since been closed. I saw many patients with measles, chicken pox, mumps, whooping cough, diphtheria, and scarlet fever as well as those with virtually every other kind of locally endemic infectious disease. I was required to make frequent trips by ambulance to pick up patients throughout the city, and many of these calls were unusual and occasionally exciting.

One day the ambulance was called to a downtown residence, a three-story building with an outside staircase, typical of many buildings in that part of the city. We had to take a stretcher up the stairs and bring down the patient, a thirty-year-old man suffering from laryngeal diphtheria and in extreme distress. When we got him into the ambulance, I put a wooden spatula behind his back teeth to prevent him from biting me and then put my finger down his throat to make him cough. As he coughed, he expelled a complete cast (pseudo-membrane) of his larynx. Although I had read about it, I had never seen this before. He started to breathe much more easily and we transported him safely to the hospital. This young man, Gerald Dempsey, was the manager of the Trans Canada Airline (later Air Canada) office on Peel Street. We became good friends, and I saw him often during the next two years.

After my rotation at the Alexandra Hospital was completed, it was time to move on to general pediatrics. The following day, September 1, 1939, two months after I arrived in Montreal and coincident with my first day at the Children's Memorial Hospital, Hitler's armies invaded Poland. Great Britain almost immediately declared war against Germany, and Canada followed six days later. From then on my life, like that of so many others, was never the same.

Along with several other residents, I joined the Royal Canadian Army Volunteer Reserve. We were assigned to the 22nd Field Ambulance Unit, commanded by Col. Dudley Ross, chief of surgery at Children's Memorial and staff surgeon at the Royal Victoria Hospital, and reported to a local armory for training one night a week. One of my fellow reservists, an American like myself, Dr. Robert Pudenz, was chief resident in neurosurgery at the Montreal Neurological Institute. After Pearl Harbor he entered the United States Navy and was assigned to the Naval Hospital in Bethesda, where his research in head injury received considerable commendation. He later designed the Pudenz valve for implantation in patients with hydrocephalus. Another member of the unit was Arthur Vineberg, a cardiovascular surgeon at the Royal Victoria Hospital, who later became famous for an innovative surgical procedure that carries his name. In this operation the patient's left internal mammary artery in the anterior chest wall was implanted into ischemic heart muscle to provide a new blood supply after a heart attack. In recent years this operation has been replaced largely by coronary artery bypass procedures.

During that first year of clinical residency, I did my share of lumbar spinal and cisternal punctures on children suffering from tuberculous meningitis, all of whom eventually succumbed to this invariably fatal disease. This was my baptism in doing those procedures. Children with rheumatic fever or typhoid fever were still encountered fairly frequently. I especially remember one twelve-year-old girl in whom Sydenham's chorea (St. Vitus' dance) was aborted by an elevated temperature resulting from typhoid fever. My interest in neurology intensified during this period, mainly because of my contacts with Francis McNaughton, a neurologist, and Arthur Childe, a radiologist, both of whom were based primarily at the Montreal Neurological Institute and provided consultation at Children's Memorial.

We saw many children with a variety of infectious diseases — in fact, most of our patients were in this category. Antibiotics had not yet been discovered, and the first antibacterial "sulfa drugs" had only recently become available. We used a red liquid preparation of sulfanilamide, marketed as Prontosil. It was considered a great advance, but as soon as World War II started, the supply became limited in the civilian sector because most of the production went to the military. Many infants and young children whom I saw had seizure disorders and for them we had only a limited number of therapeutic agents. These children usually received phenobarbital or chloral hydrate. It was not until the following year that phenytoin (Dilantin) became available. The latter medication was without doubt one of the greatest advances in the treatment of epilepsy.

In the autumn of 1939, I accepted a house staff position for the following year on the internal medicine service of Dr. Jonathan Meakins at the Royal Victoria Hospital (RVH). This included a rotation in neurology at the Montreal Neurological Institute, an RVH affiliate, that was physically connected to the hospital by a bridge across University Street.

In July 1940, my first assignment as an assistant resident was to the metabolic and endocrine ward (Ward K). I recall my two months on that service vividly because it was there that I first met C. Miller Fisher, a fellow resident, with whom I was destined to have frequent contact many years later when we both specialized in clinical neurology.

About a month after we had worked together on Ward K, Miller decided to volunteer for service in the Royal Canadian Navy, and his fellow residents gave him a send-off party in the house staff dining room. He was sent immediately to Halifax for the usual basic training and then overseas to Southhampton, England, where he joined a newly commissioned Royal Navy ship. On the second day at sea, that ship was torpedoed by a German submarine but fortunately Miller was picked up out of the water. He was taken to Germany, where he spent the next four years as a prisoner of war. Although he was repatriated before the end of the war, the experience apparently had a lasting effect for he never regained the same fun-loving spirit he once had. When we met again about ten years later, he was an attending neurologist at the Massachusetts General Hospital and on the faculty of Harvard Medical School. I was then at Baylor College of Medicine in Houston as an associate professor of neurology. (In 1989, Fisher, my oldest friend in neurology, came to

Houston as the first William S. Fields Lecturer at The University of Texas Medical School.)

My second rotation at the RVH was on the private medicine service in the Ross Pavilion. One of my responsibilities was to oversee patients who were receiving fever therapy for tertiary syphilis. This was performed either by the controlled administration of malaria or by use of what we referred to as the "hot box," which raised the body temperature to a controlled level between 104 and 105°F. One night the temperature of a patient who had been given malaria went up to about 104.6°, and was still climbing. Miss Clark, the night nursing supervisor, called me at about midnight to examine the patient. Except for the high fever, I found nothing about which to worry. I went back to bed and an hour later, when the patient's temperature had risen to 105°, Clark called me again. This time I saw no need to get out of bed once more and made what I thought was a smart remark, "When it gets over 106, sell." Apparently, Miss Clark found this not one bit funny. The next morning I was summoned to the office of the hospital superintendent, who told me succinctly that this kind of behavior was unacceptable. I agreed wholeheartedly, as I do now, and I was properly chastened.

On several other occasions, the patients that I had cared for on the medicine service were transferred to surgery and I followed them to the operating room to observe the procedure. The chief resident in medicine commented to me on one occasion that, in the hands of a certain staff surgeon, the patient was undergoing a "mutilectomy" and on another a "thoracalamity." That resident was a splendid physician, but I remember him more for his caustic remarks and catchy phrases than for his medical acumen.

I joined the Osler Society at McGill University Medical School while I was in Montreal. Later, during my early days at Baylor College of Medicine in Houston, Drs. Hebbel Hoff and Peter Kellaway, both of whom had been at McGill, organized an Osler Society, and I was invited to become a faculty participant. So, in several respects I have been an "Oslerian" for many years — first, through the contacts of my mother's family in Baltimore and, later, at McGill and Baylor. Many years later, my British friend and fellow neurologist, Dr. John Walton (now Lord Walton of Detchant), moved into Osler's former residence at 18 Norham Gardens, Oxford, when he became dean of Green College. He was surprised when I mailed him a copy of a letter from that address, written in the early 1920s by Lady

Osler and sent to my Aunt Ada Straus after Sir William's death. Both the envelope and the notepaper have black borders, as was the custom in those days.

My third assignment in the early winter of 1940 was to the Montreal Neurological Institute (MNI) for a rotation in neurology. This turned out to be one of the most memorable experiences of my postgraduate training. Almost all the Canadian residents and fellows at the institute had volunteered for military service, and the majority had joined Dr. William Cone, deputy director, to form the nucleus of the first Canadian Neurological Hospital, which had established overseas headquarters at Basingstoke, England. Those of us who remained behind were, almost without exception, Americans in clinical training or working in the laboratory. One of them, Theodore Rasmussen, who years later became director of the institute, was at that time a Fellow in Neurosurgery. The chief resident during my rotation there was Guy Odom, who, after completion of his training, went to Duke University Medical School in Durham, North Carolina, and subsequently became chairman of the department there. Guy and I became close friends and I saw him often during the ensuing years.

My assignment at the MNI was to the neurology service directed by Francis McNaughton, whom I had known from my previous contacts with him at Children's Memorial Hospital. Because the staff was very short-handed, however, I was asked to assist in the operating room whenever one of my patients went to surgery. This gave me an opportunity to scrub for surgery with Wilder Penfield, Arthur Elvidge, and Theodore Erickson. Each of these neurosurgeons had his own style and it was a revelation to me to see how differently, but competently, they approached clinical problems.

I recall one patient, a seventeen-year-old girl from Cincinnati, for whom I had been asked to do the initial history and physical examination. She was suffering from an intracranial tumor (craniopharyngioma) that had resulted in retarded puberty. She had been sent to Montreal by her family doctor for an operation by Penfield. He asked me to scrub with him as a second assistant. The patient was placed face up on the operating table for a frontal approach to the tumor. As was his custom, after the boneflap of the skull was turned, Penfield requested that a lumbar spinal puncture be performed. This was done in order to withdraw spinal fluid before he opened the dura mater covering the brain, which was under increased tension. He considered this procedure important in order to avoid herniation of the brain through the operative wound. He asked me to do the lumbar puncture. This was no small feat since I had to get down on my knees and under the surgical drapes, turn the patient's hips while she was lying face up on the table, and insert a needle into the lumbar area of the spinal canal. I placed a flashlight on the operating table to help me see what I was doing and where I was going. The operating room was hot and there was no air-conditioning in those days. By the time I was ready to insert the needle, sweat was running down my face and obscuring my vision. At about the same moment that Dr. Penfield asked me, rather impatiently, why I had not been able to complete the procedure, the needle suddenly popped into the space and spinal fluid appeared. After that, I felt that I could do a spinal puncture under almost any circumstance.

Many patients whose focal seizures were not controlled by medication were referred to Penfield for surgical intervention. During almost all of these procedures, Herbert Jasper, director of the Electroencephalography (EEG) Laboratory, recorded the patient's brain waves directly off the cortex (surface of the brain) so that the epileptogenic focus that was to be removed surgically could be identified. This required careful mapping of the operative field and the placement of multiple electrodes directly on the brain surface. Penfield pioneered this technique and perfected it with Jasper's help. These were always tedious procedures, sometimes lasting as long as six or seven hours. It was not easy to stand in the same spot for such a long time, but the nurse always provided us with orange juice through a glass tube under the surgical mask.

Although Penfield was a hard taskmaster, I realized in retrospect that he would never ask anyone to do more than he would expect of himself. Working with him and his associates was a tremendous learning experience, and the friendships that I made while at the Montreal Neurological Institute during my residency and later while in the naval service remained with me over many years.

Many patients on the neurology service were admitted with bacterial meningitis, a common disease in those days, most of the cases due to pneumococcal organisms. This was before penicillin and other antibiotics, and the best available treatment was with antiserum administered directly into the spinal fluid. This procedure required tedious and time-consuming typing of the organism grown from the spinal fluid in order to determine its sensitivity to a specific antiserum. Since repeated lumbar punctures were necessary, I was pleased that I had developed reasonable proficiency in performing the procedure while at the Children's Memorial Hospital.

Staff neurologists, in addition to McNaughton, were Arthur Young, John Peterson, and two delightful French-Canadians, Antonio Barbeau and Jean Saucier. Peterson, a very impressive clinician, was severely handicapped by gout, a disease that ended his life prematurely. He must have endured severe pain but I was impressed that he always managed to be cheerful. The electroencephalography (EEG) laboratory was directed by Jack Kershman and Herbert Jasper, two splendid clinical neurophysiologists. The latter, as mentioned previously, worked very closely with Penfield in the operating room recording EEGs during surgery. Their work, meticulously reported in many publications, received worldwide attention. Arthur Young, a psychiatrist as well as a neurologist, was engaged in, among other matters, identification of persons with hysteria and clinical management of such patients.

By the spring of 1941, virtually all of the younger Canadian doctors had volunteered for military duty, and those of us who were left behind, mostly Americans, were overburdened with work and seldom saw the outside of the hospital. I was courting my future wife at the time and thought that the best decision for me would be to interrupt my training and volunteer. Most of my American colleagues were joining the Royal Canadian Air Force, but I decided to enlist in the Royal Canadian Navy, perhaps with the idea that I would follow what had been the career choice of my recently deceased younger brother. This began a whole new chapter in my life — as it did for so many of my contemporaries.

Chapter 3

The War Years (1941—1946)

NINE MONTHS BEFORE THE Japanese attack on Pearl Harbor, I withdrew from my rotation in neurology and volunteered for duty in the Royal Canadian Navy (RCN). I cannot say that this decision was made entirely out of altruism or patriotism. So many physicians had signed up for military service that the situation at the hospital had become very stressful. Also, I was certain that the United States would be entering the war soon.

    I was sent immediately to Halifax, Nova Scotia, for basic training. After five weeks, I was seconded by the RCN to the Royal Navy and sent to St. John's Newfoundland, to join a British destroyer on convoy patrol in the North Atlantic. This turned out to be more exciting duty than I had anticipated. In 1941 submarines were numerous and active in the North Atlantic, and many allied merchant ships had been torpedoed and sunk. My ship was one of those World War I four-stackers, known by the United States Navy as "tin cans," which President Roosevelt had turned over to the Royal Navy.

    Our convoy corridor ran from Newfoundland to Iceland to the Irish Sea. My assignment to this patrol duty lasted from late April until mid-October 1941. Our crew rescued many merchant seamen after their ships had been burned, disabled, or sunk by German torpedoes. I was the only medical doctor for the flotilla, which included two destroyers and several frigates, as well as armed merchant ships, and I treated many sailors for a variety of injuries and illnesses. Once I had to perform an appendectomy on the wardroom table of our ship, with the help of a sick berth attendant who used an open ether drip for anesthesia. Necessity was indeed the mother of invention.

Twice I transferred at sea by long boat from the destroyer to a merchantman to care for seriously ill or injured seamen. I learned how to go up and down a Jacob's ladder in a high sea, which even in retrospect was a harrowing experience. The first time I used the ladder was in mid-Atlantic and the sea was relatively calm, but the second time, a stiff breeze was whipping up rough waves. As the boat approached, a crewman on the merchant ship threw a ladder over the side. I had to grab the ladder as the boat reached the top of a swell and scramble topside to avoid having my legs pinched between the boat and the ship's hull. On leaving the merchant ship, I had to jump and land in the boat while it was nearing the crest of a wave. Otherwise, the boat might drop out from underneath me and turn the short jump into a ten- to fifteen-foot fall. I was grateful that I did not have to perform such gymnastics on a regular basis.

On one trip our ship visited briefly at Digby, Nova Scotia, on the Bay of Fundy, where the sea takes a dramatic fall. The range of the tide, the difference between high and low water, in that geographic location measures among the greatest in the world. It results in "reversing falls" at St. John's, New Brunswick, and the "bore" at Moncton, where an advancing wall of water several feet high rushes up the riverbed. When our ship was tied up at the wharf in Digby, we climbed up the gangway at high tide and descended nearly thirty feet down to the deck at low tide. All of us, particularly after a few drinks, had to be mindful of the difference when returning to the ship after dark.

Many of the merchant seamen whom we pulled out of the ocean were covered with fuel oil; some even had it in their ears, nose, and eyes. If it was in the eyes, the thick oil would not permit the person to close his eyelids. When first confronted with this problem, I was reminded of a magazine advertisement for a new detergent, which I had seen a few months earlier. It showed two pictures, side by side, of a duck swimming in a pool. In one the duck was swimming on the surface while in the other the same duck was sinking in water to which detergent had been added. The next time we were in port, I bought some of the product and added a few drops to a weak boric acid solution. This mixture enabled us to wash the oil out of the men's eyes. One chap whom we rescued had an eyeball completely destroyed. I enucleated the globe and packed the socket with gauze and sulfa powder. This man, a delightful fellow named Dennis Evans from Abergavenny, Wales, corresponded with me until the middle 1950s. Years later, when a trip took me through that town, I tried to find him but to no avail.

While our ship was docked for repairs in the port of Londonderry, Northern Ireland, I met a friend from Toronto who was a radar officer on another Canadian naval vessel. We both wanted to visit the south of Ireland, so we persuaded our respective commanding officers to allow us to go to Dublin. Since the Irish Republic was neutral, the border police advised us to make ourselves inconspicuous by wearing civilian trousers, shirt, no tie, and pullover sweaters. We were told that we only needed our identity cards. We crossed the border on the train to Dublin, where we found a hotel room and then went out to a pub for lunch. We were startled to see two German Luftwaffe officers in full uniform at a table directly across the room. Apparently their planes had been shot down and they had parachuted into Ireland, where they had been interned with freedom to move about. I suspected that they were delighted to be noncombatants. This encounter left us with an uncomfortable feeling.

In August 1941, the ship was ordered into the Irish Sea and we docked at Cardiff, Wales, for a boiler refit. I decided to request a few days' leave and take the train to London, where I had never been. I found a room at the Cavendish Hotel on Jermyn Street, one block south of Piccadilly. This hotel had been named after Spencer Cavendish (8th Duke of Devonshire), a relative of Queen Victoria, and was owned by a very colorful proprietor, Rosa Lewis, who through her colorful past had earned the title "The Duchess of Jermyn Street." She was a delightful woman, who at the time must have been in her late eighties or early nineties. I learned from some of the other hotel guests that it was her strong Cockney language, the notorious parties she held, and her association with the wealthy and influential that led to her designation as "Duchess." The hotel had been a present to her from Cavendish in 1902 and she managed it like a fashionable country house, occasionally rebuking guests for treating it like a hotel. She lived in an apartment on the hotel ground floor just off the lobby, with a middle-aged gypsy woman, Edith, who looked after her.

I got to know them both well. Rosa was an undertaker's daughter who got her first job as a general servant at the age of twelve. Later she worked in the kitchens of the exiled Comte de Paris of Sheen House at Mortlake. It was there that she was introduced to Queen Victoria's son, the Prince of Wales (King Edward VII), with whom she was linked for some years. One of the earliest rose perfumes, Red Rose by Floris, was made popular by Edward VII because, allegedly, he enjoyed smelling it on Rosa's neck.

Rosa always considered me as one of her boys and saw that I was well looked after whenever I was in London. The hotel, one of the few remaining in that district, was remodeled in 1960. I was impressed, when I revisited London in September 1961, that the Cavendish had kept up its "Rosa connections" through portraits and photographs on the walls and restaurant dishes named after her, all adding to the pleasant and relaxed atmosphere.

The duty was not so pleasant on board the Royal Navy destroyer, where only one other officer, Engineer Lieutenant Ian Fraser, a New Zealander, was not from the United Kingdom. After about three months, our interpersonal relations with fellow officers had deteriorated to such an extent that one morning we found a notice from the executive officer posted on the bulletin board: "Surgeon Lieutenant William Fields and Engineer Lieutenant Ian Fraser will from this date forward be referred to as *our brother dominion officers* and no longer as *those bloody colonial bastards*." Although we were somewhat amused, this left us no doubt about our desire to be transferred to another ship.

In late October 1941, I received orders from the Royal Canadian Navy headquarters in London to return to Canada. I proceeded to Greenock, Scotland, to board a troopship, which turned out to be the former luxury liner *Ile de France*. It was sailing for Halifax, and from there I was to take the Canadian National Railway's *Ocean Limited* to Montreal and then on to Ottawa, where I would report to our naval headquarters. In Ottawa, I was informed that my next assignment would be to the recently organized Naval Medical Research Unit. How or why I had been selected for that specific duty, God only knows. I would be based at the naval barracks in Montreal and seconded to work at the Montreal Neurological Institute (MNI) with Dr. Wilder Penfield, under whose direction I had worked as a resident.

I was delighted with this assignment because I had recently become engaged to Bette Ritchie, the daughter of Dr. W. Lloyd Ritchie, professor and chairman of the Department of Radiology at McGill University and director of that department at the Montreal General Hospital. We were married on December 18, 1941, at St. Philip's Anglican Church in Montreal West. My best man was Dr. Harold Eggers, my American compatriot from Nebraska, who had been a fellow resident at the Royal Victoria Hospital. My bride and I had a brief honeymoon in Quebec City at the Chateau Frontenac. We had no desire to leave the comfortable confines of the hotel because there was a lot of snow on the ground and subzero temperature outside. (More than thirty years went by before I returned to that famous establishment. It had changed little except that it was filled with young tourists, mostly Americans.)

When we returned to Montreal, Bette went to work as a receptionist-secretary for Dr. Fred Moseley, an orthopedic surgeon at the Royal Victoria Hospital. She continued to work there for the duration of the war in Europe. Her boss was severely criticized for avoiding military service, a situation Bette often found difficult. I never knew whether this criticism was justified or not.

The director of the Medical Research Unit to which I had been assigned was Charles Best, at that time a surgeon captain. As a medical student, Best had shared the Nobel Prize with Frederick Banting for the discovery of insulin for the treatment of diabetes. He was also coauthor of the widely used *Textbook of Physiology*, which had been one of my reference sources in medical school.

Best was my superior officer for more than three years and I couldn't have asked for a better one. I assisted him in the research of motion sickness at both the Banting Institute in Toronto and the Montreal Neurological Institute. At the latter, our work was directed by Penfield, who was a member of a government committee overseeing the research. A large machine designed to simulate the movement of a ship in a heavy sea had been installed at the MNI in a room that had earlier been the squash court. Called the H.M.C.S. *Mal de Mer*, it was ready to be launched by early February 1942 to determine individual responses to the movements of the machine. Sailors from the local naval barracks, who were put through its gyrations and became sick, were then given experimental medications and subjected to a second test to see whether they could adapt to the motion without becoming sick. I was responsible for the day-to-day operation of this project for more than six months before being sent to try out specific medications under seagoing conditions.

The motion sickness research continued in Montreal, Toronto, and in field trials from late 1942 through mid-1943. After many medications had been thoroughly tested and screened in Canada and the United States for more than two years, it was finally announced in the daily newspapers that a seasickness preventive had been developed. Since the name of our drug was secret at the time, it never received the attention it deserved even after the end of the war. Instead, Dramamine, an antihistamine, was noted to offer some protection against motion sickness for some susceptible patients when they traveled to and from the allergy clinic at Johns Hopkins Hospital in Baltimore. After the war, when that drug was tested at sea by the U.S. Navy, our remedy, which contained scopolamine and hyoscyamine, was relegated to a back shelf. (Twenty-five years later, Smith, Kline and French Laboratories in Philadelphia marketed Transderm Scop, a scopolamine-impregnated adhesive disc to be applied to the skin behind the ear, as an effective motion sickness preventive. Today it is probably the most widely used remedy for this malady. Our work, which was "top secret," failed to provide me with any royalty income.)

Late one afternoon while testing some sailors on the machine, I had an unannounced visit from a senior officer of the Royal Army Medical Corps. I was working in my shirtsleeves and the visitor did not recognize me as a naval officer. He introduced himself as Maj. Gen. Reginald Dunham, Royal Army Medical Corps, and said he wanted to observe the proceedings to learn something about the program. After the last sailor was tested, General Dunham asked me to direct him to the Windsor Hotel in downtown Montreal. The way to my home was in the same direction so I offered to accompany him. When I put on my uniform jacket and he learned that I was a surgeon lieutenant in the Royal Canadian Navy, he was quite surprised. He was very gracious, however, and as we neared my residence on Peel Street, I invited him to join Bette and me for a drink. We had a pleasant visit for about an hour and then I directed him down Peel Street to his hotel, having no idea that we would ever meet again.

I made many trips overseas for the research unit. After the United States entered the war in December 1941, I visited various military installations, primarily on missions related to my work on motion sickness and also to experiment with some new ideas on improving the night vision of servicemen on lookout duty. This put me in contact with many high-level scientists in the military in Canada, England, and the United States, as well as others working in civilian laboratories. I learned about their current projects related to the nervous system. Fortunately, many of these friendships and acquaintances continued long after the end of the war.

After the Japanese attack on Pearl Harbor, I had decided that it would probably be better for me to remain as a larger fish in a small pond rather than transfer to the United States Navy. This choice created problems for my mother, who was living at that time in Flushing, Long Island, New York. She had great difficulty explaining my situation to her friends and neighbors. Every month or so some busybody would report to the local draft board that I had escaped to Canada to avoid the draft. Then my mother would have to go downtown and explain my position. Every time the personnel at the draft board changed, she was faced with the need to correct the same misunderstanding.

I returned to London in late 1942, when the bombing raids were still rather intense. One night after an air raid, I went by a building I had walked past many times before. This structure was the warehouse for Booth's Gin, a very well known brand in England. It had been hit by an incendiary bomb and was burning with an intense blue flame. I was astonished to see how many people on the street had tears in their eyes because all that gin was going up in flames.

While I was in London, I was ordered by Ottawa to visit the Royal Air Force Experimental Station at Farnborough to see how they were using the recently developed electroencephalograph (EEG), with which they were recording four separate channels of data. I was sent to learn as much as I could about what was then known as the "Berger Rhythms," named for Dr. Hans Berger, the discoverer of brain waves. The Farnborough laboratory was directed by Dr. R. Matthews, a well-known neurophysiologist. Lord Adrian, an even more famous physiologist, who was then president of the Royal Society, happened to be visiting there at the same time I was. Since much of the activity at the experimental station was top secret, I felt greatly honored to be included in such a gathering. Clinical EEG was in its infancy and did not see general use until near the end of the war. I had had the great advantage of witnessing it being employed by Herbert Jasper at the MNI.

The following week I was at the Dorchester Hotel in London's West End one evening saying goodbye to a friend who was returning to Canada. A lot of big brass were circulating in the hotel lobby, including high-ranking medical officers from the military services of virtually all the allied forces. They were there for a social affair rather than for official business. I observed a British general who looked familiar, but at first I could not identify him. I stopped for a moment and then realized that it was Major General Dunham of the Royal Army Medical Corps, whom I had met in Montreal and had invited to my apartment. I approached him and introduced myself. By this time I was a surgeon lieutenant commander. He appeared puzzled for a moment and then recalled our previous encounter. He was very cordial and, much to my surprise, invited me to join him at the dinner, which was being attended by many senior medical officers of the allied forces. Although I was rather conspicuous as the most junior officer present, I had an interesting and pleasurable evening.

In the spring of 1943, I was stationed temporarily in London at the Royal Canadian Navy headquarters, which was in an office building next to the Piccadilly Theater in The Haymarket. I will never forget that place because I had to take my turn on the roof as a fire watcher during bombing raids. In these raids the Germans dropped magnesium canisters (fire bombs) that would flare up on impact and start fires on the roofs. When a bomb landed, the watcher would rush over, pick it up in gloved hands or with a shovel, and toss it into the street. Fortunately for me, there were only two such bombs on our roof during the five nights I was on duty. I was too busy to be conscious of being in great jeopardy, and, of course, if a fire had flared up on the roof, the fire brigade would have been called. Magnesium bomb fires destroyed many areas of central London during those years.

During the early fall of 1943, while I was still in England, the Royal Navy arranged for me to live with a Russian-speaking family with the understanding that, with my acquired language proficiency, the Admiralty would send me to Murmansk as a medical liaison officer. It was a prospect about which I was somewhat less than enthusiastic. I spent three months with that very charming family — conversing, eating, drinking, playing cards — everything in Russian.

When I had been issued my winter gear and was ready to depart, the ship specified in my orders had not yet arrived in the Thames River estuary. After a short wait and in typical bureaucratic military fashion, I received notice to proceed to Gibraltar, where I remained for only six weeks. I am grateful that I never had to proceed to Murmansk. Others did and many failed to complete the journey by sea around the North Cape of Norway because of exposure to bombing by Nazi aircraft. It was almost two years later that I had to recall some of the Russian I had learned.

On one occasion, I was invited to spend a weekend with friends from Montreal who were with the Twenty-first Canadian Field Ambulance of the Royal Canadian Army Medical Corps. Their unit was stationed in a large house at Boscombe on the south coast near Bournemouth. During a Saturday afternoon break, we were in the common room playing snooker, a form of billiards, when I looked out over the sea and saw a plane heading directly toward us at low altitude. I screamed at my friend, "Johnny, hit the deck!" With that, we both went down to the floor. A German fighter-bomber came in right over the beach and was firing twin machine guns at our building. After the plane had passed, I looked around. Fortunately, no one had been injured, but the picture window was shattered and the top of our beautiful billiard table had bullet tracks carved into it. That was the closest I had ever come to disaster. The plane had maneuvered in at low altitude to get under the radar screen. We never learned the fate of either plane or pilot.

To occupy myself and enjoy good fellowship on weekends during that winter in London, I joined a discussion group on Sunday evenings at the Westminster School, in a venerable building adjoining Westminster Abbey. The gathering included some British officers, along with their wives, as well as American, Canadian, and Australian men and women. Although the session drew a few Frenchmen, it was mainly an English-speaking group, assembled to talk in depth about a subject usually selected at the previous session. On the evening of February 20, 1944, around 10:00 P.M., I started back to my quarters after an otherwise uneventful meeting. While walking up Whitehall toward Trafalgar Square, accompanied by a Grenadier Guards officer and his wife, the air raid sirens sounded suddenly. Usually, once the sirens started, indicating that German planes were approaching from the coast, we had five to ten minutes before the aircraft reached London. Consequently, on this occasion I thought I had sufficient time to reach the shelter of my living quarters at the Royal Empire Society (now known as the Royal Commonwealth Society) on Northumberland Avenue, just off Trafalgar Square. The Guards officer and his wife, however, had farther to go and did not want to chance it. When we reached the Treasury Building at the corner of Downing Street and Whitehall, they decided to stand in the recessed doorway for protection. I ran across Whitehall and toward Great Scotland Yard. As I reached that corner, a German plane dropped a stick of bombs, the kind that were designed to detonate above the ground, sending fragments in all directions. I must have been about 100 yards away when the first bomb landed in front of the Treasury Building. Immediately afterward, the second one went off behind the Treasury, in the Horse Guards Parade. They were followed by two more demolition bombs that fell in Green Park, southeast of Buckingham Palace. The first explosion blew me off my feet and into a wall. I learned later that the Guards officer and his wife had been killed.

    I picked myself up and ran the remaining block and a half to my lodging and upstairs to my room on the top floor. Although unable to turn on the light yet, I could see that the room was in shambles. The window that looked out over the Charring Cross railway station had been blown out, the blackout curtain was in shreds, and there were fragments of glass everywhere. The Germans apparently had been trying to demolish the railway terminal.

    Using only the light coming in through the window from the street, I tossed the glass-covered bedspread to the floor and climbed under the blankets with my overcoat on. The room was cold and I was rather shaken by my experience but I eventually fell asleep. The next morning I took off my street clothes, pulled on a robe, and went down the hall to the bathroom to take a shower. There was blood all over the robe and on my back. I could not see the middle of my back in the mirror, but I could feel a big lump there.

    At the Medical Corps dispensary several blocks away, the doctor on duty examined my back and found a puncture wound in the center of the lump. An x-ray showed a sliver of metal about two and a half inches long, which looked as though it had threads on it, lying against my sacral spine. I was told that the metal would have to be removed because it might "travel." I was transported by ambulance to the No. 10 Canadian General Hospital in Watford, on the northwest side of London, where an electromagnetic machine was used to extract metal fragments. Mine was removed, leaving a tiny hole and a large hematoma which was spontaneously absorbed during the next two weeks. I was lucky that the metal fragment had hit bone. If it had been an inch or two above or below, it might have cut through me. Perhaps my heavy overcoat had slowed it down. That piece of metal remained with me as a souvenir for a long time but eventually was lost.

At the military hospital I was admitted to a large ward and assigned a bed that had a thin pallet, a light blanket, and a blanket roll as a pillow. I could not find a comfortable position regardless of which way I turned. After 9:00 that first night, the nursing sister came through the ward and said, "Lights out," even though all blackout draperies had been drawn. The next thing we heard was the sound of artillery, followed by several loud explosions. Until then, none of us had been aware that there was a battery of five-inch antiaircraft guns not far from the hospital on the other side of the village common. They were being fired at the Heinckel (German) bombers that had approached the east coast at a high altitude and then dived to gather speed as they flew over London. By the time they had unloaded their bombs, the German planes were going fast enough to pull up and possibly escape the British fighter planes and antiaircraft guns. After that they flew west toward the Bristol Channel, turned left, and passed around the southwest coast of England to return to their bases in France or Belgium. These were referred to as "scalded cat" raids. I didn't appreciate the significance of these diversionary maneuvers until the week after I left the hospital. There was another night raid while I was on the street near Hyde Park, and I saw German planes caught in the cross beams of a battery of searchlights. It seemed to me as though those airmen were absolutely naked up there and everything was being turned loose on them, including rockets and antiaircraft guns. I never saw a plane hit, but they were under attack almost continuously as they flew over London.

About two weeks after my dismissal from the hospital, I was ordered back to Canada for sick leave. Unfortunately, I enjoyed only three days at home with Bette before I was ordered to report once again to naval headquarters in Ottawa. Apparently, I was needed to take an urgent assignment with the U.S. Amphibious Forces in San Diego, following which I would proceed to the Central Pacific Theater of Operations. They presented me with an airline ticket from Toronto to Chicago to Los Angeles. During the second leg of the trip, Chicago to Los Angeles, I sat next to a chatty gentleman who turned out to be a labor organizer for the United Automobile Workers. He was en route to the West Coast for discussions with union officials about working conditions in the aircraft factories in southern California. When he learned that I would have a few-hour layover in Los Angeles, he invited me to accompany him and several of his colleagues to their hotel. They introduced me to Southern Comfort, a drink I didn't relish then and have never liked since. These men, although kind and considerate, impressed me as tough, confident, and knowledgeable about labor relations.

I continued to San Diego by train, took the ferry across the harbor, and reported for duty to Capt. Frank Ryan, USN, chief medical officer at the Amphibious Training Base on the so-called "Silver Strand" of Coronado Beach. I was surprised and pleased to find that this was the same Ryan whom I had met when my brother Arthur was a patient at the Brooklyn Naval Hospital during his terminal illness in 1939. I was also pleased to learn that one of the junior medical officers stationed on the base was an army captain from Cleveland, Ohio, a pediatrician named Harold Epstein, who had been my classmate at Harvard Medical School. Another officer whom I met there was Lt. George Broyles, Jr., USNR, a Texan and a graduate of The University of Texas Medical Branch at Galveston in the Class of 1940. George Broyles turned up again in my life in 1949, after I went to Houston, where he was in practice as a general surgeon. He became a longtime close friend.

My superior officer in San Diego was Col. Henry Brockman of the Royal Marines. We were both billeted at the Hotel Del Coronado, which had been an elegant establishment in peacetime. On the veranda one evening soon after my arrival, I found Colonel Brockman having a drink with a navy lieutenant who turned out to be a reserve officer in the Royal New Zealand Navy, assigned to the U.S. Naval Air Station on Terminal Island at Long Beach, California. Assuming that the Royal New Zealand Navy was small, I asked the lieutenant whether he knew Engineer Lieutenant Ian Fraser, with whom I had served in the North Atlantic. He did not, but when I inquired about Lt. Cmdr. John A. Rhind, a New Zealand officer with whom I had shared a room at the Royal Empire Society in London, his response was positive. I was pleased to learn that he had come to San Diego to await the arrival of a mine sweeper commanded by Rhind. Rhind had brought his ship across the Atlantic, through the Panama Canal, up the west coast of Central America, and was due to arrive in port the following day. I made sure that I would be at the U.S. Naval Base in San Diego when John Rhind came ashore, and he was very surprised to see me again. We made a date to go across the border several days later to Tijuana, Mexico, with another friend of mine, Lt. Col. Worth Fulbright, a regular army officer from Fort Sill, Oklahoma, stationed also at the Amphibious Forces Training Base.

This was the first time I had been in Mexico, and the visit was memorable. We went to a restaurant where Fulbright introduced me to jalapeño peppers. He popped one into my mouth, and I thought I was ablaze. It anesthetized my taste buds so that I did not appreciate the rest of the meal. As we left the restaurant, a very persistent, ragged urchin followed me along the street for several blocks and kept asking me in broken English if I would like to sleep with his sister. I did not find that prospect very attractive.

On our way back across the border, my colleagues in uniform went through the checkpoint without any difficulty. When the immigration officer asked where I was born, I replied, "Baltimore, Maryland." This created a stir because of my Canadian uniform. He asked me to stand aside for further interrogation and I had to wait until all the others had passed before finally being allowed to re-enter my native country.

I had had a similar experience when crossing from Windsor, Ontario, to Detroit in 1942. On that occasion I was going to dinner with Cmdr. A. Ross Webster, commanding officer of the naval barracks in Windsor, and his wife, Margaret. The U. S. immigration officer detained me to ask how and why an American citizen was serving in the Royal Canadian Navy. Ross, who had been born in Duluth, Minnesota, but had spent most of his life in Canada, was never even asked about his place of birth.

My first assignment in San Diego was to test our seasickness remedy in simulated battle conditions during amphibious exercises off the California coast. These were usually carried out between San Diego and Los Angeles, near Oceanside. Working with me at that time was a civilian from the Office of Scientific Naval Research, Dr. David Tyler, professor of physiology at the University of Puerto Rico in San Juan. One day Tyler, Captain Ryan, and I visited the California Institute of Technology in Pasadena. We were seated in the office of a physiology professor, Dr. van Haareveld, when Ryan and I noticed, almost simultaneously, that Tyler had big holes in the soles of both shoes which were covered inside by folded newspaper. To both of us this was amusing because Tyler was the epitome of the absent-minded professor. No doubt, he had forgotten to go to the shoe repair shop.

I participated in several landing exercises at Oceanside, near the large U.S. Marine Corps Base at Camp Pendleton, and in another down the coast at Ensenada, Baja California, Mexico, a joint maneuver with our Mexican allies. Three weeks later, my orders came for detached duty at the headquarters of the U.S. Pacific Amphibious Forces under the command of Vice Adm. Roscoe Turner on the island of Maui. I made the five-day trip to Hawaii on board LST 1013 of the U.S. Navy. From there I was sent to Eniwetok, which was a staging area for the assault on the island of Saipan. My assignment was to one of the forward support vessels, and we proceeded to Saipan. The landing was to take place on June 15, after an intensive bombardment by carrier-based planes and naval guns. Since the seasickness remedy was being provided for the U.S. Marines who formed the main landing force, I was sent ashore as an observer with the medical detachment of a naval beach party. We arrived on the beach six hours after the initial wave of landing craft had come ashore. At that time the beachhead was only between 300 to 500 yards deep, and we were under almost continuous mortar fire from Japanese guns. I stayed on the beach overnight in a slit trench during the height of the battle, assisting from time to time with the triage of casualties that were being brought back from forward areas.

During the night I shared my poorly sheltered slit trench with a U.S. Navy medical officer. In the early morning hours a shell burst close by. I did not realize that this American officer had been mortally wounded until I shook him and he failed to respond. He had been hit in the neck by a piece of shrapnel that had severed his carotid artery. There was no way I could have saved him. The rest of us were evacuated from the beach by midmorning of the second day. As far as could be determined at that time, the seasickness preventive had worked satisfactorily and caused no serious side effects.

On the fourth day after the landing, our ship was ordered to return to Eniwetok, where mail from the United States was brought on board. I was surprised to receive a letter from the draft board in Flushing, Long Island, New York, requesting that I report for military service or be subject to severe penalty. This made me furious and, at my request, an official response was sent by the executive officer of the American ship on which I was temporarily stationed. That was the last time that I heard about shirking my patriotic duty. I learned much later that some busybody had reported that I had fled to Canada to escape the draft. It never ceases to amaze me how some people cannot resist circulating vicious rumors without foundation.

My return from the Central Pacific in early July 1944 was followed by reassignment to duty at Coronado Beach. About one week after my arrival there, I went to lunch in downtown Coronado with Captain Ryan. Later that afternoon I received a frantic telephone call from him asking me to come immediately to the base where about 150 of the navy and marine officers had literally been prostrated by acute gastroenteritis. The dispensary did not have enough space in the examining rooms to accommodate such a large number of patients; many of them were lying on blankets on the floor and in the corridors. Some were severely dehydrated as a result of almost continuous diarrhea and vomiting, and the floors were more than a little bit messy. We spent that entire evening getting an intravenous infusion started in nearly every one of them. In the midst of all of this, a frantic call came from the Hotel Del Coronado requesting my prompt return. On arrival there, I discovered that many senior officers, including the base commander, Admiral Davis, were suffering from the same acute illness.

An investigation the next day revealed that one of the cooks in the galley at the base had had an infected finger treated and bandaged the day before the food poisoning occurred. Early in the morning the man had prepared a large bowl of salad for the officers' mess and had placed it in the refrigerator to keep until the noon meal. The salad had been tossed but, unfortunately, it was in such a large container that it was still warm in the center. This provided a splendid culture medium for staphylococcus organisms. Captain Ryan and I, who had eaten in town, were virtually the only officers not infected and, with the help of a few corpsmen, we furnished almost all of the medical attention. We were fortunate to have gone out to eat that day, but, by the time this crisis was over, we were exhausted.

Back at the Del Coronado, I found myself with time on some evenings and weekends to play tennis at the hotel. One Sunday, after I had already played two sets, I was just getting out of the shower when a call came from my friend George O'Brien, the recreation and welfare officer at the base. (He had been a well-known Hollywood actor in western films before entering military service.) He told me that he desperately needed my help. The base was to have a tennis exhibition featuring William (Bill) Tilden, who had been the national amateur tennis champion for nearly two decades until he had turned professional a few years earlier. Tilden was bringing some of his colleagues down from Los Angeles and they needed another player from among the navy personnel. George begged me to put my tennis clothes back on and participate. I agreed, reluctantly.

During the first set, I was a doubles partner with Tilden. After we were defeated 6-4, Tilden refused to play the second set with me. He sat down and sulked while he was replaced by Walter Cromwell, another tennis professional from Los Angeles. Cromwell and I then defeated the same two opponents 6 2. When we retired to the Officers' Club, Tilden was so morose and unhappy about being upstaged that he refused to speak to me. After I left California and returned to Montreal, I had no further opportunity to play tennis, so my game deteriorated to the point where competition in such stratospheric company was no longer feasible or reasonable.

In mid-July 1944, one of my father's business associates, Paul McCampbell, called to tell me that Dad had died the day before. This sad news was not entirely unexpected since he had been operated on about eighteen months earlier for cancer of the colon and was living with a colostomy. I requested leave and tried to arrange transportation for my trip home to Flushing, Long Island, where my parents had been living for several years. Lt. Cmdr. William Ellis, one of my brother's classmates at the U.S. Naval Academy, who was serving as a liaison officer between the Amphibious Forces Base at Coronado Beach and the North Island Naval Air Station at Coronado, arranged for a pilot to take me to March Field in Long Beach, where presumably I would be able to catch the eastbound Military Air Transport Service (MATS) flight. As we approached the airfield and were preparing to land, the pilot said, "Doc, call the tower." He told me which switches to throw, and I asked air control for permission to land. Although this was not exactly routine and was a first for me, we made an uneventful landing. On arrival at the control center at the edge of the field, I was escorted to the office of the base commander. He was cordial when I told him of my need for transportation but said, "I'm sorry, we just received orders yesterday that we can only carry army personnel and can no longer take you navy fellows." I asked how I might make other arrangements, and he was kind enough to call for a staff car, which delivered me to the Naval Air Station on Terminal Island at Long Beach. There I learned that the eastbound Naval Air Transport flight had departed a few minutes earlier and the next one going in that direction would not leave until the following morning.

Not until departure time the next morning was I told that the first leg of the trip would take me back to North Island Naval Air Station. After twenty-four hours I had made no progress whatsoever toward getting home. I stayed on that same plane, however, and we took off for Albuquerque, New Mexico. From there we flew overnight to the Naval Air Station at Olatha, Kansas, where we were informed that the plane would not proceed further that day. In about two hours I was able to board a plane for Washington, D.C., and after an intermediate stop in Columbus, Ohio, arrived at the Anacostia Naval Air Station in the early afternoon. Later, at Union Station, I found the train north to New York City almost completely full of service personnel, and I had to stand on the platform at the back of the car throughout the four-hour trip to Pennsylvania Station in New York City. From there I took a subway train to Flushing, arriving home just as the rest of the family was coming back from the cemetery. It was a relief to get there in time to see all the relatives while being spared the agony of the funeral service. My visit had to be brief, but I was pleased that I could be of some comfort to my mother for a few days.

My return flight to San Diego was nearly as fraught with delays as my eastbound trip home. I had called the Naval Air Transport Service at Floyd Bennett Field, Long Island, to make arrangements and was told to stand by and wait for a call. Two days later the call came requesting me to report to the airfield promptly. There I learned that I would be flying in a Grumman Amphibian that was being ferried across the continent to the Alameda Naval Air Station in Oakland, California, for the admiral in command there. Our first stop was at Anacostia Naval Air Station in Washington, D.C., and from there we flew to Spartansburg, South Carolina. Next, we put down at the Municipal Airport in Atlanta, where the pilot, Lt. Joe Duncan, decided we would spend the night since he had orders to fly only during daylight hours. It soon became evident that he had arranged to spend the night with a different girl in each of our ports of call and I was left to fend for myself. Our travels then took us to Meridian, Mississippi, on to Shreveport, Louisiana, and Midland, Texas. The next day we flew to El Paso and then on to Tucson. It was only after we arrived there that Joe told me his flight plan would take him north to the San Francisco Bay area and that I would have to find some alternate way to complete my trip. He agreed, however, to deliver me to the U.S. Marine Air Station at El Centro in Imperial Valley, California, close to the Mexican border, but I had no idea how long I would have to wait in that out-of-the-way corner of the country. We had filed a flight plan, but when we arrived near the airfield, the control tower kept waving us off. Joe acted as though he never got the message and landed the plane anyway when the traffic had cleared. He was mildly reprimanded by the base commander, which seemed not to bother him at all. The plane was refueled and he took off.

About thirty minutes later, a plane piloted by a friend, Ralph Flanagan, flew in from San Diego. Ralph, who was also stationed at Coronado, had been on the U.S. Olympic swimming team in 1936. He offered to deliver me back to my base. Because there was no place to sit up front, I climbed into the back of the R4D transport plane (navy parlance for a DC-3) into a cargo bay filled with crates containing Wright Whirlwind rotary airplane engines. I lay down on top of the crates and fell asleep, exhausted from the long trip across the continent.

Flying at an altitude between 5,000 and 7,000 feet all the way across had given me a wonderful perspective of the United States. We had crossed the piney woods and the cotton fields in the South, traversed West Texas and the deserts of New Mexico and Arizona. It was the last opportunity that would come my way to see the country free of the air pollution of later years. Most people flying today have no idea what it was like in the days before jet airplanes and smog.

In late August word came that I would be staying in California for several more months. I called Bette in Montreal and asked her to join me, even though travel for civilians in those days was difficult. She planned an itinerary totally by rail and carried it out. After crossing Canada to Vancouver on the Canadian Pacific Railway, she took another train to Seattle and then a third one south to Los Angeles. In Los Angeles, she changed trains for the fourth time in order to reach San Diego. I took the ferry across the harbor and then went to the railway station to meet her when she finally arrived late in the morning. We returned on the ferry and took a taxi to the Hotel Del Coronado, where we used a rear entry. From that day on Bette maintained that I took her in through the back door because she looked so disreputable after sitting up all night on the train in a wooden seat. Not true — our room was closer to the back door than the front lobby.

The Hotel Del Coronado was a remarkable structure and a venerable southern California institution. Built before the days of the automobile, it was originally accessible only by train and horse-drawn carriage. The dining room had a high, vaulted, wooden ceiling — a magnificent piece of architecture that is still intact today. One thing especially memorable about it was that its sprinkler system would probably have guaranteed that any guests in the dining room when a fire started would drown before they burned.

One evening in the hotel bar, the famous Hollywood comedian W. C. Fields entered with three young starlets in tow. He obviously had taken on board a lot of liquor but was still able to navigate. I spoke with him a little later and jokingly told him that he had caused me no end of problems because people were always referring to me as "W. C." instead of "W. S." Fields. His answer was, "I don't give a damn who you are or what they call you, but I am the one and only W. C. Fields!" That incident led me to believe that comedians only appreciate jokes at someone else's expense, especially when they are drunk.

Bette and I remained in San Diego until early November 1944, when I was ordered to return to Ottawa. We took the train to Los Angeles and boarded the *Santa Fe Chief* east to Chicago. In the dining car it suddenly dawned on me that this was Election Day (it was the day on which Franklin Delano Roosevelt was elected for a fourth term). The waiter informed me that he could not serve me an alcoholic beverage while we were still in California because I was in uniform, but it was quite permissible for my wife to have one. I thought that this was absurd, but Bette considered it to be a reasonable arrangement.

We changed trains in Chicago on the evening of the second day and took the overnight Canadian National Railway express train to Montreal. The next morning we had a brief layover in Toronto. I left the train to get Bette the morning paper and stayed on in Toronto. My eye was caught immediately by an article on the front page with a headline, "Empire Officer Dismissed for Disobeying U.S. Naval Orders." Further on, I read that Lt. Cmdr. John A. Rhind, Royal New Zealand Naval Volunteer Reserve, had been removed from command of the ship that he was taking across the Pacific from California to New Zealand. My friend John, with whom I had only recently visited Mexico, had apparently decided, contrary to orders received in Hawaii, to take a shortcut and ran the ship aground near Fiji. I was aghast at what had happened to him. At the time I did not have the courage to write to John about his ill fortune, but more than a year later he turned up in my life for a third time.

After reporting to naval headquarters in Ottawa, I was ordered to England once more in December 1944. I took with me manuals of procedure for the handling of casualties in the Central Pacific Theater of Operations, which I was to deliver to our medical liaison in the Admiralty. This trip was made on the former Dutch luxury liner *Nieuw Amsterdam,* which was now serving as a troopship. We arrived in Liverpool on Christmas Eve. On the ship I had encountered a Royal Navy ordnance officer who had been in Canada for more than a month. We boarded the train to London together, sitting in the same compartment. In the compartment with us was an elderly civilian woman, two young women from the Women's Royal Naval Service (WReNS), and a United States Army Air Corps sergeant. The ordnance officer held on his lap a large package wrapped in newspaper. I asked him what it contained. He grinned and told us it was a frozen Gaspé salmon that he was bringing to his wife. We assured him that it was so cold on the train that the fish surely would not thaw before he got it home. The American sergeant looked at my uniform and asked if I was a doctor. When I said yes, he reached into his hip pocket, drew out a flask containing Scotch whiskey, and said, "Well, then you will know what this is good for. Would you like a swig?" I assured him that it would be a life saver and he shared it with all of us. The elderly woman seemed to enjoy it most of all.

When we arrived in London, Euston Station was enveloped in an impenetrable pea-soup fog. It was Christmas Eve and I had planned to attend a party at the Royal Air Force Club in Piccadilly with a friend, Group Capt. James Jeffs. No motor traffic was moving, and I could not possibly find my way. Traditionally in London, public surface transportation shuts down on Christmas Eve and Christmas Day. That year there was also a transport workers' strike, so underground transportation was not available either. This infuriated the English public inasmuch as the Battle of the Bulge was in progress in Belgium, and it looked as though the Germans might make a breakthrough to the coast.

Quite by chance, in Euston Station, I met a navy colleague from Toronto, the same radar officer with whom I had gone to the Irish Republic several years earlier. Although he had also planned a festive evening, he was faced with the same problem as I. We made our way to the Euston Hotel adjoining the railway station. No rooms were available because many travelers in the same predicament had preceded us there. After deciding to spend the evening at a nearby pub, we felt our way along the walls of one building to the next until we heard loud voices inside a blacked-out structure. This turned out to be the oasis we were seeking. At closing time we returned to the hotel in the same manner, and asked for blankets at the front desk. They brought us blankets and pillows and we slept right there in the hotel lobby. Jimmy Jeffs had been expecting me at the Royal Air Force Club and was unaware of my situation. I was unable to reach him by phone. He had just returned from Nassau, where he had flown with Christmas presents from King George VI for the Duke and Duchess of Windsor. (The Duke was then governor general of the Bahamas.) The next morning, when I explained my absence at the party the previous evening, he invited me to his home in Surrey for the rest of the holiday weekend.

In London, fogs of that severe density are long since a relic of the past because the residents no longer burn soft coal. If you have never been in a London fog, you have never experienced a real fog. The old-fashioned variety, as described by Sir Arthur Conan Doyle in the Sherlock Holmes stories and still seen occasionally during World War II, was not white but a shade of mustard yellow. It almost felt as though one could take it in his hands and wring it out. Needless to say, the fog was even more miserable during the wartime blackout since one could not see more than a foot or two ahead. Streets with traffic islands down the middle had posts with small blackout lights designed to keep buses and other vehicles from running up on them in the dark. How the British adapted to the hazards of the blackout in London and still kept the traffic moving never ceased to amaze me. Most people got around despite the inconvenience. The saving grace was the wonderful network of the underground railway system.

During the war, traveling on the London underground was no

problem in the daylight hours, but at night virtually all of the deeper stations were used as air raid shelters. Entire families slept there night after night. Each person seemed to have his or her own space and knew exactly where to bed down. For once, at least, one's station in life did not matter. Fortunately, during the heavy bombing attacks, many people engaged in nonessential activities were sent out of the city to rural areas, where they were assigned other work. Few children remained in London; most of them had been sent to the countryside and some even to Canada.

The difficulties encountered while living in London were inescapable, and I was always delighted to have weekend leave to go to the country. There is nothing like the English countryside, in summer or winter, if one seeks tranquility. It is the ideal place to rest and become rejuvenated.

Immediately after my brief visit in Surrey, I went to see Surgeon Capt. James Graff in the Admiralty, taking along the procedure manuals and other relevant data I had brought back from my tour of duty in the Central Pacific. After examining the materials, Graff asked me to take them to Col. Patrick Cohane of the medical department of Combined Operations, located in Richmond Terrace just off Whitehall. I spread out all the manuals for the colonel, and after briefly perusing them, he appeared to be absolutely astounded. This was surprising to me since the war in the Central Pacific was about to become more intense and I had anticipated that there would be involvement not only of the United States Navy and ground forces but other allied forces as well. That was my objective for delivery of the documents. I had no idea that there had been so little information imparted by the United States to its allies. Cohane zeroed in on one particular aspect of the report, the conclusion that modified Mark IV LSTs (Landing Ship Tanks) were not useful as hospital ships in latitudes of the Central Pacific for distances greater than 100 miles. Because of the steel decks, temperatures in the working areas often rose far too high for the transport of seriously wounded personnel. What I did not know then was that His Majesty's Government was about to undertake a large-scale shipbuilding program of Mark IV LSTs, which were to be used for this specific purpose. Cohane requested that I leave the manuals and other papers with him, and he arranged for me to be escorted to the Royal Army Medical College (RAMC) at Millbank about a mile away on the

Thames River embankment. There the commandant, Col. Russell Irvine, invited me to lunch with him and some of his staff officers.

I waited at the Medical College for a meeting at which I could provide a more detailed report of my observations in the Central Pacific. At about 2:30 I was taken to the Royal Army Medical Corps headquarters, located close to Hyde Park Gate in a spectacular Victorian mansion that had been remodeled for wartime use. There I was met by a colonel who ushered me into an anteroom and told me to wait until called. I had no idea what was in store for me. Quite a few high-ranking officers from the army, navy, and air force were coming and going as I sat in that room.

About an hour later, I was escorted upstairs to a large room with a long table covered with a green cloth and overstuffed armchairs all around. I was introduced to the senior officers present and asked to sit at one end of the table. It suddenly dawned on me that as a lieutenant commander, I was the most junior officer present. Directly opposite me was Lt. Gen. Sir Alexander Hood, director general of medical services for the British Army. To his right sat Surgeon Rear Adm. Sir Sheldon Dudley of the Royal Navy, and to his left, Air Vice-Marshal Sir Harold Wittingham of the Royal Air Force. About eight or nine other officers of lesser rank, representing the medical component of all three services, were also present as well. My manuals were placed in front of me and General Hood asked me to give a report of my experiences while at Adm. Roscoe Turner's headquarters in Hawaii and, more specifically, to describe my observations during the U.S. Marine landing in Saipan. It became evident immediately that their greatest concern was the construction program for hospital ships. Many, if not most, of the questions focused on that issue. The interrogation lasted about forty minutes and then I was dismissed, having been told to report to Colonel Cohane the next morning. I left with the impression that something big was taking place.

Next morning Cohane handed me a copy of a signal dispatch from the British Admiralty Delegation in Washington. It read: "BUMED (Bureau of Medicine and Surgery) U.S. Navy confirms that in the Central Pacific Theater of Operations the Mark IV LSTs are not suitable as hospital ships or for transporting casualties for distances greater than 100 miles." This confirmed what I had reported the previous day. Only then did I learn about the British government's building program of LSTs for hospital purposes, which was budgeted at about forty million pounds. I was astounded that the information I had brought with me from the United States via Canada had never been made available to British colleagues in Washington by the United States Navy medical authorities. I wondered how we could win the war if this was an example of the level of information-sharing between the Allies. I could understand some reluctance on our part to share certain information with the Russians or even with General DeGaulle and the Free French, but I could hardly understand why we would not be willing to coordinate our efforts with our British colleagues. Moreover, even in retrospect, it seems strange that an acting surgeon lieutenant commander of the Royal Canadian Naval Volunteer Reserve should be the one to convey such an important piece of intelligence to senior British officers.

On January 2, 1945, I was waiting for an underground train at Victoria Station when suddenly a loud-mouthed, inebriated but obviously happy man came up, put his arm around me, and said, "I'm glad that you navy chaps have just sunk the *Eisenhower*." I had no idea what he was talking about, but I learned later that the Royal Navy had observed two German warships leaving port in France and escaping through the English Channel into the North Sea. One of them was a cruiser, the *Prince Eugen*, and the other a pocket battleship, the *Gneisenau*. Several months later I told this story to some friends at the Banting Institute in Toronto. Next day one of them came into the laboratory and said, "Fields, I think it's wonderful that the Royal Air Force has just sunk the *Nimitz*." Later that day I found out that the German battleship *Tirpitz* had been discovered in a fjord in northern Norway and had been sunk by the British.

I was still in England during the uncomfortable time of the V-1 and V-2 rockets. The British called the V-1 rockets "buzz bombs." The rockets were fired across the English Channel from the coast of Belgium or northern France. These infernal machines traveled relatively slowly at a low altitude, but inevitably some of them made it all the way into central London. They were really frightening because there was no way to anticipate where they would fall. As long as the sound of the motor could be heard, however, there was time to take shelter; when the motor cut off, the bomb would fall.

The V-2 rockets were another matter because they gave no warning whatsoever. They were large, high-altitude rockets developed at Peenemunde on the Baltic Coast of Germany by Werner von Braun and other scientists who later came to the United States to work for the National Aeronautics and Space Administration in Huntsville, Alabama. These rockets were fired from Holland or Belgium and were aimed to strike at the heart of London. They would climb to a great height and then descend with a whistling noise, followed by a dreadful explosion. The damage was extensive and each always left a large, gaping crater. I thought then, and believe even now, that both types of rockets were used more for their psychological effect than for their destructive power.

Since I was one of the few commonwealth medical officers to have been in the Central Pacific, I was asked to visit Dr. E. A. Carmichael at the National Hospital in Queen's Square. Carmichael was in charge of a program, funded by the Royal Navy, to investigate how naval personnel might be affected while working in semienclosed spaces below deck in hot and humid climates. This research was being conducted in anticipation of British participation in the war in the Central Pacific. To study physiological responses, several rooms for simulating these climatic conditions were built at the National Hospital. A similar setup at the University of Cambridge, directed by Dr. Bernard Craik, focused on the psychological effects rather than physiological ones. My job was to develop liaison between the two units, and I traveled back and forth from London to Cambridge for several months before being called back to Canada.

Craik, in my opinion a brilliant but somewhat eccentric man, was killed by a motorcar while riding his bicycle in Cambridge shortly before the end of the war. This was a great tragedy, and without him the program stumbled along. This work was discontinued when the Pacific war ended rather abruptly in the summer of 1945. I have never seen any publication of the studies done in either of those laboratories.

On my return to Canada in early March, I told Surgeon Capt. Archie McCallum, medical director general (MDG) in Ottawa, that I wanted a change in assignment because I had been traveling almost continually for two years. I was called to Ottawa for what was described on the telephone as an important mission in Toronto.

At that time the Soviets were moving mine sweepers through the St. Lawrence waterway. These ships had been built for them at Sarnia on Lake Huron and were then dispatched through the Welland Canal between Lake Erie and Lake Ontario, down the St. Lawrence River, through the Lachine Locks near Montreal, and across the Atlantic. The crews were brought from the Soviet Union and billeted at the naval barracks in Toronto. I was asked to go and check out the health facilities provided for them since I was the only available naval medical officer who had even a little knowledge of Russian.

The evening after my arrival, I was sitting in the lobby of the Royal York Hotel reading a little book printed in English on one side and in Russian on the facing page, a book of fables, including *Puss and Boots*. I had bought it in London at a book stall on Charring Cross Road so that I could sharpen my Russian language skills. While sitting there, I had the feeling someone was looking over my shoulder and, indeed, standing behind me was a tall, impressive-looking man in the uniform of a Soviet colonel. He greeted me in Russian and then, as he smiled, I noticed that his two upper front teeth had crowns made of stainless steel instead of porcelain. In spite of that, he was a handsome man. He said to me, "I am Colonel Nikolai Nikolayevich Zabotin, military attaché of the Soviet Embassy in Ottawa. May I ask who are you?" After I told him, he invited me to join him for a beer. In those days all one could get in Ontario were beer and wine, so we went for a drink at the bar and then to the hotel restaurant for dinner. I saw Zabotin briefly a few times during the next day or two and he begged me to visit him in Ottawa when I was there. However, the next time I was in Ottawa, I found myself too busy to give him a call.

Several months later, in Montreal, Bette and I were having dinner with friends at a White Russian restaurant and overheard a Soviet colonel and some civilians conversing in Russian at a nearby table. I asked the officer if he knew Colonel Zabotin. He said, "Oh yes, Nikolai Nikolayevich has returned to the Soviet Union on business." A few weeks later, in Washington, DC, on detached duty and in the company of service friends, I saw that Washington's tabloid newspaper had a headline in three-inch capital letters, "BREAK RED SPY RING IN CANADA," and below was a full-page picture of Nikolai Nikolayevich. I learned then that he had been chief of Soviet military intelligence in Canada. His espionage activities had been revealed by a defector, Igor Guzenko, who had worked as a cipher clerk in the Soviet Embassy in Ottawa. Guzenko also implicated a number of Canadians who were promptly arrested. Included among them was a member of Parliament, a professor at McGill University, and numerous personnel from all three armed services. For the next couple of months I was extremely concerned that I might have been observed "fraternizing" with Colonel Zabotin. I did not know if or when my doorbell at home would ring and the Royal Canadian Mounted Police would be there to escort me away for interrogation. I was thankful that I had never had the opportunity to take the colonel up on his invitation to visit him in Ottawa, but it was pure chance that I had not. Fortunately, I never heard anything more about the whole affair except what I read in newspaper articles and, later on, in history books.

I was in the naval barracks (H.M.C.S. Donnacona) on Drummond Street in Montreal when the news came that the Germans had surrendered. That was the day well known now as V-E day. I immediately went around the corner to the office of Dr. Moseley, where Bette was employed as office manager. I remember walking in and saying to her as she sat behind her desk, "The war is over in Europe! Get your purse and let's go out to celebrate!" When Moseley came out of his office to see about the commotion, I told him that I was taking Bette out for a while. He said to me, "But we still have work to do here in the office." I replied, "That's fine, you do the work and we'll celebrate." We weren't so sure that Bette would have a job the following morning but, nevertheless, Moseley realized that there was little he could do, and she returned to work the following day as usual.

One day, while in my office at the naval barracks, I received a signal from Ottawa indicating that Surgeon Captain McCallum, the medical director general, would arrive the next morning on the *Ocean Limited* from Halifax. I obtained a staff car and met him at the railway station. As he got off the train, I saw several officers behind him, among them a tall, blond fellow with a beard. I did not recognize him until he said, "Hello, Bill. What the hell are you doing here?" It was my friend John Rhind, the New Zealander whom I had met on two other occasions in such widely separated parts of the world. I had assumed I would not see him again after the mishap with his ship on the way between Hawaii and Australia, but he had been sent back to England for a new assignment. He had been given command of a supply ship which was being commissioned on the Pacific coast of Canada. Since he was planning to stay overnight in Montreal before taking a train west, Bette and I invited him for dinner. We had a fine time recalling our previous encounters. For a long time after that I had in mind that I would see John again, but we lost touch with each other. When I finally got to New Zealand many years later, I looked for him in his hometown, Dunedin. Both in

The War Years

Auckland and in Dunedin I found several persons with that name, but none of them knew the John Rhind to whom I was referring. I could only assume that he had passed away some years before. It was really strange how our paths crossed several times during the course of the war.

Shortly before V-J day, I was visiting with three Soviet naval officers in the wardroom of the naval barracks on Drummond Street in Montreal. They were from a minesweeper that was briefly in port for refit. While we were enjoying a drink, word came that the first atomic bomb had been dropped on Hiroshima. This was exciting for all of us, although the great concern expressed by my Russian friends tempered the situation. They immediately started to press me for information, but I was as surprised as they were.

When V-J Day came along in August 1945 and the war was finally over, I was serving as principal medical officer on the staff of Capt. Thomas Kelly, RCNR, the naval officer in charge of the Port of Montreal. My responsibilities included oversight of all medical facilities in the area and the quarantine regulations for the port. This made it essential for me to stay on active duty while everyone else was being demobilized.

I was elated in December 1945 when Bette was notified by the Minister for Naval Service, Douglas Abbott, that I was to be decorated by King George VI on New Year's Day 1946 with military membership in the Order of the British Empire (M.B.E.). It was a citation for meritorious service between 1941 and 1945. I am still very proud of that honor.

My discharge orders did not arrive until May 1946, after five years in uniform. Because of the unanticipated delay, the position at the Montreal Neurological Institute, which I had been promised by the director, Dr. Wilder Penfield, had been filled by someone else.

Chapter 4

Neurology Training and First Full-time Job

IN 1946, WHEN THE TIME came for me to return to civilian life, I decided to undertake further residency training because I had been away from clinical work much too long. Doing appendectomies on the ward room table of a destroyer or doling out pills to prevent motion sickness is not exactly the most practical training for a neurologist, so I decided that I would devote my time to completing my formal education.

In January-February 1946, Surgeon Commodore Archie McCallum, medical director general, Royal Canadian Navy, in Ottawa, granted me leave to make a trip to the United States to explore the possibilities for pursuing further postgraduate study when my military service was completed. Dr. Wilder Penfield, director of the Montreal Neurological Institute, had promised me a job, but when I was not demobilized in 1945, the post went to a friend and colleague, J. Preston Robb, who also had been a medical officer in the Royal Canadian Navy. Robb subsequently became chief of neurology at the Institute.

Since I had to find another position outside of Montreal, I arranged visits to several clinics in the United States. My first stop on this trip was in Chicago at the Illinois Neuropsychiatric Institute, where I found Dr. Warren McCulloch, a neurophysiologist, working in the basement. He had recently come from Yale University in

New Haven, Connecticut. Adjacent to his research area were the laboratories of Dr. Frederick Gibbs and his wife Erna, pioneers in electroencephalography and "epileptology," who had come to Chicago from Boston soon after the end of the war. They had previously worked with Dr. William Lennox, also a well-known specialist in the study of seizure disorders in the United States. Lennox had spent much of the earlier part of his career as a medical missionary in China.

During my relatively brief visit in Chicago I stayed at the home of the McCullochs in Hinsdale, a suburb west of the metropolis. This was a very stimulating experience, both socially and intellectually. The lifestyle at their home could best be described as Bohemian. Warren and his wife were charming and highly intelligent people.

(I had the privilege of having Warren McCulloch as a guest speaker at the 10th Annual Houston Neurological Symposium in 1962. The published proceedings, which I edited with Dr. Walter Abbott, are contained in a book, *Information Storage and Neural Control*. In that volume there is a reprint of an article by McCulloch and Walter Pitts, entitled "A Logical Calculus of the Ideas Immanent in Nervous Activity." This classic paper on neurophysiological automata theory still merits reading today, almost fifty years after its publication. It is the bridge between central neural processing and modern computers. Several years before that meeting in Houston took place, McCulloch had moved back east to join the faculty at the Massachusetts Institute of Technology in Cambridge, Massachusetts.)

One of the many fascinating people I met while visiting Warren McCulloch was Ladislas Meduna, a Hungarian-born psychiatrist, then working in Chicago. Meduna was a pioneer in shock therapy for depressive psychoses. He was the man who introduced intravenous metrazol shock treatment in the United States.

After spending several interesting days in Chicago, I proceeded to St. Louis, Missouri, for a visit to Washington University School of Medicine, where neurology and psychiatry were still combined in one department under the direction of Edwin Gildea. Almost coincident with the time of my visit, James L. O'Leary, a neurologist and neurophysiologist, returned from military service. While in uniform, he had been director of the Electroencephalography Laboratory at the Naval Hospital in St. Albans, New York. During that visit I also met George Bishop, an internationally known neurophysiologist, who had been a collaborator of the Nobel Laureates Gasser and Erlanger, but unfortunately was passed over when the award was made. I was quite favorably impressed with what I saw in St. Louis and with the people there who were trying to get neurology launched as an independent department. They did not have a neurology residency training program but assured me that they had been promised approval by July 1, 1946, the date when I would be ready to start.

From St. Louis I traveled to Duke University in Durham, North Carolina, for a visit with Dr. Robert Graves, who was heading the Division of Neurology within the Department of Medicine. At the time, he had with him a younger faculty member, Frederick Hesser, whom I had first met in Baltimore when he was completing his residency training in internal medicine at Johns Hopkins Hospital in 1938 and I was a fourth-year medical student. Fred Hesser later left Duke and went to Albany, New York, where he became chairman of the Department of Neurology at Albany Medical College. Although I was very much impressed with the Duke campus and the sincerity of Dr. Graves in his desire to develop a first-rate program, I felt that they were still a long way from that goal.

From Durham I went on to New York City, where I wanted to see a couple of other hospitals. My first visit was to Montefiore Hospital in the Bronx. Dr. H. Houston Merritt was chief of neurology there. He had been one of my highly respected teachers in medical school when he was at the Boston City Hospital. I spent one memorable morning making rounds with him and his associate, Theodore von Storch. The next morning I went to Bellevue Hospital to visit Foster Kennedy, chief of neurology. I found Dr. Kennedy to be a delightful and gracious gentleman, but I had the feeling that he would be retiring before very long and it would not be in my best interest to enter that program. Furthermore, Bellevue was an immense place, with many patients, and I could envision that I might be overwhelmed. However, during the day and a half that I spent in New York with Foster Kennedy and his associates, I was well received and was invited to consider coming back for further training.

In the fall of 1952, I unexpectedly received a letter from Mrs. Katherine Kennedy, who identified herself as the widow of Foster Kennedy. She recalled in that letter that her husband had mentioned on several occasions my comments about something that he had on

Neurology Training and First Full-time Job

the wall of his office. This was a framed copy of a prayer printed in old English script with the first capital letter illuminated. At the bottom it stated, "A Prayer of the Court Physician of Saladin circa 1180." This physician was none other than Maimonides. I was astonished when she said that she would like for me to have this item for the wall in my office as a remembrance of her husband. She also mailed me a complete collection of Foster Kennedy's personal reprints, which I later sent to be bound and then placed in the Houston Academy of Medicine-Texas Medical Center Library. The framed prayer has been on the wall of my office, wherever I have moved, during the ensuing forty years. It reads as follows:

> Preserve the strength of my body and my soul so that I may be unperturbably ready to help the rich and the poor, the good and the bad, the enemy and the friend, May never arise in me the notion that I know enough, give me the strength and leisure and zeal to enlarge my knowledge and to obtain even more, our art is great and the mind of man presses ever forward.
>
> All God, thou has chosen me in thy grace to watch over the life and death of thy creatures, I am about to go to my labor, be with me in this great work that it may avail, for without thy help, nothing succeeds, not even the smallest.

After leaving New York, I went to Boston to visit the Neurological Service at the City Hospital. When I arrived, I had the pleasure of meeting Derek Denny-Brown. "Denny," a New Zealander by birth, was still in British Army uniform, having just arrived from the United Kingdom the day before I appeared on the scene. While there, I made rounds with Drs. Mandel Cohen and Denny-Brown. I also visited the Mallory Institute of Pathology.

Soon after returning to Montreal, I had letters from both St. Louis and Boston, offering me a position beginning July 1, 1946. After giving the matter considerable thought, I decided that the most suitable opportunity for me to achieve my planned goal for a career in academic neurology was offered by Washington University in St. Louis. With this in mind I accepted an appointment there as a resident and Rockefeller Postwar Fellow in Neuropsychiatry, beginning on the aforementioned date. Since then I have made every effort to avoid the appellation "neuropsychiatrist." I have continued to hold to the view that someone so designated was considered by neurologists to be a competent psychiatrist and by psychiatrists to be a fine neurologist.

I had exactly one month between the date that I was demobilized from the naval service and the date that I had to report in St. Louis. This time was used in packing personal effects and furniture and putting them in storage while I went to St. Louis to find a place for Bette and me to live. Unfortunately, I had no personal transportation because cars were exceedingly difficult to come by during the period immediately following World War II. About two weeks after starting at Barnes Hospital, I had the uncommon good fortune to have as a patient the distributor for the Ford Motor Company in the St. Louis area. When he learned of my need for transportation, he asked me to come and see him the Monday following his dismissal from the hospital. When I got there, it was not surprising to find that the selection of models and color was limited to two-door coupes painted black. However, since "beggars can't be choosers," I was delighted to be able to buy one of the first cars to come off the assembly line after the end of the war.

At that time Dr. Stanley Turkel, another member of the house staff, and I shared a room on the eighth floor of McMillan Hospital, a part of the Barnes Hospital complex. Four rooms there had been made available as quarters for residents.

As soon as I could possibly arrange to do so, I drove to Montreal to bring Bette and some of our personal effects back to St. Louis. The long drive from St. Louis to Montreal seemed endless and tedious, but the return drive was more memorable. We still had our cocker spaniel, who certainly was not going to be left behind. This family member, Brandy, loved to ride in the car but always began to bark the moment the car started to roll and continued doing so until the car stopped or he fell exhausted onto the back seat.

We drove to Windsor, Ontario, on the first day of the return trip and stayed in the best hotel in town. We had been put in touch with Harold Jex, the manager, by a mutual friend in Montreal. Since he was kind enough to permit us to keep our dog in the room with us, we decided that we would stay there and order dinner through room service. This turned out to be rather amusing. We had forgotten that there were still "meatless days" in Canada, and so we were greatly concerned about how we were going to feed the dog. Mr. Jex came to our rescue and had the hotel chef personally deliver to our room some of the most appealing rare ground beef that I had ever laid eyes on. Apparently the restriction applied only to two-legged creatures. It was extremely difficult to resist stealing some of it away from our pet. (Harold Jex turned up a few years later as manager of the Shamrock Hotel in Houston, a position which he held until the Shamrock was taken over by the Hilton chain. The Shamrock was demolished in 1988.)

We had been very fortunate to find a large apartment that was available for rent during the summer months. It was on the first floor of the so-called A,B,C,D apartment block on Kingshighway, within walking distance of the hospital. The apartment belonged to an elderly lady who always went out of town during July and August. It was much too big for us alone, so we shared it with another member of the house staff, Bill Stansbury, a resident in radiology, and his wife, Rosemary. Regrettably, we were not permitted to keep the dog in the apartment with us and it was finally arranged to board him nearby where Bette could go each day and take him for a walk.

The apartment which we were leasing had a telephone number that differed by only one digit from that of the Yellow Cab Company. It seemed that every rainy night and into the early morning hours we received many calls for taxis. When the phone company refused to change the number, we decided to take the calls and promised each customer that we would dispatch a cab. After many complaints, the cab company found out what was going on and changed its number.

It was essential for us to find permanent quarters, and we had learned that some small houses, which might be available with a GI loan, were being built in University City, a St. Louis suburban area off of Olive Street Road. After purchasing one, we were told that it would not be available for occupancy until the spring of 1947. This was bad news since Bette would be forced to return to Montreal at the end of the summer to await word that the house had been finished. Although this was unsatisfactory, to say the least, we were left with no choice. The prospect of having a house of our own for the first time since our marriage in 1941, however, tended to offset the inconvenience.

I continued to share a room at the hospital with Stanley Turkel. (He later went into the practice of psychiatry in Los Angeles.) In the room directly across the hall from us was Joseph Ogura, a Nisei Japanese, who was a resident in otolaryngology. Joe stayed on in St. Louis after completion of his training and eventually became chairman of that department at Washington University, a position that he held until his premature death at the age of fifty-two.

My situation at the hospital was unique in that I had obtained my medical degree eight years earlier in contrast to most of the other house staff members, who were recent graduates and had not been in military service. Furthermore, I was the first resident in neurology to be appointed at Barnes Hospital. Since that hospital did not yet have a neurology service as such, we were assigned beds as required on the medical wards.

The professor and chairman of the Department of Medicine turned out to be none other than an old friend, W. Barry Wood. As undergraduates at Harvard College, we had taken a class in organic chemistry together. I had encountered him later when he was an assistant resident in internal medicine at Johns Hopkins Hospital and I was doing a three-month rotation during my senior year at Harvard Medical School. Soon after completing his residency training, Barry went to Washington University as a full professor and chairman. This was a remarkable achievement at such a young age.

Barry Wood was truly an extraordinary person. During his college days at Harvard, where he graduated *summa cum laude*, he was captain of both the football and baseball teams, and was offered a baseball tryout with the New York Yankees. In addition, as an ice hockey player, he was offered a contract by the Boston Bruins. In spite of his athletic prowess, he turned down all of these offers and chose to enter John Hopkins Medical School. Not too long after I left St. Louis to come to Houston, he resigned from his chairmanship of internal medicine in St. Louis to return to Johns Hopkins as chairman of the Department of Microbiology.

Another prominent person in the Department of Medicine at Washington University with whom I had a close association was Dr. Henry Schroeder, a well-known researcher in hypertension. While serving in the United States Navy during World War II, Harry was one of the persons largely responsible for the development of the G-suit to prevent fighter pilots from blacking out when making violent maneuvers. He was all the more remarkable because he suffered from an adult form of progressive muscular dystrophy, a crippling disease which eventually caused him severe disability and ultimately took his life.

During my three years at Washington University School of Medicine, I spent nearly twelve months doing basic research, part of which time was devoted to neurophysiology with Drs. James O'Leary and George Bishop. Also working in the laboratory at that

Neurology Training and First Full-time Job

time was Robert King, a resident in neurosurgery who eventually became chairman of the Department of Neurosurgery at the State University of New York Medical School at Syracuse and later president of the American Association of Neurological Surgeons (Harvey Cushing Society).

In the spring of 1947, I worked with Bob King doing some experiments with baby rabbits. Our laboratory assistant, Henry Bramlett, a young black man with horn-rimmed glasses, took care of the animals. Henry always behaved as though he was a member of the research team, and we referred to him as our rabbit pediatrician. He remained a fixture and well-beloved character in that department until he was forced to retire in the early 1980s because of a serious illness.

In the department there was also an instrument repair and machine shop, run by a very skilled and innovative craftsman, Henry Fuchs. This gentleman had made a specially designed reflex hammer for a couple of the staff neurologists and one for me as well. This machine-tooled instrument had a lucite handle and a head two and a half inches in diameter made from the kind of rubber stopper ordinarily used to seal a large jar. In between the handle and the head there were three Kirschner wires which I had liberated from the Orthopedic Service. These were fitted as the stem of the reflex hammer. This instrument has elicited many comments from students and residents with whom I have worked over the last forty years and still survives intact in my black bag. I must decide soon to whom I shall bequeath it.

One weekend I was planning to go to Dr. O'Leary's home for a visit and decided I would bring along with me a beautiful calico cat as a pet for his two young daughters. That Saturday morning I went to the animal quarters to find the feline, which I had carefully put in a cage off in one corner, and noted that it was no longer there. I rushed down to the lab and found the cat anesthetized and stretched out on a experimental surgical table with its head secured in a frame. William Landau, then a senior medical student, had come in that morning to conduct an experiment and had selected this particular cat for his purpose. I was devastated, but there was nothing I could do about it but blame myself for not having put some kind of notice on the cage saying that this cat was not to be removed. (Landau went on to complete training in neurology and subsequently succeeded Jim O'Leary as professor and chairman of that department at Washington University School of Medicine, a position from which he retired in 1990.)

One morning while I was recording brain waves from an anesthetized rabbit and stimulating its brain in a specific anatomic area, there suddenly appeared in the record from the occipital area of the cortex a long train of spike and wave complexes which continued for an extended period of time after the stimulus was terminated. These were identical with the typical three-per-second spike and wave complexes seen in human petit mal epilepsy. Coincident with this observation, a visitor from the Mayo Clinic came into the laboratory and expressed great interest in this unusual phenomenon. Shortly afterward he returned to Rochester, where he published an article in their house journal, the *Proceedings of the Mayo Clinic*, describing his "discovery." That experience taught me to be busy with other work when certain individuals came to visit.

Arrangements were also made for me to spend three months in the laboratory of Dr. Oliver Lowry, who had just come to Washington University as professor and chairman of the Department of Pharmacology. Fortunately, Lowry was anxious to pursue his interest in neuropharmacology and I had the privilege of working with him while he was setting up some of his laboratory procedures.

In the early part of 1948, while working with Ollie Lowry, I encountered for the first time Dr. Helen Porter, a visiting biochemist from the University of London School of Agriculture. She was a research scientist in the Department of Biochemistry with Drs. Carl and Gerti Kori, both Nobel Laureates. Bette and I came to know Helen socially and enjoyed her delightful company during the year and a half that she remained in St. Louis. One day Helen introduced me to a Polish doctor, Taddeus Z. Baranowski, who was employed as an exchange fellow in Kori's department. She intimated later that she was not very impressed with Baranowski's qualifications as a biochemist and that she was also suspicious of the company he kept because he was spending a great deal of time with some well-known left-wing radical members of the faculty. This became even more apparent when we both attended the same social affairs. I mentioned my concern to one of my friends who had previously worked with the Federal Bureau of Investigation. He suggested that I call the local office and make an appointment to see the chief agent, which I did. For the next year, during the rest of my time in St. Louis, I reported regularly by phone to an agent, whom I never saw, concerning Baranowski's activities.

After I left St. Louis for Houston, I thought no more about this matter until 1953, when I was once again in contact with Helen Porter in London during my first visit to Europe after World War II. Helen told me that approximately two and a half years earlier she had been interviewed by two gentlemen from MI-5 (British Military Intelligence), who very politely queried her in great detail about Baranowski and her observations of his activities while they were both in St. Louis. She was amazed at the detailed knowledge they had of Baranowski's movements during his years at Washington University School of Medicine. I did not mention that I knew anything at all about his activities except to tell her that I had learned by chance about a year earlier that Taddeus Baranowski had been appointed as deputy minister of health in the Polish communist government in Warsaw.

In those days all candidates for certification by the American Board of Psychiatry and Neurology who were training in neurology were required to spend some time in psychiatry. I had the good fortune to be assigned to work with George Saslow in outpatient psychiatry. This proved to be an invaluable experience as it has helped me on many occasions ever since. I not only learned various ways to deal with psychoneurotic and psychopathic individuals but also became confident in my ability to recognize the cardinal signs of various psychoses. Today trainees in neurology are no longer exposed to such instruction, and, consequently, have little knowledge or experience in psychiatry. I consider this to be a real tragedy.

In retrospect, however, I feel that the most gratifying part of my residency training experience in St. Louis was the opportunity to have as my principal attending neurologists two gentlemen who were exceedingly fine clinicians, Irwin "Bud" Levy, who had trained at the New York Neurological Institute, and Andrew B. Jones, the senior neurologist on the hospital staff. "A.B.," as he was fondly called, had obtained most of his knowledge of neurology largely through personal experience, particularly during the days of the first St. Louis encephalitis epidemic in the 1930s. He was a no-nonsense type of pragmatic physician who almost always seemed to get to the heart of the problem more on the basis of common sense than through some esoteric scientific approach. Bud Levy, on the other hand, was a very well-trained intuitive clinician who was at the same time very exacting in his examination of patients. He taught me more about the nuances of the clinical neurological examination than I could have found almost anywhere else.

My boss, James O'Leary, and I had arrived on the local scene at almost the same time, both having shed our wartime uniforms only a short time before. He enlisted my help in setting up the laboratory of electroencephalography (EEG) during the 1946-47 academic year. The assignment gave me an almost unparalleled opportunity to acquire considerable knowledge about various types of epileptic seizures. This experience took place during an era when there were very few EEG laboratories around the country and even fewer persons with sufficient experience to be able to use the new tool and interpret the recordings in a clinically beneficial manner. I was able to put what knowledge I had learned to practical use during the last year of my residency (1948-49) when I was assigned the task of setting up a seizure clinic at the St. Louis Children's Hospital with two pediatricians, Gilbert Forbes and Don Thurston, and the latter's wife, Jean. This was the first seizure clinic to be developed in St. Louis.

Since the completion of my residency training at the end of June 1949 was already in sight, it was imperative for me to explore the possibility of finding a full-time position in academic neurology. Moreover, I had been out of medical school for almost eleven years and had no immediate prospect of permanent employment. I discussed my concerns with a number of people during that last year of training. My chief, Jim O'Leary, and one of the aforementioned clinical professors, Bud Levy, had been kind enough to arrange for me to accompany them to the annual meeting of the American Neurological Association in Atlantic City and the Association of Research in Nervous and Mental Diseases in New York on several occasions, so I had been provided with opportunities for meeting many important figures in American neurology and neurosurgery. As a result of these contacts and on the recommendation of Jim O'Leary, I was invited to look at several academic jobs.

First, I was interviewed for the position of chief of neurology in the Department of Medicine at the University of Washington Medical School in Seattle, which was just getting started. My friend, Arthur Ward, a fellow alumnus of the Montreal Neurological Institute, whom I had met when he was working with McCulloch in Chicago, had just accepted a position there in neurosurgery.

Neurology Training and First Full-time Job

Then, at the invitation of Johannes Neilsen, neurologist and neuropathologist, and Aidan Raney, neurosurgeon, I visited the University of California at Los Angeles (UCLA). The program there was still in an embryonic stage. They did not yet have their own hospital or even a medical school building, but I was offered a position as chief of neurology at the Birmingham Veterans Administration Hospital in Van Nuys, California, where my counterpart in neurosurgery would have been John French. Jack French later went on to become director of the Brain Research Institute at UCLA. Also working at Van Nuys at that time was Horace Magoun, a well-known neurophysiologist.

A close friend, Berne Newton, who had been a medical officer in the Royal Canadian Air Force and had lived in the same apartment building in Montreal as Bette and I, visited us in St. Louis in late 1948 on his way back to Houston, Texas. His wife, Kay, and Bette had become very good friends while we were both away in the military. He had been discharged from the service much earlier than I and had gone to Baylor College of Medicine in Houston after two years in the Department of Pathology at Yale University Medical School. He was then an assistant professor of pathology at Baylor. While in St. Louis, he asked me if I knew anything about Baylor and wondered whether I would have any interest in visiting Houston for an interview.

I had been in Texas only once following my father's funeral in 1944, when I flew across the state on a navy plane. Texas had looked great from the air at an altitude of 5,000 feet, but I wasn't sure that I wanted to move to Houston. I remember telling Berne Newton just that. Anyway, he said they were looking for somebody to develop a program in neurology at Baylor, which had moved into its recently constructed building in the new Texas Medical Center only one year earlier.

Warren Brown, chairman of the Department of Neuropsychiatry there, who had previously spent some time in both Montreal and New Haven, invited me to come down in February 1949. Bette and I drove to Houston from St. Louis. On that particular weekend, the weather in St. Louis was miserable, with snow and slush on the ground, while at the same time the weather in Houston was sunny and moderately warm. The people at Baylor gave me the red carpet treatment and told me that they were looking forward to being part of a great medical center.

That prospect was hard to visualize since all that one could see was undeveloped land, in the middle of which stood Baylor's new building, the only completed structure in the Texas Medical Center. From the front steps of that building there was an unobstructed view of the Shamrock Hotel at the corner of Bellaire Boulevard and Main Street. (The name Bellaire Boulevard was changed the following year to Holcombe in honor of the perennial Houston mayor, Oscar Holcombe. However, as late as 1991, in the area where the north side of the boulevard west of the Medical Center forms the south boundary of the City of West University, there were two signs side by side at every intersection for about eight blocks. One sign, which was blue with white letters, read Bellaire Boulevard while the other right next to it was green and labeled Holcombe Boulevard.)

In 1949 a large open drainage ditch ran from the Rice University campus to the west, along the north side of the Baylor building, across the Medical Center property all the way to Brays Bayou on the east. This ditch was located between the medical school building and Hermann Hospital. In order to go directly from the medical school to Hermann Hospital one had to cross a wooden bridge. Several years later the ditch was replaced by an underground conduit, which tunneled under the campus in front of the Jesse H. Jones Library Building and was large enough to accommodate an automobile. (Unfortunately, it could not take care of all the drainage problems within the Medical Center, and in the late 1970s there was very serious flooding. By that time the Texas Medical Center consisted of wall-to-wall asphalt and concrete, and the run-off from a heavy rainfall had no place to go. This required prompt implementation of other flood control measures.)

I was persuaded that a tremendous potential for excellence and future growth existed in Houston and on July 1, 1949, came to Baylor College of Medicine as an associate professor of neurology. The medical school was then still affiliated with Baylor University in Waco, Texas. I have looked back often since then and, presumably because I came to the Texas Medical Center as a pioneer, I consider myself a Houstonian and a Texan by adoption. I have grown up with the Medical Center, so to speak, since it was virtually in its infancy at the time of my arrival.

When Bette and I first came to Houston that summer, we needed to find a house and were advised to look in the Memorial

Drive area, which was still relatively undeveloped. A realtor took us to a house on Memorial close to its junction with Strey Lane. This was about six miles west of Memorial Park (the present Loop 610). The house was in the middle of three acres, with only woods on the south and west sides. Memorial Drive came to an abrupt end just around the corner to the west at an open ditch which ultimately drained into Buffalo Bayou. Bette and I decided then and there to buy the house if we could.

Fortunately for us, the property was owned by Horace Whittington, an executive with the Anderson, Clayton Cotton Company. His son, Horace, Jr., was at that time in his second year at Baylor Medical School in the class of 1952. Mr. Whittington was commuting regularly to Galveston, where he was in charge of the large cotton compress that was still very busy in those days. When he learned that I had come to join the medical school faculty, he agreed to sell the house and three acres for $21,500. (This sounds incredible when one considers the real estate values in that area today.)

In 1952, we added on to the house and lived there for another ten years. Those were some of the happiest years of our lives. On the property where our home once stood there is now a Christian Science church, and Memorial Drive continues for another seven miles.

Chapter 5

Baylor College of Medicine: My Early Years

BAYLOR COLLEGE OF MEDICINE had moved to Houston from Dallas in 1943, and for five years had operated out of the former Sears-Roebuck warehouse at the corner of Taft Street and Buffalo Drive (now Allen Parkway). The school did not have its own hospital, so an affiliation agreement had been executed with the city and county governments to utilize the facilities of Jefferson Davis Hospital, which was a few blocks east on Buffalo Drive. In 1948, one year before I joined the full-time faculty, the school vacated the warehouse and moved to the Texas Medical Center to occupy the newly constructed Roy and Lillie Cullen Building.

When I arrived, the Department of Neuropsychiatry at Baylor consisted of Warren T. Brown as chairman, Jack Cooper, and myself. Cooper was overseeing most of the psychiatry at Jefferson Davis Hospital, and Brown was spending much of his time as assistant dean. During my first year, Ben Boynton, a physiatrist who was chief of physical medicine and rehabilitation at the Veterans Administration Hospital, was given an appointment in our department since there was no other appropriate slot in which to put him. He spent most of his time at the hospital and was not much in evidence at Baylor.

In 1950, Brown recruited Jackson Smith, a graduate of the University of Oklahoma School of Medicine, who had trained in psychiatry at Harvard and Nebraska. I thought that he was a leading light among the available young men in the field, and he added an important dimension to our program.

Unfortunately, he did not stay very long in Houston but went on to a distinguished academic career culminating in his appointment as chairman at Stritch School of Medicine (Loyola University) in the Chicago area.

About six months later, we were joined by a British-trained psychiatrist, Vernon John Kinross-Wright. "KW," as he was known to those of us in the department, was also a relative short-termer who went on to Austin to serve as the state commissioner of mental health. His tenure in that job was marked by a lot of dissension and bickering. I have no idea who was at fault.

When I first became associated with Baylor, my only full-time faculty colleagues who were chiefs of service at any of the neighboring hospitals were James Greene, chief of medicine, and Russell Blattner, chief of pediatrics, at Hermann Hospital. Herbert Poyner, who also practiced at Hermann, was a clinical professor of surgery and ran the program at Baylor until Michael DeBakey arrived in 1948. I got to know him well as a kindred spirit since he was one of the very few fellow Harvard Medical School alumni in Houston. The aforementioned Jim Greene; Ted Hannon, an obstetrician-gynecologist; A. Burton "Tex" Anderson, a general surgeon; and two internists, A. Edward Groff and William Baird, were the other Harvard graduates in clinical practice that I came to know in those early days. There was also Hebbel Hoff, professor of physiology at Baylor, who had graduated from Harvard Medical School in 1936, and whom I had known earlier when he was chairman of the Department of Physiology at McGill University Medical School in Montreal.

There was one other physician, John Skogland, practicing neurology as a specialty in the southeast Texas area, that is to say, neurology only and not as part of a practice in either psychiatry or neurosurgery. As far as I am aware, in 1949 the two of us in Houston and one other physician in Dallas were the only neurologists between the Mississippi River and the Sierra Nevada Mountains of California, south of Denver and St. Louis. That covers a lot of territory. There were some neuropsychiatrists in Galveston at The University of Texas Medical Branch, but nobody who specialized in neurology only. It was not until the 1960s, a long time after we got a neurology program started at Baylor, that one was established in Galveston and even later in Dallas. By 1995, there were more than

140 neurologists just in Harris County, Texas, which includes Houston, and they all appeared to be busy. One can appreciate from those numbers how much the scene has really changed. It gives me great satisfaction to know that I played a part in the education and training of some of them.

At first I heard some incredible statements made by the doctors who were doing whatever neurology was being done in the Houston area. I was told, for example, that they hadn't seen multiple sclerosis in this part of the country because it just didn't occur here. What's more, they said, "Black people do not have multiple sclerosis." Well, that was the tip-off to the absurdity of these remarks because I had seen many blacks in St. Louis with a confirmed diagnosis of multiple sclerosis. In fact, one of the first black patients whom I saw at the Veterans Administration Hospital in Houston was undeniably suffering from that disease.

During the year prior to my arrival, the Baylor administration had negotiated an affiliation agreement with the Veterans Administration for staffing the large facility near the Texas Medical Center which had been constructed during World War II as the United States Naval Hospital. The war had ended before it could be fully occupied by the navy, so in April 1949, it was turned over to the Veterans Administration. The first administrator under the latter auspices was Dr. Lee Cady, a man who had had his early medical training and later a faculty appointment at Washington University in St. Louis. Consequently, we had many friends in common and this led to a pleasant relationship. He was a first-rate hospital administrator and he served in that capacity until 1962. Cady really put the place on the map, and his presence in that position confirmed my opinion that there is a great deal to be said for having physician hospital administrators. They can certainly accomplish many things that non-M.D. administrators often find difficult, and can usually, in my opinion, establish more effective rapport with the medical staff. That breed of M.D. hospital administrators has almost become extinct.

Within the first few months after coming to Houston, it seemed to me that it would be extremely important to gather together all of the potential resources for the development of an academic neurology program. Since there were no other neurologists and not many neurosurgeons, I felt that the best way to attain this goal would be to have some kind of grouping that would include people from both disciplines. There were also a few psychiatrists who had had some training in neurology and could contribute as well. These persons were all persuaded by me personally to contribute their time, but this was not a difficult task since there was usually an enthusiastic response. There already had been a great deal of publicity about the new Texas Medical Center and what was anticipated in the development of its component institutions.

During my early days at Baylor, I had both the desire and the energy to really develop neurology. I was interested in locating my program where we could have in-patients and start a teaching service. I approached Dr. Cady at the VA Hospital with a plan, and he designated half of one orthopedic ward as a location in which to start a neurology service. Needless to say, at the outset I had no residents of my own but relied on house staff personnel from internal medicine and general surgery. The staff physician assigned to be my assistant during the first year was Jess Gamble, who later became chief of hematology at M. D. Anderson Hospital. The senior resident assigned to my ward was F. Carter Pannill, who many years later was the first dean of The University of Texas Medical School at San Antonio and, still later, vice-president for health affairs at the State University of New York at Buffalo. Between the three of us, we launched a service in twelve assigned beds.

It was also important to establish an in-patient neurology training program. With this in mind, I persuaded the administration of Hermann Hospital and the chief of medicine there, Edward (Ted) Wilkerson, to send each of their residents in internal medicine to me for a rotation in the "embryo" program at Baylor. I am pleased that several prominent internists, some still practicing in the Houston community as well as others who moved away, spent three months with me in neurology, either at the Veterans Administration or Jefferson Davis hospitals.

During the latter part of 1950 and early 1951, we began to have the first of a flood of Korean War veterans admitted to the Houston VA Hospital. This influx of patients increased substantially the number of patients admitted to our neurology service, many of whom were suffering from epileptic seizures brought on by brain injuries.

In the spring of 1951, President Harry Truman summarily dismissed Gen. Douglas MacArthur from his command in Korea and ordered him home to the United States. Not too surprisingly, MacArthur returned to a hero's welcome and promptly went on a tour of veterans hospitals, which included the Houston facility. I was called upon by Lee Cady to escort the general on a tour of my ward. It was a great honor to meet this famous man and, more particularly, to witness the esteem in which he was held by the veterans, many of whom had served under his command in the South Pacific during World War II.

After I had been at Baylor for about a year, the patient load had increased to the point where I told the medical school administration that we had to have more space and additional staff. Our dean at Baylor, Dr. Walter Moursund, said that the medical school did not have sufficient funds to employ anyone else. Fortunately, Lee Cady came to my assistance once again and said, "You run the program at Baylor, continue as our chief consultant, and we'll find a full-time staff person to run this show." With that in mind, I recruited Christopher A. Iannucci, who had just completed his training in neurology and neuropathology at the New York Neurological Institute. Chris directed the service at the VA Hospital for about three years before entering private practice, in which he continued until his retirement in 1991. His assistance in those early years was invaluable. When he decided to depart for private practice, he agreed to stay on briefly to oversee the service on a part-time basis until I could recruit another neurologist. Fortunately, I was contacted by Israel Schuleman, a graduate of The University of Texas Medical Branch in Galveston and a Houstonian, who had trained with Russell DeJong at the University of Michigan in Ann Arbor. He was anxious to return to Houston. Schuleman covered the service on a half-time basis while he, too, was building his practice. That is how we got a neurology program started at the Veterans Administration Hospital and Baylor College of Medicine.

In 1950, at Jefferson Davis Hospital (the city-county hospital), I initiated the first neurology outpatient clinic and began to develop an in-patient service there as well. The staff at Hermann Hospital also became interested in establishing a neurology clinic and, with the help of one psychiatrist, Paul Walter, and an internist, Howard Evans, I was able to start outpatient services there. Consequently, I had been a member of the Hermann staff for more than twenty years before The University of Texas Medical School, in which I subsequently became a department chairman, arrived on the scene and made Hermann Hospital its principal base of operations.

I felt that it was incumbent upon me also to make every effort to establish a neurology postgraduate training program at Baylor.

The ingredients for a first-rate program were already there and needed only to be pulled together and have adequate supervision. With this in mind, I developed a proposal that a three-year training program be based upon the Baylor-affiliated institutions, namely, the Methodist, Jefferson Davis, and Veterans Administration hospitals. From each of the three hospitals, I was able to obtain funds to support two residents. This enabled me to put together a rotation, using those hospitals for clinical training and the facilities of the medical school for basic science.

The first resident to enter the program in July 1952 was James W. Crawley, who had just completed his first postgraduate year in internal medicine at Hermann Hospital. Others were Thomas H. McGuire, who was in neurosurgery training at The Methodist Hospital; Lucius Waites, who had completed his training in pediatrics at Baylor; and Floy J. Moore, who had started training in psychiatry. After completion of his training, Crawley joined me on the Baylor faculty, McGuire entered the private practice of neurosurgery in Houston, Waites became chief of neurology at the Shriners Crippled Children's Hospital in Dallas, and Moore went into psychiatry, ultimately becoming department chairman at the University of Mississippi. They were all hard workers and helped immeasurably in getting our Baylor postgraduate program launched.

Soon after my arrival at Baylor, I met Dr. John H. Perry, who was at that time an associate professor of anatomy. Perry, a Canadian originally from Windsor, Nova Scotia, and I hit it off almost right away, perhaps because of my association with Canada, but more than likely because of the fact that he had been anxious to have a neurologist with whom to work. He asked me to participate in his course in neuroanatomy and to provide some clinical correlations. This offered me a real challenge, and I jumped at the opportunity. I still see graduates of those classes from my early years at Baylor who comment with some amusement about my simulation of the neurologic deficits which occur in patients with certain types of lesions within the central nervous system.

Another source of humor in those classes was provided by my ability to draw simultaneously with both hands. This was particularly useful under those circumstances since the central nervous system (brain and spinal cord) is in reality a bilaterally symmetrical organ.

(About twenty years later a local film company was making a series of medical motion pictures for sale and distribution to medical schools around the United States. The editor of this series was Wendell Krieg, professor of anatomy at Northwestern University Medical School in Chicago. I was asked by the film director to recruit patients who would agree to be filmed for demonstration purposes. When this could not be achieved in certain spheres, they undertook to hire professional actors. During one filming session where we were trying to demonstrate a focal epileptic seizure, the professional actor was unable to accomplish the simulation, and after many attempts, he became exceedingly frustrated. I volunteered to perform in this particular segment, and it turned out to be a reasonably accurate impersonation. About a year later, after these films had been marketed, I was at a national medical meeting and several persons told me that they had seen the demonstration and suddenly realized who was on the film. One of them said to me, "I never knew that you had a brain lesion and focal fits." I guess in reality I have been, and still am, somewhat of an amateur actor.)

In those early days, if I had a patient who needed neurosurgical intervention, there were occasional predicaments. I can recall helping my friend J. Randolph "Randy" Jones, a neurosurgeon, operate on several brain tumor patients at St. Joseph's Infirmary, as it was called then. He had no one else to operate with him and, since I had had some experience in neurosurgery at the Montreal Neurological Institute, I scrubbed and assisted him at the operating table. I served as "Jack of all trades" in those days and used to go to all of the hospitals in town when requested to see patients in consultation. Sometimes I traveled as far east as Liberty, or southwest to Wharton. I even went ninety miles to Beaumont a few times. It was really very fortunate for me that I moved to Houston at a time when many physicians were returning from military service and specialists and some medical specialties were just organizing. This enabled me to have a strong voice in establishing neurology as a separate medical discipline in the southeast Texas region.

One day I received a call from Randy Jones, asking me to see a patient at Hermann Hospital in consultation. This twenty-year-old college student had just come home at the end of his sophomore year to spend his summer vacation in Houston. He had developed a low-grade fever and had lapsed into a state of drowsiness from which he could be aroused only with great difficulty and then would fall asleep again when left alone. Although I knew about the epidemic of encephalitis lethargica (sleeping sickness), which had occurred two decades earlier, I had never encountered a case myself. I went immediately to my reference books and found that the presentation of symptoms in this man fit exactly what was described for that disease. He survived, but after he recovered from the acute illness he went into a state of hyperphagia, in which he had an insatiable appetite, particularly for sweets. After returning home from the hospital, he would eat a quart of ice cream at one sitting and was nibbling constantly. He was about 5'11 but his body weight increased tremendously until he reached approximately 260 pounds. He then developed manifestations of post-encephalitic parkinsonism, including a marked change in his sleep habits. After about six months in this condition, he died suddenly of kidney failure during an emergency admission to Hermann Hospital.

The family, at my request, arranged for a postmortem examination, and I personally went to the autopsy room to remove the brain and carefully transported it to the pathology laboratory. I requested of the chief of pathology that he put it aside for special examination, but before the brain was fixed in formalin, another pathologist in the department took routine specimens plus samples from other organs that I had specifically requested. Once they were set aside for fixation, they were lost. I never forgave the pathologist and never forgave myself for letting the specimens get out of my sight. Even though I was satisfied that this was a case of encephalitis lethargica, I was deprived of making a definitive pathologic diagnosis because of the carelessness of the hospital pathologist. This was particularly distressing since there had not been a documented case of that disease reported for many years.

I could never bring myself to relate to his widowed mother, who had granted permission for the postmortem examination and whom I saw on many occasions during the next few years, exactly what had happened to the brain.

Early that same year, I received a call from Earl Hankamer, chairman of the Baylor College of Medicine Board of Trustees. He asked me if I would see a young Baptist preacher who was having "some difficulty with his head." I had no idea what this meant, but I arranged to see the man. He arrived at the appointed hour, wearing a fedora hat, which he never took off. My secretary ushered him into my office and shut the door. As he sat down, he said, "Doctor, you are going to have to do everything you can to help me." I promised that I would do whatever I could but insisted that he would have to tell me about his problem in greater detail. He then stated in an offhand manner, "I am a human radar." I asked him what he meant by this and he replied, "I will give you an example. Last Saturday I was at the Baylor-Rice football game and I could hear many of the people in the stands talking about me. Everywhere I went, there was someone saying something about me, and I found this very disturbing. I need somebody to change this so that I will not be getting these messages all of the time."

I then told him I would do whatever I could but was not sure that the necessary procedure could be done right there in my office. He pulled a gun from inside his coat, laid it on the desk in front of him, and said, "Doctor, perhaps now you will help me. It's either you or me." I told him that the machine that would help me remove those troubling electrical impulses was not kept in the office. I informed him that he should put the gun in the bottom drawer of my desk, where it would not influence the electric current, then I would go get the machine. Or, better still, he could walk with me down the hall to the room where the machine was kept. He agreed to all this quite meekly and said he would wait until I returned. I went into the outer office and told my secretary to sit quietly at her desk and not make any disturbance. I then went back into my office and, after I made sure that the gun had been placed in the drawer, asked him to follow me. When we were in the outer office, I threw him to the floor and sat down on him. The man was about 5'6 and weighed, at most, about 130 pounds. I instructed the secretary to get somebody promptly because I felt this man should be admitted to the hospital. Needless to say, there was great consternation on her part since she had no idea what her boss was up to. This was my first encounter with a psychotic patient who was threatening me with a deadly weapon.

A similar episode occurred two years later, when I was asked by an older practitioner, Walter Spencer, an ear, nose, and throat specialist in the Medical Arts Building in downtown Houston, to see a patient regarding a noise he was hearing in his head. He told me that since he could find nothing wrong with his ears, he would like for me to examine the patient as promptly as possible. I arranged to do so and, when the gentleman came, I recognized him immediately as the brother of one of my other patients, a very attractive and highly intelligent woman whose family had come to Houston from the Middle East. This man, a very swarthy type, was somewhat unkempt and apparently had not shaved his heavy beard for several days. He came in and sat down in my office. I asked him to tell me about the noise he heard in his head and he replied, "That awful noise is not the kind of noise you may think, Doctor, but it keeps telling me to go downtown and kill those sons of bitches in the Medical Arts Building." I told him that I could not help him unless he described the voices in greater detail. After listening a little while longer, I pointed out that there was nothing more to be done in the office but, if he would go with me to the hospital, I could give him some treatments to get rid of the noise in his head.

He reached under his belt, pulled out a pistol, and held it under the desk in front of me. "Now will you help me?" he asked. Although frightened, I managed to keep my cool and said once more that I would be pleased to help him if he would come to the hospital with me to arrange for his treatment. I then called the psychiatric unit at The Methodist Hospital and spoke to the head nurse, who knew me quite well. I told her that I had a patient in my office on whom I wanted to perform a prefrontal lobotomy. Fortunately, she knew that I did not do prefrontal lobotomies and suspected that something was peculiar. I arranged with her to be prepared to receive the patient when I brought him to her unit on the fifth floor. I was able then to persuade the patient to leave the gun behind in my desk and together we walked over to the hospital. We took the elevator up to the fifth floor, where we were met by the nurse whom I had phoned. We proceeded into the locked unit and closed the door behind us. I left the patient there while I made the necessary arrangements to transfer him to the care of a psychiatrist.

I cite the two foregoing episodes to illustrate that neurologists and, more particularly, psychiatrists must always be watchful. Fortunately, I have never been faced with a similar incident since then and hope that I never will again.

During the fall of 1952, some senior members of the Baylor faculty got together and thought it might be amusing to have a program in the large auditorium of the original Roy and Lillie Cullen Building. It was to be advertised as a scientific meeting, but the whole idea was to have a series of in-house presentations. My faculty colleagues, Hebbel Hoff and Peter Kellaway, prevailed upon me to be the first person on the program, billed as a visiting dignitary, Professor Sergei Ivanovich Prezbyeshevsky from the Moscow Institute of Higher Mental Activity. I came to the meeting, after having been prepared by a professional makeup artist, and was introduced to the assemblage by Peter Kellaway. With an accent which I had acquired during my association with Russians during World War II, I proceeded to deliver my lecture. Apparently, the audience was completely taken in, and even some of my close friends did not recognize me until I had almost completed my thirty-minute presentation.

I remember also that toward the end of that program, a talk was given by Vincent Collins, professor and chairman, Department of Radiology, in which he emphasized the fact that films were disappearing from the radiology department at Jefferson Davis Hospital. With a series of carefully prepared slides, he showed first a person carrying out two or three films from his department, then a person with films under each arm, next a struggling resident in a green operating suit with a pile of films, and finally, someone who was taking a wheelbarrow full of films to Dr. Michael DeBakey. DeBakey made a practice then, and still does, of keeping all of the films for his patients near his office and not in the radiology department. This, of course, was contrary to the rules and regulations of the departments in which Vince Collins had worked before coming to Baylor. Even though no names were mentioned, Collins' little skit with the wheelbarrow full of x-rays was reported to DeBakey. It has been my opinion that this incident may have ultimately contributed to Dr. Collins' untimely departure from Baylor.

One day in October 1952, I received a telephone call from my friend and neighbor, Dr. Thomas Kennerly, a general practitioner in the Memorial-Spring Branch area who, like myself, was a communicant of St. Francis Episcopal Church. I was taken aback when Tom said to me, "Bill, I don't know whether this is in any way true or not, but the word is being passed around that you are a card-carrying communist." In 1952 there was still a great furor about communists infiltrating almost all kinds of activity in the United States. Furthermore, a Senate committee, chaired by Senator Joseph McCarthy, was investigating alleged communist activities in virtually every walk of life. Needless to say, I was somewhat alarmed at first, but later I was more annoyed by this news and contacted the chief agent in the Houston office of the Federal Bureau of Investigation. He invited me to come downtown for a visit. I told him that he would undoubtedly be able to find records of my previous work with the St. Louis office of the FBI and requested that he take the necessary steps to quash the rumor.

Baylor College of Medicine: My Early Years 97

More than a year later, shortly after the opening of the Doctors' Club in the new Jesse H. Jones Library Building in the Texas Medical Center, I was approached by Irving Moody, a surgeon at Heights Hospital. I knew Dr. Moody only slightly and was very surprised when he greeted me and said, "Bill, I owe you an apology for spreading false rumors. Someone had told me that you were a communist and needed to be watched closely. I had repeated this to several other colleagues. Not too long ago, however, I was visited by an agent of the FBI who told me to cease and desist since you were, to the best of their knowledge, a patriotic citizen." I was certainly relieved that my contacts in that agency had served me well and that I would not be likely to hear anything more about this sordid affair.

In the fall of 1952, it was suggested that I attend the International Congress of Neurology the following year in Lisbon, Portugal. When I spoke to Dean Walter Moursund about participating in this meeting and visiting neurological clinics in several other European countries, he informed me that Baylor had no money available.

Since it was impossible to obtain support through the medical school, I approached one of my patients, Earl McMillian, owner of the largest Ford Motor Company dealership in Houston, with a proposal that he provide the funds needed for my trip. I had been asked, late in the previous year, to see Mr. McMillian after he suffered a disabling stroke. I had seen him first in the hospital and later supervised his therapy after he returned home. When I asked him to support my travel to Europe, he cheerfully agreed to do so.

Shortly after this request was received favorably, I was asked to see in The Methodist Hospital the wife of a Houston physician whose stepson was at that time a student at Baylor. During one of my daily hospital visits to see her, she said that she had heard from her stepson that I was interested in making a professional trip to Europe. The next day when I came to her room in the hospital, she unfastened a large safety pin holding together the breast pocket of her robe. She reached in and drew out a folded green wad and pressed it into my hand. She said, "Bill, this is for you. Use it well." I put it into my pocket without unfolding it. Later in the corridor I took a look and found five $500 bills. Never before had I seen one $500 bill, much less five of them. When I saw her the next day, I thanked her profusely. She reached over, threw her arms around me and said, "I hope that you and your wife will have a wonderful trip."

Such an experience does not come often in one's lifetime, and I shall be everlastingly grateful to this lovely lady.

The money sent to Baylor by Mr. McMillian and the amount received from the student's mother were made available to me by Dean Moursund. He said that I must take my wife and the best way to accomplish this was to have her officially recognized as my secretary. I seriously doubt that such an arrangement would be given a moment's consideration today.

Bette and I decided to travel by train to Montreal, to leave our two young children with her sister, and from there fly to England on Trans Canada Airlines (now Air Canada). In the early 1950s, flying to Europe was really quite an undertaking. We went from Montreal to Gander, Newfoundland, then overnight on the trans-Atlantic leg, landing in Prestwick, Scotland, the following morning. I will always remember our arrival in Prestwick because it was on my fortieth birthday. The phrase "life begins at forty" had taken on a special meaning that morning. As we went through customs, I recalled that my friend, Jimmy Jeffs, who had been a group captain during World War II, was back again working in the Air Ministry. I asked the senior customs officer if he knew Mr. Jeffs and was rather surprised when he said, "Certainly, he is the commandant of this airport." It was about 8:30 in the morning and I asked if Mr. Jeffs had arrived. We were informed that not only was he there but he wanted to invite us for breakfast. I was slightly nervous because the time for our departure was approaching. Jimmy then said, "Bill, relax, what are you worried about? That flight is not going to leave until I give the O.K."

We arrived forty minutes early in London and our hostess, Dr. Helen Porter, whom we had known in St. Louis, showed up at the airport just in time. She insisted that Bette and I stay in her flat. The following morning I visited the National Hospital in Queen Square to see Dr. E. A. Carmichael, a prominent British neurologist and charming gentleman with whom I had worked during the winter of 1944-45 while still in naval service. He invited me to make ward rounds with him and introduced me to other members of the staff. After luncheon I walked all the way to Buckingham Palace and from there to Hyde Park Corner in order to visit once again some of the places I had seen frequently during wartime in London.

The next evening, we were invited to the home of Col. Walter Moursund, Jr., son of our medical school dean, and his wife, Liz. At that time Walter, Jr., was serving as military medical attaché at the American Embassy in London. The other dinner guests were Dr. Francis Walshe (later Sir Francis), senior neurologist at the National Hospital, Gen. Sir Frederick Harris, director general of medical services, Royal Army Medical Corps; Col. Frank Rogers, director of the Armed Forces Medical Library in Washington; and Dr. Helen Porter, our hostess in London.

Liz Moursund, knowing that we were going to be in town, arranged for a Texas-style dinner. I will never forget the wonderful fried chicken she served. When we picked it up with our fingers and started to eat, Dr. Walshe was shocked and looked at us as if we were barbarians. He was amazed to learn that these uncouth Americans considered that acceptable.

After a weekend at Horsham with our friends, Dr. and Mrs. Thomas Ling, whom we had met in Houston several years earlier, we returned to London. On Monday morning, Bruce Lumsden, our old friend from the war years, when he was in the Royal Marines, took us to the changing of the guard at Buckingham Palace. This was really a first for both of us because during the war years the ceremony had never been as colorful.

In the afternoon, Bette and I drove with Helen Porter to Croyden Airport for our trip to Sweden. On arrival in Stockholm, we were pleased to find that we had a lovely second-floor room at the Grand Hotel overlooking the harbor. The next day I went to the Serafimerlasserettet to observe Professor Herbert Olivecrona operate. After leaving the operating room, I made ward rounds with Dr. Frykholm, one of Olivecrona's assistants.

That evening we went to the Royal Opera to see and hear *"Laeder Lappen"* sung in Swedish. It was only after half of the first act that I realized that it was the same opera which I had known as *"Der Fliegende Hollander"* or the *"Flying Dutchman."*

The next day I visited the Karolinska Institute to make clinical rounds with members of the senior staff. I was tremendously impressed by the scope of the work being done in both of the institutions I visited in Stockholm and the quality of the people working there. Several of them became close friends whom I saw from time to time during the ensuing years.

Our last day in Stockholm was spent sightseeing, and we covered as much of the city as time would allow. When we returned to the hotel, we decided that we would indulge ourselves in a really fine four-star restaurant dinner. Afterwards we felt that the decision to splurge had been worthwhile and the time and money well spent.

The following morning we enjoyed a smooth flight to Copenhagen. As soon as we were in the bus on the way into town, we realized that after having been in England and Sweden we were once again in a country where one drives on the left-hand side of the road. (Approximately two years later, the Swedish government switched the traffic from the left to the right side of the road over one weekend. With typical Scandinavian efficiency, they spent many months in preparation for the event and their diligence resulted in virtually no traffic accidents.) In Copenhagen we were again fortunate to have a front room in the Palace Hotel overlooking the city hall square and Tivoli Garden.

The next morning I was picked up by one of the assistants at the Bispebjerg Hospital and taken to the office of Professor Mogens Fog. I was very pleased to meet him since I was familiar with many of his publications. He kindly introduced me to members of his staff and invited me to accompany him for rounds and later to lunch. It was a pleasant and stimulating visit.

In the evening Bette and I went to the Tivoli Garden, directly across from the hotel. That park is unique in this world since it is located in the heart of the city and includes an amusement park, cafes, theaters, shops, and many attractive places to walk. A band came by and performed just below where we were sitting, adding charm to the occasion.

In Denmark we were fortunate to find the brother of a New York friend who provided us with a chauffeured car to take us on a tour from Copenhagen to Helsingor (where the castle is supposed to have been the scene of Shakespeare's *Hamlet*). We were able to spend the entire day driving around the island of Jutland before returning to Copenhagen.

The following morning we had a glorious flight at 8,000 feet over Holland, Belgium, and France, without a cloud in the sky. We could see Amsterdam, Rotterdam, and Antwerp from the plane. We arrived at Le Bourget Airport, the site of Lindbergh's historic landing, and the plane taxied to the ramp across the grass. The contrast between the airport in Paris and the one in Copenhagen was horrendous. It was here that we had our introduction to the planned and calculated anarchy which prevailed in France at that time. We took a taxi to our hotel, which by blind luck we finally located in spite of the fact that the driver had no knowledge of that part of the city. The hotel turned out to be only a few blocks away from the Arch de Triomphe.

After breakfast the next morning, I went by taxi to the Hôpital de la Salpétrière. After many inquiries, I found my way to the office of Professeur Agrégé Paul Castaigne, with whom I visited his service. This was a memorable experience. The wards were each as big as a barn, with no partitions between the beds, each being separated from the next only by a small bedside table on which the patient kept his or her personal belongings, more often than not including a bottle of wine. Moreover, on these wards, members of the visiting team thought nothing of pulling the covers back from the patient, whether male or female, and leaving him or her completely uncovered during the examination. No one seemed to think this particularly unusual.

Following lunch I was escorted to the laboratory and library which had last been occupied by Jean Charcot, the "father" of French neurology. I was convinced that some of the dust on the furniture and on the bookshelves had been there since the old boy died nearly sixty years earlier. However, it was an impressive historical vignette.

Bette met me later in the afternoon and we spent the rest of the time sightseeing. We crossed the Seine and walked along the left bank to Les Invalides, where we went through the Army Church and the tomb of Napoleon Bonaparte. This imposing structure is much more impressive when one sees it personally rather than on a postcard or photograph. Our guide had an appropriately funereal voice which reverberated inside the tomb and it sounded as though he was conducting high mass.

At the Musée du Louvre, during our last day in Paris, we spent three hours viewing the paintings, a truly marvelous experience. Many of these were famous artworks we had seen before only in books and on postcards.

On September 5 we left Paris for Lisbon, where I was to attend the International Congress of Neurology. We flew at a relatively low altitude over the French coast and the flat country around the Bay of Biscay. The view of the Pyrenees and the rugged terrain of the Basque country in the north of Spain and the Portuguese highlands was spectacular.

At the Lisbon airport we hired a taxi, which we shared with

American friends whom we had met on the flight, and proceeded to Estoril, up the coast from the capital, where we were to stay during the week of the Congress. Unfortunately, our pleasant drive was interrupted by a flat tire on the somewhat decrepit vehicle. With our help, and in the hot sun, the driver succeeded in changing the tire. We then proceeded without further mishap.

The following day I went with another American neurologist to register at the Congress in the city. The two of us accepted an invitation to drive into town with a Portuguese neurosurgeon, and after we got into his car I was convinced that this would be a last and fatal ride — it was absolutely wild. After registering, we went to view the harbor, then took a train back to Estoril. The return trip was a much less harrowing experience.

On the first day of the Congress, I attended an unforgettable session organized by H. Houston Merritt, professor of neurology at Columbia University, who had been one of my instructors at the Thorndike Memorial Clinic of the Boston City Hospital during my medical school days at Harvard. The meeting had been called for the purpose of organizing what was referred to as an International Panel for Multiple Sclerosis. It turned out to be a gathering of most of the senior neurologists in western Europe. Dr. Merritt suggested that Professor Monrad-Krohn of Copenhagen be the honorary chairman of that session. I remember him as a very impressive gentleman who spoke English with a distinct upper-class British accent. He gave a short introductory speech and called for suggestions. Before anyone else could take the floor, Professor Jean Barré from Strasbourg, who was sitting on the front row, stood up and spoke in French. He described in some detail, as he would to a class of students, all the signs and symptoms of multiple sclerosis. Everyone was polite and let the old gentleman finish. After he sat down, Georg Schaltenbrand from Germany arose and said he felt that the economies of the European countries had not yet recovered sufficiently from the devastation of World War II to provide much support for the proposed venture and that any concerted effort would require a considerable infusion of financial assistance from America. Following that, Professor Ladislao Minkowski from Zurich got up and, with a heavy accent, described in English his work in immunotherapy of multiple sclerosis using tissue from sheep embryos. No one present seemed to understand how or why this related to the purpose of the meeting but, nevertheless, he was allowed to finish what he had to say without comment. Then, almost before he was through, Professor Barré jumped up from his front row seat and repeated once again in French exactly what he had said before. One of his assistants finally took him by the arm and escorted him quietly from the room. It was a pathetic end to a distinguished career.

I was saddened by this turn of events. It was evident that the meeting was going nowhere fast. Fortunately, I was strategically located at the back of the amphitheater with Drs. Francis Walshe and Macdonald Critchley from London. After about half an hour into the meeting, Walshe turned to me and said, "I think I've had enough, young man. Let's go find a cup of tea." We departed from the meeting as unobtrusively as possible. In spite of the way the meeting turned out, Houston Merritt, with his consummate organizational skill, was able to put together the framework of a plan.

I was concerned about our flight reservations from Lisbon to Madrid and decided to check with the airline ticket office. I had great difficulty getting them to understand anything I said but after much pounding on the table and speaking a mixture of French, Spanish, and English, I got two "company" seats ahead of a forty-five-person waiting list. Even in retrospect, I am not sure how I was able to accomplish this. Late that afternoon, I went to the Solemn Opening of the Congress by the president, Professor Antonio Egas Moniz. Moniz had been honored before the Second World War as a Nobel Laureate for his development of prefrontal lobotomy for the treatment of psychiatric disorders. He was also the "father" of arteriography for the study of the blood vessels of the brain.

On Wednesday during the week of the Congress, time had been set aside for participants to move about at their leisure. With a couple of American friends, we hired a car for a drive through the countryside. I was fascinated by the way the houses were all painted with pastel colors and was told that this was mandated by law. This made each of the villages attractive and distinctive. At that time everything in Portugal was regulated by Antonio Salazar, who was titled "President for Life." His kind of dictatorship was quite suitable for getting things accomplished in an attractive and orderly fashion, but the people seemed to be less than enthusiastic with their lot.

When I returned to the Congress the following day, I attended the session on vascular diseases. The presentation by Professor Moniz devoted to the development of cerebral arteriography was of considerable historical interest. Another on the management of intracranial aneurysms was delivered by Professor Herbert Olivecrona, whom I had met in Stockholm. Both were informative and I was impressed with the arrangements for rapid translation into English, French, and German, which I encountered there for the first time at a medical meeting. I made a note in my diary that it was similar to what I had observed at the United Nations in New York. In those days arrangements of this kind were new and almost unique, whereas today they are commonplace.

On Thursday evening of that week, a formal banquet was held at the casino in Estoril. This was a gala affair but the seating arrangements were such that no one could hear the speakers and it appeared that no one even cared. After dinner, there was a ball; however, it was too hot for dancing in the main room and people began drifting into other parts of the casino to dance or sit at the bar. I spent some time at the roulette table with poor results. We returned very late to our hotel room, absolutely exhausted.

From Lisbon we departed for Madrid on a DC-3 which flew over the mountains between Portugal and Spain. The door between the flight deck and passenger cabin was left open most of the time and the steward was taking as much wine into the cockpit as he delivered to some of the passengers. Consequently, I was thankful when we arrived at the Madrid airport without incident.

The customs inspection in Madrid was unlike any we had gone through in other countries where it had been rather perfunctory. Spain was "Franco country" and the uniformed customs officers made us open everything. While wearing white gloves, they went through all of our baggage very thoroughly. It appeared to be a kind of calculated harassment.

When we checked into the Plaza Hotel that afternoon, we were informed that the power would be turned off all over that part of the city after 6:00 P.M. and we would have to use the stairs. This would not have been too bad except that our room was on the top floor. They explained that there had been a severe drought throughout Spain that year and the Franco government had ordered a blackout to conserve energy.

That evening, Bette and I went by bus to the Institute for Scientific Investigations to attend an homage to the memory of Professor Santiago Ramon y Cajal, the renowned neuroanatomist. We were ushered into a large amphitheater, which filled very quickly.

The ceremony began with a relatively short speech in Spanish by Professor Lopez Ibor, president of the Spanish Neurological Society, who had arranged to have a French translation at each person's seat. He was followed by Professor John Fulton, neurophysiologist from Yale University, who gave his talk in completely unintelligible French. Then Sir Russell Brain, British neurologist, spoke for thirty minutes in precise British English, which afforded some relief. After that came Professor de Wolf from Antwerp, Belgium. Before he was halfway through his presentation, the light had become so dim because of the power conservation program that he had to request a flashlight with which to read his notes. Soon it got so dark that we could creep out as inconspicuously as possible. It was evident that a lot of others had done likewise. After we departed, the next speech by Professor Oscar Trelles from Peru was followed by the closing remarks of Professor de Castro, Cajal's successor at his institute. In the middle of de Castro's speech, the auditorium suddenly became fully lighted, which revealed that of the 600 to 700 people who filled the room at the beginning of the program, no more than a handful remained. This must have really been shocking for de Castro.

Sitting on the platform behind the speakers in a very ornate armchair was a uniformed gentleman representing the minister of culture of the Franco government. He never changed his expression throughout the entire proceeding.

Following this ceremony, we went out for dinner at a nightclub and did not return to the hotel until 2:30 A.M. During our entire stay in Madrid I was struck by the hours that our Spanish colleagues worked. They arrived at their offices or laboratories at 10:00 A.M., took a *siesta* between 2:00 and 4:00 in the afternoon, returned to work and never had dinner earlier than 10:00 P.M. They seemed to thrive on this schedule, but my biological clock never adjusted.

When we departed on a British European Airways flight to London, it came as a great surprise to us, as well as to the other passengers, that we were asked to disembark in Bordeaux, France, where we were served luncheon in the airport restaurant before proceeding to our final destination. Things were done at a slower pace and in a more relaxed manner in those days.

Upon our return home and with time to reflect on our experience, I was satisfied that my first excursion into international neurology had been extremely worthwhile in almost all respects.

Chapter 6

My First Decade at Baylor

AT THE TIME OF MY ARRIVAL in Houston in 1949, most of the neurosurgery was being performed at The Methodist Hospital, where James Greenwood, Jr., was chief of service. Unfortunately, Robert C. L. Robertson and F. Keith Bradford, the other two senior neurosurgeons on that staff, were barely speaking to each other and neither one was speaking to Greenwood. During World War II, Robertson had been stationed at Brooke Army Hospital in San Antonio and Bradford at the U.S. Naval Hospital in Oakland, California. Greenwood remained behind as the only neurosurgeon in Houston. Bradford and Robertson looked askance at Greenwood because he had not volunteered for military duty. Whether this attitude was justified or not, they both gave him the cold shoulder.

In the fall of 1950 Michael DeBakey, chairman of the Department of Surgery at Baylor, recruited Moses Ashkenasy, from Northwestern University Medical School in Chicago, to be chief of neurosurgery at the VA Hospital. About six months later he also brought another young neurosurgeon, Charles Carton, an alumnus of the New York Neurological Institute, to join the faculty at Baylor. Unfortunately, the other three neurosurgeons would not give either of them operating time at The Methodist Hospital and they were restricted to working at the VA Hospital. Charlie Carton, in particular, was a quality person, and this arrangement certainly was not likely to satisfy him. I recognized that if something drastic was not done promptly, we would lose him to some other teaching institution.

The animosity between the three senior neurosurgeons at The Methodist Hospital created a terrible problem for me in the development of a neurology program. Soon it also became evident that an approved residency program in neurosurgery would be necessary as a complement to the one in neurology. Greenwood was a well-trained person and very supportive. Furthermore, he had the inside track at The Methodist Hospital, where we both believed that the best opportunity existed for the development of neurology and neurosurgery. I went to visit each of these three gentlemen in turn and heard a lot of acrimonious comment from each about the other two. I hastened to point out to each of them that we would never have a residency training program in neurosurgery, or neurology, until there was some relaxation of their strained relations.

After reasoning with the three neurosurgeons individually, I arranged a meeting in December 1953 in the board room at Baylor College of Medicine, which each agreed to attend. When we were all gathered, with me at the head of the table, I initiated the discussion with a comment to each one in turn that he should desist from pointing a finger at the other two and calling them names. I made it clear that the only way we were going to get the program moving forward was to have a formal truce. They finally agreed and all four of us signed a document which I had prepared. Then came the moment of truth. With such strong personalities, it was going to be difficult to decide who would be the one to direct the neurosurgery residency training program and obtain approval from the American Board of Neurological Surgery. I had already had a preliminary discussion regarding the problem with Leonard Furlow, who was then secretary of that board. I had known Dr. Furlow during my three years in St. Louis. He had told me that if we could get our house in order and prepare a formal application, the board would be very pleased to take the matter under consideration.

When the discussion was over, I took from my pocket three matchsticks, one long one and two others which I had broken in half. I held them between my fingers so that they all appeared to be the same length. The surgeons agreed that each would draw a matchstick and the one who pulled the long one would be the first director of the neurosurgery training program at Baylor for a period of two years, after which one of the others would take over. Robby Robertson drew the long straw, and in spite of the fact that the others were obviously not too happy, he was given the responsibility for preparing the application. The document which was drawn up for our signatures after the meeting is of considerable interest and is quoted here:

MEETING TO DISCUSS THE FUTURE PLANS
FOR NEUROLOGY AND NEUROSURGERY
December 1953

Present: Doctors Bradford, Fields, Greenwood, and Robertson

(1) Plans were discussed for better coordination of undergraduate teaching programs and post-graduate training.
(2) Proposal made for the reorganization of the Division of Neurosurgery within the Department of Surgery.
(3) Institution of some form of closer administrative collaboration between neurology and neurosurgery, and to have physical facilities in close proximity. It was hoped that this could be implemented by July 1, 1954.
(4) It was proposed to have the chairmanship of the Division of Neurosurgery on a two-year rotating basis with Dr. R.C.L. Robertson (name inserted) to be the chairman for the first two years beginning July 1, 1954.
(5) To request of the Dean that Dr. Charles A. Carton be appointed full-time in the Division of Neurosurgery as Assistant Professor. This would relieve him of his full-time responsibilities in the V.A.H. and enable him to assist in building the Neurosurgical Service at Jefferson Davis Hospital.
(6) Proposed that Dr. James Greenwood, Jr. be appointed Consultant at the V.A.H., and also that he remain as Chief of Service at Methodist Hospital to direct that part of the postgraduate training program.
(7) Proposed that Dr. F. Keith Bradford be re-appointed to the active staff of Methodist Hospital at an early date.
(8) Proposed that Dr. R.C.L. Robertson remain Chief of Service at Jefferson Davis Hospital.
(9) As a result of a letter received from Dr. Leonard Furlow, Secretary of the American Board of Neurological Surgery, it was proposed that plans be initiated to set up an integrated residency training program in the Baylor affiliated hospitals.

(10) Proposed and tentatively adopted that the four persons present at this meeting constitute in the future an unofficial policy committee.
(11) All above being mutually agreeable, we subscribe to the proposal that these plans be presented to the Dean of Baylor University College of Medicine and concerned department heads as representing our recommendations.
    (Signed) William S. Fields, M.D., Recording Secretary
    (Signed) F.K. Bradford, M.D.; J. Greenwood, Jr., M.D.;
    R.C.L. Robertson, M.D.

Once a decision had been reached about a neurosurgery program, many of the personal and emotional problems surrounding it gradually faded away. The other *quid pro quo* was that Robertson and Bradford would nominate Greenwood for membership in the American Academy of Neurological Surgery. Up to that point they had blackballed him. Fortunately, the presence of George Ehni on the staff at both The Methodist and Hermann hospitals and the arrival of Marshall Henry on the scene helped to bring a more cooperative spirit to the local scene. However, Randy Jones moved his practice from The Methodist to Hermann Hospital, where he became chief. He apparently believed that he had been intentionally left out of all of the planning and made me the target of his dissatisfaction. I had no idea that he looked upon me as the one who kept him out of all of the decision making. Another decade passed before I became aware that his aloof attitude toward me was based on such an erroneous perception.

It has never ceased to amaze me how rumors and innuendos can cause such disastrous deterioration in interpersonal relationships. I have tried wherever and whenever possible to defuse such confrontations by taking a direct approach, but even that may be regarded with suspicion and outright disbelief. I am pleased to say that Randy Jones and I worked out the problem before he died. He was a fine human being for whom I had great respect. His son, John, a 1971 graduate of Tulane University School of Medicine, has been in neurosurgical practice in Houston since 1977 and is carrying on the splendid tradition established by his father at Hermann Hospital.

Most important of all was the splendid rapport that eventually developed between the neurologists and neurosurgeons in the Houston community. Later on, in 1960, my neurosurgical colleagues nominated me for associate membership in the Harvey

Cushing Society, which shortly thereafter became the American Association of Neurological Surgeons. At the time that I was elected, I was one of only a handful of neurologists to be so honored.

Also, I was pleased that the cooperative efforts of our neurologists and neurosurgeons achieved noteworthy results. A survey of neurological and neurosurgical manpower in the United States was undertaken in 1963 by Dr. Ara Severinghaus, who, a short time before, had retired from his position as dean at Columbia University College of Physicians and Surgeons in New York. He was interested in the outcome of the teaching of neurology and neurosurgery in American medical schools. It was rewarding to learn from his survey that in the decade between 1953 and 1963 there had been more graduates, percentagewise, entering these two disciplines from Baylor than from any other medical school in the United States, with the exceptions of Harvard and Washington University in St. Louis. A lot of people in those years, particularly on both coasts, still thought of Baylor as being in the wilderness. These statistics provided me with a great sense of satisfaction.

In the mid-1950s, I had the pleasure of having as my patient Charles W. Duncan, Sr., president of the Duncan Coffee Company of Houston. We became good friends and he even granted me the privilege of calling him "Uncle Charlie." It was also my good fortune to become acquainted with his charming wife, Lillian, and both of his sons, John and Charles, Jr., who have remained my friends over the years.

In planning the development of the Department of Neurology, I felt that it was imperative to have a laboratory of neuropathology for the study of both human and animal tissue and also for the preparation of essential teaching materials. I spoke with Charles Duncan, Sr., and his brother, Herschel, both of whom were very supportive of my plan, and they agreed to underwrite a substantial portion of the budget. At that time Dr. Ellsworth C. Alvord, Jr., was still at Baylor with a joint appointment in pathology and neurology. Together we persuaded Irene Kaiser, who was preparing to retire from her position as chief technician in the pathology department at The Methodist Hospital, to come on board and take over the supervision of what was to become the Charles and Herschel Duncan Laboratory of Neuropathology. This gave the program a tremendous boost. When we moved into the new space made available for the department, a splendid laboratory facility was included in the plan.

I also believed that a departmental reference library should be an integral part of our new facilities. At about this time I was asked by Dr. Moise D. Levy, Sr., with whom I had served on the board of the Houston Academy of Medicine, to take care of a young Houston man who had just received his discharge from military service. He was in St. Luke's Episcopal Hospital, virtually paralyzed from the neck down and with an elevated white blood cell count. Laboratory tests proved this to be infectious mononucleosis with neurological complications, a most unusual clinical picture. The patient made a remarkably good recovery but with some persistent deficit. His parents, Mr. and Mrs. Isaac Brochstein, and his older brother, Raymond, were greatly relieved by his successful recovery and wanted to do something to further the development of my department. Since we were moving into our facilities in the new building, it was agreed that Brochsteins, Inc., a firm well known for its skill and craftsmanship in interior design, would undertake to build the library according to my specifications. I was thrilled at the prospect since I had admired the magnificent interiors created by their firm in other buildings in the city. This one turned out to be no exception. It was my regret that later, when my resignation was requested, these splendid facilities, the Duncan Laboratory and the Brochstein Library, had to be left behind.

Early in 1956 I was requested by the U.S. State Department to go on a round-the-world trip to report on medical school facilities in various countries. Everything was arranged for me to leave Houston in October for the Middle East and continue from there in an easterly direction. I was ticketed on Air France to Paris and on to Beirut, Lebanon, when war broke out between Israel and Egypt over the new regulations which the Egyptian president, Abdel Gamal Nasser, had placed on traffic through the Suez Canal. Britain and France had joined the Israelis in this dispute because they had a large commercial interest in keeping the canal open.

Since this war placed severe restrictions on travel through the area, arrangements were hastily made for me to travel in a westerly direction instead in order to visit in Japan, Hong Kong, and the Philippines. I was also able to persuade the U.S. Public Health Service to let me spend a couple of weeks in Guam to examine patients suffering from amyotrophic lateral sclerosis (Lou Gehrig's Disease), which had reached almost epidemic proportions among the native Guamanians.

I flew from Houston to Tokyo by way of California and Hawaii. The trip by propeller plane was long and arduous. The first leg was to Los Angeles, where I stayed forty-eight hours at the Beverly Hilton Hotel and visited some colleagues at UCLA. From there my itinerary took me by PanAm Stratocruiser to Honolulu, Wake Island, and then to Tokyo. It has been a long time since trans-Pacific flights in propeller planes made a stop at Wake Island. It seemed remarkable to me that the pilot could so easily locate in the middle of a vast ocean a small atoll that had only a landing strip and a few Quonset huts.

In Tokyo I was met by Zenjuro and Mitsunori Iwata, brothers of my resident and now longtime friend, Kinjiro Iwata, then still in training in Houston. Also, a delightful elderly Japanese, Professor Minoru Kameyama, chairman of the National Science Council of Japan, came to greet me and inform me that my accommodation had been arranged at International House, a multipurpose facility built and supported for many years by the Rockefeller Foundation.

The first full day, Sunday, was committed only to sightseeing and making some adjustment of my internal clock to the difference in time between Texas and Japan. This convinced me that a stopover of a couple of days in Honolulu would be pleasant and useful on the return trip. We visited the National Garden (Shinjuku Goyen) to see the exhibition of chrysanthemums. Not enough vases were available for the individual blooms in the early 1950s so they were carefully inserted into beer bottles on which the labels were arranged in a neat and regular fashion.

The following day, I visited the neurology service of Professor Okinaka at the University of Tokyo Hospital. We made ward rounds with his staff and I was shown several patients with a diagnosis of neuromyelitis optica, which in the United States would have been called multiple sclerosis. I was told that the latter did not exist in Japan. This discrepancy seemed to me to be a difference in definition and not in the clinical manifestations of the patients' illness.

On the third day I was a guest at Keio University. After lunch, my host, Professor Toyozo Aizawa, introduced me to the audience in a packed auditorium. During the first half hour of my lecture, I spoke about medical and surgical management of parkinsonism. My remarks were translated into Japanese by a recent graduate of the school. It seemed to me that some long paragraphs were followed by a brief translation and short ones by more lengthy remarks. It was soon apparent that the senior faculty sitting in front, while trying to be polite, were being overtaken by postprandial drowsiness. I decided to interrupt my presentation with a parable about a missionary in Africa and his encounter with a hungry lion. This aroused some attention from the audience and I proceeded with the second half of my talk. Afterward two young doctors came forward to speak to me. One of them said, "Very interesting your lecture, but we did not know that you had been missionary in Africa." I was immediately struck by the probability that my entire lecture had been translated into an unrecognizable rendition of my text. It was an important lesson in how not to give a presentation before a non-English-speaking audience.

Later that afternoon I made rounds with Professor Aizawa and his staff. Since many of the senior staff physicians had been trained in Europe, principally in Germany, prior to World War II, it was clear that the quality of medical practice was at a high level. Nevertheless, both the staff and students were intensely interested in how we were handling similar problems in the United States. This attitude had also been evident in my visit to the service of Professor Okinaka.

On my fourth day in Japan, Zenjuro Iwata and I went by train to Nikko, a resort city north of Tokyo. I was impressed by the manner in which every square meter of arable land was cultivated right up to the railway tracks. There were two trains to Nikko, running almost parallel to one another — one on a government railway, the other on a private one. Soon after our departure from Asakusa station, the conductor made an announcement over the loudspeaker pointing out the advantages of our train, which made the trip in one hour fifty-six minutes, while the other took two hours and four minutes. This was my introduction to precision in Japan.

The visit in Nikko was most impressive and the number of tourists small in comparison with what I encountered twenty-five years later when I visited there again. By that time the main street had lost most of its small-town charm.

Zenjuro and I went by cog railway up to the peak overlooking Lake Chuzenji and Kegon Falls. There were many Japanese making the trip in order to climb the sacred Mount Nantai, where in the adjacent woods we saw many wild monkeys. The return trip by motor coach over a road with sixteen hairpin turns was a hair-raising experience. The driver seemed oblivious to the fact that his passengers were all hanging on to their seats so firmly that their knuckles were white. After this wild ride, the return trip to Tokyo was anticlimactic.

The next stop on our tour was Kyoto, where my host was the well-known neurosurgeon Professor Araki, who had had part of his training in Chicago. He was busy but graciously gave me an hour of his time and then had his assistant, Dr. Wakesaka, take us on a tour of his service. Although the hospital was somewhat antiquated, the level of clinical work was excellent.

Fortunately, there was enough time to really see Kyoto, a city containing many religious and cultural gems which had not been damaged during the 1941-45 war. There were few tourists and very little evidence of the commercialism which would soon take over. Zenjuro had only been there once as a small boy and was delighted to share with me the wonders of the old city. At the Imperial Castle, which had been opened to tourists only one month before our visit, we were required to take off our shoes before entering. I was amused when the guard gave one plastic bag to Zenjuro but gave me two — one for each shoe. We stayed at the Miyako Hotel, which during a much later visit I found astronomically expensive.

On our return trip, I decided to stop overnight in Nagoya to meet Professor Hashimoto, who had been Kinjiro Iwata's chief when he started training in surgery. The professor was a charming gentleman who spoke impeccable English. He presented me with a pearl stickpin for my necktie, a gift I treasured and wore regularly for years. That afternoon Zenjuro and Mitsunori Iwata took me up the television tower in the center of the city so that I might have a good view. There were only a few new buildings, most of them made of wood. This was the consequence of fire bombing during the war, little more than ten years earlier. There was, however, a lot of construction just getting under way. Today, Nagoya is just another metropolis.

My daytime return trip from Kyoto to Tokyo seemed interminable. At every stop I would look out onto the platform and find only a sea of oriental faces and nary a single Westerner. For the first time in my life I had some appreciation of what it was like to be a member of a racial minority — a lesson that I have never forgotten. A very kind middle-aged Japanese businessman, who lived in Hong Kong, assisted me in getting something to eat on that eight-hour train trip.

That evening I stayed at a small hotel near the Haneda Airport and in the morning took off for Hong Kong. As we approached our destination, I could see nothing but hills and wondered where the British had found space to accommodate an airport. During our descent I felt as though I could reach out and touch the nearby buildings. At the terminal I was delighted to find Barney Hughes, an American whose wife, Marnie, had been my patient. He took me to their home on the Hong Kong Island side of the colony overlooking the ocean. It was an enchanting place where I could relax a little from my hectic schedule.

Hong Kong had recovered fairly well from the Japanese occupation and was still a relatively small city where life moved at a fairly leisurely pace. In those days it still had a distinctly British colonial charm mixed with the underlying Chinese culture.

The day after my arrival, Marnie Hughes arranged for me to accompany her on a trip by motor launch from Queen's Pier to the leper colony at Hay Ling Chau, an island about one hour away but still within British territory. Dr. N. D. Fraser, director of the hospital there, took us on a tour of the facility, providing me with an opportunity to see many dreadfully disfigured patients with skin, nerve, and bone lesions. In the laboratory I was shown microscopic slides of bacteria in postmortem sections of nerves. I had never before seen bacterial organisms inside a nerve sheath. Representative slides were prepared for me to take back to Houston. The excursion proved to be intensely interesting, and I came away with an appreciation of the dedication of the doctors and others who were working so diligently in this small enclave in a distant corner of the world.

The next stop on my tour was the Philippines. As the plane taxied to the airport terminal in Manila, the Chinese gentleman seated next to me asked if I knew for whom the large crowd outside was waiting. I told him that I did not. It turned out that many relatives of Roger Baisas and Leopoldo Pardo, Jr., both residents in training at Baylor in Houston, had come to greet me. Neither group knew the other. In addition, there was a delegation of army officers led by Gen. Melchor Javier, a neurosurgeon and director of the Veterans Hospital. I was literally mobbed by well-wishers.

Once I was rescued and taken to my hotel, a small group met with me to work out a mutually satisfactory plan for the next several days. My first obligation for the following day was to visit the Malacañan Palace for an appointment with President Ramon Magsaysay to discuss the purpose of my mission, namely, to obtain an in-depth review of medical education in Luzon. The president was very gracious and attentive, and he requested that a copy of my report to the Department of Health, Education and Welfare in Washington be sent directly to him. He also had as his guest that day Cardinal Spellman of New York City, to whom I was introduced. He was in Manila for a large Eucharistic Congress.

After leaving the executive offices, I was taken to the medical school of Santo Tomas University for a tour with Drs. Romeo Gustilo, chief of neurosurgery, and Gilberto Gamez, chief of neurology, both of whom had received postgraduate training in the United States. The institution itself had fine facilities but it was being misused as a factory for producing people with medical diplomas. I was appalled to learn that there were 1,200 students, about fifty percent women, admitted to the first year. It was obvious that there were not enough microscopes to go around and that in the anatomy dissecting rooms there were about ten to twenty students around each cadaver. The anatomy laboratory on the fourth floor was almost the size of a football field. I was dubious that under these circumstances the students could learn anything. Even though a large number of students failed the periodic examinations and dropped out, too many others were promoted to the upper classes. It was in these hospital buildings that the Japanese military authorities had kept American prisoners of war captured at Corregidor.

The next day I went to the University of the Far East, where I found the situation even worse. This was clearly a proprietary diploma mill from which a class of inferior doctors were being turned loose on an unsuspecting public.

On the third day, I was scheduled to give a lecture at the medical school of the University of the Philippines, or "U.P.," as it was affectionately called. Victor Reyes, chief of neurosurgery and a graduate of the training program at the Montreal Neurological Institute, met me there. Although we were alumni of the same institution, we had never met. It immediately became clear that the U.P. medical school and hospital were organized along the same lines as most accredited programs in North America. The comparison with the other schools was striking and a refreshing contrast.

That evening I was a guest of the Society of Neurology and Psychiatry at a reception held in my honor at the Manila Hotel. I presented a lecture on "The Medical and Surgical Management of Focal Epilepsy," which was enthusiastically received.

It was a great relief to be able to relax the next day and enjoy a celebration of the American Thanksgiving which was still being observed there in those days. Congressman Lorenzo Morente, an uncle of Dr. Rogelio Baisas (neurosurgery resident at Baylor), and Dr. Gamez took me to a hotel at Tagaytay on Lake Taal, south of Manila, for a turkey dinner. Unfortunately, we arrived late and had to settle for roast pork. It was a very pleasant full-day excursion in tropical surroundings, through many small villages away from the busy city. The most exciting event of the day was an encounter along the highway with a blue-eyed, albino carabao (water buffalo), which refused to get out of the way of our car.

My last day in Manila was spent at the V. Luna General Hospital (Army), where I gave a talk on epilepsy. I was introduced by Pedro Lavadia, whom I had first met when he trained in surgery with Michael DeBakey in Houston. After lunch I learned that, because of an approaching typhoon, the departure of my flight to Guam was advanced from 11:30 P.M. to 9:00 P.M., so I had to rush back to the hotel, pack my bags, and check out.

On arrival in Guam the next morning, in the midst of a tropical rainstorm, I was met by Jimmy Provencher, the business manager of the U. S. Public Health Service Hospital, who delivered me to the apartment assigned to me. Later, there was a knock on the door and in walked Sam Pieper, a 1955 graduate of Baylor College of Medicine, who was working as a U.S. Public Health Service officer on Guam. His principal assignment was an in-depth study of patients suffering from a familial type of motor neuron disease (amyotrophic lateral sclerosis, or ALS, known in the U.S. as Lou Gehrig's Disease).

By the time of my arrival in late November, Sam had already identified where the patients were located and had started a clinic. Many of those suffering with ALS, however, were in an advanced stage of the disease and had to be cared for at home. Some had been unable to provide for themselves for several years and, in spite of the burden placed upon them, relatives handled their daily needs with loving care. Although there was no promise of relief or cure, these people were always gracious and cooperative because they knew that we were there to learn as much as we could about the disease.

During my week in Guam, I went several times to Tarague Beach (U.S. Air Force Beach) with Sam and his wife and small daughters to swim and snorkel. This beautiful white sand beach is at the foot of jungle-covered cliffs. Only a few months before I arrived in Guam, a Japanese soldier had come out of the jungle nearby and given himself up. It was ten years after the signing of the peace treaty, but he had no knowledge of the fact that the war had ended.

I also visited the village of Umatac, where a small weather-worn obelisk commemorates the landing of Ferdinand Magellan, the first white man to set foot on the island. A few miles further south the village of Merizo is situated on the edge of a lagoon cut off from the open ocean by a barrier reef. The greatest depth of the water is ten to twelve feet, and Sam and I found it to be a wonderful place to snorkel in our spare time. Consequently, I was able to put together in a short time a fabulous collection of Pacific sea shells from there which I later added to ones I had collected over many years and had on display in my study at home.

We saw many patients afflicted with motor neuron disease but had little success with any therapeutic intervention. However, we were provided with a unique opportunity to study this population and contribute a little to the increasing body of knowledge about an otherwise obscure disorder.

Although I had reserved a little time for rest and relaxation while on Guam, the overall experience with the patients was extremely depressing. A few days in Honolulu at the Surfrider Hotel on Waikiki Beach and time with friends before going home more than compensated for the rest of the arduous journey. Hawaii at that time was still a territory and not a state. It was a much less hectic place to visit and, in my opinion, more attractive than I found it on subsequent trips.

In mid-July 1957, I left once again for Europe to attend the World Congress of Neurological Sciences in Brussels, Belgium. Accompanying me was my colleague, Elsworth C. Alvord, known fondly to all of us as "Buster." We left Houston at 12:30 A.M. to fly nonstop to Idlewild (later Kennedy) Airport in New York. We arrived there with only three of the four engines functioning, and as we landed, there were firetrucks screaming alongside our plane as it traveled down the runway. This was certainly not a very auspicious beginning for a long journey,

Buster and I had adjoining seats on the KLM flight to Amsterdam, in the only part of the plane where there were three persons seated together. The man sitting next to Buster insisted that he was in the proper seat when really he was not. When lunch was served, he spilled his beer over Buster, who then smelled like a brewery. There were no apologies. We thought he was a stubborn Dutchman until he got off the plane in Shannon and then we learned that he was a rude Irishman. The trip from New York took ten hours to Shannon and another two and a half hours to Amsterdam.

When we arrived at our hotel, we were told that our reservation had not been held and that they would move us to another hotel. The first hotel room had no bath and the second was no better. Finally, on the third day, we found that we had been moved to another room with a bath. We must have looked sufficiently dirty that they took pity on us. We felt that we deserved it after having been in four different rooms during the course of three days. One day was spent touring around the canals; then we hired a car for the next two days and drove to the more distant parts of the country.

From Amsterdam we flew to Brussels, not knowing that it would have been faster to take the train. We arrived on National Independence Day and had time to do some sightseeing. In the evening we went to the opening ceremony of the Congress, where King Baudoin was present in the royal box and the Cardinal of Brussels in the adjacent one. It was a very impressive event.

The next morning, in the lobby of the congress hall, I encountered Rudolf Petr, who had been my colleague while we were both training in St. Louis in the late 1940s. Rudy had returned to Czechoslovakia with the intention of bringing his wife and children to the United States to reside permanently. Within two weeks of his return to his hometown of Hradec Kralóvé, there was a communist coup that prevented him from leaving the country. From then until the day that I saw him in Brussels, we had exchanged greeting cards at Christmas but had no further communication. I asked him to have dinner with me and he said that he would have to obtain permission from the chief of the Czech delegation. This was arranged, and the following evening he came to my room at the Hotel Metropol. I had a bottle of Scotch and planned to pour us each a drink before going out to dinner. Rudy got up from his chair, looked behind the curtains and all through the room, presumably to see if there was a hidden microphone. It was only then that I realized how very uncomfortable he was and could appreciate the kind of paranoia he had developed during the previous nine years. I suggested that we go to the square in front of the hotel and sit on a bench in order to have a relaxed conversation. It was a very distressing experience. After he returned home, we continued for many years to exchange Christmas cards without any comment.

On the next to the last day of the Congress, I went to the Grand Gala Banquet at the Palais de Justice, a fantastic baroque monstrosity built in 1880 by King Leopold II. I had never before, and never have since, eaten in a rotunda with a 300-foot ceiling. On this very special occasion, I wore a tuxedo with a white summer jacket. Having seen, at the previous Congress in Lisbon, many of our foreign colleagues wearing their medals on their dinner jackets, Bette had given me miniatures of my service medals, including the award I had received from King George VI, to wear on my coat. This did not seem to me, nor to anyone else in my group at the banquet, to be of any concern. I learned later, much to my distress, that this decision had severe consequences. (By the mid-1960s, several of my departmental colleagues and other younger associates had been admitted to the American Neurological Association and I was still not a member. In fact, I had been nominated twice and turned down. I could not understand why I was being blackballed. One of my friends, who had been a member for more than a decade, made inquiry and learned that a prominent neurosurgeon at the New York Neurological Institute, who was an officer of the association, had reported that I had gone shopping in Brussels and bought some cheap medals for my dinner jacket. He considered this particularly inappropriate. There was no attempt by him or anyone else to determine the validity of this vicious rumor, but it had its consequences.)

Since Bette had taken the children to Canada to visit with her sister, I decided to spend a couple of weeks in Europe before returning home. With Dr. Jacob Chandy, a neurosurgeon from Vellore, India, who was a fellow alumnus of the Montreal Neurological Institute, I decided to travel to the south of France, rent a car, and take a tour of the Côte d'Atur and northern Italy. We flew to Nice and took off from there. Our destination in Italy was Lake Garda, where we stayed at a small country hotel. The proprietor, Carlo Lucchini, had been the interpreter for one of my Houston friends who had served in northern Italy during World War II. Jay Chandy and I traveled in a small Renault to see the countryside from there to Venice, visiting in Verona and Padua along the way. During the week that we remained in northern Italy, I spent some time each day doing charcoal pencil sketches, which are framed and still on my wall at home.

When we returned the rented car to Nice, it didn't occur to either of us that we would have difficulty with Jay's visa and Republic of India passport. He had entered France for the second time within three weeks, and the authorities wanted to detain him in the country. Since he spoke no French, I accompanied him to the local police station and was able to arrange for his departure after much wrangling with the local officials. I was thankful that I traveled on an American passport. When we arrived in Rome, he went on immediately to India. It was sad that he did not have an opportunity to visit Rome, but he was out of funds.

While in Rome, I had the good fortune to meet an elderly gentleman from Arizona who was traveling alone in Europe following a tour of England with a lawn bowling team from the United States. We decided to hire a car and tour the surrounding countryside together. A friend of my travel companion turned up the next evening with his wife. She had a plaster cast on her left arm put on by an orthopedic surgeon in Liverpool seven weeks earlier. I agreed to take it off, thinking that it would be an easy job. However, without adequate tools, it was almost two hours before I could remove it and they missed their train to Pisa. Moreover, the skin was not properly protected from the cast by a gauze bandage and, as the cast came off, so did the skin in a few places. It was really a mess.

Almost three weeks to the day after my departure for Europe, I returned home on a flight which took me from Rome to Paris, to New York and to Houston. The trans-Atlantic leg took thirteen hours and forty minutes. Thirty-five years later, one can get on a jet plane in Houston, be in Paris, Frankfurt, or London after a nonstop crossing, give a paper, and be back home on the second day. Whether this is progress or not remains for the reader to decide.

Chapter 7

The Texas Medical Center: In the Beginning

MUCH OF THE IMPETUS TOWARD the creation of a medical center in Houston originated from the vision of one individual, Ernst William Bertner. As a practicing physician in the 1930s, he understood the operation of the community's health care system and believed that it could be vastly improved through better cooperation among doctors and the establishment of improved facilities in close proximity to one another. This remained only a dream until the M. D. Anderson Foundation was funded in 1942 by assets from the estate of Monroe Dunaway Anderson. The trustees of the estate were obliged to find the most satisfactory direction in which to strategically move the money entrusted to them.

I have been told that Houston's best-informed doctors were aware of the stipulations in the trust indenture. At an informal meeting chaired by Paul Ledbetter, a prominent internist, they chose Bertner as the person to approach the trustees of the M. D. Anderson Foundation with a proposal for the establishment of a medical center. Not only did he have the stature to speak for the medical community, but he also had the determination and perseverance to pursue this goal.

To expedite matters, Bertner persuaded the trustees of the foundation to make an offer to purchase 134 acres of city-owned property adjacent to Hermann Park. Many citizens were of the opinion that this land was a part of the park, so a referendum was called in December 1943 in order to obtain a decision from the people. They voted decisively to approve the sale to the M. D. Anderson Foundation.

Earlier in that same year, Baylor University had decided to close its medical school in Dallas and find a new location. The M. D. Anderson Foundation trustees knew that the Medical Center would need to have a medical school, so they offered a site in the center plus $1 million over a ten-year span to be used for support of research. A large segment of Houston's practicing physicians were alumni of Baylor, and the majority were supportive of the idea to move the medical school to Houston. However, many other practitioners were not so enthusiastic and they were upset when they awakened one morning only to find in the newspaper an article stating that the move had been arranged. Since World War II was then in progress, construction of a medical school building had to be deferred until the end of hostilities. The school was forced to operate out of the old Sears-Roebuck warehouse on Buffalo Drive (now Allen Parkway).

After World War II ended and life in Houston began to return to normal, the trustees of the M. D. Anderson Foundation made commitments to four hospitals, two universities, and a medical library to furnish building sites at no cost. They decided to deed the 134 acres of land to a newly created nonprofit corporation to be known as Texas Medical Center, Inc., and named Bertner as its first president. Then on February 28, 1946, at an enthusiastic assembly of Houston's leading citizens at the Rice Hotel, Leland Anderson, representing his Uncle Monroe, delivered the deed from the trustees of the Anderson Foundation to Bertner in his capacity as president of the new corporation. In his acceptance speech, Bertner portrayed a comparison between the Houston Ship Channel and what he envisioned the Texas Medical Center might become:

> One made Houston's place as a trade center; the other will make Houston's place as a health center. One brought great commerce; the other will bring great blessings to mankind, and perhaps — who knows? — it will bring the answer to the cause, treatment and cure of cancer. The Ship Channel brought the captains of industry to our community; the Texas Medical Center will attract the great scientists of the world.

Bertner died of cancer in 1950 and did not live to see his dream fully accomplished. However, he lived long enough to see the completion in 1948 of the first building, Baylor's new medical school, and the initiation of construction on The Methodist Hospital and the Shriner's Hospital for Crippled Children, as well as a new addition to his old organization, Hermann Hospital, where he had been chief of staff. Although I never had the privilege of meeting the gentleman, I learned later from Dr. Frederick Elliott, executive director of the Texas Medical Center, that Bertner and I shared the same birthday, August 18. Considering the magnitude of his contribution to the establishment of the Medical Center, I have always regretted that our paths never crossed.

In April 1949, Hermann Hospital opened what was then called the Main Building and later the Robertson Pavilion. The hospital administration, the board of trustees, and medical staff were somewhat snobbish in their attitude and insisted that the Texas Medical Center ended at Ross Sterling Avenue in front of their hospital, which had stood there for thirty years, and that they were not a part of it. They have claimed to be in the Medical Center more recently, but they had no desire whatsoever to be included during those early years.

The administrator of Hermann Hospital in 1950 was a man named Jewel Daughaday, but he did not survive in that job very long. About a year later, the Hermann Estate brought in a Canadian, Lee Crozier, as hospital director. Dr. Crozier came to Houston from London, Ontario, where he had been administrator of the Victoria Hospital. I had met him previously through my father-in-law, W. Lloyd Ritchie, who had been professor and chairman of radiology at McGill University Medical School in Montreal. Both of them were graduates in medicine of the University of Toronto. Crozier was a delightful gentleman, but I remember him best as a penny-pinching Scotsman. He was reluctant to let anyone in his hospital purchase anything for anybody. Although a good friend whom I used to see socially, he was certainly anything but helpful in providing the ingredients for the development of a neurology program. Moreover, he was paranoid about Baylor and what he perceived to be the long-range intentions of its faculty. This did not make my relationship with the hospital administration particularly comfortable, although I got along famously with most of the physicians.

The first neurology clinic in Houston was started by me in 1950 at Hermann Hospital in the clinic facility on the ground floor of the original building at the corner of Fannin Street and Outer Belt Drive (now McGregor Drive). I enticed two staff physicians — Paul Walter, a psychiatrist, and Howard Evans, an internist — to work with me at the outset. It was several years before any other doctors participated. In about 1954, Lee Crozier, the hospital director, intimated that they did not need my input anymore. This was all right with me since the neurology teaching program was well established by then at the Veterans Administration and Jefferson Davis (city-county) hospitals and a private service was established at The Methodist Hospital as well.

Michael DeBakey came from New Orleans to Baylor College of Medicine in 1948, the year before I arrived. He was very eager to participate in the staff activities at Hermann Hospital as well as at The Methodist Hospital, which had not yet moved to the Medical Center. Moreover, he wanted to be chief of surgery at Hermann Hospital, largely because of its proximity to the medical school. That made good sense to DeBakey but it made no sense at all to the medical staff at Hermann Hospital. He was upset about the rebuff by the Hermann staff when James Greene, then chairman of the Department of Medicine at Baylor, was appointed chief of medicine at Hermann. The Hermann Board of Trustees told DeBakey that he could have a teaching service but they would also continue to have a private service run by staff surgeons in private practice. In those days many of the physicians in private practice were more than a little resentful of the medical school full-time doctors. This is a condition well known to every physician in a community where a medical school seeks to become established (frequently referred to as the town-gown confrontation).

The chief of surgery at Hermann Hospital at that time, George Waldron, was not about to step aside to let DeBakey have the job. The latter had to satisfy himself with operating occasionally at Hermann, running the program at Jefferson Davis Hospital, and organizing the surgery service at the Veterans Administration Hospital. He had the Dean's Committee already established at the VA when I arrived in 1949. That Dean's Committee from the outset also had a University of Texas Dental Branch representative on it. As soon as The Methodist Hospital opened in the Medical Center, DeBakey moved there and concentrated his efforts in that institution. However, they would not make him chief of the surgical service there either. I do not know how it was worked out eventually, but Methodist still has a chief of surgery, who is not on the full-time faculty at Baylor, while DeBakey has been for many years chief of cardiovascular surgery. Over the years, The Methodist Hospital has been able to work out a comfortable accommodation with Baylor without being completely dominated by the school.

Mike DeBakey and I met for the first time not very long after I came to Houston. My contacts with him during the first year or two were infrequent. I was busy at the Veterans Administration Hospital much of the time, and he did not come over there very often. I saw DeBakey more often on social occasions. Bette and I got to know his first wife and his children quite well. We also had mutual friends whose oldest son was a very good friend of DeBakey's oldest son, Mickey (Michael, Jr.).

One Sunday shortly after I arrived at Baylor, I received a call from DeBakey asking me to accompany him to the home of Ben Taub, a prominent local businessman, who was chairman of the board of the Harris County Hospital District. In my opinion, the gentleman was almost prostrated by labyrinthine vertigo. I could find no ready explanation for it except that Mr. Taub had had a recent upper respiratory infection. There was very little that I could do except to give him some medication to reduce the unpleasant sensation. What I used in those days was some of the anti-seasickness remedy with which I had experimented previously in the navy. This seemed to work reasonably well and a few days later, when I went back to visit him, he was virtually over his bout of acute discomfort. He was very grateful for my assistance and in his quiet and reserved manner subsequently did me a great favor.

About two weeks later I encountered Mr. Taub at Jefferson Davis Hospital and he asked me how things were going since my arrival at Baylor. I mentioned that as soon as my wife and I were settled, we were thinking about adopting a family. Bette and I had been unable to have children of our own and we had hoped in the near future to seek the help of an adoption agency. Taub suggested that I contact Grace Knox, the administrator of DePelchin Faith Home, and arrange a visit for my wife and me. What I did not know was that the Faith Home had a long waiting list and prospective adoptive parents often had to wait a year to eighteen months before they had any response whatsoever. A week later we were guests at the home of Warren T. Brown, professor of psychiatry and my chief at Baylor, where we met Thomas Ling, a prominent psychiatrist from London, England, and his wife. During that pleasant social visit we mentioned our desire to adopt a family and our frustration with having to wait.

In early April 1950, only a matter of a few weeks after our initial visit to the Faith Home, Bette and I were surprised to receive a call from Mrs. Knox informing us that there was a nine-month-old girl in their custody whom we might want to visit. We were delighted at the prospect and, when we saw the child and spent some time with her, we were enchanted. We decided on the spot that the baby, whom we named Susan, would fit perfectly into our household, and within a week we took her home. It was many years later that we learned from Camille Smith, director of social service at DePelchin Faith Home, that Ben Taub, who was chairman of the board there, had interceded in our behalf. This resulted in cutting out all the red tape and the long delay. Unfortunately, at the time we learned of this, Mr. Taub was very ill and living at The Methodist Hospital. Since he was allowed no visitors, I never had the opportunity to thank him in person.

What we did not anticipate was a telephone call in mid-September from Dr. Ling in London telling us that he and his wife had under their wing a young American woman, studying in England, who had just given birth to a little girl and found it necessary to put the child up for adoption. Mrs. Ling said that she, herself, would be coming by ship to New York in late January 1951, and would bring the baby with her. We agreed and another adoption was consummated. As a result we went from a two- to a four-person family in less than one year, but we were ecstatic about the prospect of fulfilling our hopes and desires. My mother, who was living in Baltimore, went to New York, met Mrs. Ling, and brought the baby, later christened Anne, to Houston by plane.

In the late 1940s, there had been established a Texas Children's Foundation, the ultimate objective of which was the construction of a Texas Children's Hospital in the Medical Center. Members of the board of this foundation included Leopold Meyer, Malcolm Lovett, and two pediatricians, David Greer and George Salmon. This group was very supportive of Russell Blattner, chairman of pediatrics at Baylor, in his efforts to get a first-class pediatric program established in Houston.

Russell Blattner and I had met previously in St. Louis in 1947, while I was completing residency training after my discharge from naval service. I remember visiting with him on several occasions at the St. Louis Children's Hospital when I was on the neurology consultation service and later when I was participating in the Seizure Clinic in the spring of 1947. By the time that I left St. Louis to come to Houston, Russell was already at Baylor.

When I arrived in Houston, the pediatric department of Baylor was operating the Junior League Children's Clinic at Hermann Hospital. This clinic had been run by George Salmon, who decided to step down as director after Russell Blattner arrived. Blattner had been promised that he would be made head of pediatrics at Hermann Hospital, then the only pediatric unit in Houston, but Baylor and Hermann Hospital were never able to consummate an affiliation agreement. However, James Park, one of the premier pediatricians in the city, who was the head of pediatrics at Hermann, indicated he was not interested in keeping that position. He had told Blattner during a recruitment visit to Houston that, if he took the job at Baylor, he would see that Blattner was appointed chief of pediatrics at Hermann Hospital. From that time until the mid-1950s, Blattner was reappointed each year as head of pediatrics, not because he was at Baylor, or under any formal affiliation agreement, but because they recognized him as someone capable of running a good program. The money to fund thirty pediatric beds at Hermann was provided by the M. D. Anderson Foundation, although Russell Blattner told me years later that he had for a long time believed that this support had come from the Hermann Estate.

During the summer of 1949, a devastating epidemic of poliomyelitis flared up in Houston. Soon after my arrival, I was recruited by my friend, Blattner, to participate to the fullest extent possible in the development of a program for the care of polio victims. There were only inadequate facilities in Houston for the care of these patients, especially the adults. Mr. and Mrs. Lamar Fleming, two of the finest people ever to be connected with the Texas Medical Center, had given money to construct a transitional unit geared toward home-living at the old Jefferson Davis Hospital. This area was ready to be occupied by patients who needed rehabilitation, but the Flemings were prevailed upon to turn it over to the National Foundation for Infantile Paralysis to establish the first regional center for polio.

That was a very hectic time. The Department of Medicine at Baylor, under the chairmanship of James Greene, refused to have anything to do with polio patients. It fell largely upon Russell Blattner and the department of pediatrics to assume responsibility, not only for children, but also for the many seriously ill adult patients who were in "iron lungs."

Blattner had been serving as a consultant at Brooke Army Medical Center in San Antonio and during one of his visits there he met William A. Spencer, a Johns Hopkins Medical School graduate who was in the military at that time. He was so impressed by Bill Spencer's intellectual capabilities and his presentation at a conference on endocrinology that he eventually convinced Spencer that his future belonged in Houston. After Spencer finally accepted the challenge to come, he immediately began to apply his genius to many problems being encountered in the use of the "iron lung" and other kinds of resuscitation devices. Everybody lent a hand and we struggled along, but the ultimate responsibility rested with Bill Spencer. It was not too long after he arrived that he emerged as director of the Southwest Polio Respiratory Center adjoining Jefferson Davis (City-County) Hospital. He was instrumental in helping us get funds from the National Foundation to develop research activities as well as teaching and patient care. He was also responsible for bringing Dr. Robert Jackson to Houston. Bob made many significant contributions to our rehabilitation effort before moving on to the Craig Rehabilitation Center in Denver, Colorado.

I was reminded many years later of my association with the Southwest Polio Respiratory Center when Prentice Findlay, a senior pediatrician on the faculty of The University of Texas Medical School at Houston asked me if I was the Fields who had written a manual for the care of paralytic polio patients in the early 1950s. He was very much surprised to learn that I was the author of that small booklet, and I was equally surprised to find someone who remembered.

It soon became obvious to all of us associated with this effort that it would be necessary to find a facility where adults facing post-polio problems could be institutionalized for long periods. Available for this purpose was the Pauline Sterne Wolf Home, located near the Medical Center and controlled by a group of Jewish people who had inherited money from the Wolf family estate. They were looking for a way in which to use their physical plant in a meaningful manner and were quickly persuaded to establish a unit there for the long-term care of polio victims. This unit included three buildings, beautifully situated on land where the Southwest Freeway now runs.

Ben Taub, who was also chairman of the board at the Wolf Home, asked Russell Blattner if he could use the buildings in some manner. This resulted in the creation of a rheumatic fever convalescent unit patterned after Rich Farm in St. Louis. During that same era, my former teacher at Harvard, T. Duckett Jones, was running the Good Samaritan Hospital in Boston for rheumatic fever victims. It was he who had developed a definition of rheumatic fever and prepared a list of criteria, known to all of us as the "Jones Essentials."

At about the same time, Mary McArthur, the daughter of the famous actress Helen Hayes, acquired polio and died in New York City. Her mother, of course, was heartbroken. Mary had bulbar polio, which went undiagnosed, and she was dead before anything could be done to save her. Helen Hayes was connected in some way with the Boston Children's Hospital, which was very active in polio research, and they requested that the Baylor group allow them to open the Mary McArthur Polio Respiratory Center in Boston before officially opening the unit in Houston. Russell Blattner, Bill Spencer, and others graciously consented to that. So, while the Baylor group was the first to operate such a unit, credit was given to Helen Hayes and her associates in Boston, a decision which those of us at Baylor never regretted.

Shortly after the rheumatic fever unit in Houston was established, however, the advent of the new era of antibiotics resulted in the organizers being left with empty buildings at the lovely Wolf Home. Fortunately, Sadie Epstein, director of Wolf Home, was capable, eager, and willing to move into another area of concern. Ben Taub, a strong-willed person, was desirous of using his money to advantage but reluctant to give up control of it to anyone else. It was at this point that Bill Spencer conceived the idea of developing a halfway house at the Wolf Home in which polio victims partially independent of institutional care could reside and accommodate to their disabilities while living in a domestic setting. As a result, he acquired a great deal of knowledge about rehabilitation and with his mechanical and mathematical bent he fell right into the restorative aspects of physical medicine. This ultimately led to the development of a department of rehabilitation medicine at Baylor, independent of the physical medicine department. Bill Spencer advocated the need to differentiate between preventive, curative, and restorative aspects of the disabilities which came to the attention of his group.

When polio began to decline as a prevalent national health

problem, Spencer switched over to taking in patients with spinal cord injuries. I can recall that one of the first such patients was an unfortunate youth from Kinkaid School who had suffered a broken neck while playing football. His father, George Broyles, Sr., a general surgeon in Houston, was the team physician at Kinkaid School. He had the horrifying experience of being on the bench and witnessing the event when his son was injured. This was the same Broyles whom I had met in 1944 when we were both in military service at the U.S. Amphibious Forces Training Base in Coronado Beach, California.

Later, in 1956, the Fleming Department of Rehabilitation Medicine was established at Baylor and the aforementioned institute was opened in February 1959. This facility now occupies a prominent place in the Texas Medical Center and ranks among the best-equipped, best-run rehabilitation units in the United States. Lamar Fleming was instrumental in assisting Spencer with the financing of this venture. It seems to have been a predestined arrangement. Blattner and his associates had taken away from Mr. Fleming the unit to be used originally at Jefferson Davis Hospital for geriatric rehabilitation. In its place he was provided with the opportunity to assist in the development of an even better one — the Texas Institute for Rehabilitation and Research in the Texas Medical Center. Lamar Fleming did a great deal to stimulate others like the Cora and Webb Mading Foundation, the M. D. Anderson Foundation, and the Clayton Fund, as well as the Macashan Research and Education Trust, to provide major funding for this remarkable unit.

When I first joined the staff of The Methodist Hospital in 1949, it was situated on the northwest corner of San Jacinto and Rosalie streets in an old building, long since demolished, which was attached to a second and older building. The latter was known originally as Norsworthy Hospital after World War I, but it eventually became part of The Methodist Hospital. The administrator when I arrived was the late Mrs. Josie Roberts, whom I came to consider as one of my mentors and dear friends. She helped me in many ways during my early days in Houston, particularly by promptly making certain that I met all four of the local neurosurgeons (James Greenwood, Jr., Robert C. L. Robertson, F. Keith Bradford, and J. Randolph Jones). The five of us used to meet in a private dining room at the hospital every Tuesday at noon for lunch, and then have a clinical conference with about three to four others in attendance.

In 1951, when The Methodist Hospital in the Texas Medical Center was completed, we all moved out to the new facility.

In 1948, Mrs. Roberts and The Methodist Hospital Board of Trustees had recruited a young man from St. Louis, Ted Bowen, whom I had known slightly when he was a resident in hospital administration at Barnes Hospital and I was a resident in neurology. He had trained there with Dr. Frank Bradley, administrator of the Washington University Affiliated Hospitals, who was well known for having initiated one of the first accredited residency programs for hospital administrators anywhere in the country. Ted Bowen came to Houston a few months before I did and also worked at the old hospital on Rosalie Street. He assisted "Miss Josie" in putting the plans together for the new building and overseeing its construction. However, I am sure that she insisted on being involved as well in every detail. She was getting close to retirement and during that period she aged a lot. She finally decided that she had achieved her goal and retired to New Mexico in 1953, having remained on the job for a period just long enough to see the new hospital up and running. Then Ted Bowen took over the administrative responsibilities. Mrs. Roberts lived well into her nineties and in her latter years was back in Houston living at St. Anthony Center on Almeda Road. In fact, my second wife, Alma, and I brought her to our home for dinner not too long before she died. She was still very bright and articulate until a few months before she passed away. About ten years after Mrs. Roberts' retirement, Ted Bowen was given the title of president of the hospital. In the late 1960s, after the separation of Baylor College of Medicine from Baylor University in Waco, he was appointed vice-president of the Baylor-Methodist Complex.

At The Methodist Hospital, during the formative years of the relationship with Baylor, L.L.D. "Dewey" Tuttle was the chief of surgery and Michael DeBakey was chief of the cardiovascular service. They did not have a neurology service as such and there were no other neurologists, so I became chief of neurology by default. In those days that was an exception for a full-time Baylor faculty person.

When Russell Blattner and I had first talked about training neurologists, I reminded him that I had completed a residency in pediatrics before going into the Canadian navy, and then after returning to civilian life had had further residency training in both adult and pediatric neurology. I asked him if he would accept me as a pediatric neurologist. He replied, "I don't believe so, Bill, but you could train one." His response seemed to me to be contradictory then, and even many years later we still laughed about it. We had talked about setting up a children's neurological clinic, as well as a seizure clinic, which was also of great interest to Peter Kellaway, a clinical neurophysiologist. Peter had also preceded me to Houston by one year. Although I never knew him before, he, too, had come to Texas by way of Montreal, Canada. We were able to form between us a nucleus upon which to build a child neurology program.

Prior to entering a career in neurophysiology, Kellaway had been a student at McGill University Medical School through the first two years. He then dropped out of medical school and went on to complete studies for a Ph.D. under the tutelage of Hebbel Hoff, professor and chairman of the Department of Physiology at that school prior to coming to Baylor as head of physiology. Kellaway clearly had ambitions to be a medical doctor, but he never returned to finish his years of clinical education. After my arrival in Houston, I did everything in my power to try to persuade him to complete the work for his medical degree. This he refused to do, which I think was largely because he felt that he would be much older than the other students, many of whom he had previously taught in classes of physiology. However, throughout his career, Peter has behaved as though he was in the practice of medicine without ever having achieved the necessary academic qualifications or licensure. This always created a rough interface between him and me when it came to dealing with the clinical programs in neurology at Baylor and in The Methodist Hospital.

At a meeting of the American Epilepsy Society at the Waldorf-Astoria Hotel in New York in December 1953, I was approached by Drs. Frederick Gibbs, William Lennox, and Robert Schwab of Boston, the leaders in that organization. They asked me whether I felt that Peter Kellaway, who was a Ph.D. and not an M.D., would be a suitable candidate for secretary-treasurer of the Society, but clearly they had some misgivings about his nomination. Since he was a colleague at Baylor and in my opinion was competent, particularly in the area of clinical electrophysiology, I agreed that it might be reasonable for him to fill that position. This judgment came back to haunt me later.

The conflict between us was evident in the management of the Blue Bird Clinic for Children's Neurological Disorders at The Methodist Hospital and also in the operation of the EEG Laboratory. With respect to the latter, I was asked in the late 1950s by Ted Bowen, the hospital administrator, if I would like to take over the supervision of the EEG Laboratory in that hospital. Until that time, it had been the fiefdom and the responsibility of Peter Kellaway. I declined to accept this offer since I felt that Kellaway was doing a satisfactory job and my intervention would have been looked upon with disfavor by his boss at Baylor, Hebbel Hoff. Once again, I lived to regret my decision.

Russell Blattner, Peter Kellaway, and I were approached by the Ladies Auxiliary of the First Methodist Church, which had been supporting work in orthopedics. When the orthopedic needs of the disadvantaged children in the community were assumed by the Shriner's Hospital, these women found themselves without a project, so someone recommended that they contact Blattner about what they might do. He came up with the suggestion that they start an epilepsy clinic. They did not take kindly to the word "epilepsy" and it was suggested therefore that it be called the "Blue Bird Circle Clinic for Neurological Disorders." That turned out to be a much more suitable name because as subsequent events developed, it embraced not just epilepsy but a broader spectrum of children's neurological disorders.

Together Russell, Peter, and I persuaded the ladies of the Blue Bird Circle that it would be a splendid idea for them to have this clinic as a project on which to focus, and they accepted responsibility for its support. This was at the time when The Methodist Hospital was still located at San Jacinto and Rosalie streets. There was a small building at the rear of the hospital that was turned over to us for the operation of what eventually became our pediatric neurology clinic. When we started that operation, we did not have a formal director and desperately needed to find some full-time people to staff it. The first one to be brought on board was Charles Bielstein, who had been in general pediatric practice in Baytown, Texas. He stayed with us until 1952, when he moved to Oklahoma City to start a seizure clinic of his own. The second person to be recruited was Dora Chao, a pediatrician, who had only recently come to the United States from China. She was born in Harbin, Manchuria, and was a graduate of the Peking Union Medical College. Peter Kellaway was given day-to-day responsibility for the operation of the clinic and the EEG Laboratory.

In those days (late 1940s) our doctors were seeing black patients, as well as whites, in the children's neurology clinic behind the old hospital. That was considered perfectly acceptable under the circumstances. However, an elaborate new floor was built for the clinic at The Methodist Hospital in the Medical Center, and when the clinic moved to its new quarters in 1951, the hospital administration began talking about not admitting black children. Blattner and I objected strenuously and said that those children needed care just as much as white children did. So a meeting of the women's group was held at a lovely home in River Oaks. The women present were all pretty much against admitting blacks to our clinic. One of the women asked, "Dr. Blattner, what would you do if somebody put a black child in the same room with one of your children?" He replied that he would say, "Suffer the little children to come unto me and forbid them not for such is the kingdom of heaven." Well, that touched a sympathetic chord and there wasn't a dry eye in the house. They voted unanimously to let the black children come to the clinic, with one restriction: that there would be one separate room for black patients. Russell and I were willing to go along because we knew that such an arrangement could not survive very long. It turned out that Dora Chao, the only full-time physician in the clinic, became pregnant, much to her surprise, and when she delivered a nice normal little girl, Mei-Su, she used the room which had been set aside for blacks as a nursery for her infant while she was at work. Consequently, we never really used it for black patients but infiltrated the whole area with whatever children were referred for diagnosis and treatment.

The women of the Blue Bird Circle have been enormously successful in everything they have undertaken. They have supported The Methodist Hospital in a very substantial way. They dyed Easter eggs, sold dishcloths which they hemmed by hand, and carried on all kinds of activities in order to raise money to support their project. These funds were the nucleus from which we could expand the work in the Blue Bird Clinic to include not only teaching and clinical care but research as well.

In late 1951, when the Blue Bird Clinic for Children's Neurological Disorders moved to the fourth floor of the new Methodist Hospital, the staff consisted of myself as the clinical director, Peter Kellaway in charge of the Electroencephalography Laboratory, Ralph Druckman, a neurologist whom we had brought to Houston from the Montreal Neurological Institute, and Dora Chao, who had been with the clinic since its inauguration at the old hospital further downtown. Although children with many different kinds of neurological problems were seen there, the majority suffered from seizure disorders. This emphasis was largely due to the research interests of Druckman and Kellaway. Their activities subsequently led to the publication of a splendid and very useful book entitled *The Management of Epileptic Seizures in Children*, by Kellaway, Druckman, and Chao. Ralph Druckman remained for about three years and then decided that he would join an old friend, James Stevens, a British emigré, at the University of Colorado Medical School in Denver.

Dr. Charles Dickson, an ear, nose and throat specialist, was also involved in the Blue Bird Clinic. We made a triumvirate of sorts — Charles Dickson, Russell Blattner, and I. Later we were joined by Jim Greenwood, chief of neurosurgery. Charles represented The Methodist Hospital staff and his wife was a Blue Bird. It was really quite difficult at times to get him to listen to what we thought should be done to expand the clinic program because he was always primarily concerned with whether our proposal would be in the best interest of the hospital. Fortunately, we had functioned quite successfully in the old building and had developed a substantial number of patient referrals even before we moved to the Medical Center.

Along the way, during the first ten years or so of the clinic's existence, problems developed among factions of the Blue Bird Circle, and Dora Chao got caught in the crossfire between two opposing groups. Unfortunately, I could not avoid being in the middle of all the turmoil as well. This crisis occurred at the time that Ralph Druckman was getting ready to leave for Colorado. Dora had had the goal from the time she left Manchuria as a young woman that she was not only going to be a physician and take care of little children but that she was also going to have her own clinic one day, of which she would be the director. Unfortunately for her, the ladies did not see things quite that way. Although they recognized that she was competent in taking care of children, and most of them were extremely fond of her personally, many were opposed to her being placed in charge. We had numerous meetings at that time of the Clinic Advisory Board, appointed by the hospital. This board consisted of Blattner, Greenwood, Dickson, and myself. Finally, it came down to a decision where I was asked by this advisory group not only to remain as a member but also to serve as director of the clinic.

All of this furor caused a rather significant split among the Blue Birds, and a number of them eventually resigned. The real tragedy was that we lost Vivian Smith, wife of Houston business tycoon R. E. "Bob" Smith, who had worked actively in the clinic and also had been extremely supportive. Unfortunately, she had an unreasonably proprietary attitude about the clinic and this was resented by some of the other ladies. For a long time afterward, Vivian Smith looked upon me as her enemy because she felt that I had sided with the opposition and against her personally. Actually, I had attempted not to side with anyone but, nevertheless, I got caught in the middle of the fracas. The clinic chairperson was the individual with whom I had to deal and that chairperson was opposed to what she perceived as Mrs. Smith's interference. Because of being on the hot seat, so to speak, I was hopeful that I could find someone soon who would be capable of directing the clinic on a full-time basis. With this in mind, I recruited Thomas Zion, a pediatrician, to our training program. I had come to know Tom fairly well at Wilford Hall Air Force Hospital in San Antonio, where he was on active duty and I was a civilian consultant. He proceeded to spend two years with me as a neurology resident at Baylor and then I arranged for him to go to the Massachusetts General Hospital in Boston to finish his training in pediatric neurology with Philip Dodge. As soon as he returned to Baylor on a full-time basis, I stepped aside and he took over the management of the clinic, of which he remained director until 1990. The activities of the Blue Bird Clinic over the years have continued to serve as a very significant part of both the neurology and pediatric training programs at Baylor.

It is important at this juncture to emphasize that the original concept of the Texas Medical Center was for each hospital to concentrate and excel in some specialized area. Since Jim Greenwood was well known in neurosurgery and neurology, The Methodist Hospital became the natural location for the pediatric and adult neurology programs to be developed. As time went by, however, each of the major hospitals decided to pursue multiple interests and the original concept of specialization within each hospital failed to survive. This serves to explain why, in the pediatric training program, neurology was split off to The Methodist Hospital, where it has remained even though many people thought that it should have been located at the Children's Hospital when that institution opened. There has been an active movement more recently to duplicate or to transfer the neurological program to Texas Children's Hospital under the direction of Marvin Fishman, a relative newcomer, who still cannot understand why Blattner and I allowed the Blue Bird Clinic to develop at The Methodist Hospital. However, this decision was made even before the Texas Children's Hospital came into existence and we could have never visualized the great strength that each of these institutions would eventually achieve.

During those years, I participated in the training of several other pediatric neurologists who are still active in Houston. Robert Zeller started his postgraduate studies at Baylor and then went to New York to complete his training. Another one, Fabio Fernandez, became a resident in the Baylor neurology program with me after qualifying for certification in pediatrics. He is still active at the Blue Bird Clinic. Fabio is a competent clinician who has contributed in a meaningful way and has been accepted by the new regime in pediatric neurology.

It was in this manner that a small, simple beginning in a clapboard building eventually resulted in major support for a pediatric neurology program, and the neurology programs in general, in the Texas Medical Center. As I understand it, in 1967, just about the time that I was getting ready to depart for Dallas, the Bintliff family along with some other donors provided a large amount of money to develop the Neurosensory Center at The Methodist Hospital. This infusion of funds provided a major boost to the clinical research activities in this particular discipline. That more recent development has been of great importance for the program, but its roots were in the original Blue Bird Clinic.

In 1953 a new dean was appointed at Baylor. To fill this position, the Search Committee had chosen Stanley W. Olson, dean of the University of Illinois College of Medicine in Chicago and former staff member of the Mayo Clinic in Rochester, Minnesota. One of the first things Olson did after his arrival was to appoint a search committee for a successor to Warren Brown, professor and chairman of the Department of Psychiatry and Neurology, who had resigned and moved to New Mexico. Until a new chairman could be recruited, Eugen Kahn, formerly Sterling Professor of Psychiatry at Yale, whom Warren Brown had enticed to come to Houston after his retirement, served in an acting role. He was a delightful and very knowledgeable person with whom to work. After a somewhat prolonged search, the committee offered the position to William

Lhamon, a professor of psychiatry at the University of Washington in Seattle. Soon after Lhamon's arrival in Houston, the Texas Research Institute of Mental Sciences in the Medical Center was completed and an affiliation agreement with Baylor was consummated. Lhamon was appointed the director of that institute (later The University of Texas Mental Science Institute).

I didn't know Bill Lhamon before he came to Houston, but soon learned that his brother and mine had been classmates at the U.S. Naval Academy. He bought a house in our neighborhood and we were both communicants of St. Francis Episcopal Church, where we also served together on the board of directors of the newly established day school sponsored by the congregation. This made our relationship more pleasant and close.

In February 1954, approval for funding was received from the National Institute of Neurological Diseases and Blindness in Bethesda, Maryland, for postgraduate training in neurology at Baylor. This provided the impetus necessary to launch a residency program and recruit residents for the full three years required by the American Board of Psychiatry and Neurology. The program was designed to enable the graduates to sit for the specialty board examination after the three required years of supervised training. This was the first big step toward the development of neurology as a medical specialty in the Southwest. Within the year following Lhamon's appointment, it was agreed that neurology should become a semi-independent division within the Department of Psychiatry.

By the fall of 1958, the growth of neurology as a discipline seemed to me and to Bill Lhamon to warrant the separation of our unit from psychiatry and the establishment of an independent department. I wrote to Dean Olson requesting that this change be considered by the Academic Council:

> For ten years I have been associated with Baylor College of Medicine and can look back over a period of continuing growth of neurology as a discipline. In 1949 we had no beds, no staff, and virtually no teaching of neurology. Now, we have ten active beds at Jefferson Davis Hospital with an ever increasing out-patient service, 42 beds and two staff men at Veterans Administration Hospital, and an active service at Methodist Hospital, including the Blue Bird Clinic.
>
> Where we had one resident and a two-year approved resi-

dency training program in 1952, we now have a three-year approval supported by a graduate training grant from the National Institute of Neurological Diseases and Blindness. There are four residents currently in training, two of them graduates of Baylor. In addition to these trainees, we have assumed the responsibility of neurological training for residents in neurosurgery and, in the past, in psychiatry and internal medicine as well. Conversations have recently taken place with the Acting Chairman of the department of medicine regarding the re-establishment of a rotation for residents in internal medicine as well.

During the past four years our staff has been expanded to include Dr. Ellsworth C. Alvord, Associate Professor, Drs. Ralph Druckman and James W. Crawley, Assistant Professors, and Dr. Paul C. Sharkey, Instructor. Another instructor, Dr. John S. Scott, left in June for an appointment as Assistant Professor at the University of Colorado School of Medicine.

With the increase in staff, it has been possible to expand our teaching program to undergraduates throughout the four academic years. We are now participating in the teaching of neuroanatomy for freshmen, have a 22-hour course in applied neuroanatomy and neuropathology for sophomores, as well as didactic neuropathology in lectures and laboratory exercises, a clerkship (inadequate time), a lecture course for juniors, and outpatient teaching at Jefferson Davis Hospital for seniors. Time is also devoted to the neurological examination in the sophomore course in physical diagnosis.

This augmentation of teaching activities has stimulated the interest of many of our better students to pursue research interests and further education in the neurological sciences. Summer clerkships have attracted more applications, and seven students were appointed during the past three summers. Of the seven students thus far appointed, five have elected to continue their careers in neurology or neurosurgery. This is a substantial improvement over the situation in previous years.

The Division of Neurology has operated on a separate budget for several years. Four years ago this amounted to approximately $12,000, and today it amounts to slightly over $97,000, including grants.

We have been very happy with our association with the Department of Psychiatry and Dr. Lhamon and his staff have assisted materially in the growth of neurology. Now, the Department of Psychiatry is looking forward to embarking on an important new venture in the development of the Houston State Psychiatric Institute, and our staff feels that this will inevitably reduce the amount of time which the chairman has available to deal with the distinctly different problems of neurology. I believe, therefore, that the time has come to raise the question of departmental status for neurology.

I respectfully submit this request for departmental status for neurology and would appreciate your bringing this matter to the attention of the Academic Council. (Signed: William S. Fields, M.D., Professor and Head, Division of Neurology)

With the sanction of Bill Lhamon and the dean, and subsequent approval by the Academic Senate, the separation was accomplished. Dr. Lhamon remained in Houston until 1962, at which time he left to take a position as professor of psychiatry at Cornell University Medical School in New York and also assume the responsibility of director of the Psychiatric Institute in the New York Hospital complex.

The chair in psychiatry did not remain vacant very long. Shervert Frazier was brought from the Mayo Clinic, Department of Psychiatry, to be the new chairman. I soon learned that this was the same Frazier whom Stanley Olson had asked me to take into our residency training program in neurology soon after the latter's arrival in Houston. Frazier at that time had been in general practice in southern Illinois in association with a Baylor graduate of the class of 1952, my friend James Wimpee, who later became a successful and respected orthopedic surgeon in San Angelo, Texas. At the time that his request was made, we had already appointed the residents for the following year, but I told the dean that I would be pleased to take on one more resident if he could find the funds. Baylor did not have the resources at that time to provide another stipend, so Frazier went to Rochester, Minnesota, to enter residency training in psychiatry. When he assumed his new administrative duties in Houston, it became apparent that he coveted neurology as a part of his overall domain, and I could see that he was preparing to create serious problems for me.

Chapter 8

Texas Medical Center: Growing Pains

A CONCEPT THAT HAD been instilled in me many years earlier by Dr. Wilder Penfield was that the basic and clinical neurosciences were most likely to flourish when they were drawn together, as he had done at the Montreal Neurological Institute (MNI). He had reached this conclusion while visiting numerous clinics in Europe. In those which were most effective, the neurology and neurosurgery units worked closely together. Furthermore, he had realized that it was the integration of clinicians and basic scientists that in the long term would lead to successful study and treatment of disorders of the nervous system. He once wrote, "The problem of neurology is to understand man himself." It is, in my opinion, a fitting quotation to grace the clinical and research pavilion of the MNI, named in his honor in 1978.

In the 1950s The Methodist Hospital did not extend out to Fannin Street, so the space on the west side of the building was used as a parking area. Early in 1952, Milton McGinty, architect of The Methodist Hospital, had prepared for Jim Greenwood and myself detailed plans for a neurological institute such as the one in Montreal to be built on part of that parking lot behind the hospital. Warren Brown, associate dean at Baylor, Josie Roberts, who was still administrator of The Methodist Hospital, and Thomas Anderson, nephew of Monroe D. Anderson, were all extremely helpful in promoting the project.

The events which followed were very interesting. It appeared that Mrs. Roberts, several members of The Methodist Hospital Board, the dean of Baylor College of Medicine, Dr. Walter Moursund, and Dr. Brown felt very keenly that this additional structure should be called "The Neurological Institute of The Methodist Hospital" and that I should be appointed as director and given the responsibility for developing it. However, the outcome of this plan was unfortunate, and I say in all due deference to my longtime friend, Jim Greenwood, that we would have had that institute in the 1950s if he had not become upset about my being asked to be its director. He was chief of neurosurgery at The Methodist Hospital and thought he should be so designated. He was an old Houstonian, whose father had been in practice in the community for many years. I didn't know until years later that it was he who had killed the proposal. It took a long time, from 1951-52, when we first conceived this plan, until 1969, when The Methodist Hospital erected the Neurosensory Building, for this idea to come to fruition. I have been reminded about it on several occasions since then by both Tom Anderson and Milton McGinty.

I remember well the old Rice Stadium on the corner of University and Main streets. The first game I attended there was between Rice and Baylor. On that occasion Tobin Rote was the quarterback for Rice and Adrian Burke was the quarterback for Baylor. Rote later played professional football for the Washington Redskins and the Detroit Lions and was elected to the Football Hall of Fame in Canton, Ohio. Burke was a Southwest Conference official for many years. In spite of not going to a postseason bowl game in many years, Rice University still fields teams that can be competitive in the Southwest Conference.

I still have some photographs of the Texas Medical Center which I took in 1955 from what I thought were strategic points, including the roof of The Methodist Hospital. (See photo section.) From the roof one could see all the way to the recently constructed Rice Stadium, the architect for which was the aforementioned Milton McGinty. One of the photos is really incredible. Where the graduate school dormitories of Rice University (originally the Tidelands Motor Hotel) are now located, there was a Sinclair service station on the corner. I remember it well because I used to stop there to fill up with gasoline. The fellow who owned the station and pumped gas suffered from neurosyphilis, manifested by tabes dorsalis. I, personally, had not seen a case of tabes for several years before that because it had virtually disappeared after the advent of penicillin. This fellow walked with a typical slapping gait, had slurred speech and poor vision, but he was still able to manage the gas station. I persuaded him to be a subject at one of my case presentations to the medical students and residents.

Just a little farther south, in the same block of Main Street, there was a small dirt track. I used to take my daughters there on weekends, when they were preschoolers, to let them ride the Shetland ponies. In another photograph looking just a little farther south, one could see the steel framework of the Medical Towers on Dryden Street between Fannin and Main as it was being built in 1955. At the same time the Hermann Professional Building was adding the second half of its present structure, extending out to Main Street. Like The Methodist Hospital, the east half was built first, and the other half, on the west side facing Fannin and Main streets, was completed later.

In the early 1970s I tried to take pictures from approximately the same locations as before but in many instances was thwarted by the presence of newly constructed intervening buildings.

The Kelsey-Leary Clinic was the first multi-disciplinary private institution to be established in the vicinity of the Texas Medical Center. It was started in the mid-1950s by two Mayo Clinic alumni, Mavis Kelsey and William Leary, both of them internists. Mavis Kelsey, a graduate of The University of Texas Medical Branch in Galveston, had returned to Houston from the Mayo Clinic in January 1949 to begin private practice. He was joined, approximately two years later, by Dr. Bill Leary and then by a third partner, William Seybold, a general surgeon, who had also trained at the Mayo Clinic. For a while, Bill Seybold left the partnership and went into practice on his own with two other surgeons, but he maintained a relationship with the clinic through patient referrals. Later Leary dropped out of the partnership to join the full-time staff at M. D. Anderson Hospital, and Seybold returned, after which the facility became known by its present name, Kelsey-Seybold Clinic.

In 1955 the clinic developed an affiliation with St. Luke's Episcopal Hospital when it opened its doors in the Texas Medical Center. That association has continued to the present time. The Kelsey-Seybold Clinic activities have grown exponentially over the years and the facility has expanded to include several satellite operations elsewhere in Harris County. In many aspects it was modeled after the Mayo Clinic, where Drs. Kelsey, Leary, and Seybold all had their training.

I got to know Bill Seybold in the early 1950s when his wife, Frances, developed multiple sclerosis and became my patient. He was then in practice on his own during the interval when he was independent from the clinic. He was scheduled to operate on Bette, my first wife. She had had profuse intestinal hemorrhage on several occasions and we could not locate the source of the problem. Her internist, Dolph Curb, after putting her through every conceivable diagnostic test, arranged for an operation at The Methodist Hospital by Seybold, who was going to do an exploratory of Bette's abdomen to try to find the source of her hemorrhaging. It was planned for John Wall, her gynecologist, to do a hysterectomy at the same time while she was under anesthesia because she also had been having a lot of trouble from fibroid tumors of the uterus. The morning that she was scheduled for surgery, John Wall was to proceed with his part of the operation first. When this was completed and it was time for the exploratory, there was no Bill Seybold in sight, and no one seemed to know where he was. Denton Cooley happened to be located in the adjacent operating room finishing his own case (he was still on The Methodist Hospital staff at that time). So John said, "Get Denton in here right away." Cooley agreed to assist him and in exploring Bette's small bowel, he located the source of the problem. It turned out to be a benign tumor, an exceedingly rare lesion in that location, the surface of which had become eroded and an artery within it bled profusely. This was the cause of Bette's problem and she was effectively cured by its removal.

That morning Bill Seybold had gone to the Tuberculosis Hospital on West Dallas Street to a conference which he attended regularly. He had completely forgotten that he was due in the operating room. Needless to say, he was terribly upset by the incident, particularly since his wife was my patient. Fortunately, there were no long-term consequences and all of us remained good friends.

Abe Hauser, a senior neuropsychiatrist, and one of my most ardent supporters, persuaded me to join the Central Neuropsychiatric Society in 1956 and I attended a couple of their annual meetings. Then together with several other colleagues in the Houston-Galveston area we prevailed upon the Society to select Houston as the site for the 1959 annual session. That meeting was memorable, in my opinion, only with respect to the social program.

Some local entrepreneur, knowing of Dr. Hauser's desire to have a social affair at his home on South Macgregor Boulevard, sold him on the idea of air-conditioning his backyard. The promoter was anxious to use the occasion to demonstrate this novel idea in order to stimulate his business. Fifteen-foot-high poles were strategically placed around the spacious yard and sheets of green canvas were stretched between them. Then a large compressor was installed in one corner of the yard and refrigerated air was pumped in. The cold air, being heavier, displaced the hot air upward and maintained the yard at a surprisingly comfortable temperature in spite of the heat radiating from the crowd which attended the party.

This was, I believe, a first for Houston and it received sufficient publicity to compensate the promoter and provide him with more orders in the future. Those in attendance, particularly guests from out of town, were astonished by the arrangement and many commented that this could only happen in Houston, Texas.

Although by 1953 Michael DeBakey was working exclusively at The Methodist Hospital, where he was developing a cardiovascular surgery service, my own close professional association with him did not come about until the late 1950s. He had already been joined by several young stars, including Drs. E. Stanley Crawford, Denton Cooley, and Oscar Creech. Oscar, however, left The Methodist after a couple of years and went to the Veterans Administration Hospital as chief of surgery and from there to Tulane as chairman of the Department of Surgery. Tragically, he died at an early age, not too long after assuming the latter position.

DeBakey at that time was frequently performing thoraco-abdominal graft replacements of the aorta and several of his patients became paraplegic. I was asked to see them in consultation. It was my opinion that these neurological problems were secondary to interruption of the thoracic spinal cord circulation through the small arteries originating from the aorta near the level of the diaphragm. In most cases the collateral circulation by way of other arteries below and above that level was adequate, but when it was not, infarction (due to impaired circulation) of the spinal cord might ensue during or following surgical intervention even though every effort had been made to determine preoperatively whether the collateral circulation was adequate or not. This activity brought me into almost daily contact with Mike DeBakey.

My interest in carotid surgery as a means of preventing stroke was stimulated by the fact that it had been shown once again in 1951 by my longtime friend and former fellow resident in Montreal, Miller Fisher, that there might be a relationship between atherosclerotic lesions of the carotid arteries in the neck region and infarcts in the brain (strokes). It was thought then that the obstructions in the neck vessels produced brain symptoms by interference with blood flow and reduction of perfusion pressure. It had been suggested by a number of people that if one could remove or bypass the obstruction and improve the flow of blood to the brain, one might prevent a stroke. That was the principal reason why I became involved in this work with the vascular surgeons. Today the whole concept has changed. It is not only the narrowing of the artery that is significant but, more importantly, the roughened or ulcerated internal surface of the affected vessel at, or near, a point of narrowing in the neck. From there aggregates (clumps) of blood elements (mostly platelets) wash off and go downstream and plug up smaller vessels in the brain. Today, we think in terms of medical, as well as surgical, means of handling these offending lesions which might be the site from which clots go downstream to block the smaller arteries and cause strokes. That is how prophylaxis with aspirin, a method in which I first became interested in 1968 while in Dallas, also got into the picture later.

Early in 1955, Stanley Crawford and I became involved in extracranial arterial surgery for the prevention and treatment of stroke. He was a fellow Harvard Medical School alumnus and had been a resident in surgery at the Massachusetts General Hospital in Boston. Together we worked up a series of patients at both The Methodist and the Veterans Administration hospitals.

Meanwhile, Denton Cooley performed an endarterectomy on a patient with a narrowed carotid artery at Hermann Hospital in Houston in 1956. That patient had an asymptomatic bruit (noise heard with stethoscope) on the left side of his neck which was transmitted upward, producing a disturbing intermittent swishing sound in his left ear. Denton was assisted in this procedure by a neurosurgeon, Charles Carton, who was working then with me at Baylor, and a surgical resident from Iraq by the name of Yousef Al-Naaman, who later became professor of thoracic and vascular surgery at the

University of Baghdad. They published their case but, unfortunately, their report, which introduced an innovative operative technique, received little attention because the surgery had been performed for reasons other than threatened stroke.

Between 1955 and 1958, Stanley and I collaborated on a study to determine the role of extracranial arterial surgery in the prevention of stroke. Together we worked on seventy-one patients who had proven extracranial arterial stenosis (narrowing) or occlusion (blockage). I did the neurological evaluations, both pre- and postoperatively, and Stanley operated personally on all of these patients, using techniques which he had devised for carotid bypass and endarterectomy. The results of this study were compiled by the two of us and presented for the first time by me at the American Academy of Neurology meeting in Philadelphia at the end of April 1958. This article was published several months later in the journal *NEUROLOGY*. The authors were listed as Fields, Crawford, and DeBakey, with the latter's name being included as a courtesy since he was chairman of the Department of Surgery. The report created quite a sensation at the meeting, and after the platform presentation, I was interviewed by a reporter from *The New York Times* at the Bellevue-Stratford Hotel, where the meeting took place. This occurred on a Saturday morning, and the article about our work appeared on the front page of the Sunday edition and was given prominent coverage nationwide by the Associated Press.

When I returned to Houston on Tuesday morning, Mike DeBakey requested that I come to his office to discuss with him a mutual patient at the hospital. I noticed immediately that *The New York Times* was strategically situated in front of him on his desk. He made no comment whatsoever about the article but it was obvious that he wanted to make certain that I saw the newspaper in front of him. His name was given some prominence in the article, but I had been the one interviewed, and I was the one who had reported on our experience. Crawford, unfortunately, was barely mentioned. From that point on DeBakey became the "father of carotid surgery."

At about the same time, another paper was published in which Crawford's and my name were associated. This article dealt with vertebral endarterectomy for the prevention of infarction in the territory of the posterior intracranial circulation. The authors were listed as Crawford, DeBakey, and Fields. Again, I had worked up the patient from the neurological point of view and Stanley Crawford had done the surgery.

As a result of the report of our experience with carotid artery surgery in the prevention of stroke, I was invited to participate in the Eighth Latin-American Congress of Neurosurgery in Santiago, Chile, in April 1959. This was to be the first of many trips to South America. The flight on Panagra (an affiliate of Pan American Airways) from Miami was a long one, so I decided to make two intermediate stops. I flew to Panama City, where I stayed overnight at the Hilton, and in the morning went by taxi to see the Canal. I stayed long enough to watch several large oceangoing vessels pass through the Miraflores Locks, then went to the airport for the next leg of my trip to Lima, Peru. When I reached my hotel late that afternoon, I was met by Amador Awapara, a general surgeon, whose brother, Jorge, a professor of biochemistry at Rice University in Houston, had provided me with a letter of introduction. He had arranged to take two days away from his office to show me the city and its environs. It was an exceedingly pleasant way to break the long journey by propeller plane from Houston to Santiago.

While in Peru, I decided to avail myself of the opportunity to go to Machu Picchu, the Inca capital northwest of Cuzco, high in the Andes. In those days one flew there from Lima in a propeller-driven Fairchild monoplane which was unpressurized. Because of the altitude, it was necessary to wear a clip on one's nose and breathe oxygen by mouth through a tube. This arrangement was certainly primitive but the trip was well worth the time and effort. On arrival at the hotel in Cuzco, I lay down for several hours in order to adjust to the high altitude. The next morning, I went down by cog railway to the ruins of the ancient city which had been discovered by an American, Hiram Bingham, only thirty-five years earlier. It was the kind of experience one never forgets.

My stay in Cuzco was brief and, immediately after returning to Lima, I took off on the next leg of my flight to Santiago. Since there were four days before the opening of the Congress, I accepted the invitation of my former resident (trainee), Jorge Weibel, to go farther south to his home city of Concepcion. The flight there was in a twin-engine DC-3, and we landed in a large field without a paved runway and only a small hut in one corner which served as a terminal building. I was the only passenger to disembark and I stood waiting anxiously for some minutes before Weibel arrived in an antique Ford driven by his chief at the medical school, Eduardo Skewes.

They drove me to the City Hotel where a Rotary luncheon was just getting under way. I was seated at the head table and was expected to make a few remarks before the main program began. When I spoke in Spanish, Weibel was astonished since in Houston I had made it a point never to address him in Spanish in order to force him to learn English.

The following day I gave a lecture at the medical school of the University of Concepcion and was made an honorary member of the faculty. That afternoon I drove farther south with Manuel Donoso, a neurosurgeon, to see a patient at the town of Lota, where the coal mines extend out under the Pacific Ocean. While there, I was introduced to the director of the welfare program for the miners, one Guillermo Campos. I informed him that I was "Guillermo Campos del norte" (William Fields of the north), a bit of information about which we both enjoyed a hearty laugh. We drove back to Concepcion and the next morning I returned to Santiago for the opening of the Congress.

My official invitation to come to Chile had been received from Professor Adolfo Asenjo, president of the Congress, but I was there primarily to present a paper in a symposium organized by A. Earl Walker, professor of neurosurgery at Johns Hopkins Medical School in Baltimore. The night before the symposium, Earl asked all of the participants to meet with him in his hotel room. Included were two of my friends from Boston, Derek Denny-Brown, professor of neurology at Harvard, and H. Thomas Ballantine, neurosurgeon at the Massachusetts General Hospital. The other member of the panel was John Bates from London, England. We were told by Earl that the presentations were to be made in English. This was very disturbing to Tom and me since we had spent considerable time and effort preparing our talks in Spanish. Denny interceded for us and said that as long as we had made the effort to give our talks in Spanish, although he had not, we should be permitted to do so. But Earl was adamant. Then Reinaldo Poblete, a neurosurgical assistant of Asenjo, went to the phone to call his chief. The latter was very generous in stating that we could use whatever language we preferred. This decision obviously upset Earl Walker, but he made no further protest. The presentations went very well and the audience was obviously appreciative of our efforts to prepare our material in the language of the host country.

The next day at a large reception, I encountered, much to my surprise, Eileen Flanagan, who had been director of nursing at the Montreal Neurological Institute when I was an assistant resident there in 1940-41. She had come to Chile as a guest of the Nurses' Association and was delighted to see a friend among all of the Spanish speakers. I knew that she had recently retired and was doing consulting work concerned with neurosurgical nursing. She asked me to sit with her at the formal dinner that night and serve as her interpreter when necessary. She had always been extremely kind to me, so I was delighted to be of some assistance.

This was my first involvement as an active participant and not just an attendee at an international meeting. It was during this congress in Chile that I first met Nestor Azambuja, a Swedish-trained neuroradiologist from Montevideo, Uruguay, who later became one of my closest friends and collaborators in Latin America.

In the early 1960s, Mike DeBakey and I were both attending a meeting of the Association for Research in Nervous and Mental Diseases at the Roosevelt Hotel in New York City. He had been asked to talk about carotid artery surgery, and at the end of his presentation, there was a scheduled discussion period. A prominent neurologist from Boston asked DeBakey whether he had ever considered undertaking a series of randomized patients, some of whom would be operated and some who would not, since he really couldn't know if what he was doing was all that beneficial. DeBakey said without hesitation that he was absolutely certain it was beneficial because he could see a great difference in the patients postoperatively and he did not feel that there was justification for randomization. He said, "We never randomized appendectomy and yet we all recognize that as something good for the patient." So, when they started to press him for answers to more questions, he looked at his watch and said, "Sorry, I have a plane to catch. I hope you will forgive me." Then he walked off the platform. As he passed me he said, "Bill, please pick up my slides and bring them home." With that he disappeared and I retrieved his slides.

There soon developed a stream of patients admitted to The Methodist Hospital following an article by a science writer who interviewed DeBakey about carotid surgery and had written it up for

Reader's Digest. DeBakey was quoted as saying that this operation of "reaming out the carotid artery in the neck" (terminology used by the writer) improved the cognitive functioning of the patient. He also reportedly said that there were people who had told him that they felt better generally and some said they felt as though there was more blood going through their brains.

When these quotes ascribed to DeBakey appeared in print, there was plenty of criticism coming from many directions. He proceeded to set up a meeting with William Lhamon, chairman of psychiatry at Baylor, Sanford Goldstone, chief of the Division of Psychology, and me, for the purpose of planning a study. We met in Bill Lhamon's office to discuss a proposal for evaluation of these patients pre- and postoperatively in order to determine exactly what change, if any, could be demonstrated in their cognitive abilities and their performance. DeBakey had shown great interest in this idea until, during the discussion, he asked, "Do you think that some of these people might become worse?" Lhamon answered, "If we knew the answer to that question, we wouldn't be interested in doing the study." Consequently, the study was never done because the minute DeBakey was told that we thought there might be a chance that an operation he performed might make somebody worse, he was no longer willing to participate.

I was chairman of another department in the same medical school where Michael DeBakey was chairman of the Department of Surgery, but one could not fail to see that in his view I, like many other of his fellow faculty associates, was just someone upon whom he could call at his convenience. I can recall one evening, at a time when I was seeing many of his patients in consultation, that I had just returned by plane from Washington. When I arrived at Hobby Airport, which was then the only airport in Houston, I called home to tell Bette that I would be late because there were patients to be seen at the hospital, some of them mine and others were DeBakey's. I went directly to The Methodist Hospital to make rounds. I started to enter one patient's room just as DeBakey was coming out, followed by a retinue of students, residents, and fellows. He asked, "Are you going to do a pneumoencephalogram on this patient?"

I told him that I did not think it was indicated because we already had the answer to her problem without doing a procedure that could be so very uncomfortable.

"Well that is what she was sent here for," he said.

"That may be, but I don't think it is necessary to put her through such a painful examination," I replied.

With that he turned and addressed his whole entourage, "I have trouble with all of you people, am I going to have trouble now with my consultants too?"

I just walked away and left them. I certainly did not appreciate his dressing me down in front of the medical students and residents.

DeBakey went to the next room and I proceeded to the floor below to see another one of his patients, a wealthy rancher from California. I had taken care of this gentleman when he was in the hospital on several previous occasions. Before I got to his room, I heard my name being paged. It was DeBakey's resident, who wanted to know if I had seen that patient already. I told him that I was on my way there.

He said, "Would you call Dr. DeBakey later at home after you have seen him?"

I said, "Is Dr. DeBakey still there with you? If he is, please put him on."

When DeBakey came to the phone, he asked, "What's the problem?"

"If ever again you dress me down in front of the house staff and students, there will be no accounting what might happen as a result," I said. That was the last time that ever occurred.

I took care of the gentleman from California over a long period, following which he gave a substantial gift to the DeBakey Surgical Foundation and never paid my bill.

In the early 1960s, I became more and more closely involved with DeBakey's vascular surgery service. During some of the major procedures which were being done on his service at that time, there was occasionally an amount of blood loss sufficient to produce a fall in blood pressure, particularly during the immediate postoperative recovery period. Some of these patients failed to wake up or had strokes during or after the operation. As a neurologist, I was of the opinion that these individuals might also have severe atherosclerotic disease with narrowing of the carotid arteries in the neck. Under these circumstances, a sudden fall in blood pressure might produce significant alteration in the dynamics of cerebral circulation and be the cause of the strokes. I proposed to DeBakey and Crawford as well that, as a part of the routine evaluation of all their patients who were about to undergo a major vascular surgical procedure, someone should listen with a stethoscope over the carotid arteries. This was something that was not generally done in those days. If one could detect with the stethoscope a swishing sound (bruit) over the carotid artery in the neck, or if the patient gave a history of brief stroke-like symptoms (transient ischemic attacks- TIAs), then it would be best to identify by x-ray and then operate on the carotid lesions first and follow later with the thoracic, abdominal, or lower limb procedure. When the vascular surgeons started doing that, there was a significant decrease in peri-operative strokes. Needless to say, the surgeons doing these major operations had considerable anxiety about such complications, and I felt that it was my responsibility to try to be as helpful as possible in managing the neurological aspects of the patient's care.

Unfortunately, as I became more involved with DeBakey's ever-growing vascular surgery service, I was expected to be available on a moment's notice and virtually around the clock. My participation in this "assembly-line operation" began to take its toll on what I was trying to accomplish with other important aspects of the neurology program at Baylor. DeBakey clearly wanted me to be available to him full-time. However, while working with him in what ostensibly was a consulting role, I found that I really wasn't serving in that capacity but was being called upon, more often than not, to confirm what he had already decided to do. That was a role in which I felt extremely uncomfortable and I was reluctant to continue.

DeBakey and I frequently had differences in terms of my recommendations for his patients whom I was seeing in consultation. This applied most often to the ones who were having stroke-like symptoms or signs and also included those who had undergone major vascular surgical procedures and developed postoperative cerebrovascular complications. I was seeing many, if not most, of these patients at that time.

The fact that I had assisted DeBakey in promoting carotid artery surgery eventually proved also to be for me a personal disadvantage. Neurologists across the country tended at that time to be extremely conservative in their approach to stroke and many of them were virtually nihilistic when it came to treatment. Moreover, they considered the vascular surgeons to be interlopers in a territory that they considered their own. Neurosurgeons, except for a few stalwarts such as Francis Murphey in Memphis, J. Garber Galbraith in Birmingham, and E. S. Gurdjian in Detroit, had practically abdicated their position to the vascular surgeons at that time. When I spoke to neurologists about the work that we were doing together as a team in Houston, I was considered a traitor, and it cost me a great deal of credibility in the neurological community. I was advocating surgical intervention into what they felt was their province. They could not accept the fact that surgeons were intervening successfully in what they considered to be a medical problem.

One Saturday morning about two years before I departed Houston, Mike DeBakey was in his office at The Methodist Hospital. On Saturday the operating rooms were closed for all but emergencies and that was about the only time one could get his attention long enough for him to listen. I was there to discuss with him several of his patients whom he had asked me to see in consultation. I remember that on that particular morning Robert Bloodwell, a Baylor medical graduate, was also present. He had just completed his training at Johns Hopkins with Alfred Blalock, the well-known cardiac surgeon, and had come back to Houston to work as an associate of Denton Cooley. I had known Bloodwell as a Baylor student, and he apparently thought a good deal of me. He and several others were there when DeBakey suddenly lit into me and said, "Bill Fields, if you persist in your attitude about the matters with which we have mutual concern, you will never have a job anywhere again." At that time I was still chairman of another department in the same medical school. Needless to say, I did not feel that I could allow someone with that kind of messianic attitude to control my future. Rather than respond in a like manner, although I was sorely tempted to do so, I turned and walked out. What bothered me most about the episode was the fact that Bloodwell walked out of that office with me and we crossed the parking lot together. He never even spoke to DeBakey before leaving. I was still naive enough to think that I could work things out with DeBakey.

DeBakey did not like it, either, that Denton Cooley would call me to see patients in consultation at St. Luke's Hospital, even though at that time Denton was still a Baylor professor. Denton was then, and still is, a good friend of mine and a respected colleague.

In the spring of 1961, I received a letter from Dr. J. Preston Robb of Montreal, who was then secretary of the Canadian Neurological Society. Preston and I had been fellow medical officers in the Royal Canadian Navy during World War II. He invited me to London, England, to present a paper at the joint meeting of the Canadian Neurological Society, of which I was a member, and the Association of British Neurologists (ABN). That year the president of the latter society was Sir Russell Brain (later Lord Brain), whose *Textbook of Neurology* I had recommended to our medical students for many years.

I was informed in the letter of invitation that Dr. William Feindel, at the Montreal Neurological Institute, had raised funds to provide a new stone for the grave of Sir Thomas Willis in Westminster Abbey to replace the old one that had become quite worn as a result of many footsteps crossing over it since it was laid. This was to occur on the 300th anniversary of Willis' description of the anatomy of the communicating arteries at the base of the brain. In view of this, I decided to present at the London meeting a paper on arteriography of the Circle of Willis and its importance in collateral circulation of the brain. Preparation for this presentation led me several years later to write a monograph entitled *Collateral Circulation of the Brain*, with the assistance of two of my younger Baylor colleagues, Martin Bruetman and Jorge Weibel.

The meeting in London was held in September 1961, prior to the International Congress of Neurology in Rome. It was an interesting meeting from both the scientific and social point of view. I was provided with an opportunity to speak with many colleagues from Canada and Great Britain whom I had not had the pleasure of meeting previously but whose contributions were already familiar to me. The conference concluded with a splendid black-tie dinner at the Savoy Hotel.

Following the London meeting, I flew to Munich to participate in the International Congress of Neuropathology. It was there that I first met Klaus Zülch, a professor of neurology in Cologne, West Germany, who subsequently became one of my closest friends. During a reception at the Rathaus, I also encountered Henri van der Eecken, professor of neurology in Ghent, Belgium. Henri had visited his old friend in Houston, neurosurgeon Marshall Henry, about eighteen months earlier, and I had seen him at that time. He greeted me enthusiastically and said, "Bill, I am very happy to tell you that my wife and I have a new baby made in Texas by Belgians." Apparently, while in Texas, he was impressed by stickers he had observed on the rear window of many new Ford cars which read, "This car made in Texas by Texans."

From Munich I traveled by train to Zürich, Switzerland, where

I met one of my Baylor associates, William Lucas. Bill was very helpful during our stay there inasmuch as he had been a medical student at the University of Zürich ten years earlier. Shortly after my arrival in Zürich, I met Hugo Krayenbühl, professor of neurosurgery at the Kantonsspital. The following day, after making rounds with his assistant, I had an opportunity to visit with Krayenbühl in his office. I recall very well his saying to me, "Dr. Fields, it has been a great pleasure to meet you and to have you visit my service. I had expected someone quite different. On a recent visit to me, Dr. Raymond Adams of Boston made some poisonous remarks about you. I am happy to know that there is no truth in what he said." This revelation came as a great surprise to me since Ray Adams was someone whom I had invited to be a participant in the 1959 Houston Neurological Society Symposium and was otherwise really not well known to me, nor I to him.

Also on the occasion of that visit, I met Krayenbühl's assistant, Gazi Yasargil, a Turkish national, who had come to Switzerland for his postgraduate work and stayed on as assistant to the professor. At that time Yasargil spoke very little English. He visited me several years later in Houston. The night after his arrival I took him to a baseball game at the Astrodome on which occasion he informed me that it was his fortieth birthday.

I went on from Zürich to Rome to attend the International Congress of Neurology. I visited the Eternal City briefly in 1957, and, once again I had a fabulous time seeing as many of the historical sights as possible during the week that I was there.

In the middle of my week in Rome, I picked up an English-language newspaper and noted in a box on the front page that a large, dangerous storm (Hurricane Carla) had hit the Gulf Coast in the vicinity of Houston. I tried to get through by telephone to talk with Bette, who was at home with our children, Susan and Anne, aged twelve and eleven. However, many of the telephone lines were down in Houston, particularly in the suburban areas, and it took three days before a connection could be made. When I finally reached Bette, it was a relief to learn that, although we had lost a number of trees on our three acres, there had been no damage of consequence to the family, house, or the horses which we kept on the back acre of our property.

My next trip to Europe took place in October 1962. I had been invited to participate in the annual meeting of the Czechoslovak

Medical Association to be held in Prague in celebration of the 100th anniversary of Jan Purkinje, a renowned neuroanatomist. This invitation came from Professor Rudolf Petr of Hradec Kralóvé, whom I had first met in St. Louis when we were both residents at Barnes Hospital. Although I continued to receive a card from him each year in December, I did not see him again until 1957 at the World Congress of Neurological Sciences in Brussels. On the latter occasion, I had invited him to dinner.

I learned from another former colleague, Edmund Smolik, a neurosurgeon in St. Louis, that he had also been invited by Rudi Petr to attend the meeting in Prague. Although American-born, he was going to present his paper in Czech and I decided to make a valiant attempt to do likewise. I had encountered two young surgeons from Prague who were observers with DeBakey at The Methodist Hospital, so I contacted them and asked them to help me prepare a draft of my paper in Czech. After the paper was translated, I wrote the proper pronunciation phonetically between the lines of the manuscript. A short time after we had completed that task, DeBakey was visited by a professor of surgery from Bratislava. My young friends arranged for me to give the paper, complete with slides, in his presence. Afterward the professor began to ask me some questions in Czech. We all laughed because there was no way that I could understand the questions, much less respond to them other than in English. My young friends were satisfied that I had learned my lessons well.

Subsequently, during the Congress in Prague, my paper was assigned to one of the plenary sessions. At the end of my presentation, the audience stood up, applauded, and cheered. It was hard to understand why I should have such an accolade for what I had considered to be a pedestrian kind of paper and I thought that it must be because I had made the effort to give the talk in Czech. Later, Rudi told me that the audience was very pleased that I had given the paper in Czech because most of the Russian doctors, who had come to hear me present it in English, could understand very little of what I had said.

The Cuban "missile crisis" took place during my visit to Prague. Since I could not read the Czech newspapers, I was virtually in the dark and almost completely isolated. My family was in Houston and, like everyone else in the southern part of the United States, they were very concerned about what was going on and fearful that I might not get back from central Europe if war broke out. I actually had no idea that the situation was that serious until I returned to Paris at the end of the Congress in Prague and was able to call home.

In October 1963, I was invited to Buenos Aires to participate in the Congreso Latinoamericano de Neurocirurgia (Latin-American Congress of Neurosurgery). This came about as a result of our recently consummated affiliation with the Institute of Neurology at the University of Montevideo, Uruguay, as a participating institution in the Joint Study of Extracranial Arterial Occlusion, supported by the National Heart Institute in Bethesda, Maryland. For me this trip had several important aspects.

Before leaving for South America, I had gone to New York and planned to take a nonstop flight from Idlewild Airport (now the John F. Kennedy International Airport) to Buenos Aires. I recall going to a cigarette machine in the airport terminal and putting in fifty cents to obtain a pack of Pall Malls. Those were king-size cigarettes without filters, and I was smoking nearly two packs a day. After a few puffs on the first cigarette, which I lit while waiting for the plane, I started to cough. I was so disgusted with myself that, for the first time, I took the full pack, threw it in a trash receptacle, and got on the plane without buying another. When I arrived in Argentina, I found that I could not tolerate smoking the cigarettes available there. From that day to the present, I had only a cigar on rare occasions during the next two or three years but never again smoked cigarettes. I might not have been able to break the habit if I had tried to do so, as on several previous occasions, while at home and with Bette still smoking.

In February 1964, on a return trip from New York, I found myself seated in the coach section of the plane next to Col. John Glenn, the astronaut, who was trying to be as inconspicuous as possible. I had never met Colonel Glenn before, although his wife, Annie, had been referred to me as a patient because of a severe speech impediment. For the next three and a half hours, during the flight to Houston, we had quite an interesting and animated conversation. I had no idea that I would be seeing him again so soon. However, in March I received a telephone call from the commanding officer at Wilford Hall Air Force Hospital in San Antonio, where I was a civilian consultant, informing me that John Glenn had been admitted there following a head injury. Glenn had already declared himself a candidate for the Democratic nomination to the U.S. Senate from Ohio. While trying to hang a mirror in the bathroom of his rented apartment in Columbus, he slipped on the bath mat and fell against the bath tub, hitting the side of his head just above the ear. As a result, he sustained a concussion and was suffering from marked rotational vertigo.

When I saw Colonel Glenn in the hospital, he was still trying to conduct, from his bed, the business associated with his political campaign. However, he had found that when he would turn his head too quickly to one side or the other, he would have severe vertigo and, on several occasions, had vomited as a consequence. This was an intolerable situation, which was being made even worse by the stress placed upon him by others as well as himself. After examining him, I suggested that he ought to retire from the Senate race. He was loath to do this because he felt a sincere obligation to his many ardent supporters. Then I portrayed a picture to him wherein I asked how he would respond if he were on a statewide television talk show back home in Ohio and when asked a question by a member of the press, he would turn his head quickly, become nauseated, and perhaps even vomit in front of the television camera. Shortly after that, I left his room and told him that I would return in the morning to reexamine him. Perhaps then he would want to discuss the matter further. I suspected later that the scenario which I had laid out for him helped to influence his decision to withdraw from the campaign.

Two years later, he had an opportunity to run again and on that occasion won the nomination and later the election. He has been in the Senate ever since, and from time to time I have had contact with him. Fortunately for him, the vertigo ceased after about three months and in six months he requalified for pilot status.

(John called me during the 1988 Democratic National Convention and told me that his name had surfaced as a potential vice-presidential candidate. He had given my name, as a contact, to the managers of the campaign of Michael Dukakis. As a result, I received a call from a physician in New Haven, Connecticut, who wanted to know the details of Glenn's injury in 1964 and whether there had been any long-term consequences. I assured him that, in my opinion at least, there were none. Nevertheless, the governor of Massachusetts chose another running mate.)

In 1963, not too long after Shervert Frazier had come to Baylor as chairman of the Department of Psychiatry, I began to appreciate that there was an undercurrent of activity which was going to make my job difficult, if not untenable. This came from several directions. First and foremost, it was apparent that DeBakey wanted me to devote as much of my time as possible to his immediate interests, particularly with respect to his patients at The Methodist Hospital. Inasmuch as Frazier coveted neurology as a part of his fiefdom, it soon became obvious to everyone on the faculty that he wanted to move neurology from independent status into the Department of Psychiatry. There was little doubt in my mind that this was a reflection of his attitude toward me, resulting, at least in part, from my inability to accommodate him with a residency position ten years earlier.

It also became obvious that Peter Kellaway had aspirations of being director of a neurological institute within The Methodist Hospital complex, and he began a campaign which made it extremely difficult for me to function satisfactorily as chairman of the Department of Neurology at the medical school, acting director of the Blue Bird Clinic, and chief of the Neurology Service at The Methodist Hospital. I did not appreciate how far this agitation had progressed until September 1965, when I was on my way back from a meeting in Caracas, Venezuela, where I was a participant in planning for the second PanAmerican Congress of Neurology to be held in Puerto Rico. In Miami, on my way to Venezuela, I had met my friend, Richard Schmidt, professor and chairman of neurology at the University of Florida Health Sciences Center in Gainesville, and we had flown together to Maracaibo and then on to Caracas. On the return flight, when we were nearing Miami and I was about to say farewell to Dick Schmidt, he informed me that he was not returning directly to Gainesville but would be accompanying me on the same flight to Houston. He had been invited by Peter Kellaway, and I am not sure who else, to look at the chairmanship of the Department of Neurology in Houston. All of this occurred without my ever having been informed that I was about to be replaced. Dick apologized profusely for not having told me earlier and said that he had refrained from doing so because he realized when we were together that I knew nothing about his scheduled visit and that I would have been very upset. He told me that he had little or no interest in the job but thought that, out of courtesy to those who had pressed him to come, he would go to Houston and have a look.

It was not too long after Dick Schmidt's visit that I was informed that A. Earl Walker, who was about to retire from the chairmanship of neurosurgery at Johns Hopkins Medical School, would be coming to Houston to visit the medical school as a prospective candidate for the chair of a combined department of neurology and neurosurgery. This had also been done without any information having been given to me prior to the day of his arrival. Earl, who had been a friend of mine for many years, was astounded when I told him that I had not been informed of his visit and was unaware that I was to be replaced. This was extremely embarrassing for both of us, but just another part of the game that was being played at my expense.

During the first week of October 1965, I was in Atlantic City attending the annual meeting of the American Neurological Association. On the second day of the meeting, I was standing in line waiting to enter the hotel restaurant for lunch when I was approached by John Stirling Meyer, chairman of neurology at Wayne State University in Detroit. He informed me that he would soon be visiting Houston to look at the chairmanship of the department of which I was still the incumbent. Then he said, "Don't worry, I am really not interested, but I am coming out of courtesy to Dr. DeBakey." That's when I started to be concerned. Meyer had been invited one year earlier to be the national director of the stroke portion of the Regional Medical Program organized by Michael DeBakey and initiated by President Lyndon B. Johnson.

Meyer's subsequent visit did not engender much enthusiasm from the faculty members who visited with him and so it was almost three years later, after DeBakey had become president of Baylor College of Medicine and I was in Dallas, that his appointment was finally consummated.

In mid-October 1965, a meeting of the executive committee of the faculty was convened at the home of James R. Schofield, assistant dean, to discuss a recommendation by DeBakey that I be removed as chairman of neurology. I was unaware of the meeting at the time but learned about it later from some of the other chairmen who had been present.

On October 28, 1965, I was visited in my office by Raymond D. Pruitt, chairman of the Department of Internal Medicine and also chairman of the executive committee of the faculty, and Jimmy Schofield. They informed me that they were requesting my resignation from the chair in neurology effective November 1. This was done without any explanation or warning and only took place after Dean Stanley Olson had departed on a trip out of the country. None of them had the courage to confront me while he was still in Houston.

At Dr. Pruitt's request I prepared a letter which read as follows:

> It has become increasingly difficult during the past year to operate the Department of Neurology without being able to exercise the usual prerogatives of a Chairman. To continue this situation will not be of benefit to Baylor or to me. The time has come for me to resign from the chairmanship. I would like for this to become effective immediately, since I wish to pursue my academic work in my present tenured appointment as a Full Professor by devoting more time and energy to my own personal research and teaching. This would entail a continuance of work already in progress in the Cooperative Study of Extracranial Vascular Disease for which I am Director of the Central Registry. In addition, we could continue our role as institutional participants in the Cooperative Study. There is also work related to the Study of Aneurysms and Subarachnoid Hemorrhage. Aside from the Neurology Training Grant, these three grants concerned with cerebrovascular disease, constitute a major source of support for personnel presently employed in this department.
>
> I hope that as soon as possible after receipt of this letter, you will make arrangements to inform the members of the department of neurology of my decision. I know that you will want to assure them that there is no immediate alteration in their status contemplated.

It had become very clear to me that I could not be involved in work with someone who had fixed ideas and a single-minded egocentric goal and take a position opposite the one which he espoused. Moreover, whether I was right or wrong had no relevance. If I accepted the position of being a rubber stamp to someone else's decisions, I could have continued. However, what I was being asked to do contravened my principles and my integrity, and so I decided that I could not remain in that mode. In retrospect, I appreciate that this entire affair did more for me than I realized at the time. It was a difficult lesson in character building but I was determined to continue a career in academic medicine. Therefore, it was necessary to stay the course even though it ran through a jungle and would never be easy to follow. Under such circumstances there were inevitably sacrifices that needed to be made, and the injury to my pride took time to heal.

On Monday, November 8, 1965, one week after the executive committee of the faculty had accepted my resignation, I received a visit from Shervert Frazier, professor and chairman of the Department of Psychiatry, and David Friedman, an associate professor in that department. Frazier sat down opposite me and placed his tape recorder on my desk, saying that he wished to record our conversation to make sure that there would be no misunderstanding. I told him that before he turned his machine on, he should wait until I had my tape recorder, which I then retrieved from a drawer in my desk. I put it in front of me and said, "Now turn yours on and I will turn mine on also." I certainly had no faith in what Frazier would do with his recording of our conversation. I regretted having to resort to this kind of defense, but, unfortunately, this approach is what one can anticipate in some academic circles. I was often amazed at the backstabbing and underhanded politics present among supposedly well-educated professional adults. At least I was taught some lessons that subsequently enabled me to cope with this kind of behavior and not be burned again.

On that same date I sent another memorandum to Ray Pruitt spelling out for him in some detail the space needs for the Cerebrovascular Research Program of which I was the principal investigator. I also wrote a letter to Dr. Murray Goldstein at the National Institute for Neurological Diseases at the National Institutes of Health in Bethesda, Maryland, informing him that I had resigned as chairman of the Department of Neurology and, as a consequence, would be relinquishing my responsibility as director of the neurology residency training program, which was supported by a government grant.

During the first week of November, I invited the trainees in our neurology program to come see me individually in my office and told each one that I had been asked to resign as chairman and director of training. They were very disturbed about the events which had taken place, but I assured them that I would not allow their training to be interrupted since I felt responsible for their having come to Baylor in the first place. I then spent several hours on the phone talking to colleagues around the country who were also directors of training programs. Before the day was out, I had each of the residents placed in a program elsewhere beginning July 1, 1966. One went to the University of Iowa, two to Washington University in St. Louis, while the fourth, who was about to complete his final year at the end of June 1966, went on to a teaching position in northern Illinois. I am pleased to say that all of them were most appreciative of my efforts in their behalf and I have continued to maintain contact with them during the intervening years. Very soon after my resignation became generally known, several other members of the department decided that their future would be better served elsewhere.

I moved my base of operations from the medical school building to the Texas Institute for Rehabilitation and Research, upon receiving an offer to relocate from Dr. William H. Spencer, director of the Institute. I remained there for two years doing my work, taking care of patients, running my research program and trying to find a new location to which I might want to move. Nevertheless, I felt as though I was the bastard son at the family picnic. Several of the more junior faculty colleagues have said to me since then that I made tenure mean something at Baylor and they thanked me for it. I had no intention of closing up shop, going across the street and starting a private practice. That just was not on my agenda.

One event in which I was peripherally involved and which received national attention occurred in 1966, after I was no longer chief of the neurology service at The Methodist Hospital. I am referring to the widely publicized episode relating to the implantation of the first mechanical left ventricular bypass. This was not an artificial heart but an "assistive device" designed to provide a period of rest for the left ventricle, that part of the heart which does all the hard work of pumping. By temporary implantation of this prosthesis, the heart would theoretically be allowed to recover from injury and then after an undetermined interval would be reconnected to the rest of the circulatory system. I knew that this device had been under development for several years but had no idea when the time would be appropriate for it to be placed in a patient. When the day finally arrived for it to be used clinically, I was preparing to go to St. Louis for a meeting of the Harvey Cushing Society (later known as the American Association of Neurological Surgeons). It wasn't until the next afternoon in St. Louis that I realized why all the extra lines and the temporary telephone booths had been placed in the corridors of The Methodist Hospital. With all of the excitement, I knew only that something spectacular was going to take place. Of course, what the world outside of Texas did not know was that April 21, San Jacinto Day, is an important local and state holiday. That day had been chosen because the operating schedule at The Methodist

Hospital would not be routine and the regular crew would have the day off. Only DeBakey's team was on hand.

Ted Bowen, administrator of The Methodist Hospital, called Don Macon, who had until then been narrating all of the motion picture films of DeBakey's operations, a day or two before the surgery and asked him to serve as a liaison in order to handle the press. Macon told Bowen that if he wished to preserve the anonymity of the patient and also provide access to the equipment, he should not invite a large number of the press, like the pool that covers the White House. However, because DeBakey wanted to have national coverage, Bowen instructed Macon to press on and he called NBC in New York. The NBC man handling the pool that particular month sent out the word to pool members that they would meet in Houston the following day at 3:00 P.M. Everybody and his brother were there.

It was arranged that Gene Davis, the surgical motion-picture photographer at Methodist Hospital, would shoot the entire operative procedure on film while one of his assistants would shoot the highlights of the surgery in still photographs. Then these materials would be distributed throughout the press pool in the usual fashion. The time was worked out as well as the deadlines. Then the group voluntarily declared a moratorium on all information until a specific time the next day. Macon told me when I returned that they were about to conclude this meeting in the hospital conference room when DeBakey entered wearing his operating room scrub suit, holding in his hand a prototype of the device to be implanted which everyone had wanted to keep a big secret. This shot the previously arranged moratorium completely to pieces. I also learned from Don Macon that Gene Davis took the surgical motion pictures as planned and sent duplicates around the world in a fashion similar to what had been done with the space materials from NASA. Regrettably, all of these films and still pictures had to be retrieved soon afterward because no one in all the haste had taken the time to obtain proper signed releases. Meanwhile, DeBakey had made his own arrangement with a well-known photographer from *Life* magazine, which was very big in those days, to let him have, exclusively, still pictures of the procedure in exchange for DeBakey's appearance on the cover of the magazine. His picture did appear a few weeks later. As a result, the man in charge of public affairs at Baylor College of

Medicine resigned in disgust or despair shortly thereafter. He told me that he could no longer tolerate his situation.

I learned about some other details of this surgery in a strange way, three years later. At a medical meeting in another city, I met the former surgical resident who had been on the inpatient service at The Methodist Hospital during this event. He told me that DeBakey was committed to implanting his experimental device into a patient on Thursday, April 21, 1966. The night before, he made rounds on the inpatient service with this resident and selected for the procedure a gentleman from southern Illinois, not too far from East St. Louis. When DeBakey and the resident went to see the patient, DeBakey said to him, "I plan to take you to surgery tomorrow." Then he gave him the news. "You will be the first man anywhere in whom we will use an artificial heart." According to the resident, the patient, as I have witnessed many of Mike DeBakey's patients do, responded excitedly, "Oh, Doctor, I am so pleased that you are going to have me as your patient."

As a corollary to what I have said in regard to the press coverage, a local reporter in the patient's hometown in Illinois met the patient's wife as she was coming out of the supermarket later that morning, April 21. He immediately asked, "How do you feel about your husband being the first man in the world to receive an artificial heart?" She said, "What?" In their haste to schedule the surgery, Ted Bowen, the hospital administrator, and DeBakey forgot to notify the wife that her husband was going to surgery.

Tom Fourquean, in those days a high-level associate hospital administrator who had considerable power, was, like me, out of the city. He told me that when he returned and checked into the details of what had transpired in his absence, he insisted that all the film be retrieved from around the world.

The patient's wife called The Methodist Hospital on the telephone as soon as she got home. DeBakey and Bowen were so upset when they realized that she had not been notified, and that there was an item already in the press to the effect that she did not know, they arranged to send a private jet to Illinois and immediately bring her to Houston. This placated her somewhat.

During my stay in St. Louis for the neurosurgical meeting, I was very upset by two things. While driving on Thursday evening out to the house of my former chief, Dr. James O'Leary, with another friend, Dr. Clinton Woolsey, a neurophysiologist from the

University of Wisconsin, we were listening to the radio in the car. There had been bulletins reporting on the patient's clinical status every fifteen to thirty minutes since he was, after all, a "local" personage who came from just across the Mississippi River near East St. Louis. The next morning, the *St. Louis Post Dispatch* had on its front page a picture of DeBakey and my neurology resident, who had no authority whatsoever to make any statement, standing by the bedside of the patient. The caption underneath the picture said, "Neurologist says brain damage only temporary," quoting the resident. You can imagine what a shock it was to me to learn that this fellow had presumed to make such a statement. That resident had been recommended to me by the chairman of neurology at the University of Tennessee in Memphis, Robert Utterback. I learned later that Utterback had been told by his faculty and housestaff that if he didn't fire the resident, they would all resign. After finishing his neurology training, this fellow went into private practice in Houston. He was a highly intelligent man who subsequently completed law school for the express purpose of being able to handle cases for plaintiffs who were suing doctors. He died a few years later of a malignant brain tumor.

When I returned to Houston on Saturday morning, April 23, I went to see DeBakey's patient, who had been placed in a special isolation room with continuous EEG recording on the third floor of the hospital. Dr. Peter Kellaway, chief of the Electrophysiology Laboratory, walked in while I was there and informed me, "This man's EEG was flat when he came from the operating room." This condition was indicative of isoelectric or nonfunctioning brain. What we were seeing on the EEG tracing was being produced by severe twitching of the scalp muscles.

It is ordinarily a difficult decision to turn off a life support system even if one believes that a patient is "brain dead." However, in this case one was confronted with a patient who was not only not breathing on his own but still had an artificial pulse produced by a mechanical device. This created a dilemma regarding when to turn off the respirator. While Kellaway and I were standing there, DeBakey came in. He said, "Bill, I am glad you're back." Then pointing to the spikes on the tracing, he went on, "Look at this brain activity." Without further comment, he turned on his heels and left the room. The machine was not turned off for four more days.

It was of interest to me that not too long before all these events took place in Houston, Adrian Kantrowitz, a cardiovascular surgeon in Brooklyn, New York, had placed an aortic assist pump in a patient who had lived for three days. This latter feat had been reported in great detail and with a diagrammatic representation in *TIME* magazine.

The only article known to me in which these events were criticized publicly came to my attention a few months later, when I was traveling to Europe on an Air France flight. On board was a copy of *Paris Match*, a popular French periodical. The article, in French, was written by a reporter who had been in Houston during the entire affair. His conclusions and his comments regarding what had taken place were not too dissimilar from mine.

Gradually, in the mid-1960s, the strained relationship with DeBakey created more and more of a problem for me and apparently for him as well. There is little doubt that DeBakey is a superb organizer and he has probably done more than any other man, with the possible exception of Dr. R. Lee Clark at M. D. Anderson Hospital, to put the Texas Medical Center on the map. Unfortunately, matters came to the point where there was virtually a complete rupture of our relations resulting eventually in my departure from Houston.

I was informed by several close friends in other cities that my association with DeBakey had delayed my admission to the American Neurological Association, where I was turned down twice. Two of my former residents were admitted to that organization before I was elected to membership. It wasn't until 1967, when it became known that I was leaving Baylor to go to Dallas, that Dr. H. Houston Merritt, who had been professor of neurology, director of the New York Neurological Institute, and then dean at Columbia, as well as president of the American Neurological Association, wrote me a letter stating that he would be pleased to nominate me for membership. That only happened after I disassociated myself from Baylor and, more specifically, from DeBakey. The only comment that I ever heard from DeBakey was through a mutual friend to whom DeBakey had said, when that person inquired about me, "Sure, I know him well; he is a damned good neurologist!" I thought that was grudgingly complimentary.

Several years later, when they dedicated the DeBakey Building for Medical Education and Research at Baylor, I wrote Mike a letter and told him how pleased I was that he had received this recognition and honor and that I was sorry that on the occasion of the dedication I would be out of the city. I received in return a very nice "Dear Bill" letter signed "Mike." I assumed that the hatchet had been buried but I am still not sure. My association with him provided me with an opportunity to see an amount of vascular disease that I would never have seen otherwise. My principal quarrel with him was on an intellectual level. I felt that such a tremendous amount of clinical material as was available to us should have been looked at from a more scientific and academic aspect than by merely counting numbers of abdominal aortas replaced and coronary arteries by-passed. Maybe I was wrong and he was right, but I soon realized, when I left Baylor and went on to conquer other worlds, that I slept better at night. Although it was very unpleasant, and in an even greater respect, unfortunate, I do not think this soured relationship put the brakes on my career. It taught me several important lessons.

When my appointment in Dallas was announced, I was tremendously pleased by the number of letters and telephone calls that I received from former colleagues and friends across this country and overseas, as well as a large number of former students, wishing me well in my new post at Dallas. It was certainly gratifying that there were, in fact, 186 communications in all. These letters still remain in my personal file. One in particular summarizes what most of the correspondents wrote:

> Thank you for your thoughtfulness in writing about your new position. Shortly after your letter arrived, I also read about it in the news section of *Neurology*. The new position sounds fine and I am sure that it will not only be stimulating for you, but even more, I hope that you will continue with many of your activities that were so well started and so well received during your stay at Baylor.
>
> I am well aware of many of your problems at Baylor and I am sure that you know that most of your friends, both in neurology and neurosurgery throughout the country, admire your ability to face up to the real facts in neurological and neurosurgical results. In doing so you have performed a great "moral" service for all of us who feel that perhaps the most important thing in medicine is complete intellectual honesty.
>
> Please consider this letter as wishing you the greatest success and happiness in your new bailiwick.

Although it is a distinct advantage to have the most money, the biggest guns, and most exalted position, these elements are not always the key to ultimate success.

I was very sad about the circumstances which resulted in my leaving Baylor College of Medicine after an association lasting eighteen years. I had grown up with the institution, so to speak, had started the neurology program, and was satisfied that I had developed it into something worthwhile. We had an established residency training program, our own clinical service, and worked in all of the affiliated hospitals. The residents rotated through the Veterans Administration Hospital, Jefferson Davis Hospital, and later Ben Taub Hospital, as well as The Methodist Hospital. Some of them even went out of town for specific rotations. I was, and still am, very proud of the department which I developed at Baylor. The student teaching and residency training programs in neurology expanded and the recipients appeared to be delighted with the results.

Fortunately, I still had my Cerebrovascular Research Program intact and a sizable amount of other grant support. In fact, it totaled $258,000 for the academic year 1965-66. Each of these grants was renewed for another three years at the end of the grant period, and I was able, as principal investigator, to move all of them to Dallas when I left, taking with me the Central Registry for the Joint Study of Extracranial Arterial Occlusion and support for my part in another large study of aneurysms and subarachnoid hemorrhage. I had absolutely no intention of leaving behind what I felt I had rightfully earned.

Shervert Frazier, once he had taken on the responsibility of acting chairman, insisted that all of the publications which might emanate from the Department of Neurology had to pass across his desk. One of my papers concerning phantom limb pain, on which I had collaborated with Dr. Eugen Kahn, was completely appropriated by him, a fact that I did not fully appreciate until after I had left Houston.

In the late 1970s I was appointed a member of the National Advisory Committee for Psychiatry and Neurology of the Veterans Administration in Washington. After accepting the invitation, I found out that the chairman was none other than Frazier, who was then professor of psychiatry at Columbia University College of Physicians and Surgeons in New York. He was not overjoyed to see me there. He subsequently went on to Harvard as professor of psychiatry and director of MacLean Hospital. Along the way, he was elected president of the American Psychiatric Association.

In 1988, Shervert Frazier was faced with serious difficulties himself, having been accused of plagiarism by a graduate student. He was investigated by a faculty committee at Harvard and dismissed from his academic post. The dean of Harvard Medical School, Dan Tosteson, after having removed Frazier from his faculty position at the recommendation of this special *ad hoc* committee, was treated to a barrage of abuse. I spoke with him several weeks after this event had been reported in print and had become a *cause célèbre* in the academic community. I told him about my previous experience. He was perturbed only to the extent that he had never received any input about Frazier's career in Houston before he went to New York and then later to Boston. Evidently, neither Dean Tosteson nor his search committee had ever asked Frazier's former Baylor associates for any comment or recommendation.

It is also of more than passing interest that Frazier, in the biographical sketch which he submitted to the *Directory of Medical Specialists,* states that he was a fellow at the Mayo Clinic from 1951 to 1953 when, in fact, he was in general practice in Harrisburg, Illinois, for at least part of that time. In 1953 he turned over his practice to Dr. James Wimpee, a graduate of Baylor College of Medicine, class of 1952. (Jim Wimpee has been for many years in the practice of orthopedic surgery in San Angelo, Texas.) For certain, the adage "The higher you go, the harder you fall" is still applicable today, or one might say, "What goes around, comes around."

I look back upon my experience at Baylor with considerable nostalgia. While there, I made many long-lasting friendships. It was an exceedingly enjoyable time of my career until the last two years. Even though those final years were very disturbing and stressful, I was fortunate to have the time available to find a more suitable location. Still, Houston had been my home for eighteen years and the community had been good to me. One of my daughters had grown up there. When I was offered an opportunity to return less than two years later, I jumped at it.

Chapter 9

The Harris County Medical Society and The Houston Academy of Medicine

IN THE LATE 1940s AND EARLY 1950s, there was a good deal of concern among practitioners in Harris County regarding the role of a medical school and its faculty in the delivery of patient care. This apprehension was expressed most vehemently by doctors in the areas of Harris County remote from the new Medical Center rather than those who were already nearby in southwest Houston and who might become affiliated with the new institutions.

These matters came to a head in the early part of 1952, when a lengthy detailed letter was sent to Dr. Byron P. York, president of the Harris County Medical Society (HCMS), by Dr. Wendell H. Hamrick, chairman of the society's Medical Jurisprudence and Public Relations Board, regarding lay publicity by doctors, particularly the Baylor full-time faculty. Indignation was voiced by many private practitioners over what they perceived as unfair competition by full-time salaried physicians. This scenario was not unfamiliar among physicians in other urban locations where a new medical school had been inaugurated in the midst of older established patterns of practice and referral.

On June 9, 1952, a report was received by the executive committee of the Medical Society from the Medical Jurisprudence and Public Relations Board over the signature of Dr. Hamrick. This letter laid out in detail a meeting which had been held with Dean

Walter Moursund regarding publicity by members of the Baylor faculty. Basically, the whole issue was that of full-time faculty engaging in what was referred to as "private practice." Earlier that year a letter was sent to the president of the Medical Society by Dr. Hamrick regarding the affiliation between Baylor College of Medicine and Houston-Harris County Hospital District Board of Managers. The Medical Society was insistent that society membership be a prerequisite for staff membership at that hospital. Later in the year, Dr. Hamrick directed his concern to what were referred to as "private beds" at M. D. Anderson Hospital. Subsequently, another letter was sent to Dr. York by Dr. John Glen, a pediatrician and president-elect of the Medical Society, concerning sixteen beds which were being set aside for private patients at M. D. Anderson Hospital, then under construction.

In those early days, things went along pretty well with Walter Moursund, Sr., as dean. Baylor had a fairly small cadre of full-time doctors in the midst of a flourishing medical community, and although their presence did not cause a whole lot of friction, they were not completely without it. Consequently, I was taken by surprise when, in late 1952, I was asked to run for a position on the executive board of the Harris County Medical Society. There was no one on the board at that time who had any association with full-time activity at the medical school. My opponent for the position was Herbert Duke, Sr., from Baytown. I was told later that he defeated me by a mere four votes and that the reason for my defeat was that the membership preferred to have representation from eastern Harris County, where there had been none previously. Other than that nomination and serving later as chairman of the Grievance Committee, I really did not have too close an association with Medical Society politics.

In May 1954, at the request of Dr. Charles Reece, then president of the Harris County Medical Society, Dean Stanley Olson, Dr. Moursund's successor at Baylor, agreed to the establishment of a liaison committee that would meet regularly to discuss the interface between the medical school and the Medical Society. Everett Lewis, a prominent surgeon at Hermann Hospital, and I were the two most active members of that committee.

According to Dr. Lewis, not everyone could talk to Stanley Olson because "he had been to The Clinic in Rochester, Minnesota, and was therefore superior to the country bumpkins in the culture-barren wastelands of Texas." But Everett Lewis had been to the Mayo Clinic before Stanley, and for a longer period, so he ended up doing most of the talking to him. During one committee meeting, he led Dr. Olson on to make statements that even the other representatives from Baylor, including me, agreed were absurd. On more than one occasion the liaison committee scolded Olson for some of his actions. Since little was accomplished by this effort to have more cooperation, the so-called "liaison committee" just faded away.

It was a most unfortunate situation because there were a number of persons on both sides who felt that it did not have to be that way, but Stanley Olson had his views and his set of facts, which he was always ready and willing to present. If the listener did not buy the facts as they were presented to him, he was obviously ill-informed.

Finally, it reached the point where Olson was telling various department heads how to plan their next year. He even tried to direct Mike DeBakey. Olson later reminded me that one does not argue with John Hunter (a famous British surgeon of the eighteenth century).

When James Pittman became HCMS president in 1955, he appointed a committee which would explore the need for a new city-county hospital. I was asked to serve as a member. This had become a real burning issue with the Society membership. The committee, with Dr. C. Forrest Jorns as chairman and me as secretary, was to interview nationally recognized hospital planners to determine whether or not a new hospital was needed by the community. We spent virtually all of the Christmas and New Year's holiday period interviewing these consultants. We invited James Hamilton of Booz, Allen and Hamilton in Minneapolis; Dr. Anthony Rourke, a hospital consultant from the New England area; and Ross Garrett from Chicago, who had done considerable work for Sears-Roebuck, to come to Houston for consultation. We were very impressed with what each of these men had to offer, but Garrett with his previous track record and the price that he quoted appeared to be the most reasonable choice. He said he would charge $10,000 to undertake the research and planning and provide us with a recommendation. Any proposal for spending that amount of money required approval of the Medical Society membership. Jim Pittman asked that I withhold the information about the proposal until after the installation of his successor, Everett Lewis. In mid-February 1956, Dr. Lewis called a meeting specifically for the purpose of presenting to the members the proposal submitted by Garrett.

Several meetings of the Society had been held previously to discuss whether there was even a need for a new hospital. I remember very well that at one of them Stanley Olson had requested time to make a presentation. He had arrived with a stack of prepared charts to inform the Society members about "the facts." There was so much emotion involved, particularly at that time, that the members were not about to receive any "facts" from Dr. Olson, especially since, from the time of his arrival in Houston in 1953, he had not endeared himself to the Society by his comments regarding their lack of a cooperative spirit.

At the special meeting called by Everett Lewis, it was evident from the outset that the large turnout would be hostile. I made a presentation for the committee in as factual and dispassionate manner as possible considering the circumstances. During my presentation I pointed out to the members present that the price of Ross Garrett's proposal was extremely reasonable. However, payment would have to be covered by a special assessment or from a special fund of the Society and required approval by the membership. I emphasized further that if the Medical Society was not going to take the initiative, it was a certainty that the Texas Medical Center and the county commissioners, together with the Hospital District Board of Managers, would invite Garrett to undertake the project for them for at least three times what it would cost the Society.

This was followed by a question-and-answer period. A number of members got up and made what I thought were rather inane remarks. One stated, "We don't need any new place for *those people*; they go now to Jefferson Davis (City-County) Hospital in their Cadillacs, leave them in the rear parking lot, and go into the clinics for free medical treatment." Another said, "Those people are not indigent in the sense that we think of poor people needing to get medical care. We certainly don't need to pamper them." Frankly, I never have been able to figure out who *those people* were. This haranguing of the assemblage went on and on until finally the time had arrived for Everett Lewis to cut off discussion and put the matter to a vote.

The outcome of the vote was a foregone conclusion. Not too surprisingly, the members turned down the proposal by a substantial margin. I then asked Dr. Lewis if he would permit me to make a few remarks before he adjourned the meeting which had been called specifically for this purpose. I expressed my disappointment with the outcome, especially since I, along with a number of other colleagues, had spent so much of the holiday season trying to get this urgent business on the table early in the new year. I concluded by saying that in my opinion the vote which had just been recorded could best be described as "taking one of the first steps to repeal the twentieth century." Needless to say, that comment was not greeted with a lot of enthusiasm.

Less than a week after that special called meeting, there was a picture in the *Houston Chronicle* of Dr. Frederick Elliott, executive director of the Texas Medical Center, Harris County Judge Bob Casey, and Houston Mayor Lewis Cutrer with Ross Garrett. The accompanying article said that the latter had agreed to develop a plan for the City-County Hospital District and that his fee would be $30,000.

They eventually hired Garrett, with at least some persuasion from the executive committee of the Harris County Medical Society. At a meeting later that year, Garrett was invited to come before the Society to present the report which he had developed for the Hospital District. I had never before seen a gathering of adults who behaved in such an immature fashion. When Garrett presented his proposal to the assemblage, he was booed and hissed. It was an unbelievably bad scene.

The book of plans has since disappeared, but it was very interesting. At the time Ross Garrett was reviewing the hospitals in Houston, the cost of a private room was about $25 per day. He reviewed the cost per occupied bed per day using a system that most hospital administrators did not like. He took the total cost of operating the hospital and the number of occupied beds and days and figured out the cost per day. At that time, Jefferson Davis Hospital cost about $28-29 per day; Hermann Hospital, which was still mostly charity, about $30-32; The Methodist Hospital, where the cardiovascular surgeons were getting a lot of expensive equipment, was about $37; the Veterans Administration Hospital, in wards, was $85 a day. However, this should not be construed to indicate that the federal government could do it better.

My recollections of the Houston Academy of Medicine and its library go back to 1949, the year that I came to Houston to join the faculty at Baylor College of Medicine. At about the time of my arrival, the Library Committee of the Academy Board of Trustees was exploring the possibility of joining together the libraries of Baylor and the Academy. At the September 29, 1949 meeting of the Academy Board, Dr. Claude C. Cody, Jr., gave a report for the Library Committee giving their approval of the proposed agreement to consolidate the libraries. This agreement had been drawn up by Dr. Cody and Dean Walter Moursund. It was moved by Dr. Hatch Cummings and seconded by Dr. Theodore R. Hannon that the proposal be approved and that a special meeting of the Fellows be called for October 12 to consider the matter.

In October 1949, a discussion was held by the executive committee of the Harris County Medical Society regarding a hall of health which was to be planned for the new Houston Museum of Natural History. It was at this same meeting that the proposed plan for combining the Houston Academy of Medicine and Baylor libraries was first presented to the executive board.

The Harris County Medical Society and the Houston Academy of Medicine during those years met at the Medical Arts Building downtown. Since the membership of the two organizations was identical, there was ordinarily only one joint meeting each year. There was bound to be opposition to the proposal on the table at the October 12 meeting because some of the leading doctors in the community were not very pleased that Baylor College of Medicine had moved to Houston in the first place.

A heated discussion ensued. The most vehement opposition came from Dr. J. Edward Hodges, who had been president of the Harris County Medical Society in 1907, Dr. John T. Moore, president in 1938, and Dr. Charles W. Klanke (later president in 1965). Three other former presidents, Dr. Everett L. Goar (1922), Dr. L. L. D. "Dewey" Tuttle (1947), and Dr. Benjamin F. Smith (1932) spoke eloquently in favor of the proposal. Meetings of the Academy were ordinarily rather perfunctory and not well attended by the members, and it was sometimes difficult to get a quorum. However, on this occasion the room was packed and the debate lasted nearly two hours before the matter was put to a vote. The man who really carried the day was Dr. Tuttle, then chief of surgery at The Methodist Hospital, who made an impassioned plea to have the libraries joined. He expressed the opinion that the library of the Academy would not be taken over by Baylor and that by combining their holdings, they could serve a larger constituency and at the same time save money by not having to duplicate accessions. He was sufficiently persuasive that the members voted for the merger by a substantial majority.

In 1950 the Academy moved its books from the downtown location to the Medical Center, where it was housed at the north end of the first floor of the Roy and Lillie Cullen Building of Baylor. The Baylor librarian, Mrs. Pendergrass, was pregnant and about to retire, so Helen Holt, the librarian for the Houston Academy of Medicine, took over responsibility for the combined collection.

No one could anticipate that Baylor would give up all its books and turn them over to the Academy, but it did, although during the time that Helen Holt remained there as librarian, separate records were kept on them. That arrangement continued for several years, but by the late 1960s the entire collection, including many duplicates, had been turned over completely to the Academy. It very soon became evident that the Baylor location would be inadequate for the collection and would not permit the anticipated expansion.

The Academy owned for many years a piece of land diagonally across the street from the Warwick Hotel on Fannin and Ewing streets. There had been consideration at one time of putting the library there. However, after the M. D. Anderson Foundation offered land in the Texas Medical Center, the Academy sold the tract at Fannin and Ewing because it was felt by the board that the library should be at the hub of the new center.

At the regular meeting of the Academy Board of Trustees on November 16, 1951, Dr. Cody moved that the trustees of the M. D. Anderson Foundation be notified that the contingency of their gift to the Academy for building construction had been met by a substantial sum, raised by the membership.

In his annual report to the membership of the Academy in 1951, President Moise Levy reported that some members were trying to sabotage the library plans by circulating rumors that the space then being occupied at Baylor was adequate for the library's needs. Dr. Levy said that the members should not be misled by these rumors and that the board had already signed a contract with Cameron Fairchild and Associates, architects. He then went on to report that the actual date for construction to start could not be determined under the existing conditions. He further stated that the Texas Medical Center, Inc., had been offered space in the proposed library building as had the Medical and Dental Service Bureau. Dr. Levy indicated, however, that no decision had been made with respect to offices for the Harris County Medical Society. It was also planned that the building would include an auditorium suitable for meetings of the membership and leased upon request to other medically related organizations.

When 1952 rolled around, it was evident that there was some friction developing between the boards of the Houston Academy of Medicine and the Harris County Medical Society. A letter was received by the Society from Drs. Burt B. Smith and John E. Skogland, dated February 25, 1952, regarding plans for offices in the new library building. In this letter they also raised the question of the relationship of the Houston Academy of Medicine and its various sections to the Harris County Medical Society. Moreover, Dr. Skogland was quite vocal in his opposition to the Houston Academy of Medicine soliciting funds for construction independently from the Harris County Medical Society.

On March 25, 1952, a joint meeting of the board of trustees of the Academy, the building committee, and the executive committee of the Medical Society was held. The group was informed by Dr. Levy that the cost of the building and equipment would be $1,250,000 and that Cameron Fairchild, architect, had estimated the cost of the building for which he had drawn plans at between $800,000 and $900,000. At that meeting Dr. John Skogland asked if the two upper floors could be eliminated. Skogland, who had been opposed from the beginning to moving the library from downtown, inquired whether it would be possible to eliminate the two upper floors and do away with some of the more "dreamy" parts of the building. This was not surprising in view of Skogland's outspoken opposition to the conjoined library plan.

In a letter dated April 3, 1952, Dr. Moise D. Levy wrote Dr. Skogland, who was then secretary of the Harris County Medical Society, indicating that the Houston Academy of Medicine did have the authority to solicit funds for construction.

There are probably not many people in the Houston community who know how the last of the funds required to build the Jesse H. Jones Library Building were obtained. Dr. H. Grant Taylor, who was chief of pediatrics at M. D. Anderson, knew about it, as well as Dr. Frederick Elliott, who was then executive director of the Texas Medical Center.

There were very few neurologists in Houston in the early 1950s. Therefore, it was not surprising when one day in April 1952 I got a call from Dr. Moise D. Levy, Sr., one of the oldtimers who had come to Houston in 1922 to practice internal medicine. When he called me, he said, "Dr. Fields, I would appreciate your helping me out with a clinical problem. One of my VIP patients is in Memorial Baptist Hospital downtown following surgery the day before yesterday. Dr. George Waldron removed his gall bladder and now the patient is behaving very strangely. He is out of his head, he's confused and combative." Then he asked, "Do you know Mr. Jesse Jones?" I replied, "No, I do not know Mr. Jones but I remember that he was chairman of the Reconstruction Finance Corporation during the first Roosevelt administration in the 1930s, and I know that he owns the *Houston Chronicle*."

I got in my car, drove downtown to the Memorial Baptist Hospital (as it was called in those days), and parked in the lot across the street. That was before they built the Memorial Professional Building downtown (both of those buildings have been torn down since). I went up to the private suite on the tenth floor. Mr. Jones was in one room while Mrs. Jones, his nephew John T. Jones, Jr., Mr. and Mrs. Fred Heine, the cook, butler, and the chauffeur were assembled in the outer adjoining room (Mr. Heine was Mr. Jones' colleague and business confidant).

I could hear Mr. Jones in the next room, bellowing and making a terrible racket. After formal introductions, I excused myself and went into the patient's room, closing the door behind me. Mr. Jones was sitting upright with the head of the bed cranked up, stripped to his waist and with an intravenous infusion running into his left arm. He had restraints on all four limbs to keep him from climbing out of the bed. There was a male nurse and two females — another nurse and a nurse's aide — trying to keep him in bed. Before I did anything else, I stood at the bottom of the bed and watched him for a while. He was just looking around at random as though there was no one present at all. I noticed that the right side of his chest was not expanding quite as much as the left side. I said to the nurse, "I think he may have a collapse of his right lower lung." This is not an uncommon complication of gall bladder surgery since the gall bladder is just under the diaphragm on the right side. Percussing his chest and listening with a stethoscope confirmed my suspicion. It was not necessary to do any neurological examination. So I asked the nurse, "Would you get me a syringe full of Coramine?" Coramine was a respiratory stimulant widely used in those days. She brought me a 20 cc syringe containing the medication, and I inserted the needle into the tubing of his intravenous infusion. After I had injected about a third of it, I could see that his respirations were becoming a little less labored. By the time I had half of it in, he had quieted down and began to look around the room. In about a minute or two, he said, "Who the hell are you?" Those were his first words that were coherent. I told him who I was, we talked a bit, and then I withdrew the needle and syringe. I had satisfied myself that he was merely underventilating and that his brain was not getting sufficient oxygen.

This situation was embarrassing, to say the least, because the clinical problem was clearly not neurological. I decided that I had better bring the family in before he relapsed into his confused state. They came in and spoke with him. Mrs. Jones was so thrilled and said it was "Just like a miracle, my husband has been brought back to life." I excused myself as soon as I could, wrote a note on the chart, and took the elevator down. When I got to the doctors' lounge, I called Dr. Levy in his office and said, "I am embarrassed, Dr. Levy, to tell you what has been going on." I explained to him that I had not said anything to the family about the nature of the problem but had brought them into Mr. Jones' room and that they were very pleased. He immediately said, "We are going to get things taken care of promptly. Leave a note and I will call Waldron." He thanked me profusely, and I went about my business.

I anguished over the bill I should send Mr. Jones. In those days, a big bill for a consultation when one had to get in his car and go to another hospital might be $40 or $50. I thought, however, that this was an exceptional situation, and I sent a bill for $250. I knew that whatever was paid wouldn't go to me anyway, it would go to Baylor in accordance with my contract. I didn't think any more about it until about four months later when I received a call from Mr. Jones' office. A woman said, "This is Mr. Jesse Jones' secretary. Mr. Jones would like to know if you can pay him a visit soon." I said, "Yes, I will rearrange my schedule. Please assure Mr. Jones that I will be there tomorrow morning." She told me that his office was on the fourteenth floor of the Lamar Hotel. I had no idea what he wanted, but the next day I was in his office at the appointed time.

Before leaving Baylor and on the way to my car in the parking lot, I passed by the entrance to the library. At that time the consolidated library was housed in the north wing of the first floor in the original Baylor College of Medicine building. I saw Helen Holt (later Mrs. Helen Holt Garrott) seated at her desk near the door. I stopped for a moment to visit with her, and to pass the time of day.

She commented somewhat offhandedly, "We desperately need some place to put this library. We are just bursting at the seams."

I proceeded downtown to Mr. Jones' office and was soon ushered into his presence. I remember him as a tall, patrician gentleman. He came around the corner of his desk, put out his hand, and said, "Doctor, I am so pleased to meet you. I hope you will forgive me but I have no recollection of having seen you before and I wanted to see what you looked like. My family tells me that you saved my life."

I replied, "Oh no, Mr. Jones, that's certainly an exaggeration."

"Doctor, don't tell me any differently because my family has told me you saved my life. So, please sit down, I want to visit with you."

I remember the conversation as if it had taken place yesterday. I replied, "I do have to see patients this afternoon." So we just sat there and talked.

He said rather abruptly, "Young man, you have got a hell of a lot to learn."

I didn't know what was coming next. "I'm sure, Mr. Jones, there is a lot I need to learn, but I don't know to what you are referring."

He said, "I want you to know that Waldron charged me several thousands of dollars to do my surgery and Levy charged me at least another thousand to take care of me while I was in the hospital. Then I get a bill from you for a lousy $250, and my family tells me you are the one that saved my life." He then went on saying again, "Doctor, you've got a hell of a lot to learn. I want to do something nice for you, so you tell me what can I do?"

I said jokingly, "Mr. Jones, you could give me a membership in the River Oaks Country Club, and I couldn't pay the dues. Or you could buy me a new Cadillac or a Lincoln Continental, and I probably could not maintain the upkeep."

He said, "Now seriously, please tell me, what can I do for you?"

Then through my mind flashed the brief conversation I had had with Helen Holt in the library as I had come out of the Baylor building. I also recalled the tremendous amount of time and effort that Dr. Levy had spent over many years to see his pet project come to fruition. It occurred to me that here was a chance to be of some help to Dr. Levy in this regard, so I replied, "You know, Mr. Jones, there is something you could do for me that would help the entire medical community."

He asked, "What's that?"

I responded, "Your doctor, Moise Levy, Sr., is the president of the Houston Academy of Medicine. Their financial statement shows that between 1915, when it was founded, and today, they have raised from among the doctors in the community and from a few private contributions a total of $600,000. The Academy desperately needs a building in which to house its library which was recently (in 1949) combined with the Baylor medical school library. A facility is needed in the Medical Center that can be made available to the entire medical community as an educational resource."

He said, "What will it cost me, Doctor?"

I made a wild guess and replied, "Perhaps, Mr. Jones, if you would match the $600,000 that has already been collected by the Academy, there could be a building out in the medical center with your name on it. That's what you can do for me and for Dr. Levy." We visited a little longer and then I left.

I was told many years later by Helen Holt Garrott that the final arrangement was consummated soon afterward by Mr. Jones and Dr. Levy at the River Oaks Country Club. Shortly after that, the Houston Endowment provided the money to match the funds already raised by the Academy. That was in September 1952.

At its regular monthly meeting on October 2, 1952, the board of trustees of the Academy was told that the balance of the funds needed for the construction of the building had been received from a donor who wished to remain anonymous. It was agreed to announce the new library building in the Houston newspapers, and a date for the groundbreaking was set.

On October 15, 1952, thirty-seven years since the founding of the Houston Academy of Medicine, the groundbreaking ceremony took place on the site provided by the board of the Texas Medical Center. On that occasion an announcement was made by Dr. Levy that the previously anonymous donors who had provided the funds for completion of the building were none other than Mr. and Mrs. Jesse H. Jones and that the amount of their contribution was $600,000. This would match the $600,000 previously on hand, of which $300,000 had been provided by the M. D. Anderson Foundation and the remainder obtained over the previous thirty-seven years from Fellows and other interested friends of the Academy. I was extremely pleased that my small part in the fundraising had been of some value.

At the regular meeting of the Academy board on January 28, 1953, Dr. Thomas Kennerly, representing the Harris County Medi-

Author's maternal grandfather, William L. Straus, at the Maryland Air Races, 1912.

William S. Fields with his maternal grandmother, Pauline Gutmann Straus, and sister, Lenore, August 1919.

William S. Fields, age four months.

Author with his father, Arthur Mortimer Fields, and his brother, Arthur, Jr., 1919.

Author's mother, Lenore Straus Fields, June 1930.

Top left: *William S. Fields, Harvard College, A.B., 1934.*
Top right: *Arthur M. Fields, Jr., Harvard College, Class of 1936, United States Naval Academy, Ensign, U.S.N., 1939.*
Bottom: *William S. Fields (second from left) escorting Gen. Douglas MacArthur (third from left) on his visit to the V.A. Hospital, Houston, September 1952.*

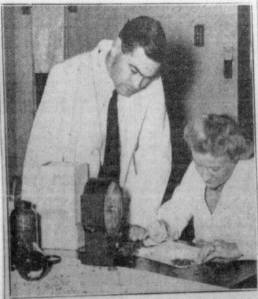

"*Prevention of Seasickness*," Montreal Gazette, *November 13, 1943.*

Top: *Planning Committee, First PanAmerican Congress of Neurology, Sao Paulo, Brazil, September 1965. Foreground, Eduardo de Robertis, Argentina. Background, left to right, Paulo Pinto Pupo, Brazil; Jorge Voto Bernales, Peru; and William S. Fields, United States.*
Bottom: *Second visit to Moscow, September 1973. Left to right, V. M. Smirnov, William S. Fields, E. V. Shmidt, N. I. Kanarekin.*

Top: *William S. Fields addressing the Philippine Neurological Society at the Manila Hotel, November 1956.*
Bottom: *Visiting scientists from the Soviet Union, November 1969. Left to right, N. V. Vereschagin, A. P. Romodanov, interpreter, William S. Fields, E. V. Shmidt, A. N. Konovalov, V. M. Ugrumov.*

Top: *Klaus J. Zulch, Cologne, Germany, William S. Fields, and Paniotis Balas, Athens, Greece, at Fourteenth World Congress, International Union of Angiology, Cologne, Germany, July 1986.*
Bottom: *Address delivered at the dedication of the Chi Omega Building of the Center for the Retarded, Houston, 1983.*

Top and bottom: *Texas Medical Center, same location from 1955 to 1975.*

Top: *1955 Texas Medical Center Library, Hermann Hospital in background.*

Middle: *1975 Texas Medical Center Library in background; in foreground Institute of Religion.*

Bottom: *Baylor College of Medicine, 1955, view to the northeast from the roof of the Methodist Hospital.*

Top and bottom: *University of Texas M. D. Anderson Cancer Center, from 1955 to 1975.*

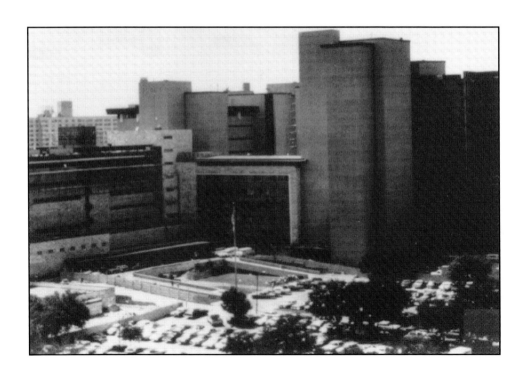

Top: *View to the southwest from the Methodist Hospital, 1955, Shamrock Hilton Hotel in background.*
Bottom: *Growth of the Texas Medical Center, view to the southwest from the roof of the Methodist Hospital, 1975.*

Top: *St. Luke's Episcopal Hospital, 1955, in background Prudential Life Insurance Building.*

Bottom: *St. Luke's Episcopal Hospital and Texas Heart Institute, 1975, in background University of Texas Main Building (former Prudential Building).*

Top: *The author's last group of faculty and residents at University of Texas Health Science Center at Houston, June 1982.*
Bottom: *William S. Fields with Milam Leavens, chief of neurosurgery, faculty and fellows of University of Texas M. D. Anderson Cancer Center, May 1987.*

Above: *Division of Neurology, Baylor College of Medicine, 1952. Back row, residents left to right, J. W. Crawley, L. Waites, T. M. McGuire, F. J. Moore. Front row, faculty left to right, C. A. Iannucci, William S. Fields, and Peter Kellaway.*

Right: *William S. Fields in the Chairman's Office, Department of Neurology, Baylor College of Medicine, 1965.*

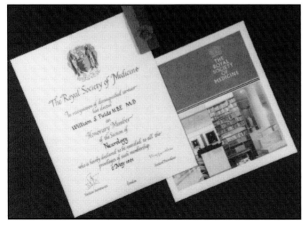

Left: *William S. Fields inducted as Honorary Fellow, Royal College of Medicine, London, England, May 1991.*

DOCTORS HOPEFUL — FRONT PAGE

Aspirin May Help Save Your Heart

From Chicago Tribune, AP and UPI

NEWPORT BEACH, Calif. — When your doctor tells you to "take two aspirin and go to bed," he may be treating you for health problems that neither of you suspects you have.

Use of aspirin to treat and prevent conditions causing heart attacks and strokes continues as a promising research area, Dr. William Fields, chairman of the University of Texas neurology department, told the American Heart Association's Science Writers Forum here.

In a recent study, Fields said, victims of minor strokes treated for furring of the arteries, or atherosclerosis, fared 50 percent better when they took four aspirin tablets daily than did a comparable group of patients given inert pills instead of aspirin.

Although Fields' study was cut short because of the funds shortage, he said that long-term studies in Canada also have found a 50 percent improvement in chances for stroke patients who take aspirin regularly.

A recently completed study by doctors in West Germany and Austria also found that people who suffered one heart attack had fewer second attacks when they took aspirin.

Aspirin has been in use for 80 years to relieve aches and pains and to lower temperatures, some physicians over the years

This aggregate also is called a white platelet plug, and it can break loose from the artery wall to wash downstream and block a smaller artery.

Aspirin released into the blood makes the platelets unable to stick together. By taking four aspirin daily, Fields said, a person can keep 90 percent of his platelets "acetylated" or unable to adhere to each other.

ALTHOUGH THE EFFECT of aspirin in limiting strokes and heart attacks was observed first about 20 years ago, the

---

Doctors tell science writers

Aspirin is termed effective in averting some strokes

By JULIAN DeVRIES
Republic Medical Editor

NEWPORT BEACH, Calif. — If aspirin had been discovered in modern times instead of 80 years ago the chances are good the U.S. Food and Drug Administration wouldn't approve it, Dr. William S. Fields of Houston said Wednesday.

Fields is professor and chairman of the department of neurology at the University of Texas School of Medicine. He spoke at the fifth annual Science Writers' Forum of the American Heart Association.

"Aspirin is a useful drug, but some people become very ill because of it and others can develop stomach ulcers from its use, so the FDA probably would withhold approval of it if it was a new drug," Fields said.

Despite the drawbacks, however, Fields said studies show that aspirin, in addition to being useful in the treatment of arthritis, can be used to prevent strokes in some cases. Additional

"Aspirin works in the prevention of strokes and possibly heart attacks by preventing the clumping together of blood platelets which form an artery blocking clot," Fields said. "However, when the artery also has an occluding cholesterol plaque, aspirin will not be effective."

Heparin, a naturally occurring body substance, also is used to prevent the formation of blood clots, according to Dr. Robert D. Rosenberg, associate professor of medicine at Harvard University Medical School in Boston.

Although it is not as efficient as aspirin, it can be used by patients who have an allergy to aspirin or where aspirin causes the stomach to bleed, paving the way to an ulcer, Rosenberg said Wednesday.

"Only a very small fraction of the heparin molecule is effective in blood clot prevention; it requires the presence of a naturally occurring protein

Newspaper reports of author's talk to the Science Writers' Forum of the American Heart Association, January 1978.

Top: *Alma and "Bill" Fields at the dedication of the "William S. Fields Neuroscience Library" in the Department of Neurology at University of Texas Medical School.*
Bottom: *William S. Fields receiving Distinguished Service Award from Dr. James Bowen, vice-president for academic affairs, University of Texas M. D. Anderson Cancer Center, June 1987.*

cal Society, moved that the board accept the suggestion of Dr. Claude C. Cody, Jr., that plans be formulated for the inclusion of a doctors' club in the library building. A committee was appointed which would report back at a special called meeting of the membership. It was agreed at that meeting that the cornerstone on the new building should read "Jesse H. Jones Library Building of the Houston Academy of Medicine for the Texas Medical Center." At that same meeting, Dr. Louis E. Williford was elected to fill the unexpired term of Dr. A. M. Parsons.

In November of 1953 there was a special called meeting of the membership of the Academy to discuss plans for a doctors' club. This club was to stand on its own feet, controlled by a board of governors and not by the Academy.

In December 1953, I received a phone call and the voice at the other end said, "Bill, this is Moise Levy." (It had been "Dr. Fields" previously.) "I don't know whether you know or not that I'm president of the Houston Academy of Medicine Board of Trustees. You may have seen in the newspapers that "Skinny" Williford died recently." I only knew that Williford was a general surgeon who had just been elected president-elect of the Harris County Medical Society and that he had died before he could take office. Levy then told me, "Skinny was on the board of trustees of the Academy and as president, it is my prerogative to fill with a substitute his unexpired term which runs another four years. The board has approved your appointment unanimously. We have never had an institutional man on this board. Would you do us the honor of serving?"

Clearly, this was Levy's way of saying thank you to me for what I had recommended to Mr. Jones. He never made any other comment. I was astounded because I knew that the board was made up of some very prestigious older members of the medical community.

I said, "Fine, I'll be pleased to accept your invitation."

Dr. Levy followed up the phone call with a formal letter dated February 18, 1954, and I sent him a letter of acceptance the following day.

I began service on the Academy Board in 1954, when I was forty-one years old. There wasn't another man under fifty years of age on that board, which included, in addition to President Levy, such senior members of the medical profession as Claude C. Cody, Jr., Jared E. Clarke, H. J. Ehlers, J. Griffin Heard, Cecil F. Jorns, Frederick R. Lummis, Jack Mayfield, and John H. Wootters. Six of these gentlemen had served as president of the Harris County Medical Society. Dr. Heard resigned on February 26, 1954, and Dr. Hampton C. Robinson was appointed soon thereafter to fill out his unexpired term.

I remember an amusing incident which occurred when Jesse Jones came to inspect the new building, and Hampton Robinson and I were asked to show him around. It was in the spring of 1954, the building was nearly finished, and we were about to accept it from the contractor. Cameron Fairchild, the architect, and the fellow who was his construction superintendent, Lemuel Bottoms, conducted the tour. The restrooms which are in the front of the building on the first floor have windows going from the top to the bottom of the building. When one entered either restroom, there was nothing between "him or her" and the sidewalk outside. One could look directly into the men's restroom and see the urinals. Mr. Jones took one look and said, "Fairchild, is this the way you have it at home?" Fairchild's face became bright red and he did not know what to say. After that episode, a barrier was placed there as well as Venetian blinds. (Years later, when Fairchild presented his plans for the addition to the library building in the 1970s, I joked with him about that incident.)

On April 20, 1954, Cecil Jorns was appointed chairman of the Doctors' Club Organizational Committee by Levy. He promptly called a meeting of the members of the Houston Academy of Medicine on April 28 for the purpose of setting up such a club.

The Jesse H. Jones Library Building was dedicated on September 9, 1954. I was appointed later that month to the recently established board of governors of the Doctors' Club and also served in a liaison capacity between the club and the Houston Academy of Medicine. In May 1955, a special committee of the Academy, of which I was a member, met with the Blood Bank Committee of the Harris County Medical Society to discuss construction of a building for the blood bank behind the library. It was decided by the board to defer any decision on this matter, and ultimately it was shelved.

Baylor turned over all of its books, and, although there was a great deal of duplication in the holdings of Baylor and the Academy, all the volumes were moved from the Baylor building into the new library building in the summer of 1954. That was the only time that I can recall the library being closed. The original plan was to have the Houston Academy of Medicine Library alone serve the needs of the entire Texas Medical Center, including The University of Texas M. D. Anderson Hospital and The University of Texas Dental Branch. However, the Anderson Hospital administration decided that a library was required in their own building, and then the Dental Branch insisted that it also needed its own library.

At the annual meeting on January 25, 1956, Hampton C. Robinson was elected president of the Academy of Medicine to succeed Moise Levy, who had held that position for so many years. I was elected vice-president.

Miss Holt had resigned and intended to leave the library at the end of 1956, but since a replacement had not been found she was asked to stay on until another person arrived. She remained on the job until the end of 1957, after having been with the Academy for thirty years.

When my three-year term as vice-president expired at the end of 1959, I was reelected for another term. During the next several years I found that I was often "pinch hitting" for the president, Hampton Robinson, because personal problems were taking up much of his time. He eventually found it necessary to resign in 1961 because his wife had become very ill. Upon his resignation I succeeded him as president.

Moise Levy retired from clinical practice in 1960 and he and Mrs. Levy took a long-delayed trip to Europe. He had not taken time to enjoy a vacation in many years. His lovely wife, Sarah Levy, had become known to me for the first time when she served on the board of the Houston Speech and Hearing Center, of which I was also a member. They decided to fly to Europe and their first "port-of-call" was Amsterdam. On their second night there they went to a famous restaurant called "The Three Flies." During the meal, Levy had a dizzy spell. Mrs. Levy got him back to the hotel in a taxi, but he was complaining of double vision, his speech was slurred and he was unsteady on his feet. This lasted for about an hour or two and then everything cleared up. She called me in the middle of the night to express her concern about her husband. I told her to get him on the plane as soon as possible and bring him home. When they returned to Houston, I admitted him directly to The Methodist Hospital for what I was convinced had been a vertebrobasilar transient ischemic attack (a minor stroke). An arteriogram showed advanced atherosclerosis involving the vessels at the base of the brain including both vertebral arteries. Shortly thereafter, he had a stroke, and subsequently a heart attack, which took his life two years later. This was a real tragedy since he had worked so long and hard during his lifetime and never got to enjoy his retirement.

Shortly after Dr. Levy's death, Mrs. Levy invited me to come to their home. She said that her husband knew I had been a navy man and he had left something for me. She presented me with a small velvet-covered box in which there was a set of gold cufflinks, each in the shape of a ship's propeller. A diamond was set in the hub of the propeller. These were the most beautiful cufflinks I had ever seen and I was delighted to have them as a memento of Moise Levy.

Toward the end of 1962, Thomas Royce, a Houston ophthalmologist, led a group of doctors who had decided that something drastic had to be done about the Academy and its fiscal management. This, no doubt, also had to do with the fact that the Academy had its separate sizable portfolio of assets. He and James Sammons, who later became executive director of the American Medical Association, wanted to take over the Academy, which was far too independent from the Medical Society, in their opinion. I was up for reelection as president of the Academy and, for the first time in anybody's memory, these doctors rounded up a lot of members for the annual meeting and elected their own hand-picked candidate. At most of the previous annual meetings, it had been extremely difficult to obtain a quorum.

There has been a Library Board since the mid-1950s and a full-time executive director of the Academy since 1972. The Library Board is made up of persons representing each of the major participating institutions. The fiscal affairs are overseen by the Houston Academy of Medicine. During the 1970s Paul Jordan, the executive director, was taking care of the financial affairs of the Academy. James Hickox, who was then, and until his retirement in 1990, the executive director of the Harris County Medical Society, had believed for many years that he should have both jobs. He finally succeeded in accomplishing this goal.

Moise D. Levy, Sr., and Claude C. Cody, Jr., both founding members and past presidents, had very carefully, beginning in 1915, put together a portfolio, the income from which was to be used specifically for Academy business and library support. Originally, there was a large block of Humble Oil Company stock (now Exxon) as well as some other blue chip issues. The Harris County Medical Society (HCMS) had for many years coveted that money.

In the late 1970s, some members of the executive board (HCMS) tried to keep a certain Houston doctor from joining the Society. Although this might not have been totally unjustified, they attempted to exclude him without due process when the time arrived to elevate him from provisional to active membership. Unfortunately, they did not even abide by their own by-laws. The doctor sued the Medical Society and subsequently won a judgment against it in federal court, as well as against members of its executive board and board of censors, individually. Money was not readily available to defray these substantial costs and, in order to avoid going to the membership to request an assessment, they took over the portfolio of the Academy of Medicine and used those monies to pay the legal fees. The general membership was never made aware of this and the entire episode was kept under wraps. Had the members known about this sordid affair, they might have been up in arms.

Because of the growth of the Texas Medical Center and its component institutions, an addition to the library building was deemed necessary in the early 1970s. On the Library Board in 1971 were R. Lee Clark and Robert Hickey, representing The University of Texas System Cancer Center, and Cheves Smythe, who had just come to Houston as dean of the new University of Texas Medical School. The Baylor representatives were Joseph Melnick and Wilson Fahlberg. John Armstrong, as president, represented the Academy of Medicine, and Richard Eastwood, executive vice-president of the Texas Medical Center, was chairman of the board. It was a rotating chairmanship.

One day I got a call from Dick Eastwood, whom I had known almost from the day that he had arrived in Houston from the University of Alabama in Birmingham. We had become good friends. He said, "Bill, at yesterday's Library Board meeting, Dean Smythe volunteered your services to write the application for a matching grant for federal funds to build an addition to the Jesse H. Jones Library Building. The dean really extolled your virtues, saying that, after all, you are about the only person around here who has been on the Baylor faculty as a department chairman, now with The University of Texas in a similar capacity, has been president of the Academy of Medicine, knows the medical community and is well known by many physicians and surgeons. He thought you would be the ideal person to undertake this task."

I said, "Thanks, but no thanks."

He pleaded with me and I finally accepted, but only after he agreed to convene another meeting of the Library Board so that I could state my requirements. The plan was contingent upon my writing an application for funds to match the $600,000 that had been set aside in equal portions ($300,000) by two local foundations, the Houston Endowment and the M. D. Anderson Foundation. The boards of these foundations agreed that if we would press forward with a grant application, they would provide their share of the funds. It always struck me as ironic that the figure we were after — $600,000 — was exactly the same amount that Jesse Jones provided for his gift the first time around.

A meeting was called within the next two weeks. I informed the board that if I was going to do this job for them, I needed to become better educated about libraries. I also told Lee Clark, who was in attendance, "If you will allow me to have the services of your very fine research librarian, Marie Harvin, to assist me in this project, then, and only then, will I accept the responsibility for preparing a grant application."

He said he thought they could manage that, and it was arranged. Then I pointed out that I needed some money so that Ms. Harvin and I could visit some of the outstanding medical libraries elsewhere in the United States. Those funds also were provided promptly and enabled Marie and me to make some trips to the East Coast and several places in the Midwest.

The day after I had accepted this responsibility at the special called meeting of the Library Board, I received a call from Cheves Smythe, my next-door neighbor. He invited me to come over to see him that evening. I had no idea what he wanted until we sat down in his study. That was the one and only time that I ever visited with him there. My bottom had hardly hit the chair when he said, "Fields, I don't believe you have gotten the message."

Well, I already had the impression that Cheves spoke tangentially about a lot of things.

"Perhaps I have not," I said. "What message was I supposed to receive?"

He replied, "I'm referring to the Library Board meeting yesterday when you agreed to take on the responsibility for writing the grant application for the new library building. I hope you realize that we are going to have our own library in our new medical school building. So we are not going to worry too much about that joint library project across the street."

I said, "Then what were you doing when you volunteered my services?"

"I just don't think you should devote a whole lot of time and effort to the project," he said.

I looked at him and said, "Do you mean to tell me that you volunteered my services for a project at which I am supposed to fail?"

"Now you have the message," he said.

With that, I got up and walked out.

Marie Harvin and I then proceeded to make several trips. We went first to the Countway Library at Harvard Medical School, then to Stonybrook on Long Island where the State University of New York Medical School had a new library, which was temporarily housed in what had been a local grocery store. The librarian there had formerly been at The University of Texas Medical Branch at Galveston, so he was well known to Marie and was very cordial and helpful. From there we drove to Rutgers in New Brunswick, New Jersey, where they had just opened their medical library. On a subsequent trip, we went to Omaha, Nebraska and Denver, Colorado. At the latter location, the librarian was Col. Frank Rogers, who had previously been director of what was originally known as the Armed Forces Medical Library. That library later became the nucleus of the National Library of Medicine in Bethesda, Maryland. Many years earlier, I had met Frank Rogers at a dinner party in London, England, given in my honor by none other than Col. Walter Moursund, Jr., son of Dean Moursund at Baylor. Colonel Rogers had retired from the army and was organizing the library at the University of Colorado Medical School. We received some excellent ideas from him.

After we returned to Houston, I began to prepare the written application. In the meanwhile, the Texas Medical Center library was trying to recruit a new librarian. After several months, at about the time that I had put the proposal together, Sam Hitt was appointed. I offered to step aside and let him put the finishing touches on it, which he did, because he wanted the library to include certain features of interest to him. While the grant application was being completed, Dick Eastwood and I made a trip to Bethesda, Maryland, to talk to the people at the Facilities and Resources Branch of the National Institutes of Health to ascertain what the possibilities were of obtaining the funds we were seeking. They offered little encouragement but told us to proceed anyway. Not too long after our trip, we noted in the newspaper that President Nixon had impounded a large portion of the construction funds which had been appropriated by Congress, so we thought that our chances of success were somewhere between slim and none. However, much to my surprise, we got word about three months later that the Review Committee had met and had awarded us $588,000. I was ecstatic but Dr. Smythe was not happy because his application for $40 million to construct The University of Texas Medical School Building, which was in the same batch of applications, had been turned down. Needless to say, that was another mark against me in his book. That, however, was a matter clearly beyond my control.

This was an irony that I did not come to appreciate until about six or seven years later when I was talking with Col. Dan Kadrovach, who had been director of Hermann Hospital when The University of Texas Medical School first opened in Houston. He had left Houston and was at that time administrator of the Veterans Administration Medical Center in New Orleans. We were sitting in his living room when I commented about the Jesse H. Jones Library Building and he said, "I don't believe I ever told you, but I was on the committee of the National Institutes of Health that considered that batch of applications. When yours and that of the Medical School came along, I absented myself from the room while the discussions were taking place. On the second day of our meeting, when we were about to adjourn, we found that we had $588,000 available that we had not yet allocated. The committee scurried around looking for an application and located yours for $600,000. Because of my Houston associations, I again absented myself from the room while the others considered it. I learned later that they had found it attractive and approved it because of the multi-institutional aspects of the proposal and the fact that it would serve as a facility and resource for the entire medical community."

I said, "Well, Dan, it was written with that in mind. I am particularly pleased because that is the premise on which the library was first founded and the way we wanted to keep it."

That was how it came to pass that I was involved in the planning and construction of both halves of the present library building.

I have had a long and abiding interest in that library and in libraries in general. Over the years, I had developed a rather extensive collection of my own and always had my journals bound. In 1980 I had all of my personal books and journals appraised and gave them to The University of Texas Medical School as a permanent collection for a Library of Neuroscience. I was joined in this effort by my longtime colleague, Joe Wood, chairman of neurobiology and anatomy, and by Richard Ruiz, chairman of the Department of Ophthalmology. I subsequently learned that the Division of Neurosurgery in the Department of Surgery had also become involved.

Shortly before I retired from the medical school on August 30, 1982, Dean Ernst Knobil arranged for the dedication of that library. Much to my surprise and pleasure, it was named the "William S. Fields Neurosciences Library." My colleagues requested that I go downtown to Giddings Studio to have a portrait made. This picture still hangs in the Neurosciences Library at the medical school. I used to go out every year to raise money for new books, and I had hoped that my successor would also seek the support necessary to continue the development of the library. Unfortunately, that has not been one of his priorities, and furthermore, my name has never been placed on the door as we had agreed.

The Harris County Medical Society leadership eventually packed the board of the Academy with candidates of their own choosing and took it over. They reorganized the structure, and none of the people previously on the board remained. The board as such no longer exists. Now there are just officers, and I do not have a clue regarding their responsibilities. The business of the Academy is conducted out of the office of the executive director of the Harris County Medical Society.

During the years that I was on the Academy board, and later on the board of the library, there were some very substantial physicians and surgeons as members. The character of the board changed completely in about 1963, soon after my defeat for reelection as president.

I would like to know the status of the Houston Academy of Medicine now, and I have tried to figure it out several times. John Armstrong, one of the last presidents nominated and elected by the membership, said to me not too long before he died in 1988, "They took the Academy away from us." (They, meaning the hierarchy of the Harris County Medical Society.) On that occasion we were sitting together at a meeting, and he did not have an opportunity to provide me with the details.

Chapter 10

The Houston Neurological Society and Neurological Symposia

ON FEBRUARY 24, 1951, I WROTE a letter to James Greenwood, Jr., chief of neurosurgery at The Methodist Hospital, promoting the idea that we give consideration to the formation of a Houston Neurological Society, one that would be devoted to both neurology and neurosurgery. In that letter I stated:

> I am very much inclined to agree with you that we should make it our principle at the outset that this Society will be devoted to Neurology and Neurosurgery. Or, if one would care to put it another way, medical and surgical neurology. It has been my experience in the past, as it has been yours, that if this were to be a neuropsychiatric society, that it would suffer from exactly the same difficulties as has every other society of the same name. By this I mean that it would become a psychiatric debating club.
>
> It might also be worthwhile considering the inclusion of some of the practicing neurosurgeons and medical neurologists in Galveston, if they should so desire. Of course, their participation will become a great deal simpler once the superhighway is completed between here and Galveston. It may be possible to sound out such people as Sam Snodgrass and Ira Jackson, but again we run into the difficulty that most of the medical neurological practice in Galveston is done by neuropsychiatrists.
>
> I really do not have any definite ideas as to what one should

consider as the necessary qualifications for membership. However, it has been mentioned to me in discussion with others in town that one should have either the neurology or neurosurgery boards, or an equivalent amount of training. You will notice in the list that I have attached that there are several persons who are primarily in basic science work and who are Ph.D.'s and not M.D.'s. It would have to be taken up in the organizational meeting as to whether they could become full members or would be associate members. I really do not have any feeling one way or the other regarding this.

Dr. Greenwood responded enthusiastically since such an organization would serve to further the ambitions of both of us. With his help a preliminary meeting was held at Ye Olde College Inn on South Main Street at Dryden near the Medical Center. The eighteen persons who attended this organizational meeting were: F. Keith Bradford, James Albert Brown, George Ehni, James Greenwood, Jr., J. Randolph Jones, Claude Pollard, Jr., Robert C. L. Robertson, neurosurgeons; William S. Fields, Christopher A. Iannucci, John Skogland, neurologists; Abe Hauser, Paul J. Walter, neuropsychiatrists; Howard L. Evans, internist; Bela Halpert, Berne L. Newton, pathologists; John H. Perry, neuroanatomist; Hebbel Hoff and Peter Kellaway, neurophysiologists. Thus the Houston Neurological Society was organized in 1951 for the purpose of promoting interest and research in neurology, neurosurgery, and allied basic sciences without limiting interest to clinical subjects. At its inception, the Society included both clinicians and basic scientists, with no requirement that a member be certified by a nationally recognized board, or that he be a member of the county or state medical association. The physicians and basic scientists from Galveston, who had met with the Houston group previously for many years as the Houston-Galveston Neuropsychiatric Society, were invited to apply for charter membership in the newly established organization. It was considered especially appropriate that residents and fellows in neurology and neurosurgery attend the meetings as associate members.

Beginning in 1951, regular meetings were held on the second Friday of each month except July and August. At each meeting a scientific program was presented with program content selected by a standing committee. The presentations varied widely, always taking advantage of the presence of outstanding guest speakers from out of town who were visiting the Texas Medical Center. The monthly meetings were first held in a private dining room of the Ship Ahoy Restaurant on South Main Street, later in a special dining room at The Methodist Hospital, and eventually at the Doctors' Club in the Jesse H. Jones Library Building. The December meeting for many years has been strictly a social affair designated as a Christmas party for members and their spouses.

In 1952 the members voted to designate the March session as the annual meeting with speakers and other guests from out of town and abroad. The first annual meeting was devoted to clinical neurological and neurosurgical presentations and the proceedings were published in abstract form in the *Journal of Diseases of the Nervous System*, 14:1-8, 1953. (This journal died a slow death many years ago.) Because of the rather surprising and enthusiastic reception of this first gathering and the published material, it was decided to make this an annual affair. The second annual meeting, in 1953, was held as a joint session with the Southern Neurosurgical Society, which was already scheduled to meet in Houston, and the proceedings were not published. I was less than enthusiastic about this arrangement since it was my sincere belief that the Society needed to maintain its own identity. The following year an annual session was held, but once again the proceedings were not published.

Nevertheless, in 1955, it was decided that the Society would sponsor an annual symposium which would take the place of the annual meeting in March. The subject chosen for the first meeting was "Hypothalamic-Hypophysical Interrelationships." The main theme was the interdependence of the brain and the various endocrine organs. Arrangements were made to record, compile, and edit the proceedings for publication in a hard-cover volume. One anonymous reviewer of the initial book published under these auspices stated that although the book would not have a general appeal, it would be read by those interested in the central nervous system and, in his opinion, represented a frontier upon which we might expect many future accomplishments. He then went on to say that it was inspiring to see that the Houston Neurological Society had published a book of eight papers, together with their discussions from the third annual meeting. From this modest beginning the annual meeting of the Society eventually became well known to clinicians and basic scientists both in this country and abroad. Many neurologists, neurosurgeons and others expressed the opinion that this was the best scientific session of the year and the Houston Neurological Society worked hard to maintain this reputation.

The following year, the symposium, which I organized on my own, was devoted to "Brain Mechanisms and Drug Action." This represented pioneering work in neuropsychopharmacology, which at that time was a relatively new field. The published volume was considered an important source of information on the action of drugs on the brain, with particular reference to the problems of behavior. It was an introduction to several of the most basic concepts in the pharmacotherapy of neurological and psychiatric disease.

The 1957 meeting was devoted to the epidemiological and clinical aspects of viral encephalitis. I received invaluable assistance from my friend and colleague at Baylor, Russell Blattner, who helped put the program together and edit the proceedings. Russ had been an avid student, and later an expert, on this subject during his days in St. Louis, beginning with the first epidemic there in the late 1930s. In a book review in the British periodical, *BRAIN*, Henry Miller of Newcastle, England, stated, "This stimulating and useful book could be published only in the United States, not merely because of the expense of presenting such a wealth of topical information in so elegant and permanent a form, but also because the extended medical symposium, given by experts for experts and particularly appropriate for the presentation of work on the fringe of medical knowledge, is a typical and still almost unique American form of medical communication." This commentary pleased me immensely.

The following year the symposium was entitled "Pathogenesis and Treatment of Parkinsonism." After receiving a copy of the published volume, Stanley Olson, dean of Baylor College of Medicine, wrote: "The conference and the publications are an elegant ornament that Baylor wears with pride." This gave me a tremendous sense of satisfaction, particularly when later that same year neurology was recognized as an independent department at the medical school.

Although the Houston Neurological Society had had its birth in 1951, it did not become a formal entity until 1958. Application for a charter of incorporation was submitted to the Texas secretary of state on September 6, 1958, by three of the original members, James Greenwood, Jr., Abe Hauser, and myself. In addition, three others — R.C.L. Robertson, F. Keith Bradford, and George Ehni — were named as directors.

In 1959 the attendance was even larger than in previous years and almost filled the conference hall of the Jesse H. Jones Library Building in the Texas Medical Center. The subject was "Pathogenesis and Treatment of Cerebrovascular Disease." Denis Williams, editor of *BRAIN*, wrote, "The resulting volume, excellently arranged, illustrated, and published, gives a vivid picture of each aspect of these dynamic problems with extensive access to the present literature upon them."

The following year, the symposium in March was devoted to "Disorders of the Developing Nervous System." The meeting was also well attended by an audience which included many pediatricians and obstetricians. This time the book review in *BRAIN* was somewhat less enthusiastic and the reviewer stated that the title of one of the chapters, "How to design and build abnormal brains using radiation during development," seemed to be a macabre comment upon the time in which we live and our efforts to extend life and health. However, one could not escape the fact that nuclear war or other nuclear catastrophe was always a threat to humanity. Another reviewer was more generous and stated, "This book is a good summary of our knowledge of nervous system diseases in the developing brain and spinal cord. It contains much valuable material for those who may wish to find some answers to the vexing problems concerning hereditary and congenital factors in nervous system disease."

The 1961 meeting was a pioneering effort in the biology and treatment of intracranial tumors. The reviews were generally complimentary and in one it was stated, "It is doubtful that James Poppen's magnificent chapter on extracerebral tumors will ever be out of date."

In organizing the program for the 1962 meeting on "Information Storage and Neural Control," I was assisted by Walter Abbott, Ph.D., a colleague at Baylor. After the printed programs had been distributed, I received a communication from my former chief and mentor, Dr. Wilder Penfield, director of the Montreal Neurological Institute. In it he said, "Good luck to you in the conduct of your already famous annual symposia." It was especially pleasing to me that a man of his stature and reputation would consider our local effort as being "famous."

The annual symposium of the Houston Neurological Society became well known to clinicians and basic scientists in the United

States and abroad. Frequent inquiries were received regarding forthcoming meetings, and many people expressed their desire to be on the mailing list. Also, at national meetings many spoke of this symposium as being the best scientific session of the year in neurology and neurosurgery. The Houston Neurological Society was desirous of maintaining this reputation.

In 1963, with the help of Bobby R. Alford, another Baylor colleague, a splendid program was put together on "Neurological Aspects of Auditory and Vestibular Disorders." Much to our surprise and pleasure, nearly 500 persons from across this country and some from overseas attended the event. It focused considerable attention on the Houston Neurological Society and the Texas Medical Center. Bobby Alford subsequently became vice-president of Baylor College of Medicine, a position in which he has served with distinction.

The 1964 meeting on "Intracranial Aneurysms and Subarachnoid Hemorrhage" was attended by 350 physicians and surgeons. I was assisted in the organization of the program by Adolph L. Sahs, professor and chairman of neurology at the University of Iowa. Several months later a very gratifying editorial appeared in the *Journal of Neurosurgery,* which stated: "The annual meeting of the Houston Neurological Society has won a special place in the hearts of neurosurgeons and neurologists from all over the country. This is one meeting that everybody looks forward to and makes every effort to attend."

The last in this series of "famous" symposia took place in March 1965. It directed attention to new neurological diagnostic techniques which were just appearing on the horizon or were undergoing refinement, including cerebral biopsy, muscle biopsy, radioisotope scanning, clinical electroencephalography, radiographic subtraction, air myelography, and selective arteriography.

Although I had anticipated continuing to organize these annual symposia, it soon became apparent to me that the political climate at Baylor and my unsought involvement in academic politics was going to make it impossible. The final blow came when I was asked to submit my resignation as chairman of the Department of Neurology. Two years later, I resigned my faculty position after accepting an appointment at The University of Texas Southwestern Medical School at Dallas.

Neurological symposia in the Texas Medical Center went into limbo until I returned from Dallas in 1969, following which I undertook once again to put on an annual session of the same quality as the previous ones. Two of these meetings in the 1970s deserve more than passing comment.

The one in 1972 was especially interesting in that it had significant moral and social implications which resulted in widespread repercussions. The idea that it might be appropriate to conduct a symposium in Texas on the "Neurological Aspects of Violence and Aggression" evolved from several conversations I had with my friend, William H. Sweet, chief of neurosurgery at Massachusetts General in Boston, beginning shortly after a tragic event which occurred on the campus of The University of Texas at Austin.

On the afternoon of August 1, 1966, a young ex-Marine, Charles Joseph Whitman, poured down a deadly rain of gunfire from the University Tower, killing thirteen people and wounding thirty-one others with his sniping. He had killed his wife and his mother earlier that day. Shortly after the Austin tragedy, John B. Connally, governor of Texas, established a thirty-two-member panel, which included Bill Sweet, to make a detailed study of the case. Following its deliberations, the committee suggested, among other recommendations, that more substantial support be given to research into the relation of brain function to behavior — particularly violent and aggressive behavior — so that approaches to clinical management of this problem could be pursued on a sound and logical basis.

In planning this symposium, it was our expressed intent from the outset to have it directed toward scientific discussion of brain mechanisms and behavior so that as many persons as possible might have a better appreciation of the available basic information. Clinical and, more importantly, surgical intervention in these problems were to be given a relatively minor role. It was unfortunate that then, and even today, many neurologists and neurosurgeons, as well as psychiatrists, are uninformed in this area. We had hoped that the proceedings of this symposium would have an impact that would permit all of us, as physicians, to understand and alleviate some of the distressing symptoms which occur in persons who suffer from violent episodes. To achieve this would benefit many. We most assuredly did not anticipate the repercussions which our decision would engender.

The program was finalized by the end of May 1971, before I left for a four and one-half week lecture tour in the Soviet Union. A brochure announcing the program, its content, and the names of the invited participants was printed in November of that year and nearly 5,000 copies were mailed before the end of December. The mailing list included basic research neuroscientists as well as clinical neurologists, neurosurgeons, psychiatrists, and psychologists. It was not surprising, therefore, that the symposium received a considerable amount of advance publicity. The prompt response from registrants in all parts of the United States and Canada was very gratifying. There was no hint of the surprising events that would take place during the meeting until less than two weeks before it was convened.

On February 28, 1972, we first became aware of a letter which had been sent to all of those listed as participants in the program, other than Bill Sweet and myself. This omission was not an oversight but clearly deliberate. A copy was also addressed to Dean Cheves Smythe at The University of Texas Medical School. The letter presented a carefully planned and precisely timed campaign to take over the symposium and alter the intent of its program. In part it stated:

> Since it is generally recognized that the major causes of violence are social, not neuropathological, and that this is more strikingly epitomized within the framework of the coercive closed society which the prison system embodies, any proposals for the control of such behavior by drugs and especially by surgery administered under the aegis of prison authorities inescapably become suspect, no matter how well-intentioned the proponents and surgeons may be. Malpractice becomes an issue. Moreover, threats of brain surgery issued by administrators to coerce prisoners cannot be prevented. There is serious question whether informed consent, free of coercion, and the conditions of trust essential for therapeutic rapport are possible on the part of prisoners. The ethical problems inherent in this situation cannot be denied. It appears that proponents of brain surgery on prisoners are prominently represented on the agenda of the Houston conference. While we do not know every individual scheduled to participate, it appears to us that physicians active in opposition to experimental neurosurgery on prisoners and attorneys actively involved in legal challenges to the abuse of prison medicine are either not represented or substantially under-represented.

This letter was signed by Philip Shapiro, M.D., co-chairman of the Prison Health Committee, Medical Committee for Human

Rights, San Francisco Bay Area Chapter; Edward M. Opton, Jr., Ph.D., of the Wright Institute; and George H. Hogle, M.D., clinical assistant professor of psychiatry, Stanford University and University of California Medical School, San Francisco.

Enclosure 7 (entitled "Statement of Agenda") of the above-mentioned letter requested the recipient to sign the following statement: "I request the conveners of the Houston Neurological Symposium on Neural Bases of Violence and Aggression to broaden the agenda to include individuals who have been involved in active opposition to neurosurgical experimentation on prisoners."

After careful consideration and with full awareness of the risk involved, we decided to offer the authors of the letter a place on the program for a speaker of their choice. This was done in the hope of avoiding a menacing confrontation. Before this could be accomplished, however, I received a telephone call from Dr. Peter Roger Breggin, a psychiatrist in Washington, D.C., during which he virtually insisted that he be given an opportunity to present his views. Subsequently, the California group acknowledged Dr. Breggin as their spokesman. He was accorded a spot on the program for his presentation, and at his own insistence was included in the panel on psychosurgery. This request seemed to be somewhat strange in view of the expressed concern of those who protested the formulation of the program that "issues of medical ethics be dealt with not only in the abstract." One would have expected them to have directed their attention more specifically to the important moral and ethical problems, but instead they focused their attention on "experimental neurosurgical procedures on prisoners," which had not even been considered as a subject for discussion. In fact, surgical intervention in these problems, which Bill Sweet and I thought deserved to be discussed, had been given only a small place on the program. It was difficult, therefore, to conceive of their motivation as medical and scientific rather than political, and as the events unfolded, this became increasingly evident. I discussed the matter with Dean Smythe, who promised to enlist the help of The University of Texas Police in keeping the situation from getting out of control.

In answer to the circulated letter of Shapiro, Opton and Hogle, Dr. Frank Ervin, director of Stanley Cobb Laboratories for Psychiatric Research, Harvard Medical School at Massachusetts General Hospital, and a founder, continuing sponsor and member of the Medical Committee for Human Rights, wrote a comprehensive, thoughtful reply to these gentlemen. In the view of Bill Sweet and myself the response dealt completely with the questions raised by them. Ervin, in the closing paragraph of his letter, stated: "I look forward to your group participating in discussion in Houston, hopefully, in a creative fashion."

Shapiro, given the floor at the Houston meeting, raised none of the points in Ervin's letter, although it should be noted that Dr. Ervin's closing paragraph invited further discussion in Houston. We, therefore, assumed that Shapiro shared our opinion that his points were answered by Ervin to the satisfaction of a reasonable man.

Time had been allocated at the end of the scientific sessions for presentation of essays directed toward the moral, legal, and ethical aspects of violence and aggression. The essayists were Krister Stendahl, dean of the Harvard Divinity School; Albert E. Jenner, Jr., a well-known Chicago attorney who had been senior counsel to the Warren Commission and a member of the National Commission on Causes and Prevention of Violence; and Henry K. Beecher, professor emeritus at Harvard Medical School and a nationally recognized medical ethicist. The moderator of the panel discussion to follow was the late Hyman Judah Schachtel, a highly respected Houston rabbi.

During the coffee break preceding these presentations there was a loud clamor in the hall outside and banging on the door leading to the meeting room. Rabbi Schachtel and I went out to confront the leaders of a group of unruly demonstrating students, recruited by Peter Breggin from the campuses of Texas Southern University and the University of Houston. These young people had come with the intent of disrupting the meeting and creating enough disturbance to attract the attention of the media who had already been notified by Breggin. We agreed to let a representative group enter the room and also allow their spokesman to speak after the other scheduled presentations.

In the meanwhile, because of concern for private property, the management of the hotel where the meeting was being held had called the Houston Police, and four squad cars were dispatched to the scene. After granting permission for representatives of the protesters to attend the meeting, the situation calmed down and the police left without making any arrests.

An opportunity was provided for Stephen Eisenberg, who purportedly represented members of the Students for a Democratic

Society, Workers Action Movement, and Progressive Labor Party, to speak. He had agreed to present a one-page resolution but proceeded instead to present an eighteen-minute polemic and diatribe which made it clear that further rational, dispassionate, and scientific discussion would be impossible. Eisenberg finished by requesting that the audience adopt the following resolution: "We call on this body to take a stand against racism and oppression by absolutely opposing the use of psychosurgery."

Then as co-chairman of the symposium, I rose and made the following closing statement: "We thank you all for coming; we appreciate the expression of your varying points of view. I feel as you do that they needed very much to be presented. This has been a meeting with very serious social and ethical implications. I want you to know, as the organizer of this symposium, that most of these questions were taken into account from the very day in May 1971, when the symposium program was formulated prior to the time that I left Houston for a visit to the Soviet Union as a guest of the Ministry of Health. While I was there, I had an opportunity to observe many of the matters about which you have spoken. It has been stated at this meeting that such procedures are outlawed in the Soviet Union, which I can assure you is untrue. Time does not permit me to go into the details at this point.

"I think that we all agree that the matters which we, as thoughtful individuals, have discussed here need to receive a considerable amount of further investigation and careful, thoughtful consideration by many groups. This was not convened as a meeting at which manifestos would be adopted or any votes taken. This is not a parliamentary body but an academic, scientific assembly, and I now call it adjourned. Thank you."

The abrupt termination of the meeting without further discussion completely surprised both the invited guests and those who had come to disrupt it. Most of the latter very quickly dispersed and disappeared since they probably had little or no idea why they were recruited to attend in the first place. Rabbi Schachtel was very disappointed that rational discussion was impossible. Immediately after the adjournment, I was asked to appear on network television. Peter Breggin, who was also interviewed, honored me by saying that I was "the most hostile man he had ever met."

In the ensuing months after the meeting, there appeared in local, national, and international news media a vast number of references to what had occurred during the scientific discussions and in the events peripheral to the meeting itself. I was so stressed by the entire affair that I wound up in the hospital with a bleeding stomach ulcer shortly afterwards. Moreover, I was particularly upset that Dean Smythe, knowing of the threat which faced us and, after promising to request assistance from The University of Texas Police, did nothing to prevent a potentially explosive situation from occurring.

The reader of the published proceedings, *Neural Bases of Violence and Aggression* (Fields WS and Sweet WR, Warren H. Green, Inc., St. Louis, Missouri, 1975, 551 p), may fruitfully consider Dr. Breggin's other activities in order to better judge his contribution to the meeting and to the book. Having generously given us the benefit of his thoughts in Houston, he traveled in the summer of 1972 to Great Britain. There his views received widespread coverage by the daily press and he debated them on a television program with Professor William Sargent, who for many years had been in charge of the Department of Psychological Medicine of St. Thomas' Hospital in London.

Breggin's extraordinary statements led to a careful analysis of their merit by Dr. Henry Miller, one of Britain's major medical statesmen and distinguished neurologists, then vice-chancellor of the University of Newcastle-upon-Tyne. Miller stated that, "The treatment of severe mental illness by lobotomy is not a subject for denunciation or prohibition, but for cool, continuous scientific assessment that should be applied to all problematical forms of treatment." In his thoughtful commentary, he objected to the sweeping scope and the absence of supporting evidence for Breggin's condemnations. Furthermore, he pointed out that Breggin's presentation in the *Congressional Record* (24 February 1972) prior to the Houston meeting "is partial and tendentious, the language that of the emotional crusader rather than the seeker after the truth." The opportunity the editors gave Breggin to publish in a reputable scientific volume was not used by him to present one iota of data about patients he had personally observed.

During the next four years successful symposia were held under the same auspices and published in hard-cover volumes. One was entitled "Neurological and Sensory Disorders in the Elderly" and was considered timely in view of concern over the increasing population of senior citizens. Another entitled "Neural Organization and its Relevance to Prosthetics," undertaken with the collaboration of the late Lewis A. Leavitt, professor and chairman of the Department of Physical Medicine at Baylor, was directed toward interdisciplinary collaboration between the medical, paramedical and bioengineering professions in providing a systems approach to rehabilitation of the physically handicapped and the development of adequate patient services.

The last of this series of symposia was another resounding success. However, I was unable to attend this meeting which was concerned with "Neurotransmitter Function: Basic and Clinical Aspects" because I was stricken once again with a bleeding ulcer. This time it was from stress related to refusal of some members of the scientific community to accept the preliminary results of a cooperative study of aspirin in the prevention of stroke, of which I was the coordinator, and also the threat of a delay in approval of our neurology residency program at The University of Texas Medical School at Houston after residents had been appointed. Fortunately, my collaborators for the symposium, Drs. Dianna Redburn, Joe Wood, and Philip Gildenberg, supervised the conduct of the proceedings in a splendid manner.

As a result of the pressure of other matters, it was my own personal decision to retire from organizing annual symposia. Unfortunately, none of my colleagues was prepared to devote the time or the effort to continuing them. I look back now on those scientific sessions as having focused attention on the efforts of those of us in Houston in basic and clinical neuroscience and clinical practice to enhance knowledge in our professional community and to disseminate that information to as wide an audience as possible.

Since those earlier days, there has been a proliferation of medically related scientific symposia, both in this country and abroad. Most of them have been sponsored either by large foundations, pharmaceutical companies, or the makers of scientific instruments. Moreover, medically related institutions which sponsor such meetings do so today in a more formal manner through offices of continuing education with a paid staff. The fact that we were able to launch and maintain the momentum of this annual effort on a local basis for so long was in itself no small achievement, and I am greatly indebted to those whose help along the way was invaluable.

When I returned from Dallas, the members of the Houston Neurological Society were very kind to elect me once again as president and I served in that capacity for two years. The Society still flourishes. In 1994 it had more than 150 members and the six meetings a year were well attended. The November meeting has been set aside for the annual William S. Fields Lecture in Neurology and the February meeting for the George Ehni Memorial Lecture in Neurosurgery. The late George Ehni was professor of neurosurgery at Baylor and director of the neurosurgical residency training program.

In 1995, of the six persons who signed the original charter of the Society, I am the only survivor.

Chapter 11

Participation in Community Affairs

IN MID-1949, ALMOST COINCIDENT with my arrival in Houston, a group of parents of some twenty children who had been denied admission to the Houston Independent School District because of low mental ability met at a nursery school to try to set up and finance a special class.

The organizational meeting was held on July 29, 1949, in the parish house of Trinity Episcopal Church, at the corner of Main and Holman streets, because of its central location. Prior to the meeting, there was some media publicity and more than seventy parents of mentally retarded children attended the session. Permission for this meeting was granted by the rector, Rev. Arthur S. Knapp, who never dreamed that three years later his wife would give birth to a son with Down's syndrome. A decision was reached to make application to the Texas secretary of state for a charter in the name of the Houston Council for Mentally Retarded Children as a nonprofit organization.

The first time that I had had any personal contact with a mentally retarded individual was while I was in medical school. At that time my brother was dating a very attractive young lady who lived with her parents in a high-rise apartment on Park Avenue in New York City. She had a retarded younger sister with Down's syndrome. The family was very wealthy and the mother insisted on keeping the mentally retarded daughter at home and even taught her to play a few tunes on the piano. I recall visiting there and the mother insisting that I stay after lunch to hear the girl perform. It was a tragic and yet very revealing experience.

After I was demobilized from military service in 1946 and had started my neurology training at Barnes Hospital, I was asked to go to the St. Louis Children's Hospital to assist two pediatricians in setting up a seizure clinic. Among the patients that we saw with epilepsy were some who were also mentally retarded.

When I arrived in Houston in July 1949, Russell Blattner, professor of pediatrics at Baylor and my friend at St. Louis, urged me to become involved in the care of retarded children since his attention had been diverted to other matters as a result of the polio epidemic and he did not have time to participate. It soon became evident that the parents of these children, who had developed an organization, needed a lot of professional guidance and I accepted the challenge. Eventually, I saw most of the retarded family members of that group as regular patients.

The first project of the Parents Council was to organize classes in the back room of a store on South Shepherd Drive. The group remained there until the fall of 1952, when they expanded to a more ambitious program and opened the first "Opportunity Center" in a rented six-room frame house located at 1511 Bissonnet Street. They took over the premises following a three-month renovation program, in which they were assisted by members and friends from organizations such as the Painters' Union and the Houston Lighting and Power Company. The center was to provide a base for three special classes and twenty-four-hour care of retarded persons for two-week periods.

The three-person staff consisted of supervisor, teacher, and nurse. The nurse was in charge of the residential care planned to provide a short break for parents. It was exceedingly disappointing to the Council that it was unable to keep the two residential beds occupied because parents could not bring themselves to let go of their handicapped children for even that short time. Education of parents to free their children for more independent living was to be a long and painful process, but it took only about a year and a half for the Council to learn the hard way what was meant by *nonprofit*.

In the summer of 1952, a retarded son was born to Rev. Arthur Knapp and his wife, Betty. The Knapps had been introduced to the parent group through Episcopal Bishop and Mrs. Clinton S. Quin, who lived next door to Mr. and Mrs. Charles E. Ames II, parents of a retarded child and members of the original Council. When a financial crisis arose, and at the request of the Council, Rev. Knapp went for advice to Leopold L. Meyer, a wealthy retail merchant who was also a well-known community leader and philanthropist. Meyer had had a long and abiding interest in the welfare of handicapped children and was a member of the board of directors of the new Texas Children's Hospital.

Meyer eventually agreed to help the Council if he were permitted to form a lay board of governors from the community. The Council members realized that they would have to give up control of the program but voted to do so in 1954, with several members of the original parents group serving on the new board. The primary concern of the board of governors was to raise funds as well as formulate service programs and establish the overall policies and procedures of the Council.

Through the intercession of Mrs. Marian Ames, the Walter Fondren home at 3410 Montrose Boulevard (now the Colombe d'Or Restaurant) was acquired for housing the Opportunity Center in larger and more adequate facilities. Purchase of this building was made possible through a telethon arranged by Leopold Meyer. In 1955 the Council moved into the large three-story Fondren home and remained there for the next eleven years. Mrs. Fondren continued to pay the taxes and maintenance costs of the building and provided it rent-free to the Council. Late in 1955, the Council was admitted to the United Fund. Meyer had been one of the founders of the original Houston Community Chest, forerunner of the United Fund (later the United Way), and his presence on the board was invaluable.

Now that more adequate space and better funding were available, Meyer proposed to the board that the time had come to bring in professional help. He was remarkable in recruiting people for participation in the support of many community activities related to the needs of children. I had never met him until he became interested in the needs of this organization. After we became better acquainted, we began to appreciate the contribution that each of us could make, and he would look to me for guidance in professional matters. Meyer was a neophyte with respect to mental retardation but, when he was told that there was a great need for a program in the Houston community, he became sold on the idea and persuaded several of his close friends to get things moving. Among the more influential persons in the early days of the Center was Harris Masterson, another Houstonian noted for his community service, who initially supported the effort handsomely. One of the original buildings of the present Center still carries his name as well as that of Meyer.

Leopold Meyer approached in a very businesslike manner the task of finding someone to direct this agency. He asked professional organizations around the country to give him a list of names of younger people whom they thought had some promise in the field of mental retardation. It was our good fortune that the name of Frank Borreca happened to be on that list. In the latter part of 1954, he was contacted by Meyer, as were several of his acquaintances in New York City. Borreca met Meyer in New York and talked with him at great length about community development. Borreca's work previously had been primarily in the public arena, with a heavy concentration on fostering parent groups that were emerging in New York City and focusing attention on schooling for retarded children. Meyer described to him what had been accomplished by the parent group in Houston and mentioned my name and that of Russell Blattner. When Borreca came for a visit and interview, he met with Meyer, Masterson, and me for lunch at the recently opened Doctors' Club in the Jesse H. Jones Library Building. We decided during that meeting that if Borreca came to Houston, I would take responsibility for organizing a professional advisory committee and become a member of the recently organized board of governors.

From that time on, there was a continuing involvement of professionals including, initially: Fred Taylor, a professor of pediatrics at Baylor College of Medicine; Jack Wheeler, a clinical psychologist; Nancy Greenridge, a special education adviser for the Houston Independent School District; and Theresa Monaco, from the School of Education at the University of Houston. Later on I invited Fred Dorsey, an internist and geriatrician, to join us since many of our clients were older retarded persons. Our aim was to convene a gathering of disciplines both within and outside of medicine. These people were dedicated to the task at hand and attended meetings faithfully. Frank Borreca told me before he retired to New Mexico in 1991 that what seemed unique to him was that, over many years, the considerable progress made by the Center for the Retarded in the medical area started from this small committee of volunteers which had been put together in those early days. Initially our members were concerned not only with medical matters but also with such problems as the ethics involved in our relations with the community of practicing physicians and the kind of publicity that should be given to the program. This was before many of the laws now on the books came into effect. I knew that we faced the risk of getting into serious difficulty if we did not tread carefully and avoid offending any official bodies, such as the Harris County Medical Society or the local hospitals.

The opportunity soon arose for my personal involvement at the Center for the Retarded in other matters which had nothing to do with medicine, such as deciding on program expansion and location. My participation in those early days was not only in the planning for a permanent facility, but also in the actual acquisition of the land. Frank Borreca and I had many sessions with the architect, Howard Barnstone. The latter and Leopold Meyer were at each other's throats all too frequently, and we served as peacemakers. We were strapped for funds at the time, but if we had to replicate today what we built then, it would most assuredly cost at least three times as much.

I came up with the idea of meeting with the State Board of Health and making application for Hill-Burton construction funds, which the federal government had allocated for hospital construction under the aegis of the State Board of Health. In my opinion, what we were planning was a health facility and I was convinced that we would be able to persuade the State Board to provide matching funds. At that particular time the chairman of the State Board, which had the responsibility for allocation of these federal funds, was Dr. Hampton Robinson, a well-to-do general surgeon and a good friend, whose wife was my patient. Hamp Robinson had a suite of offices in a high-rise building in downtown Houston, where he conducted his nonmedical business affairs. I recall going there with Frank Borreca to ascertain whether he thought the State Board would be receptive to a formal application from us.

We went with no prior preparation except what I had in my head and whatever data Frank considered relevant. I did most of the talking and described to Hamp who and what we represented. Then I asked whether he thought it would be reasonable for us to prepare an application for presentation to the State Board as a health-related facility. The answer was, "Yes, it sounds like something that would be very appropriate."

Leopold Meyer was very enthusiastic about our proposed plan and we were determined to request funds in the amount of $500,000. It was decided that he would accompany Frank and me to Austin for our presentation. We flew there from Hobby Airport in James Abercrombie's private plane. Abercrombie had been one of the leading benefactors of the Texas Children's Hospital. I have always felt that the members of the Board of Health were so startled by our audacity in approaching them for funds, that they were persuaded to award them to us. This was the beginning of a whole new movement and the opening up of a number of related facilities around the country under similar auspices.

Russell Blattner and I were invited to New York to attend the first Kennedy Foundation Awards dinner at the Waldorf Astoria Hotel on February 5, 1964. This dinner had been postponed from early December 1963 because of the assassination of President John F. Kennedy. President Lyndon B. Johnson made the presentations in his stead, and the Honorable Lester Pearson, prime minister of Canada, gave the dinner address. I had the good fortune to sit at a table between Adlai Stevenson, former governor of Illinois and Democratic Party candidate for president in 1956, and Princess Lee Radziwill, sister of Jacqueline Kennedy. I did my best to promote our effort in Houston. During the day prior to this social function, a scientific symposium had been held concerning research in mental retardation. The genetic aspects of the problem occupied an important place on the program.

About one month following this New York trip, it was announced in the local newspapers that the Houston Council for Retarded Children would be launching a drive to raise $1,220,000 for a medical and training site on Allen Parkway. More than 100 campaign workers, parents, and city officials met on March 30, 1964, for the groundbreaking ceremony in a tent on land leased from the city. On that occasion, I was the guest speaker and discussed recent developments in the treatment of mental retardation. I pointed out that in an age of automation, individuals with minimal skills and abilities were becoming increasingly handicapped. Moreover, we needed to think and plan boldly and that it was imperative for adequate medical services to be provided for large segments of our population during pregnancy and infancy. The new research and treatment center, on a five-acre site, with sheltered and outdoor play areas, was expected to be completed in September 1965. When finished it would accommodate between 500 and 600 children and would have about fifty professional staff members.

Unfortunately, in 1967, there was an interruption in my participation because I no longer had an administrative position or an academic program at Baylor. I departed Houston on July 1 of that year after having accepted an appointment to the faculty of The University of Texas Southwestern Medical School at Dallas. Frank Borreca came to me before my departure and asked me to recommend someone to take over the committee functions where I had left off. I suggested Fred Taylor, who had been very active with me in this work for several years. This turned out to be an an excellent choice. During my absence from Houston, Fred chaired the Professional Advisory Committee. I never dreamed that I would be returning so soon, but I was back in Houston on March 1, 1969, only twenty months later. Almost immediately I resumed my involvement and, not too long afterwards, Dr. Taylor, for health reasons, decided to step down as chairman. It was then that I suggested that the Professional Advisory Committee assume a slightly different orientation and requested permission from the board to bring some additional persons aboard. Within the next couple of years after my return, we enlisted the help of Sarah Howell, a pediatric psychiatrist, William Riley, a neurologist in private practice, and Kay Lewis, a pediatrician who had been medical director at the Richmond (Texas) State School. The assistance of all three proved invaluable.

At that stage the board of the Center began planning for a residential facility and an infirmary. Several members of the board of governors, myself included, pointed out that many of our clients were no longer children and that we should have some way of accommodating the long-range needs of retarded persons. Frank Borreca and Earl Pierson, a dedicated board member, whose son, Wendell, was one of my patients, enlisted my help with the designing of medical facilities and in discussing the matter of staffing. Soon thereafter Frank completed his studies for a doctoral degree in education at the University of Houston. The Cullen Residence Hall was completed in 1974, and I was there for the dedication of the building, at which time Congresswoman Barbara Jordan gave a heart-warming speech.

By 1991, the board of governors was ready to address the need for planning the care of an aging population in the residential facil-

Participation in Community Affairs

ity. What Frank and I had preached about earlier was clearly coming to pass, and geriatrics became the focal point of a lot of the new programming. It is well known that premature senility is frequent in this population of retarded persons. The Professional Advisory Committee was convinced that the next big thrust should be in geriatrics, in all its aspects, not only medical but social as well, and so advised the board of governors. It was also with this in mind that Fred Dorsey, a geriatrician, was invited to join the committee.

My compensation for the time and effort which I have devoted in over forty years to the needs of the retarded comes from the dedication of the others with whom I have been associated, the program which developed, and the clients whom we served. I have gained great personal satisfaction from all three aspects and take considerable pride in the results.

Another Medical Center institution in which I participated almost from its inception was the Houston Speech and Hearing Center. This clinic, from a small beginning, subsequently became the Speech and Hearing Institute of The University of Texas Health Science Center at Houston.

The Community Council of Harris County, Texas, in 1943, had asked the Health Section of the Council to review Houston's needs in the area of speech and hearing. A committee consisting of laypeople and physicians was formed. After visits to community and university speech and hearing centers elsewhere, it was decided that the establishment of such a center in this city was desirable.

W. D. Sutherland, president of Henke-Pillot Grocers (the predecessor of Kroger Grocery Stores in Houston), had a hearing problem for which he had consulted J. Charles Dickson, who was at that time chief of the ear, nose, and throat service at The Methodist Hospital. These two gentlemen enlisted the help of two others, James W. Rockwell and Forrest Lee Andrews, in applying to the Texas secretary of state for a charter as a nonprofit, benevolent, and charitable private corporation known as the Houston Speech and Hearing Center. The charter stated that the corporation was formed for the purpose of observing, testing, analyzing, diagnosing, and treating those persons afflicted with speech and hearing abnormalities, defects, and disorders, regardless of race, creed, or color, and for the related purposes of furnishing facilities for the instruction in the studies relating to speech and hearing afflictions and disorders, and of serving as a center for research and studies related to speech and hearing defects, abnormalities or afflictions. It was agreed also to vest the direction and management of the affairs of this entity in a board of directors of not less than five, nor more than fifteen, persons. This charter was sent to Austin and was approved by the secretary of state on September 18, 1950.

While this document was being prepared, a search was begun to recruit a director for this new entity. Jack L. Bangs, Ph.D., came for an interview in the fall of 1950 and was subsequently offered the position as director of the clinic. His wife, Tina, was just completing her work toward a doctorate at Stanford University, so he agreed to take the job with the provision that Tina would be made assistant director. The clinic was to be located in The Methodist Hospital, then under construction in the Texas Medical Center. Jack and Tina were asked to prepare plans for the clinic in the basement of the hospital in space which was rather small and cramped. Unwittingly, what they prepared while still on the West Coast failed to take into consideration the continued existence of segregation in Houston; they had planned on having integrated drinking and toilet facilities for all clients. Under the circumstances the plans were carried out without further discussion, but at that time such an arrangement probably would not have received approval from the board of trustees of the hospital. Nevertheless, it became a *fait accomplit.*

When Jack and Tina Bangs arrived in Houston in July 1951, Jack started working at the old Methodist Hospital on Rosalie and San Jacinto streets, where the clinic was housed until the new hospital was completed. Tina, however, did not participate in the clinic until the facility was moved to the Medical Center in the fall of 1951. Almost immediately a search was started to recruit a board of directors. The original board included the aforementioned W. D. Sutherland and Forrest Lee Andrews as well as Drs. J. Charles Dickson and Herbert H. Harris, both otolaryngologists and members of The Methodist Hospital staff. Important additions to that original board were Mrs. Gus Wortham, and Mrs. Nina Cullinan, both wealthy, philanthropically minded Houstonians.

At that time, I was busy with organization of the Blue Bird Clinic in the new Methodist Hospital. Nevertheless, I had considerable interest in the program for diagnosis and management of speech and hearing impairments, particularly as they affected children. In the latter part of 1952, I was asked to serve on the board of directors of the new center. This was a position in which I continued until I left for Dallas in 1967 and to which I was invited to return when I came back to Houston in 1969.

After one year at The Methodist Hospital, it was obvious that the clinic was not going to be able to support itself on fees alone, and application was made to become an agency of the United Fund (later the United Way). This funding was approved and has been continued to the present time.

From the very outset the caseload increased exponentially and the small quarters at The Methodist Hospital soon became inadequate to accommodate the diagnostic and treatment services. These were therefore expanded to a rented house on Crawford Street, and additional teachers and therapists were recruited to meet the need.

As the Center grew, many community organizations became involved in contributing to its support. Those included the Junior League of Houston, whose support of both the clinical and research functions continued until the early 1960s; the Kappa Alpha Theta Sorority, which from 1962 until 1971, when The University of Texas assumed control, donated monies from their annual antique show to help establish the research and development division; and the Delta Zetas, whose hobby shows helped build the institute's television studio, which produces videotapes for educational and therapeutic purposes. In addition to these organizations, a group of volunteers banded together in 1959 to become the Women's Auxiliary. These individuals gave much of their time and effort to both personal service and fundraising.

A program was developed which covered a broad range of services. Four general areas were to be addressed, namely, diagnosis, therapy, research and teaching of students who would become specialists in these fields. Classes for children were organized for auditory training and language development for those hard of hearing and those with speech problems. Facilities for diagnosis of speech and hearing problems in adults were included. Also, special instructions in speech were made available for those who had lost communication skills through an operation or following a stroke or head injury.

Almost within the first five years, the rapid growth of the Houston Speech and Hearing Center made it apparent that a new facility would be needed to house its several departments. Application was made for Hill-Burton funds, along with matching local funds raised by the board of directors. With Jack Bangs' hard work and the dedication of the board, a new building adjoining the Texas Institute for Rehabilitation and Research in the Texas Medical Center reached completion in 1959. For the first time the entire staff, which had grown to eighteen persons, was under one roof. Several new board members from the Houston community were added at the time of the move, including Sarah Levy (Mrs. Moise), Nancy Adams (Mrs. Kenneth "Bud"), and Katherine Hannah (Mrs. David). Additional representatives were appointed from the University of Houston and the Houston Independent School District.

With the completion of the new building, the diagnosis and therapy divisions of the Center's service program were able to flourish. The new building had state-of-the-art sound-treated rooms and an anechoic chamber which was to be used for research purposes. A research director, James Jerger, Ph.D., was appointed but after a couple of years he departed to join the Department of Otolaryngology at Baylor as chief of audiology. However, it was always the dream of Jack and Tina Bangs, shared by many of us on the board, that research and teaching would become an integral part of the Center's program. The plan was to create a multi-disciplinary research institute devoted to the study of human communication and its disorders. Construction of a 40,000-square-foot adjoining research building was initiated in 1967 and completed in 1969. It was opened and the staff moved in almost coincident with my return from Dallas. A plan to bring together specialists from medicine, psychology, and communications was promptly submitted to the board of directors. Unfortunately, the expansion, in my opinion, came too quickly and the Center was unprepared for it.

It became apparent that in order for the Speech and Hearing Center to prosper, it could no longer remain a free-standing institution but instead would have to seek a closer affiliation with one of the major institutions in the Medical Center. Both Baylor College of Medicine and The University of Texas M. D. Anderson Hospital and Tumor Institute had been affiliated with the Center for many years with respect to specific programs in speech diagnostics and training. This activity was directed toward a variety of handicapped persons, including those in whom the larynx (voice box) had been removed because of cancer. Overtures were made to both Baylor and The University of Texas in an endeavor to arrange a favorable affiliation. Michael DeBakey and Bobby Alford, by then chairman of the Department of Otolaryngology at Baylor, made a concerted effort to incorporate the Speech and Hearing Center into the Department of Otolaryngology of that institution. However, Jack Bangs, along with the chairman of the board of the Center, Joseph S. Cullinan III, decided that it would be more appropriate to affiliate with The University of Texas in order to emphasize the educational aspects of the program. A proposed agreement had been considered in 1970, but was delayed at that time by the university, pending clarification of other affiliation agreements previously entered into by the Center.

Joe Cullinan agreed to appoint an executive committee from his board to work with The University of Texas if Dr. Charles LeMaistre, then chancellor of the university, agreed to explore the possibility of making a formal affiliation. Cullinan suggested that an executive committee of his board, including James A. Baker III (later secretary of state in the Bush administration), William S. Fields, Kenneth Fellows, and Ross Stewart, take responsibility for exploring a mechanism for transfer of the Center to the university. It appeared to all concerned that this was an ideal time for negotiations because (1) the Center was essentially free of indebtedness, (2) a new director had to be appointed, (3) the program needed to be expanded to include proper medical participation, and (4) the University of Texas needed a facility for both the Graduate School of Biomedical Sciences and for the affiliated programs of the other units of the University of Texas in Houston.

I resigned from the board and from the committee appointed by Joe Cullinan to avoid any conflict of interest since I had been an employee of The University of Texas Graduate School since my return from Dallas. Shortly thereafter I accompanied Dr. R. Lee Clark to Austin to obtain approval from the central administration of the university for the orderly transfer of ownership.

On March 2, 1971, Joe Cullinan wrote to L. F. McCollum, chairman of the board of Baylor College of Medicine, informing him that the executive committee of the board of directors had elected unanimously to reject Baylor's proposal and cast their lot with The University of Texas. He stated in his letter that three major issues determined the board's decision: (1) the history of continuing inactivity of the affiliation agreement with Baylor College of Medicine, which the board felt to be clearly a one-sided relationship, (2) the declaration by Dr. DeBakey that the facilities could not be enjoyed by other institutions through multiple affiliation once the transfer had occurred, (3) the desirability of being under the umbrella of The University of Texas Graduate School of Biomedical Sciences. Cullinan further stated that it continued to be the overriding philosophy of the board of directors that the Center should neither be the sole province of medicine, or arts, or sciences and that an affiliation with the university would serve the foregoing purpose. Moreover, he offered to keep open the Baylor affiliation since he felt that both sides would benefit by keeping it functioning. Last but not least, the board of directors felt that this arrangement was best for the pursuit of the goals and purposes set forth in the original charter of the Center.

Several options for affiliation were under discussion but the final decision was for the actual transfer of ownership to The University of Texas, with an understanding that the ongoing program of the Houston Speech and Hearing Center, supported by the United Fund, would continue under full operational management of that university. It would provide a budget for operation of all pertinent activities with the exception of those supported by the United Fund and fee-for-service clinics. In addition, those who were on the board of the Houston Speech and Hearing Center would continue in an advisory capacity for the development of a program for the future. This group would constitute a board of visitors. It was also agreed that an expanded program in communication research and teaching, under the auspices of the Graduate School of Biomedical Sciences and other units of The University of Texas at Houston, would be envisioned.

Once this move was accomplished, the Speech and Hearing Center became known as the Speech and Hearing Institute and, for educational purposes, as the Division of Communication Disorders in the Graduate School of Biomedical Sciences, under the direction of Dean Alfred Knudsen. Members of the board of directors were called the board of visitors. Unfortunately, Dr. Knudsen left for Philadelphia within about eighteen months after taking over this additional responsibility.

Because it became clear to them that it would be difficult, if not impossible, to maintain the Speech and Hearing Center as a freestanding unit, Drs. Jack and Tina Bangs resigned after accepting positions with the University of Cincinnati. Once they had decided to move from Houston, they sold their house, but before they could vacate the premises, Jack died suddenly of a heart attack in May

1971. Since I lived nearby, I was the first one to arrive after receiving a call from Tina, who was devastated by her husband's untimely death. Tina's situation at the Institute immediately changed. She was asked to remain in her position and, at the request of the new administration, she became interim director of the Center and subsequently, director.

It was during the administration of Charles A. Berry, as the first president of the newly formed University of Texas Health Science Center that Tina Bangs officially became director of the Speech and Hearing Institute. When Dr. Truman Blocker succeeded Dr. Berry, he decided that there was a need for a new director with a more medical orientation. He felt that the Speech and Hearing Institute should be closely allied with the medical and dental schools rather than with the graduate school, although the latter could still serve as a unit from which trainees received their graduate degrees. With this in mind, Blocker undertook to find a new director to replace Tina Bangs.

There had always been a close association of neurology and neurosurgery, and also pediatrics, with the Center. The only rough interface came with respect to relations with the Division of Otolaryngology in the Department of Surgery at The University of Texas Medical School. It was soon clear that this adversarial relationship would create more problems.

At the end of February 1978, Dr. Blocker established a committee advisory to him regarding the activities of the Speech and Hearing Institute. He requested that I assume the responsibility of chairman. The other members of the committee were from otolaryngology, plastic surgery, dentistry, oral surgery, pediatric psychiatry, and pediatric neurology. Over the course of a few months, we interviewed several outstanding candidates from across the country. The one whom we felt was the best qualified was Dr. Charles Berlin, director of a similar facility at Louisiana State University School of Medicine in New Orleans. The committee recommended him to Truman Blocker. Blocker, on the other hand, felt that Berlin's acceptance requirements would be more than the university was prepared to meet at that time. He thought that one of the other candidates whom we had interviewed, Dr. Walter Carlin from Ithaca College in upstate New York, might be more suitable. I, personally, was not entirely sold on Carlin and persuaded Blocker to defer an offer of appointment. A day or two later, I was in conference with Blocker in his office during midmorning when a tan-colored Mercedes drove up just outside of the window and out stepped Carlin. On entering the office, he informed us that he had arrived ready for work. This was an extremely embarrassing situation since no offer had yet been made to Carlin. Blocker decided that under the circumstances he could not back off and proceeded to go ahead with Carlin's appointment. It subsequently turned out that Carlin's credentials were substantially different from what he had presented to the committee and that he had led Truman Blocker into believing he was the ideal man for the position.

The appointment of Walter Carlin was an unmitigated disaster. He turned out to be an erratic and incompetent administrator. Moreover, he was an alcoholic and this particular problem had followed him wherever he had gone throughout his career. Carlin's appointment was, in my view, uncharacteristic of Truman Blocker, who was ordinarily a forceful, direct, and perceptive person. How he could have been deceived by this man into making such a disastrous decision is still incomprehensible to me.

Not too long after Dr. Roger Bulger assumed his duties as president of the Health Science Center, Carlin disappeared. He never said farewell to anyone and his whereabouts are still a mystery to his former associates in Houston. Bulger appointed Dr. R. William Butcher, the new dean of the Graduate School of Biomedical Sciences, as director of the Institute and Dr. Joan Lynch as deputy director. The latter had originally been recruited by Jack Bangs.

Twenty-three candidates were awarded master's degrees between 1975 and 1977, and three postdoctoral fellows trained at the Speech and Hearing Institute. Four of the twenty-three entered Ph.D. programs and one later graduated from medical school.

Tina Bangs resigned in 1984 and was subsequently designated professor emeritus. The dean did not replace her, or any other faculty member who resigned from the Institute, and phased out the graduate degree program. The future of The University of Texas Speech and Hearing Center as a free-standing entity became very much in doubt and in 1992 it ceased to exist.

During the latter half of 1973, I had received inquiries from several colleagues in neurology around the state of Texas regarding the possibility of forming a section of neurology within the Texas Medical Association (TMA). On November 15 of that year, I wrote to C. Lincoln Williston, executive secretary of the TMA, requesting an

Participation in Community Affairs 223

up-to-date listing of physicians around the state with the designation of neurologist so that I might contact them. Independently, in January 1974, Robert McMaster and Edward Liske of San Antonio began a similar initiative. They were kind enough to send me a copy of their letter addressed to Mrs. Dale Willimack, coordinator of the annual session, which was to be held in Houston in early May 1974.

During the annual session, a meeting of interested neurologists was held at the Towers Hotel on Holcombe Boulevard across from the Shamrock Hilton Hotel, and I was asked to chair the session. Twenty-four neurologists were in attendance. A motion was made and passed unanimously that a statewide society of neurologists be established within the framework of the TMA and that the inaugural session take place the following year. This was approved by the parent organization and a Section of Clinical Neurology was established, with its first meeting to be held in San Antonio on May 2, 1975.

Peritz Scheinberg from the University of Miami, Florida, and Manuel Gomez from the Mayo Clinic in Rochester, Minnesota, were the invited guest speakers. I was asked to speak at the luncheon on the historical evolution of medical neurology in the state of Texas. The thirty-five neurologists in attendance signed a prepared document as charter members of the Texas Neurological Society.

Chapter 12

To Dallas and Back

WITH SOME REGRET AND CONSIDERABLE NOSTALGIA, I took my leave of Baylor and Houston at the end of June 1967, after accepting a position offered to me as professor of neurology at The University of Texas Southwestern Medical School at Dallas. One year earlier they had recruited a new chairman, David Daly, who had been for many years at the Mayo Clinic in Rochester, Minnesota, and had come to Dallas by way of the Barrow Neurological Institute in Phoenix, Arizona. I arrived on the same day that Charles Sprague came from Tulane to begin his tenure as dean. Subsequently, he was promoted to president of The University of Texas Health Science Center at Dallas when that entity was created and held that position until his retirement in 1987.

Bette and I had sold our house in Houston, to be ready for its new occupants on August 1, but had not yet found a suitable home in Dallas. She came to visit a couple of times and we went shopping for a house, finally locating one in Farmers Branch on the north side of Dallas. It was a delightful house with a swimming pool in the backyard, but it certainly could not compare with what we were leaving behind in Houston. The move from Houston was also exceedingly difficult for both of our daughters. Susan had her eighteenth birthday on July 2, the day after I departed for Dallas, and Anne had just finished her second year in high school. She faced being separated from her friends and having to adjust to a new school for her last two years. This certainly was not easy for either of them or for Bette. While awaiting their arrival, I stayed in a garage apartment behind the home of Dr. Daly. His wife, Harriet, was extremely kind and generous with her hospitality, but I was most assuredly happier after my family arrived.

I was delighted to be able to remain in Texas, where I had developed so many friendships and professional contacts. Unknown to me, however, was the fact that most of Dave's former colleagues at the Mayo Clinic had been very surprised when I accepted his offer to join him in Dallas. They knew Dave well and assumed that I did too. They were convinced that it would be only a short time before there would be serious conflict between us. For reasons best known to them, they never mentioned their concerns to me until later, when I decided to leave Dallas and return to Houston.

Fortunately, I was able to transfer the Central Registry for the NIH-supported Joint Study of Extracranial Arterial Occlusion to Dallas. This large grant provided me with the funds necessary to pay for secretarial and editorial help as well as for a neurologist to assist me. In the latter capacity, Richard North, who had been a trainee and junior faculty person with me at Baylor, accompanied me to Dallas. Later, after I decided to return to Houston, he established a successful private practice. Robert Maulsby, a recent Baylor graduate, also decided to come along after being invited by Dave to take over and run the day-to-day operation of the EEG Laboratory. Three others also moved with me to Dallas: Mary Macdonald, our biostatistician; Joan Chambers, my editorial assistant; and Omkar Markand, a resident in his last year of postgraduate training. I was grateful for their loyal support. Dr. Markand subsequently left Dallas for Indiana University, where for almost twenty years he has been a professor of neurology and director of the EEG Laboratory. Ultimately, several other people were recruited to round out the program. Bassett Kilgore, a radiologist, returned home from St. Louis, Missouri, where he had been on a fellowship in neuroradiology, and accepted a full-time faculty appointment and a staff position at Parkland Hospital. Anthony D'Agostino was recruited as neuropathologist in the Department of Pathology. This provided a splendid nucleus for the development of a program in cerebrovascular research and education, which could be relatively independent of other research and patient care activities in the department that

Dave was developing. His clinical and research interests were primarily in the field of epilepsy.

When we arrived in Dallas, there was no space available in the medical school building for me or the colleagues who had accompanied me. At the suggestion of a Houston friend, I went to visit Trammell Crow, a prominent Dallas real estate developer. He told me that there was vacant space available in a shopping center just south of the tower on Stemmons Freeway in which he had his office. The university agreed to rent that space from Mr. Crow so that I could accommodate my research staff, secretary, and personal library. This provided me with a certain amount of autonomy which, unfortunately, did not last very long. Dave Daly decided that he needed to keep us under close observation and moved his entire operation from the medical school to the same suite which we were occupying in the shopping center. I was by no means happy with this decision and it became apparent, at least to me, within a very short period of time that I was quite correct in my assessment of what was likely to happen. He was obviously fearful of my having any autonomy within his department and being located at a distance from his office.

Almost coincidental with my arrival in Dallas, the Regional Medical Program of Texas was being mobilized. This activity was run out of an office at The University of Texas at Austin under the direction of Charles "Mickey" LeMaistre, who in 1967 was vice-chancellor for health affairs. Charles McCall had come there at LeMaistre's invitation to be the medical director of the program for the state. This federally funded activity had three arms: one in heart disease, another in cancer, and a third in stroke. I was offered the opportunity to be coordinator of the stroke program. I convinced the authorities in Austin that it would be worthwhile to develop in Dallas a demonstration stroke care unit under the aegis of the Regional Medical Program. This unit, along with an already established Stroke Registry, would provide another venue for the overall project. The relatively new Presbyterian Hospital of Dallas appeared to be the ideal location for such an undertaking. I visited with the hospital administrator, Roderic Bell, and persuaded him to consider providing space for this effort on the top floor of the east wing of the new hospital, an area which was still unfinished. He arranged for me to present a proposal, which I had put together, to his hospital board. Two of the more active members of that board, Toddie Lee

Winn and Donald Zale, were favorably impressed with the proposal and provided the impetus required to get it started.

During the construction of the hospital, Rod Bell had been approached by a professor from the Texas A&M University School of Architecture at College Station regarding the feasibility of introducing a new modular concept in interior hospital design. Initially, the trustees had turned down this proposal, but when I convinced them of the need for a stroke unit, they decided that it might serve as a suitable place in which to test this type of structural design. The hospital was able to obtain a grant of $317,000 from the U.S. Public Health Service to launch the program. I immediately started to work enthusiastically with the architects to develop a plan.

The generous support from many sources which I received in this endeavor to get a comprehensive stroke research and treatment program started was tremendously gratifying. Enthusiastic cooperation was also forthcoming from Dr. Howard Coggerhall, an internist, who had just been designated director for the Regional Medical Program in Northeast Texas. It was reported in *Texas Medicine* in July 1968 that the first operational project to be funded by the Regional Medical Program of Texas was under way in Dallas. The University of Texas Southwestern Medical School announced also that it would cooperate with the Presbyterian Hospital of Dallas in establishing a Stroke Treatment Demonstration Unit, which would be dedicated to the continuing education of physicians and allied health professionals. As part of the announcement, it was stated that the goals of the overall program were:

1. To collect information which would assist in identifying persons who were likely to have stroke;
2. To continue the Cooperative Study to determine which categories of patients were best suited for surgical intervention;
3. To provide demonstration facilities in which physicians and allied health professionals could be trained to establish more effective programs in their local communities.

It was also mentioned that I would be the director of a Stroke Registry in the Department of Neurology at Southwestern, the registry being a cooperative venture in which twenty-three university medical centers in the United States and one in Montevideo, Uruguay, would continue to collect exhaustive records and analyses of stroke patients. The information in the Data Bank at that time had been collected from nearly 8,000 patients over the previous ten years. In 1968 additional support was provided by the National Heart Institute in the amount of $315,000 for the next three years. Another area in this broad attack would be the establishment of a Cerebrovascular Clinical Research Center at Southwestern Medical School and Parkland Memorial Hospital, funded by the National Institute of Neurological Diseases and Stroke with a planning grant of $400,000. For the overall program additional specialized personnel would be recruited. By mid-1968 almost $1.5 million had been awarded for the stroke program by various agencies.

About four months after my arrival in Dallas, I was introduced by Dean Sprague to a young physician, Howard M. Siegler, who was working with him as an administrative intern. I was not exactly sure what the young man's responsibilities were and I had the impression that Sprague was not sure either.

When LeMaistre gave me the responsibility for supervision of the stroke arm of the Regional Medical Program of Texas, Sprague asked me if I would take Siegler under my wing and have him work with me on this statewide project. Siegler was moved out of the school to the offices on Stemmons Boulevard, where the Department of Neurology was then located, and given an office in the suite adjacent to that department. This was organized by Howard Coggerhall.

At that time Siegler, unfortunately, was involved in a lawsuit that his wife and members of her family had against the Bank of the Southwest and others in the city of Houston and in Louisiana. He had to devote a great deal of time responding to questions from lawyers on both sides and spent more time on the telephone with them than he did attending to the affairs of the program to which he had been assigned. It soon became obvious that he would be unable to fulfill his obligation and that his time would be taken up even more with the events in Houston. He therefore resigned from his position in Dallas and, after finding a suitable dwelling, he and his family moved to Houston. I did not know then that I would be seeing him frequently after my return to Houston in early 1969.

In the spring of 1968, I was invited to participate in a symposium on carotid artery surgery, which was planned for a regional meeting of the American College of Surgeons at the Hilton Hotel in Dallas. The others on the panel were Jesse Thompson, chief of vascular surgery at Baylor University Hospital in Dallas; Sterling Edwards, professor of surgery, University of Alabama, Birmingham; Malcolm Perry, associate professor of surgery at The University of Texas Southwestern Medical School in Dallas, who was the moderator; and E. Stanley Crawford, professor of surgery at Baylor College of Medicine in Houston, a colleague with whom I had previously collaborated.

I presented my paper first, followed by Thompson, Crawford, and Edwards, in that order. When Stanley Crawford spoke, he referred to me as a "crepehanger," presumably because in his opinion I had not been sufficiently enthusiastic about endorsing a surgical approach to the stroke problem. I was of a contrary opinion. During a round table discussion at the end of the session, I was able to respond to his comment. I pointed out that neurologists and vascular surgeons obviously had a different approach to many more problems than the one under discussion. Another, for example, was what to do if an elevator door was about to close as you were approaching. I suggested that the neurologist would put in his hand to protect his head, while the surgeon would put in his head to protect his hand. For a moment there was a pregnant silence among the audience of about 600 surgeons; then they all broke up and had a hearty laugh. The only other non-surgeon present to my knowledge was my neuroradiologist friend and a colleague at Southwestern, Bassett Kilgore, who had accompanied me to the meeting. I was often reminded of this incident over the ensuing years by persons who had been in the audience.

The following year I was invited to Milwaukee as a member of a panel on medical and surgical management of stroke. The other members were the aforementioned Jesse Thompson, F. J. "Jack" Wylie from San Francisco, Joseph Foley of Boston, and Mark Dyken from Indianapolis. When I got up to speak, I could not resist the urge to jokingly comment that it must be difficult for Mark to be on the same panel with all of us Harvard alumni. However, when his turn came, he had the last word. He mentioned a physician in Indianapolis who had two sons, one at Indiana University and the other at Harvard. When the doctor was asked whether this created any problem, he replied that the only difference he could tell in their progress through college was that the Harvard son, when asked to comment on some controversial topic, responded by saying, "Extraordinary," while the one at Indiana said, "Horseshit."

Since the Houston Neurological Society and its annual symposia had achieved such great success, both locally and nationally, it occurred to me that a similar effort might be worthwhile pursuing in Dallas. I discussed with some of my colleagues at the medical school the possibility of forming a Dallas Neurological Society. It was clear that this would be neither reasonable nor possible within the academic community alone, so I approached some of the neurologists and neurosurgeons in the private sector. This was a novel concept for them since there had been very little fraternal relationship between "town" and "gown" in the Dallas area. The idea caught on surprisingly well and an organizational meeting was planned. We prepared a mailing to all persons in the Dallas-Fort Worth medical community whom we thought might be interested, and there was a sufficiently enthusiastic response that a meeting was convened. I declined to serve in any capacity other than secretary, so Glenn Cherry, a neurosurgeon in private practice, was elected president. During the next year meetings were held every other month except in July and August of 1968.

I discussed with Dean Sprague the possibility of having a Dallas Neurological Symposium similar to the ones I had organized on an annual basis in Houston. He told me to proceed and gave me permission to talk to prominent people in the community who might provide financial support. At that time it came to my attention that Sarah Cole, an attractive young woman referred to me by the dean's office, was willing to assist me in this effort. It soon became evident that she was a first-rate fundraiser. Together we visited some very important people in the Dallas business community and were able to raise a sufficient amount of money to underwrite the expense of the proposed meeting. Unfortunately, there was no place at that time within The University of Texas Southwestern Medical School to hold such a large meeting. With the assistance of some prominent local citizens, space was provided for us at the Dallas Apparel Mart in March 1968, during an off-season period. This unusual venue turned out to be an ideal place for such a meeting.

After some discussion with William Willis, professor and chairman of the Department of Anatomy, it was agreed that it would be most appropriate to have a symposium concerned with "The Cerebellum in Health and Disease." This would enable Bill Willis to organize the basic science portion of the program and for me, with the help of my colleagues, to put together the clinical portion. The symposium was a great success both scientifically and socially. It was well attended and the proceedings were compiled and published soon thereafter. As had been my habit in the past, I began planning for the 1969 symposium as soon as the 1968 meeting was over. Unfortunately, the events which unfolded during the ensuing months threw cold water on this effort, and the entire program was abandoned when it became known that I would be returning to Houston. Likewise, much to my disappointment, the Dallas Neurological Society disbanded.

In September 1968, I received an invitation to present a paper at the International Conference on Cerebral Circulation to be held in Salzburg, Austria. When it came to the attention of the late Professor Roger Gilliatt, then medical director of the National Hospital, Queen Square, London, England, that I would be in Europe at the end of September, he invited me to come as a visiting lecturer to that venerable and esteemed institution. For a neurologist, particularly one in academic pursuits, this was much like making a pilgrimage to Mecca. When I submitted my leave request to go to Europe for this dual purpose, Dave Daly agreed that I could go to the Salzburg meeting but refused to give me approval for the invited visit to the National Hospital. He told Dean Sprague that there was no way that I could be spared for that long a time from my clinical and teaching responsibilities in Dallas. I never received a second invitation.

Dr. Daly's refusal to sign my leave request to visit London after the meeting in Austria was, I thought, based on a mean-spirited nature and paranoia. It appeared to be in keeping with what his former colleagues at the Mayo Clinic and in Phoenix had suspected would happen when I became a member of his department in Dallas. Not a single one of them saw fit to forewarn me; they just awaited the predictable eruption.

After my trip to Europe, I learned that during my absence Dave had asked his administrative assistant, nicknamed "Jinx," to obtain from my secretary the keys to my private files. The latter was reluctant to oblige but they were very insistent. Upon my return she told me what had happened and I confronted Dave. I requested that he provide me and my cerebrovascular program with some autonomy within the department or perhaps move us elsewhere within the school. Regrettably, he refused to accede to either request.

The situation became more and more unbearable from my point of view, and the friction between Dave Daly and me became obvious to every member of the department, particularly to those who had accompanied me from Houston and some senior faculty persons in other departments as well. Consequently, I requested permission from Dean Sprague to speak with Mickey LeMaistre about my concerns the next time I went to Austin for a visit to the offices of the Regional Medical Program. Mickey expressed regret over the deteriorating situation and suggested that I return to Houston as soon as I could arrange to settle my affairs in Dallas and transfer with me the movable portion of my grant support. He told me that he would arrange with Lee Clark, president of The University of Texas M. D. Anderson Hospital and Tumor Institute, for me to have an appointment at the Graduate School of Biomedical Sciences while awaiting the inauguration of the university's new medical school in Houston.

Following my return to Dallas after this visit in Austin, I informed Charlie Sprague of my desire to return to Houston and then proceeded to make arrangements with the funding agencies to move all of the grants for which I was the principal investigator back to Houston. This was a sizable undertaking. The institutional grant support for which I was coordinator had to remain behind. The amount involved at the medical school, Parkland Hospital, and Presbyterian Hospital altogether exceeded $2 million (a tidy sum in those days). Much of this funding was not renewed when I left and the program virtually expired.

The target date for my return to Houston was March 1, 1969. Bette and both of our daughters were still at our home in Farmers Branch on the north side of Dallas. I made a trip to the National Institutes of Health in Bethesda, Maryland, to make final arrangements for the transfer of the grant funds. While there, I arranged to visit my mother in Baltimore. I was pleased to find her in good health and surprisingly active in spite of the fact that she was somewhat handicapped by a fractured hip which had been pinned about two years earlier (when she was eighty-four years old). Prior to that she had planned to go on a trip around the world with her younger sister, Ada. Unfortunately, this accident prevented her from doing so.

After spending the night at Mother's apartment, I left Baltimore, went to the National Institutes of Health in Bethesda, and then later that day flew to Houston to make arrangements for transfer of my equipment. That night, while still in Houston, I received word from Bette in Dallas that my mother had passed away unexpectedly. The previous evening, after my departure, she had gone to the Baltimore Symphony Orchestra concert with one of her neighbors. When she returned, instead of having her usual tea before bedtime, she retired immediately because she did not feel well. Shortly thereafter, she experienced severe chest pain and called her family physician. He, in turn, called an ambulance but she was dead on arrival at Johns Hopkins Hospital. Frankly, I can think of no better way to depart this life than to succumb unexpectedly and suddenly at the age of eighty-six, without a long terminal illness. I knew from my visit with her the day before that she was in good spirits and remarkably alert mentally, reminding me at times of things that I had forgotten. I returned immediately to Dallas, where I met Bette, and together we went to Baltimore for my mother's funeral.

I was very much saddened by the fact that, although I had been able during a period of less than two years to develop a sizable research and educational program in cerebrovascular disease while in Dallas, much of this effort would be dissipated. It was even more disappointing that Dean Sprague had not seen fit to give me an opportunity to move that program out of the Department of Neurology. Not surprisingly, soon after I left Dallas, two things happened. First, the neurology program itself began to come unglued, and second, Dave Daly, because of his erratic behavior, was removed from the chairmanship and replaced by one of the associate deans, who then served as acting chairman. I have always regretted this turn of events and I know that Charlie Sprague did likewise, but he always made me feel as though it had been my fault that all that grant support went down the tube. Nevertheless, I was pleased to return to Houston, which had been my home for eighteen years. What I did not know then was that I would be starting what was to become for me virtually a second career.

When Mickey LeMaistre invited me to consider coming back to Houston in anticipation of the inauguration of a new University of Texas Medical School, I accepted the challenge with enthusiasm. It was somewhat of a gamble because the medical school in Houston was not yet a reality. There had been an enabling act passed during the 1967 session of the state legislature, so I knew that one day, and I hoped soon, there would be such a school, but at that moment it was only a promise. The legislature, however, did come through and appropriated the funds during its regular session in 1969. At the end of the session, Governor Preston Smith came to Houston and signed the bill at a special convocation in the auditorium of the Jesse H. Jones Library Building in the Texas Medical Center. I believe that I was the only person present who subsequently became a full-time member of the faculty of the new school.

I was returning to Houston at a time of great change and uncertainty. Baylor University College of Medicine had disassociated itself from the parent institution in Waco and was now known as Baylor College of Medicine. Seven clinical chairmen had departed from the local academic scene to pursue their careers elsewhere, and DeBakey was now in the driver's seat at Baylor. The University of Texas Medical School, which had only been a dream, was officially a reality.

It came as a great surprise to me to learn that The University of Texas planned to have its new medical school affiliated with Hermann Hospital as a primary teaching unit. Until then, Hermann Hospital had never considered itself to be a part of the Texas Medical Center and the dividing line between them was Ross Sterling Avenue, on the south side of the hospital. It was apparent to me, and I am sure to a few other old-timers, that Hermann was not yet ready to become a base for a full-scale academic program, particularly in the face of competition from Baylor College of Medicine, which was across the street.

Hermann Hospital had had its own teaching service for a long time. For a residency program the administration and staff had always used the clinic building (later called the Cullen Pavilion) that faces the corner of Fannin Street and Outer Belt Drive (now North MacGregor). This building had housed the original Hermann Hospital, which was on the southern outskirts of the city when it was built. In fact, only one block away, the electric trolley car that operated until World War II had terminated its line at Outer Belt (now North MacGregor) and Main Street across from the entrance to Rice Institute (now Rice University). The tracks were finally covered over with asphalt the year before I came to Houston.

A few days after my return to Houston from Dallas, I was coming out of The Methodist Hospital when I saw a young friend, Domingo Liotta, crossing the parking lot between Methodist and St. Luke's hospitals with a large briefcase in hand. Liotta, a well-qualified surgeon, had come from Argentina for further training with DeBakey, and had been assigned to his laboratory to work full time on the artificial heart program. I had known him earlier while I was still on the faculty at Baylor. I inquired about what he had been doing during my twenty-month absence from the city and whether he was still working in the laboratory for DeBakey. He said, "No, as a matter of fact, I'm on the way today to work with Dr. Cooley." In answer to my surprised "Why?" he went on to explain that he had gone to DeBakey and told him that as a surgeon he felt that he was losing touch with clinical practice while doing experimental surgery and working only with animals. He had been told that his continuing presence was required in the laboratory and so he had decided to quit working on DeBakey's artificial heart program. He told me that in his briefcase he was carrying a prototype of the mechanical heart and was taking it over to Denton Cooley, who had promised him that he could also work in the operating room at St. Luke's Hospital. I didn't have the faintest idea then that shortly thereafter Denton would implant the prosthesis in a patient. Moreover, this would not have occurred to me since the device had been removed from the Baylor laboratory without DeBakey's permission. It wasn't very long after this encounter that I read in the newspapers about a Haskell Karp, who had had an artificial heart implanted by Cooley. Then it suddenly dawned on me that Liotta was the intermediary, and perhaps the culprit, in that undertaking.

This sensational episode immediately brought the wrath of Mike DeBakey down on Denton Cooley and resulted in a widely publicized lawsuit. It was also the culmination of a long period of friction between the two and, to the best of my knowledge, they have not spoken to one another since.

About a year later, Domingo Liotta returned to Argentina and I thought that I had heard the last of him. However, in the early 1970s I was in Argentina and learned that Liotta had become the minister of health in President Juan Peron's cabinet only a few days before the latter was overthrown and forced to leave the country. Although Liotta was in the government for only a brief time, it certainly did not enhance his reputation. Once Peron was gone, Domingo had the misfortune of being identified as one of his close associates, which was certainly not the case since he had been out of the country for many years. I then lost track of him until 1990, when I was once again in Buenos Aires, where I had been asked to give a talk at the Hospital Italiano. I learned that Liotta was planning to come to the lecture. However, when I spoke with him on the telephone, he apologized and said that he could not make it because of an emergency, so I did not get to visit with him after all.

I am very grateful to Domingo Liotta for having arranged other opportunities for me in Argentina. While Domingo was in Houston in the 1960s, Jack Wylie, chief of vascular surgery at the University of California in San Francisco, and I went to Uruguay and Argentina. During that trip several unusual things happened. First, we met Mahels Molins, a thoracic surgeon who had worked with Raul Carrea, a neurosurgeon and close friend of mine, in the performance of the first successful carotid operation for management of stroke. Molins spoke very little English and Wylie spoke no Spanish, but the two of them had one thing in common — they were both inveterate sailors and so they went sailing together on the River Plate. Having some common interest can often help in circumventing or overcoming a language barrier.

Later Jack and I were invited to present lectures in Cordoba, Argentina, a city in the north central part of the country. This visit also was arranged by Domingo Liotta, who was an alumnus of the Catholic University in that city, and by the professor of vascular surgery there, Norberto Allende, who earlier had had some of his training with DeBakey in Houston. It was during that visit that I was introduced to an *asado,* which is a barbecue, Latin-American style. This took place at an *estancia* west of Cordoba near the town of Carlos Paz. The food vas delicious but the meal was very filling and better suited to a lumberjack than an itinerant neurologist.

Early in 1969, shortly after I returned from my sojourn in Dallas, there was another considerable controversy about an eye transplant done by Dr. Conard Moore, a full-time member of the Department of Ophthalmology at Baylor. Louis Girard, chairman of that department, was away in Spain as a visiting professor at the Instituto Barraquer when the incident occurred. One of his friends there read about the eye transplant which had been done in Houston by Moore and asked Louis about it. The latter tried unsuccessfully to reach Conard Moore by telephone at his Baylor office but finally made contact with him at home. Conard explained that he had done an enucleation (removal) of the patient's eye and decided that he would put a transplant into a shell of the sclera. He was contacted shortly thereafter by a reporter who had been notified of the event by a nurse in the operating room. Girard advised him to stay away from the newspaper and television reporters. Conard was contacted, however, by Mike DeBakey and Ted Bowen, administrator of The Methodist Hospital, who wanted him to appear at a news briefing which they had set up. He was advised by Louis Girard to cancel this. However, after further discussion with DeBakey, the news conference was held. Unfortunately, Conard stated at the news conference that he had been doing research on this technique while at New York University, where he was completing a basic science rotation as part of his training in ophthalmology. This was completely at variance with the facts.

When Girard returned from his overseas trip, he told DeBakey that he should request Conard's resignation. DeBakey, however, refused and took the matter out of Girard's hands. The latter had a meeting with his faculty and told them that they should refrain from discussion of this unseemly affair in order to avoid a serious blow to the entire department. Nevertheless, Milton Boniuk, a full-time member of the faculty, and Whitney Sampson, a part-time member, started agitating for some action. They persuaded the Ophthalmological Society to throw out Dr. Moore. The Harris County Medical Society also wanted his license suspended, but Girard appeared before the Board of Censors, which then backed off. The members finally compromised by agreeing to a motion of censure only.

Sampson, Boniuk, and Richard Ruiz, chief of ophthalmology at Hermann Hospital, wrote to DeBakey and demanded that Louis Girard resign as chairman of the Department of Ophthalmology. They appeared before the Academic Senate at Baylor College of Medicine, as did Girard himself, and were told that no action would be taken by that body. Regrettably, this did not satisfy those gentlemen and they went to virtually every ophthalmologist in the city with a petition. This even included Everett L. Goar, who had been Girard's mentor and predecessor as chairman of the department at Baylor. After all of this maneuvering, DeBakey suggested that Girard resign, but he held on to the letter of resignation for a long time. When DeBakey finally accepted Girard's resignation, he told him that he could stay on and do research.

A search committee recommended that Dr. David Paton from the Wilmer Eye Institute at Johns Hopkins be recruited as chairman of the Department of Ophthalmology, a move that Girard wholeheartedly endorsed. However, when Paton arrived, Girard was still in the chairman's office and was seeing patients in the Jones Building at Baylor. Negotiations were under way regarding disposition of his equipment and other financial concerns. Paton needed to know what he would have to acquire for the department if Girard's equipment was removed. After about three to four months of feeling like a guest in his own department, Paton asked Alfus Johnson, the business manager at Baylor, to notify Girard that he would have to move out of the building. Girard then went to DeBakey, who informed him that he would have to abide by a decision made at the discretion of the new chairman. Louis Girard was distressed very much by what he perceived as political games. Fortunately for him, he had interests outside of the academic arena which he was able to pursue and in which he has been very successful.

When I returned to work in Houston, I brought with me a group of co-workers in addition to my rather substantial grants. We were employed by the Graduate School of Biomedical Sciences, then administered through The University of Texas M. D. Anderson Hospital. I was given the position of assistant to the dean, Dr. H. Grant Taylor, a longtime friend and adviser during my Baylor days. When I requested office space, I was told that there was no place for me or my group even though I had a sizable number of persons paid by grant funds working with me. Since no space was available to accommodate us, I visited St. Anthony Center, an extended care facility on Almeda Road about one mile east of the Medical Center. This building was owned and administered by the Sisters of Charity of the Incarnate Word, who also owned St. Joseph Hospital in downtown Houston. I persuaded the Sisters to lease for my group some space until such time as the university could provide more permanent quarters. It turned out that the space which they very generously renovated in their basement was more than adequate. Little did I know then that the Department of Neurology of The University of Texas Medical School would continue to be housed there until 1976, when we were all transferred to the new medical school building in the Texas Medical Center. Frankly, we were delighted to remain there during that time because the medical school was located in much less comfortable quarters in the Center Pavilion at the corner of Braeswood and Holcombe boulevards. That building had been opened in the early 1960s as an apartment hotel. It was demolished in 1990.

The University of Texas Medical School had its first Christmas party for faculty and staff in 1970 in our basement offices at St. Anthony's. I still have a guest book with the signatures of all those who attended — four faculty and nineteen administrative or classified personnel. Of the latter, eight worked in my cerebrovascular research program. However, after that the relative numbers changed quickly.

About six weeks after my return to Houston, I was visited in my office at St. Anthony Center by John Stirling Meyer, who had come to Baylor College of Medicine from Wayne State University in Detroit only a few months earlier as professor and chairman of neurology. I remember our conversation precisely since it was very clear in my mind what machinations had occurred in order to put him in the chair that I had occupied. He began by explaining that we should make every effort to cooperate and that since I knew the community well, I could be of great assistance to him. I responded, "That will be fine, John, but don't expect me to just *coo* while you operate." That ended the discussion without further comment.

It came as no surprise to me that Meyer, who thought he could offer DeBakey consultation about his stroke patients, soon found out, as I had, that this was not what was expected of him. It was not very long before there was serious disagreement between the two of them, and John Meyer was relieved of his responsibilities as chairman in much the same manner as I had been several years earlier. His successor, Stanley Appel, has had the good fortune, and good judgment as well, to be working primarily in an area of neurology totally unrelated to surgery or amenable to surgical intervention.

While at St. Anthony Center, I had an opportunity to devote more time to geriatrics by serving on the Executive Committee there, an activity which I found very rewarding. It was also extremely worthwhile to have this older patient population available for the instruction of medical students and, subsequently, our first group of neurology residents at The University of Texas Medical School.

The research project to which I was devoting a major portion of my time was the Joint Study of Extracranial Arterial Occlusion. This was the same project which had been initiated ten years earlier by the National Heart Institute when I was associated with Mike DeBakey. I found myself shorthanded and in need of professional help but was not quite sure where I was going to find any. One day during the first few months that I was at St. Anthony's Center, I was approached by Dr. Noreen A. Lemak, the wife of Leslie Lemak, a radiologist at St. Joseph Hospital, with whom I had been acquainted for many years. This exceedingly capable woman was serving as a volunteer at the Center. After graduating from Wayne State University Medical School in Detroit, she had been in general practice for a year or two but soon gave up her professional career to raise a family. By 1969 she had decided that she had the time to change course and do something more closely related to medicine, and so she had offered her services. I jumped at the opportunity of having Noreen join me, and once my research program was transferred from the Graduate School of Biomedical Sciences to the Medical School, I arranged for her to have an appointment as a research associate on a half-time basis. She continued to work with me in this capacity for nearly twenty years. During this very fruitful association, we completed the ten publications of the Joint Study of Extracranial Arterial Occlusion and numerous other articles related to two subsequent multicentered controlled clinical trials in which we were both involved.

In the mid-1960s, I had seen many patients with headache and had the opportunity to follow a large number of them over several years. I found that those who took aspirin regularly, many of them in the older age group, appeared to have fewer strokes and heart attacks during the period that they remained in my care than I would have anticipated. Although I did not recognize immediately the significance of this observation, I mentioned it to several of my friends and colleagues. They all ridiculed it.

In June 1969, I received a phone call from a friend, William K. Hass, a neurologist at New York University Medical School, one of those to whom I had made a comment earlier about aspirin. He asked me if I had seen the abstract of a paper presented by Harvey Weiss, a hematologist in New York City, at a recent meeting at Atlantic City. In it the author had mentioned that aspirin appeared to be an excellent inhibitor of platelet aggregation, an important step in the coagulation of blood. This was the stimulus that I needed in order to proceed with a plan to study aspirin as a preventive of ischemic stroke.

I told Bill Hass that I would contact Sol Sherry in Philadelphia, who was at that time chairman of the Committee on Thrombosis of the National Heart Institute. He suggested that Bill and I travel to Bethesda at an early date to make a presentation to the committee in order to ascertain their level of interest in recommending a controlled trial of aspirin in the prevention of stroke (cerebral infarction). The reception we received from the committee was a very enthusiastic one, and we were encouraged to assemble a group of investigators who would be willing to participate in such a venture.

Coincident with this plan, Bill Hass and I organized a small closed meeting by invitation in Houston in the fall of 1969 for the purpose of exploring the possibility of undertaking a clinical trial of aspirin for the prevention of stroke. The proceedings of this meeting were published in a small volume entitled *Aspirin, Platelets and Stroke, Background for a Clinical Trial*.

One of the invited participants at the meeting was the aforementioned Harvey Weiss at Roosevelt Hospital in New York City and a professor on the faculty of Columbia University College of Physicians and Surgeons. During that small conference, Weiss recalled attending a meeting the previous year at which he proposed the study of aspirin as a possible prophylaxis against recurrent myocardial infarction (heart attack). He reported that after the meeting, while sharing a taxi to the airport with several colleagues, one of them mentioned a publication on this subject that he vaguely remembered reading in a regional medical journal about fifteen years earlier.

Upon returning home, Dr. Weiss gave this fragmentary information to the hospital librarian, who within an hour found the article to which his taxi companion had undoubtedly referred. It was written by Lawrence L. Craven of Glendale, California, and published in the *Mississippi Valley Medical Journal* in 1956. This obscure journal, published in Quincy, Illinois, went out of business in 1958.

Dr. Craven had practiced general medicine for over forty years. He reported on his use of aspirin for prophylaxis of coronary and cerebral artery thrombosis during the previous ten years. His rationale for prescribing aspirin was based on his observations that aspirin occasionally caused a mild bleeding tendency. He then argued that since bleeding and thrombosis (clotting) were in a sense on opposite sides of the same coin, perhaps a drug that produced a mild bleeding tendency might also prevent thrombosis. He therefore prescribed two aspirin tablets a day to 8,000 men. His results obtained over a period of seven to ten years were stated in bold type, "Not a single case of detectable coronary or cerebral thrombosis occurred among patients who have faithfully adhered to this regimen."

Unfortunately, in spite of this observation, Dr. Craven conceded that he did not know how or why aspirin worked. He argued, though, that a similar statement could be made about quinine therapy for malaria and electroshock therapy in psychiatric disorders. Craven reiterated his intention of continuing to use aspirin as an antithrombotic agent. However, since his studies lacked proper control, his very astute observation failed to receive the attention it deserved.

After this preliminary meeting in Houston, Bill Hass and I proceeded to prepare an application for a federal grant to support a proposed multicenter controlled trial. This trial, organized in 1971, was designated the Aspirin in Transient Ischemic Attacks Study (AITIA). Funding was approved and the trial began in January 1972. It was requested of the investigators in participating hospitals across the country to use aspirin in patients with a history of one or more episodes of transient paralysis or bouts of transitory blindness in one eye. All patients entering the trial were subjected to arteriography to determine the location and extent of the obstruction in the arteries leading to the brain. Depending on a decision made at the discretion of the patient's doctor, one group would have surgery to reduce the possibility of a major stroke while the other would not. Within each group, patients were randomly allocated to either aspirin or a placebo (inert, innocuous medication). I was assigned the responsibility of organizing and supervising the Central Registry for the trial. Once again I had the invaluable assistance of my co-investigator and associate, Noreen Lemak. This was a very worthwhile exercise, but we had considerable difficulty in recruiting subjects and also in maintaining the long-term financing of the project.

When the time came to prepare an application for continuing support to be presented to the National Institutes of Health review committee, I was in Europe. Noreen had collated the data and sent it to our biostatistician at The University of Texas School of Public Health. He promised to have all of the analyses completed in time for a presentation at Bethesda. What I did not know, and could not accommodate for, was that this young man was found to have a skin lesion on his back which turned out to be a highly malignant melanoma (black mole). He had had to enter the hospital for a biopsy and further diagnostic studies. He was so upset emotionally that he put all of our material aside without any notification to either Noreen or me and left us totally unprepared for our meeting with the committee. Although the members of the review board were sympathetic concerning our dilemma, they did not give our application a priority score high enough for funding. This had a devastating effect on our relations with the principal investigators at several of the collaborating institutions who were dependent on the institute's support for their participation.

I turned to Sterling Drug Incorporated, the firm which was supplying the tablets being used in the trial, and requested that they make up the difference in the continuing support. With supplemental funds from that source, we were able to stagger through the trial. Although it appeared clear that aspirin reduced the probability of stroke and death, the effect was not statistically significant. We had only 178 patients recruited into the trial but there appeared to be a reduction in the broader category of unfavorable outcomes such as death, a major stroke, or the frequency of transient ischemic attacks.

In January 1976, with the approval of the Executive Committee of the study, I presented our data in a preliminary form at a Stroke Conference in Princeton, New Jersey, and was roundly criticized. I was literally called a charlatan and other equally uncomplimentary terms as well. One of the prominent neurologists at the Mayo Clinic led the charge. To make matters worse, the editors of the proceedings of the meeting deleted my report. It was in this way that I learned that my fellow neurologists would prove to be even more skeptical about the efficacy of aspirin than I had suspected.

Following this, matters became progressively worse. I received a phone call from a friend who informed me that the NIH did not believe my report and they wanted to send a site visit team to Houston to examine our data. Mark Dyken, from Indiana University, and Raymond Bauer, of Wayne State University in Detroit, both participating investigators in the trial, came to Houston to help me defend our data before the visitors. The deliberations before this committee continued throughout the morning and into the afternoon. After Dyken and Bauer had left for the airport, members of the committee grilled me about the integrity of our trial. It had been planned for me to present a paper for our study group at the First Annual Stroke Conference of the American Heart Association in Dallas the following month. The NIH site visitors demanded that this presentation be withdrawn and also insisted on sending referees to determine whether the data which had been presented to them were valid. I was absolutely stunned and at the time could not understand the reason for the hostility shown by some members of the committee.

About six weeks later I was leaving to attend the annual meeting of the American Academy of Neurology, which was being held in St. Louis. The stress that I had been under was terrific since I felt keenly the responsibility for maintaining the integrity of the trial which represented the efforts of many people, not just my own. I decided to drive to St. Louis with Bette. The morning after our arrival, I was in the bathroom at the hotel when I started passing blood and then fainted. My friend, Henry Barnett, professor of neurology at the University of Western Ontario and coordinator of a concomitant Canadian stroke study, came to our hotel room and arranged my transfer to a hospital by ambulance. Several days later, we flew home and a friend drove my car back to Houston.

A short time later, two senior neurologists, Fletcher McDowell and Richard Janeway, came to Houston at the request of the NIH to have an in-depth look at our data. They subsequently reported that they could find no fault with the data and recommended that we be permitted to proceed with publication. I spent much of the remainder of 1976 with my colleagues, Noreen Lemak and two biostatisticians, Ralph Frankowski and Robert Hardy, writing up the results of this aspirin study for publication in *STROKE* the following year. This was the first reported clinical trial to demonstrate the efficacy of aspirin as a preventive medication for occlusive vascular disease. The Canadian trial, which had been conducted coincidentally with ours, was completed shortly thereafter and published in 1978.

I was extremely angry, not only for myself but also for my collaborators, that our study had been held up long enough to lose its unquestioned priority. It was clear that had the representatives of the NIH not gone through this unusual exercise, we could have had our report in print much earlier. Never before in my career had I been accused of fabricating data. The reason for the inexplicable hostility became apparent later when I learned that the same federal agency had initiated the Aspirin Myocardial Infarction Study (AMIS) only shortly before I first announced our preliminary findings at Princeton in January. No doubt, if it had become public knowledge that aspirin had already been found to have some impact on death, major stroke, and the frequency of transient ischemic attacks (TIAs), there was grave concern that recruitment of subjects into that large and expensive study would have been affected adversely. It was, in my opinion, appallingly unfair on the part of the government's representatives.

Sterling Drug Incorporated, the company which had supplied the aspirin for our trial, decided in 1979 to submit an application to change the labeling for over-the-counter aspirin. Using the results of our study and those of the Canadian group as a basis for the application, Dr. William Soller, medical director of Glenbrook Laboratories Division of Sterling, sought to have aspirin approved for the prevention of stroke in persons suffering from transient ischemic attacks. The application was submitted to the Food and Drug Administration Advisory Committee on Peripheral and Central Nervous System Drugs in September 1979. The principal investigator for each of the studies which were to be the basis for the petition, namely Barnett and myself, appeared before the committee in support of Sterling's application. Bill Soller came prepared to fight for approval of the application, only to learn that the committee had apparently already decided to approve it. When the testimony was finished, the chairman said to me, "Can you live with what we have just decided?" I replied in the affirmative and that was the end of it.

Although the Canadian data convinced the committee that the approval should be limited to men, the professional indications for aspirin use were expanded to cover prevention of TIA and stroke. This was a landmark decision and a reward for both Barnett and me, as well as for all of those who had given so much time and effort to these trials.

Following completion of this cooperative venture, we became involved in another study comparing aspirin alone with aspirin plus dipyridamole (Persantine), another supposed platelet inhibitor, in the prevention of stroke. This was a joint American-Canadian venture and it, too, lasted nearly five years, ending with a definitive publication in *STROKE* in 1986. In spite of the fact that the data showed conclusively that Persantine contributed nothing to the aspirin effect, the drug continues to be one of the most widely sold worldwide. The power of advertising and promotion clearly outweighs the lack of scientific evidence.

Chapter 13

The University of Texas Medical School at Houston: Early Development

THE BOARD OF THE HERMANN HOSPITAL Estate was anxious to bring another medical school to Houston. Unfortunately, Dr. Lee Crozier, hospital director, was reluctant to do so and declined to participate. He had experienced a similar situation in London, Ontario, when he resigned as director of the Victoria Hospital to come to Houston. In my opinion, he had felt somewhat threatened by the inauguration of the medical school of the University of Western Ontario. Dr. Crozier recommended his associate, Col. Dan G. Kadrovach, recently retired from the army, to the chairman of the Hermann board as his successor. Charles Hooks was the chairman of the board of the Hermann Hospital Estate when they interviewed Dan Kadrovach for the position in 1965.

The board of the Hermann Hospital Estate had several members at that time who were currently or formerly powerful figures in The University of Texas hierarchy, including Walter Sterling, a university regent, Jack Josey, a past regent, and John Holmes, an alumnus of The University of Texas who understood best the economics of hospital management. The other members of the board were John Coffey, a graduate of Rice University, John Dunn, Walter Mischer, Sr., and Corbin Robertson. Coffey participated every day in the operations of the Estate. He was a "wheeler-dealer" and almost inevitably his actions were confirmed at the board meetings. Corbin

Robertson seldom participated in board meetings, whereas Walter Sterling always came.

During this period, Dixon Manly was the full-time director of the Hermann Hospital Estate. Manly died of leukemia in the fall of 1974 and his position was taken over by his assistant, Neil Amsler. At that time Bill Ryan, the garage manager, was given a more exalted status by Amsler. Both of these promotions had serious repercussions later.

Col. Dan Kadrovach had come to Houston in 1966 from Johns Hopkins Hospital in Baltimore, where he had been assistant director since retiring from the army on January 1, 1962. He was responsible for the construction of the Children's Medical Center at Johns Hopkins, which was built to replace the Harriet Lane Pavilion. Following completion of the center, Colonel Kadrovach was made its director, a position which he held until his move to Houston.

Once the Children's Medical Center at Johns Hopkins was completed, Kadrovach began looking for other things to do. The challenge of changing a community hospital to a teaching hospital affiliated with a medical school in Houston was appealing to him. When he arrived in Houston in 1966, the Clinic Building, which had housed the original Hermann Hospital, was being used for black patients only, while the Main Building, later called the Robertson Pavilion, was used for white patients. The staff at that time numbered around 860 physicians, about a third of whom were regular staff members while the majority used the hospital only occasionally as courtesy members. Colonel Kadrovach later recalled that only about 125 of those doctors were enthusiastic about teaching and willing to sacrifice the time to do so. The key players on the medical staff who were interested in bringing a medical school to Hermann Hospital were Louis Dippel (Chief of Staff/Obstetrics and Gynecology), Everett Lewis (Surgery), Frank Parish (Orthopedics), Rodney Rodgers (Medicine), and Richard Ruiz (Ophthalmology).

I met Kadrovach during the year before my departure to Dallas, but I did not really get to know him until my return to the Graduate School of The University of Texas early in 1969. Like myself, he was present at the ceremony in the Jones Library Building in June of that year when Governor Preston Smith signed the appropriation bill which included funds for the new University of Texas Medical School (to be affiliated with Hermann Hospital).

Almost from the time of his arrival in Houston, Kadrovach worked on a master plan for building the medical school and also adding a large private pavilion to the hospital (known later as the Jones Pavilion). It was designed to be contiguous with both the medical school and the Robertson Pavilion. He also started the remodeling of the Clinic Building, put together a Trauma Center at the east end of the Robertson Pavilion, and built the heliport on the roof over the Emergency Room. Further construction included renovation of the Main Building and also construction of the Dunn Chapel and the parking garage. The entire Hermann Hospital complex as it exists today was "planned" by Dan Kadrovach.

The architects for both the Hermann addition and the medical school were with the firm of Max Brooks in Austin, Texas. Kadrovach had been working on the hospital plan prior to the arrival of the dean of the new medical school in 1970 and also on the plan to have the school's building physically attached to Hermann Hospital. R. Lee Clark, president of M. D. Anderson Hospital, Truman Blocker in Galveston, and Grant Taylor at the Graduate School all helped Kadrovach with plans for the new school. Although the Clinic Building, since 1949, had been solely for black patients, Kadrovach proceeded to put black and white obstetrics patients together in a unit in the main building. This move alienated most of the staff physicians. Dr. Louis Dippel, chief of staff, was an exception and he contributed materially to the reorganization, modernization, and affiliation of Hermann Hospital with the new school.

Planning was already well along for the hospital and also for the medical school prior to the arrival of a dean in the summer of 1970. Kadrovach had already written an affiliation agreement with the school by the end of 1968, but this was inevitably to be modified after the dean's arrival. It was clear to Kadrovach that the medical staff at Hermann Hospital wanted medical school appointments but were not prepared to contribute much to teaching. Rodney Rodgers, who had been helpful in persuading the medical staff not to oppose the coming of the medical school, tended to waver a bit between the two camps.

In the fall of 1969, I received a telephone call from John Hickam, a professor of medicine at Indiana University, whose name was prominent on the list of candidates for dean of the new medical school. I had known him since our days at Harvard Medical School, where he graduated one year behind me. He had called to inquire about the job and I urged him to consider coming for a visit. Tragically, before his visit could be arranged, he succumbed suddenly to brain hemorrhage from a ruptured aneurysm while in a Chicago hotel attending a medical meeting. Since I had spoken to him so recently and was looking forward to his coming, I was shocked at the news of his unexpected and untimely death.

In May 1970, Cheves Smythe's appointment as dean of the new University of Texas Medical School at Houston was announced. I was still a professor in the Graduate School. Smythe was coming to Houston from the Association of American Medical Colleges, where he had been on the senior staff for several years. Prior to that, he had been dean at the Medical University of South Carolina in Charleston. When I heard that Smythe had been appointed, and before I met him, I phoned him at his office on his first or second day to welcome him to Houston. He was occupying an office located on the first floor of the Jesse H. Jones Library Building in the Medical Center. During the course of that conversation I inquired whether he had found a house, since I knew that he had come without his family. He said, "Yes sir, in fact, I just signed a contract on a house yesterday." I asked, "Where is it?" He replied, "Out in the Memorial area." I replied, "That's a big area. Just where is the house? I live out there too." He said, "On Stoney Creek." I then inquired further, "What number?" When he gave me the number, I said, "You're going to be my next door neighbor." I thought I heard him drop the phone. That was an interesting first encounter which had many ramifications later, not the least of which was his refusal to appoint me as director of the program in neurology.

Kadrovach believed that when the affiliation with the university was consummated, the allocation of money from the Hermann Estate would increase because of the commitment made to convert from a community hospital to a university teaching institution. When this did not materialize, the new service chiefs recruited by Smythe felt deprived of their expectations because neither the dean nor Kadrovach could deliver what had been promised. Unfortunately, Hermann Hospital, until the 1990s, suffered from the withholding of resources by the Estate.

It was not too long after the arrival of Dean Smythe in 1970 that the staff of Hermann Hospital began to have second thoughts about the affiliation agreement with The University of Texas Medical School at Houston. Most of the service chiefs were of the opinion that they should be professors in the new school and continue to run the day-to-day operation of the services which they had controlled until then. They had had excellent independent residency programs and Hermann Hospital was recognized as one of the largest privately owned teaching hospitals in the United States without government subsidy of its programs. They wanted to keep it that way.

When it became obvious that the dean was not going to waver from his position that the department chairmen at the medical school would be the service chiefs at the hospital, the physicians in private practice requested a meeting with the trustees. This was arranged and held at the home of Corbin Robertson in River Oaks. The trustees of the Hermann Estate, Dean Smythe, the hospital director, Col. Dan Kadrovach, and representatives of the staff were present. The trustees could not understand that the doctors wanted to take care of their own patients and not have them under the control of residents and students selected and assigned by full-time faculty of the medical school. The trustees refused to be pressured and suggested that another meeting of the staff doctors be held with Dean Smythe. At this latter meeting, Cheves spoke in a manner calculated to alienate just about everyone. He was determined to pursue the course he had set and stated that he knew that some of them would leave the staff right away and some would go within the year, while those who saw the advantages of participating in the educational activities of the school would remain. This attitude convinced those present that their future lay elsewhere, and they began to make plans for building their own hospital. Thus began the second exodus of a large number of staff doctors from Hermann Hospital. The first had resulted in the building of the Diagnostic Clinic and Hospital, further south on Fannin Street across from the Medical Center, while the second produced the Park Plaza Hospital on the north side of Hermann Park facing the Medical Center to the south.

The University of Texas Medical School at Houston finally got under way after the appointment of Dean Smythe. My appointment in the new school and transfer to that faculty did not occur, however, until his formal arrival in September 1970. In the meantime, I continued with my research in cerebrovascular disease, which constituted one of the principal academic activities of the medical school during its first few months of existence.

Smythe, I believe, accepted me grudgingly as one of the first two full-time professors on his new faculty roster to begin September 1, 1970. At that time there was no faculty organization or structure. The other member who joined us then was Joe G. Wood, a Texan and a neurobiologist who had received his Ph.D. degree at the University of Texas Medical Branch in Galveston and who had been on the faculty of the University of Texas Medical School at San Antonio. He was appointed professor of anatomy and also associate dean for student affairs. At least the basic and clinical neurosciences got off to a good start. Joe Wood had an office with Smythe on the first floor of the Jesse H. Jones Library Building.

Regrettably, as one of Dean Smythe's faculty who had been on the local scene before he came, I felt that I was immediately suspect, of what I never knew. I am sure that he had heard stories about me, some true and others largely invented. More importantly, however, and perhaps unfortunately as well, there were a lot of folks, including Michael DeBakey, who had suspected that Mickey LeMaistre was bringing me back from Dallas in anticipation of appointing me dean of the new medical school. Such an appointment had never been discussed with me and no such arrangement was ever contemplated. I was careful not to comment to anyone about the matter one way or the other. No doubt, Smythe, too, had heard some of these rumors and they did nothing to enhance my relationship with him. Moreover, he wanted a young faculty and in this regard I did not qualify.

Soon after Joe Wood and I joined the new faculty, the next two chairmen to be appointed were part-time. Gerald Dodd, who was chief of radiology at M. D. Anderson Hospital, became, in addition to his other responsibilities, professor and chairman of radiology at the medical school, and chief of radiology service at Hermann Hospital, and Richard Ruiz, who had an ongoing program in ophthalmology at Hermann Hospital, became clinical professor and chairman of ophthalmology, a position which he still holds although he is primarily in private practice and director of the Hermann Eye Center. Nevertheless, in this capacity he has been able to support and administer an excellent training and research program.

Our first faculty retreat was held at the Flagship Hotel in Galveston, where we gathered with Dean Smythe to discuss the direction in which he thought we ought to proceed with the many aspects of the new school's program. By the time of that meeting, C. R. "Bob" Richardson had been appointed by the system administration in Austin as associate dean for business affairs. Bob Richardson subsequently departed to become president of Sul Ross University in West Texas and later returned to Houston as vice-president for business affairs at Baylor College of Medicine. The next person to be appointed to the faculty late that same year, 1970, was Robert Tuttle, who came to Houston from Bowman Gray School of Medicine, Winston-Salem, North Carolina, as associate dean for academic affairs. I remember Cheves telling me, "We can bring to Houston a whole group to work in endocrinology, population studies, etc." Frankly, I could not envision how this accomplishment, no matter how meritorious from a scientific viewpoint, might be expected to enhance an infant academic program. Nevertheless, with this in mind, he recruited Drs. Emil and Anna Steinberger from Albert Einstein Medical Center in Philadelphia.

Cheves was confronted with the problem of finding classroom space since none had been identified and Hermann Hospital could not accommodate us. As soon as the school started, the first class of fifteen students was enrolled. One-third of these students started their basic science classes in each of the other three medical schools of the university. The plan was to enroll thirty-two students into the next first-year class the following year in Houston, despite the fact that we still did not have a site at which to hold classes and provide laboratory facilities.

During those years, J. Walter Kilpatrick, my insurance adviser and fellow member of the vestry at St. Francis Episcopal Church in Piney Point Village on the west side of Houston, was treasurer of the board of trustees of St. Luke's Episcopal Hospital. St. Luke's at the time was disenchanted about its affiliation with Baylor College of Medicine, which was trying to regroup after its separation from Baylor University in Waco. St. Luke's board of trustees and the hospital administration felt that their interests were low on the priority list of Baylor College of Medicine, which was directing almost 100% of its attention to The Methodist Hospital. I was personally of the opinion that St. Luke's would be receptive to the idea of establishing an affiliation then and there if The University of Texas Medical School so desired. Because of my own need for an office closer to the school, I thought it might be worthwhile for the dean to also explore with their board of trustees the possibility of occupying several of the upper floors of the recently built tower of St. Luke's Hospital, which still were unfinished and unoccupied. Walter Kilpatrick conveyed to several members of the board of trustees of St. Luke's my idea of converting some of the space into classrooms, offices, and laboratories. The trustees expressed considerable interest in entering into negotiations with the dean, but Cheves dismissed the entire idea as unworkable.

The University of Texas Medical School could easily have been an active participant at St. Luke's Episcopal Hospital in 1971 instead of at the Center Pavilion, which turned out to be a much less adequate and less desirable facility (that building was demolished in 1990). My neurology group was fortunate because while the medical school was struggling at the Center Pavilion, we were at St. Anthony Center enjoying what was eminently suitable space for our needs. Our offices were in the basement at one end of the building and the examining rooms were halfway down the hall. It was disadvantageous only because we were at a greater distance from Hermann Hospital, which was the medical school's primary affiliate, than our other clinical colleagues. Nevertheless, we developed a neurology service, established a residency program, and continued working there until 1976, when construction of the new medical school was completed.

The Hermann board set aside $1 million a year for charity purposes in order to meet some of the requirements. Kadrovach knew the Estate was making about $10 million a year and felt that a $3 million reservation for expansion was not going to help him very much. He wanted $7 million but the board of trustees refused to discuss his plan. Those trustees were on the boards of several large banks in town, which paid cash for real estate in order to get the most favored price. When the board refused to meet Kadrovach's request, which he felt was necessary to meet the needs of the new hospital-medical school affiliation, a big commotion ensued and Kadrovach was asked to resign. He left Houston on August 1, 1975. It was largely through his efforts that the Hermann Hospital-medical school relationship was developed and that Hermann Hospital grew from a small community facility to an academically oriented institution. During the ensuing years, his contribution to the hospital and his almost ten years of painstaking effort toward the establishment of The University of Texas Medical School have been overlooked. The dedication of Cheves Smythe in pursuit of this goal has also been largely forgotten.

The charity support plan that had been worked out by Kadrovach and Smythe was washed out. Pressure on the board to do more was not received with any enthusiasm, and unless the Estate was prepared to do more the hospital was destined to be in constant financial straits.

Another issue which created a problem for Kadrovach and Smythe was the desire of Richard Ruiz to have Hermann Hospital build an Eye Center in the new building which was being constructed. John Coffey was behind Ruiz in this endeavor, but Kadrovach objected to providing space for what he believed amounted to a private clinic. Consequently, Ruiz became very confrontational and complained that Kadrovach's management of the hospital was poor and that, even though construction was occurring at every entrance, the hospital was dirty. Ruiz had the ear of Coffey and Jack Josey and eventually this contributed to the decision by the trustees to persuade Kadrovach to leave.

An interesting figure involved in Hermann Hospital's affairs at that time was an attorney, Wayne Gillies, who was a self-appointed volunteer. Gillies had had a very colorful career. For several years, during the Vietnam conflict, he had been in Southeast Asia doing civilian undercover work, the exact nature of which was never revealed to me. He claimed that he had a number of important clients who would put the Hermann Estate into their wills. He was given an office in the Hermann Professional Building, rent free, by the board and made his role one of encouraging his clients to give money to the Estate. He proclaimed great success but, as far as I am aware, very little materialized. This was confirmed to me much later in a discussion with Dan Kadrovach.

Unfortunately, Gillies was a heavy drinker and this frequently got him into difficulty. One night he drove his sports car off Memorial Drive into a culvert and was killed in the accident. Dr. James "Red" Duke, who had temporarily become his housemate, was away on a hunting trip when he got word of Wayne's demise. He was informed by the deceased's legal representative that the house was sealed and that in order to get in and retrieve his personal effects he would have to be accompanied by the representative. What Wayne kept there that did not warrant public scrutiny has remained a mystery, but it was suspected by some of us who knew him that it had something to do with his work in Vietnam.

The Medical Board, as designed in the affiliation agreement by Smythe and Kadrovach, included the chairmen (referred to by Smythe as program directors) of psychiatry, medicine, surgery, pediatrics, obstetrics and gynecology, and three members of the voluntary staff. The latter three almost always had a different perspective and a separate agenda. This made the organization of the hospital staff somewhat cumbersome and difficult.

Beginning in 1968 and continuing until 1971, one year after the arrival of Cheves Smythe, Lee Clark had sponsored what he referred to as U.T. Houston luncheons. He felt that it was important to pull together all of the university units in Houston and used this venue as a means to accomplish that goal. The meetings were attended by Robert Moreton, an assistant to Clark; John Victor Olson, dean of the Dental Branch; Reuel Stallones, dean of the School of Public Health; Alton Hodges, dean of the School of Allied Health Sciences; Grant Taylor, dean of the Graduate School of Biomedical Sciences; Dan Kadrovach, director of Hermann Hospital; Jack Bangs, director of the Houston Speech and Hearing Institute; and Janet Aune, dean of Texas Woman's University-Houston Center. To no one's surprise, the staff at Hermann Hospital were very suspicious of Lee Clark's intentions, and the members of the Hermann Estate board were also wary.

The Hermann board always had a chairman and a president. The chairman, Charlie Hooks, died in 1968. Walter Sterling, who had been president, moved up to be chairman and Corbin Robertson became president. The board at that time consisted of Sterling, Robertson, Josey, Coffey, Holmes, Dunn, and Mischer. The latter was a very astute solid citizen, who came infrequently to the board meetings, although, according to Kadrovach, he always contributed when he was there. Dixon Manly, director of the Hermann Hospital Estate, was more involved with the Estate than the hospital. Neil Amsler, his assistant, was in contact almost exclusively with John Coffey, who came every day to monitor the activities of the Estate, as well as the hospital.

Over the next couple of years, my relationship with Cheves Smythe was cool, to say the least, and he absolutely refused to appoint me as the head of his program in neurology. He had decided that he was not going to have departments but would install entities called "programs" instead. This arrangement would, in his view, I suspected, prevent the directors of programs from becoming powerful department chairmen.

It soon became obvious to all concerned that I was an experienced faculty person who had already developed a successful neurology program in another medical school and the one doing the majority of the teaching in that discipline. When Smythe approached the directors of other programs and asked whom they might suggest to head neurology, they unanimously recommended my appointment. They agreed that I should be appointed since I was already on the scene, had a national reputation in the field, and, lastly, that I was well known in Houston. Smythe said that he was not prepared to do that. He then proceeded to circulate what amounted to a subtly worded character assassination letter to many prominent neurologists around the nation, soliciting names of candidates. Very promptly, I heard from some of my out-of-town friends who wondered what was going on behind my back. Not too surprisingly, several of them sent me copies of the letter which they had received. I considered this activity on the part of the dean to be both insulting and demeaning.

The word about all this maneuvering reached Dr. "Mickey" LeMaistre in Austin. He had been the person primarily responsible for my coming back to Houston from Dallas. By then he had become chancellor of The University of Texas System. He informed Dean Smythe that he would like to come down from Austin to discuss the matter and asked him to set up a meeting with the clinical chairmen. After they had reviewed the situation at a gathering in Smythe's office, LeMaistre asked each one in turn whom he would nominate and what should be done. Unanimously, they said that I should be appointed. Then LeMaistre asked Smythe, who replied once more that he was not yet prepared to take that step and wanted to think about it a little more. Of course, the longer he thought about it, the deeper he was digging his own grave. This was just symptomatic of how Cheves Smythe interacted with his senior faculty. Consequently, there was a lot of grumbling and the next thing I knew, we were meeting as a group at the Warwick Hotel at noon every Saturday to discuss our mutual concerns about the progress, or lack of same, of the medical school and its programs. Pretty soon the various clinical chiefs started to compare notes and found out that a number of them had been promised a little piece of the territory of one or more of the others, and it was clear that this would result in a lot of squabbling and in-fighting. This technique appeared to us to be Dean Smythe's preferred way of doing business. I am still of the opinion that he found it very difficult to accept me because I had been in the community since 1949, knew virtually everyone in the medical fraternity and, in addition, a lot of important people downtown whom he did not know and might never meet.

The foregoing was best illustrated by an amusing encounter with Cheves not too long after he had arrived at Houston. This occurred at a reception at the River Oaks Country Club that had been arranged by Howard Boyd, who at that time was the chairman of the board of El Paso Natural Gas Company. He was a friend of another gentleman who was also a close friend of mine, John R. Hubbard, then president of the University of Southern California (USC). Jack Hubbard, a graduate of The University of Texas at Austin, was also serving on the El Paso board. This reception was held in his honor, presumably to assist him in fundraising for USC in the Houston area.

I went to the River Oaks Country Club by myself and, when I arrived, I met Mrs. Gus Wortham, whom I had come to know well when we were both members of the board of trustees of the Houston Speech and Hearing Center. On that occasion she was in a wheelchair because of some difficulty she was experiencing with her legs. Mr. Wortham, chairman of the board of the American General Insurance Company, had not yet arrived, so I offered to shepherd her around at the party and she gracefully accepted. There was a receiving line at the door and Jack Hubbard had said to me as I went by, "When this is all finished, come on back. I would appreciate a chance to visit with you." There were in attendance a number of important guests whom I knew, including Leland Anderson, president of the Texas Medical Center, Presley Werlein, a fraternity brother of Jack Hubbard and my personal attorney (later a district judge in Houston), and others. When the receiving line broke up, I went back to a location near the entrance to the room and started speaking with Hubbard.

While we were standing there, Cheves Smythe came in wearing a string tie and tennis shoes. As he came up to me, he said, "Fields, what are you doing here?" I was tired of hearing from him remarks such as this.

However, I replied, "I would like for you to meet the honoree for this occasion, an old friend of mine, Jack Hubbard, president of the University of Southern California." Then I said, "Cheves, there are a lot of other people present whom you should get to know and to whom I would be pleased to introduce you." He replied, "No, no, I'll take care of myself," and with that he went off to the refreshment table and that was the last I saw of him. Hubbard asked me, "Who was that?" I replied, "That's the dean of our new University of Texas Medical School." He then went on to say, "He certainly is a strange one and not very cordial." Needless to say, my relationship with Cheves was never exactly smooth.

Shortly after Cheves Smythe arrived, I had occasion to talk by telephone with Juan Franco Ponce, a longtime friend living in Lima, Peru. I had known Franco, a neurosurgeon, for a number of years and had visited him in Lima on several occasions. He told me that because of the political situation in Peru, where a left-wing military government had just come to power, he would like very much to emigrate and wondered if it would be possible for him to come to Texas and take the State Board examination. Since I knew him and was aware of his ability, I thought it might be reasonable to employ him on a part-time basis as a research associate to assist me with work we were doing in our large stroke grant. He could easily do this while devoting the remainder of his time to studying for the exam. With that in mind, and not even considering him for a faculty position, I called Smythe on the telephone and said that I had a neurosurgeon whom I wanted to bring to Houston to work with me on a part-time basis and, as a courtesy, wished to inform him before making a formal offer to Juan Franco. Cheves' response was, "Now look here, Fields, I am not having any banana boaters on my faculty." I was incensed because I had known Franco for a number of years and he was no "banana boater." He was, first and foremost, a member of a well-respected family in Peru and was also a competent neurosurgeon who had trained in the United States. (In a subsequent Peruvian government under President Francisco Belaunde Terry, a graduate of The University of Texas, Juan Franco Ponce served as minister of health.) After that remark by Smythe, it would have been impossible for me to recruit the man, even if he still wanted to come.

However, before I could hang up the phone, Smythe said to me, "Fields, I need to explain something to you. If you are going to be on *my* faculty, there is a course in required reading." I asked him to please enlighten me. Whereupon he told me that for starters in this course there were three books; namely, *The Prince* by Machiavelli, Goethe's *Faust*, and any William Faulkner novel of recent vintage that I would care to choose. I was outraged and slammed down the phone. My attitude toward Cheves was pretty much cast in stone after that conversation, and I knew that it was going to be extremely difficult from then on for me to function in a medical school where a man with this attitude was dean.

Difficulties were also encountered in obtaining adequate time for a student clerkship in neurology, largely because of barriers put up by Smythe. Eventually the clinical clerkship was put into the fourth year, making it almost impossible to recruit house staff to our residency training program from among our own medical students. Consequently, the selection by the senior class of residency positions for which to apply began in the fall of the final year before more than a handful of students had had virtually any contact with neurology patients or neurology staff physicians. This was then, and still is, a serious impediment to recruiting residents from among our own students, with the possible exception of the few who might choose to have additional elective time in neurology in the third academic year. As I stated earlier, I had always taken great pride in the number of students who rotated through neurology at Baylor and then chose to enter postgraduate training in that discipline. The allocation of our teaching time to the final year seriously inhibited the new department from having equal access to students.

Early recruits to the medical school as program directors, in addition to those already mentioned, included John DeMoss (Biochemistry), Stanley Dudrick (Surgery), Louis Faillace (Psychiatry), Berel Held (Obstetrics and Gynecology), R. Rodney Howell (Pediatrics), Eugene Jacobson (Physiology), and Alan Robison (Pharmacology). That was the original group. Walter Kirkendall, chairman of internal medicine, came on board a little later than the rest of us. There have been a lot of changes over the last few years, and from the original group of chairmen only Jack DeMoss remained in place at the end of 1990 and he retired soon after that.

Gage Van Horn, a 1963 graduate of Baylor College of Medicine, whom I had known as a medical student when he took a summer fellowship in neurology, was the first full-time faculty person to join me at The University of Texas Medical School. He had gone to Chicago for his postgraduate training at St. Luke's Presbyterian Medical Center, and following that to the University of Pittsburgh as an assistant professor of neurology. Gage was eager to return to Texas and I was delighted to have him. He had visited in the summer of 1973, at which time I spoke to him about returning. During that visit he met Dean Smythe, who wrote me a letter afterwards to tell me that he was not very impressed with my choice. I suspect that this assessment had little or nothing to do with Gage's credentials and that Cheves would not have been enthusiastic about any recommendation that I made. Before Gage's departure, Bette and I had dinner with him at the airport and I offered him an appointment.

At the time that Gage arrived in January 1974, Harry Lipscomb, an internist and 1952 graduate of Baylor College of Medicine, was medical director at St. Anthony's Center. I served with him on the Executive Committee of the staff at the Center along with two internists, Dominic Moore-Jones and Philip Bellegie; a radiologist, Charles Yates, Jr.; a general surgeon, John Bardwil; and a geriatric psychiatrist, Charles Gaitz. By serving in this capacity, I felt that we could in some small measure repay the Sisters of Charity for making it possible for the Department of Neurology to have a base of operations until the new building for the medical school was completed in the Medical Center. Gage Van Horn became chairman of the Utilization Review Committee, which had oversight of bed allocation at St. Anthony's Center in accordance with governmental regulations. The gracious Sisters of the Sacred Heart of the Incarnate Word shall have my everlasting gratitude for their support and assistance in helping us to get our program launched in a satisfactory manner.

It seemed logical to me that the next person to be recruited to the neurology department faculty should be a pediatric neurologist. A name suggested by several people was that of Ian John Butler, an Australian who was just finishing a fellowship at Johns Hopkins Medical School. In the spring of that year, while I was attending the annual meeting of the American Academy of Neurology in Washington, I arranged to go to Baltimore to meet with Ian at my Aunt Ada's residence. I was delighted to make his acquaintance and felt that he would be a real asset. He decided to accept my invitation to visit Houston with his wife, Patricia, a pediatrician. Rodney Howell, chairman of pediatrics and a Johns Hopkins alumnus, was very enthusiastic about my bringing Ian to the medical school and offered him a joint appointment in his department.

While in Houston, Ian met with Dean Smythe and he described this encounter to me later. Cheves, wearing sneakers, was seated on a chaise lounge in his office. He asked Ian why he would want to leave an established institution and come to a new school. After this inquiry he took him over to a cabinet in the office and pointed to some black shark teeth and commented, "The sharks out there will get you." After his return to Baltimore, Ian wrote to me saying that he would not come as long as Smythe was dean. This put recruitment of a pediatric neurologist on hold for a while.

It was not until after Cheves' forced resignation that I reopened negotiations with Ian. The only possible deterrent to his coming was the need to find his wife an appointment in the Department of Pediatrics. She, however, solved the problem by accepting an appointment as a resident in the Department of Psychiatry.

Ian joined the department in March 1976 and for a short while officed with Gage and me at St. Anthony's Center. It soon became evident, though, that the pediatric patients would have to be seen elsewhere, so he transferred to an office in the John H. Freeman Building of The University of Texas Medical School in the Medical Center. He shared a laboratory at the Center Pavilion with Dr. Sam Enna of the Department of Anatomy and Neurobiology until we all moved to the seventh floor of the new medical school when it was completed. It was the last floor to be finished. Although the Sisters at St. Anthony's Center had provided us with a "refuge" for more than seven years, we were delighted to be allocated office and laboratories in the medical school building. In retrospect, I believe that we were fortunate to have been somewhat insulated in our remote location from much of the turmoil surrounding the first few years of the new school.

Each chairman had been allocated funds to use for designing and furnishing an office suite in the medical school building. I could not have been more pleased than when Raymond Brochstein, whose father had furnished my library at Baylor fifteen years earlier, accepted the contract to complete my new office.

It was only after our move into the new building that I was able to recruit a fourth faculty member, Howard Marmell, who came to us from New York University. Howard, in addition to being board certified in neurology, had completed formal training in physical medicine and rehabilitation, which added a new dimension to our program.

One day in late May 1972, I had gone to one of the upper floors at St. Anthony's Center to visit a patient. As I was about to get on the elevator to return to my office, the acting director of nurses, Ms. Robbie Snow, got off the elevator with a lady wearing a long white lab coat. Ms. Snow stopped me and said, "Dr. Fields, I would like to introduce you to our new director of nursing and assistant administrator, Ms. Foulks." I noted on the lapel of the woman's lab coat a pin that looked very familiar to me. I identified it almost immediately as the distinctive pin worn by graduates of the nursing school at the Royal Victoria Hospital in Montreal where I had had my residency training in 1940-41. When I asked her if that was a "Vic" pin, she answered in the affirmative and wanted to know how I recognized it. I replied, "I'm an alumnus too but probably way before your time." She looked again and said, "You want to bet?" Then it dawned on me who she was. I asked, "Weren't you Alma Sicard?" She replied that she was one and the same and wanted to know how I knew. I said, "You may remember me because you dated Harold Eggers, who was my good friend and fellow resident at the 'Vic.' He was my best man when I married in 1941." No doubt both of us had changed more than a little bit in thirty years.

Late in the summer of 1972, Bette and I separated and I moved out of the house, a step I had been reluctant to take until both of our daughters, Susan and Anne, had graduated from high school. Shortly thereafter, I invited Alma out for dinner and we began dating. We continued to see each other occasionally during the following year and a half. After my divorce in October 1974, Alma and I were married at her home by Reverend Frank Balch, a minister of the Church of Christ and Protestant chaplain at St. Anthony's Center, a Roman Catholic institution. The others in attendance were my daughter, Susan, and her husband, Richard Hendricks, Alma's son and daughter-in-law, Jay and Cathy Foulks, and some friends, Dr. Bernard Flanz and his wife, Ruth. Since Alma is a Presbyterian and I am an Episcopalian, it was a very ecumenical affair. Almost immediately afterwards, we departed for a honeymoon in South America.

On that trip we went first to Rio de Janeiro, then to São Paulo. As a special treat we elected to fly to Iguaçu Falls on the Parana River, which borders Brazil, Argentina, and Paraguay. That was an absolutely unbelievable experience. When we arrived by jet plane at the airport, seven miles away, we could already hear the roar of the falls. We stayed in the Cataratas Hotel on the Brazilian side. In the afternoon of our first day there, we walked along a path beside the river to a platform below and to one side of the main falls. We stood there transfixed, looking up at this gigantic body of muddy water flowing from the Brazilian and Paraguayan jungle. Below the falls, large birds were diving into the rapids to retrieve fish which had been washed over and stunned when they struck the bottom. In the trees and bushes around us there were literally clouds of multicolored tropical butterflies. We were astounded by the noise around us, the magnitude of the flow of water, and the lush foliage of the tropical jungle. It was almost like a religious experience, and it made us feel so insignificant in nature's scheme of things.

The next morning, much to my surprise, Alma agreed to a trip below and above the falls in a helicopter with a Brazilian ex-navy pilot. We were too busy taking pictures to concern ourselves with the hazards of the flight. The photos I took were really spectacular.

We then flew to Buenos Aires, where we had hoped to spend a few days. However, after learning that a bomb had been exploded in the lobby of the Sheraton Hotel there as an anti-American symbolic gesture, Alma persuaded me to change the itinerary and go directly to Uruguay, where we spent the remainder of our trip in Montevideo and at the seashore in Punta del Este.

When we returned from our trip, we visited frequently with the director of Hermann Hospital, Dan Kadrovach, and his new wife, Nancy, with whom we were kindred spirits. At Christmas time that year, they gave a party and were serving drinks out of their kitchen. Alma and I were there getting drinks when Cheves Smythe and his wife, Polly, arrived. I had been their next door neighbor until I moved out of that house in late 1973. Right away Cheves said, "Bill, I want to meet your new bride." I introduced him to Alma and then turned to speak to someone else. Their conversation was later reported to me by a third party. Smythe, in his usual manner, started probing as to who she was, where she was from, what was her family background. Having heard a great deal about him, she had little patience with the interrogation. She finally said, "You know, Cheves, you really need to be better informed about me. I was a hooker in New Orleans and came to Houston in order to marry a university professor." He turned on his heel and quickly walked away.

Historically, The University of Texas Medical School at Houston had no preconceived form and was a sort of nebulous concept until Cheves Smythe was recruited to organize and develop it. One must give him a tremendous amount of credit for his accomplishments. Most assuredly, he was the right man for the job at that point in the school's history. In my opinion, he would have been remembered as a great figure in the history of the Medical Center if he had stepped down after the initial phase of the school's development was completed.

By that time The University of Texas Health Science Center had been formalized and the acting president, John Victor Olson, dean of the Dental Branch, had returned to that school and the first full-time president, Charles A. Berry, formerly the director of Medical Programs at the National Aeronautics and Space Administration (NASA), was appointed. The festering problems at the medical school soon came to Dr. Berry's attention, and he decided to arrange a meeting with the clinical chiefs. We all met with him one evening to discuss our concerns. Everybody present agreed that Cheves Smythe had done a splendid job of getting the new school launched. However, all were also of the opinion that his ability to bring the institution to maturity left much to be desired. Shortly thereafter, Berry prepared two letters for presentation to Smythe, one of which was a letter of resignation, and the other a letter stating that he was fired.

A meeting of senior faculty members was convened in the president's office on the eighth floor of the Fannin Bank Building, where Cheves was confronted with President Berry's ultimatum in the presence of his senior faculty. He signed the resignation letter. At that particular moment, I was in St. Luke's Episcopal Hospital having *elective* surgery. (I emphasize *elective* since I was very pleased to be somewhere other than at the unpleasant meeting.) I considered this scenario to be a very clumsy and demeaning way in which to remove a man who had contributed so much to the medical school's early development.

Chapter 14

The University of Texas Medical School at Houston: Toward Maturity

FOLLOWING CHEVES SMYTHE'S FORCED resignation, Robert Tuttle, who had been associate dean for academic affairs, was appointed dean. Soon thereafter, and adding to the turmoil, Charles Berry was asked to resign. That also followed a very interesting series of events.

The development officer in Dr. Berry's administration was Jon H. Fleming, the son of Durward Fleming, a longtime friend of mine and formerly senior minister of St. Luke's Methodist Church in Houston and then president of Southwestern University in Georgetown, Texas. The full-time legal counsel for the Health Science Center was a young black man named William Lyons, whose appointment had been arranged by Frank Irwin, chairman of The University of Texas Board of Regents. On several occasions, these two gentlemen, Lyons and Fleming, whom I had come to know quite well, informed me that President Berry, for reasons best known only to him, would have hour-long meetings, trying to decide how they were going to get rid of that so-and-so Fields. It seemed to both of them that this was not a very profitable exercise. However, considerable time was devoted to this subject, and for what reason, I do not know to this day. Those in attendance at these meetings in Berry's office were James Landry, assistant to the president; Charles Franklin, vice-president for business affairs; Lysle Peterson, vice-president for external affairs; Edward McLaughlin, vice-president for programs, who had come with Berry from NASA; Milton DeLucchi, director of Sponsored Research; Fleming and Lyons.

One day, quite by chance, I was coming out of the Fannin Bank, where I had done my banking business for many years, and met a young black man named Ray, who was the driver for Dr. Berry and ran errands for him. He was a pleasant fellow and I had come to know him well. On this occasion I encountered him at the entrance to the bank and asked, "Ray, where are you off to?" He replied, "Oh, I'm going down to NASA for Dr. Berry to get him some recording tape." I asked him why he couldn't get the tape in the Village or down on Main Street somewhere. He said, "No, this is very special recording tape that Dr. Berry uses for the machine that is in his briefcase." This information was rather enlightening. I began to notice that at meetings Berry always set his briefcase down beside him. I also realized that Berry was wearing something in his lapel that I assumed to be a remote microphone. With this very sophisticated equipment, obtained from NASA, he was apparently recording all the conversations in his office and at meetings, even the remote ones from the corner of the room, on the tape concealed in his briefcase. Then I learned from Bill Lyons that he was taking these tapes home at night and reviewing them. I thought that was rather paranoid, to say the least.

Berry, who had been with NASA as the coordinator of their medical program and worked closely with the astronauts from the standpoint of their medical concerns, had virtually no academic credentials and most of us in the Health Science Center were astounded that he had ever been appointed president in the first place. He had done little of note in the medical field since he had served an internship after medical school. This very quickly became apparent to those of us who had been in academic medicine for any length of time. Several years later, Scott Carpenter, who was one of the seven original astronauts, said to me, "Chuck Berry is the only man that I have ever encountered in my life who can anticipate the click of a camera from fifty feet." Berry was always available to have his picture taken with every important visitor.

The final straw between Berry and me was broken on the occasion of the launching of the *Apollo-Soyuz* joint mission with the Soviets. I received a call from Christopher Craft, director of operations at the Johnson Space Center at Clear Lake. His secretary, a very nice young lady, had been a patient of mine. Chris asked me if Alma and I would like to go to Florida with a group of guests of Rockwell International, one of their prime contractors, to watch the launch. I thought that would be a unique experience for both of us and quickly accepted his invitation. It turned out that the group invited by Dr. Craft included the former mayor of Houston, Louie Welch; Don Hudson, chief executive officer of the Houston Light & Power Company; Alfred Neuman, chancellor of the University of Houston at Clear Lake; Norman Hackerman, president of Rice University; and a number of other well-known persons from the Houston community and their spouses.

The first evening we were all invited to travel from Orlando by Greyhound Bus to Coco Beach for a special reception at the Holiday Inn. The bus parked alongside the hotel next to a high hedge, and we went into the pool area through a break in the hedge. The first people that Alma and I encountered as we entered the grounds were Chuck Berry and his wife. He took one look at me and said, "What in the hell are you doing here?" I replied, "I've been invited to come just as you have." At that moment someone grabbed my arm, spun me around, and said, "Good Lord, Bill, how are you? It is so nice to see you here." The speaker was none other than Senator John Glenn, the former astronaut. You should have seen Chuck Berry's face, he was so shaken. He asked John, "How do you know this man?" John replied, "He's been a friend of mine for a long time. He's the one that took care of me when I struck my head and had a medical problem during my first political campaign in Ohio."

That incident certainly did not serve to improve my relationship with Berry. The next day we went out to the viewing area near the launch site and sat in the bleachers along with the military observers. Being that close to the launch of a Saturn rocket was a once-in-a-lifetime experience that really could not be fully appreciated when viewed on a television screen at home.

When we returned to Houston, I called Chris Craft to thank him. He immediately said, "By the way, Bill, you and your wife ought to come down this afternoon. The administrator of NASA, Dr. Gilruth, will be here and we are going to have a closed circuit interview with the people up in space." We drove down to Mission Control at Johnson Space Center and, much to our surprise, Alma and I were the only others present besides Craft and Gilruth, who had come down from Washington. On a big TV screen on the wall in the front of the control room we watched an interview with the Soviets and Americans in the vehicles docked in space, which was also being communicated to and from Moscow by satellite. It was really an exciting and exceptional experience.

My participation in all of these events relating to NASA stemmed not from my professional association with Chuck Berry, which was incidental, but by virtue of the fact that I had been asked professionally and personally to do certain chores for individuals within the NASA family. Unfortunately, to his detriment, Berry was a fellow who always had to be in the limelight, and he did not want someone else casting what he perceived to be a shadow on him.

After Berry's resignation as president of The University of Texas Health Science Center at Houston, the central administration in Austin appointed Truman Blocker, Jr., as interim president in Houston. Truman had recently retired from his responsibilities as president of The University of Texas Medical Branch at Galveston. Rather than move into the space at the Fannin Bank Building previously occupied by Berry, Blocker elected to be closer to the medical school and had a suite of offices renovated on the first floor of the John H. Freeman Building. From my point of view, this was a very fortuitous decision since Truman soon placed upon me a considerable amount of responsibility. He continued to maintain his home in Galveston largely because his wife, Dr. Virginia Blocker, had her medical practice there and also because he planned to return after a limited time in Houston. Truman found living quarters in the Shamrock Hilton Hotel so that he could be close to the Medical Center. He would come to Houston at noon on Monday and return to Galveston in the afternoon on Friday. Whenever both he and I were in town, he expected me to appear in his office at 6:30 in the morning, after which we would have a brief discussion over coffee regarding the affairs of the past few days and the duties which he wanted to assign me during the next week or so. At about 7:15 I would leave and he would then work on his daily crossword puzzle.

It was a great pleasure to work with this fine gentleman, who had had such a wealth of administrative experience. I found his open style very refreshing and was pleased that he took me into his confidence. The nearly two years during which he served as acting president were among the most pleasant of my entire career. Unfortunately, he was prevented by the administration in Austin from implementing many of his ideas. This attitude, in my opinion, was a serious impediment to progress within the institution.

Knowing of my interest and concern regarding medico-legal matters, Truman Blocker had requested that Dean Robert Tuttle appoint me as chairman of a Professional Liability Committee made up of members of the clinical faculty. The establishment of this committee became a necessity in view of the burgeoning number of malpractice suits being filed in the Houston community. The committee was charged with reviewing cases in which the conduct of clinical practice had been questioned in petitions filed in Harris County, Texas, by plaintiffs' attorneys. Although many of these petitions were frivolous, some were not and we assumed the responsibility for investigating these matters with the defendant physician and often with the university attorneys as well. This was an assignment which was interesting, but which required a great deal of tact and understanding. It was not designed to always win friends, but it did influence some people and altered the behavior of others. Some of the attorneys in Austin in the Office of General Counsel of the university acted at first as though we were meddling in an arena which was strictly theirs. However, most of them eventually were persuaded that we could contribute to the adjudication of these issues in a helpful manner. Over the years, I have been interested in legal process and have continued to the present time to serve as a reviewer and, on occasion, as an expert witness for both plaintiff and defense attorneys. Looking at these matters from both sides has provided me with a reputation for an honest and straightforward appraisal of each situation. This has enabled me to develop some expertise as a consultant and as a credible witness in court proceedings.

In the fall of 1978, Margery Shaw, professor of genetics in The University of Texas Graduate School of Biomedical Sciences, who was an attorney as well as a physician, enlisted my help in making a proposal to President Blocker regarding the establishment of a health-law institute. Truman was enthusiastic about setting up such an entity between the University of Houston Central Campus and the Health Science Center. He appointed an organizing committee consisting of Dr. Shaw, William Lyons, an attorney from his office, and me to meet with representatives of the University of Houston, namely, George Hardy, dean of the Bates College of Law, Professor Leonard Riskin, and Dr. Andrew Rudnick, vice-president of the university. A plan was devised for what came to be known as the

Institute for Interprofessional Study of Health Law. This proposal was approved in October 1978 by the boards of regents of the two universities. The press release which followed stated that the Institute would "engage in teaching, research, and services relating to health laws and policy and would try to foster understanding between lawyers, doctors and laymen in areas of mutual concern and interest." The organizing committee subsequently became an executive committee.

Toward the end of Truman Blocker's tenure as acting president of The University of Texas Health Science Center at Houston, I became involved in an interesting incident. A full professor at the Speech and Hearing Institute, which was administered through the Graduate School of Biomedical Sciences, was found to be working a second job at the Veterans Administration Hospital. She had been told to give up this job if she wanted to retain her full-time appointment at The University of Texas. However, she continued with the outside employment in spite of the admonition from the president. This forced Blocker's hand, and he summarily dismissed her from her post in spite of her tenured appointment. She threatened to sue the university and Dr. Blocker for improperly terminating her appointment. This required that he convene a tribunal to hear her case, and he requested that I serve as chairman. Included were three other faculty members, one of whom, the aforementioned Margery Shaw, was an attorney as well as an M.D. and Ph.D.

When the tribunal was convened, the dismissed faculty member enlisted Larry Watts, a well-known Houston civil rights attorney, to serve as her personal counsel. The university sent a representative from the Office of General Counsel in Austin. As chairman of the tribunal, I insisted that the proceedings be carried out in a quasi-legal fashion and that there be strict adherence to the rules of procedure. This seemed to cause no problem for the outside attorney representing the faculty member, but the attorney for the university repeatedly interrupted and tried to take over. I refused to allow him to do so. Each of these gentlemen evidently wanted to prolong the process, hoping to be able to postpone the decision until another day. I made certain that this did not happen and insisted that everyone present stay until the members of the tribunal were ready to adjourn the hearing. We remained until about 2:00 in the morning, at which time everybody had had his or her say and I adjourned the session. The decision of the panel was to recommend support of

President Blocker's dismissal of the tenured faculty member. A transcript of the proceedings was forwarded to The University of Texas Board of Regents in Austin. Relief for the plaintiff was subsequently denied by the federal court.

About six months later, when I was in Fort Worth attending a convocation at Texas Wesleyan College, where my young friend Jon Fleming was being inducted as president, I was introduced to Tom Law, then a member of the Board of Regents of The University of Texas. He informed me that as the only member of the board with legal training, he had been asked to review the transcript of the aforementioned proceedings. I was pleasantly surprised when he complimented me for the orderly manner in which the hearing had been conducted by someone without a legal background.

In October 1978, I had been asked to see in consultation Vincente Recto, president of Merchants Development Corporation, a quasi-governmental Philippine company operating during the presidency of Ferdinand Marcos. Recto, who was only fifty-seven years old at that time, had already had one episode four years previously in which he apparently had suffered a cerebral transient ischemic attack (minor stroke). At the time of his first visit to my office, he had recovered remarkably well and appeared to have virtually no neurologic deficit. During the ensuing year, I corresponded with his neurologist in Manila, who wrote that the patient was doing well. A second similar episode had occurred in August 1979, at which time his blood pressure was noted to be elevated. He returned to see me before going to New York on business.

One morning in early September 1979, I was attending a meeting with some of my senior colleagues in the office of the recently appointed president of The University of Texas Health Science Center, Dr. Roger Bulger, when the latter's administrative assistant entered and told me I had a long distance call from the president. Everyone seemed surprised since we were in the president's office. I went to the telephone in the corner of the room and, upon hearing the voice at the other end of the line, said, "Yes, Mr. President, what can I do for you?" The caller had identified himself as President Ferdinand Marcos, calling from Manila. He wanted to inform me that his good friend and associate, and my patient, Vincente Recto, was at the Roosevelt Hospital in New York City, following a stroke. Marcos told me that he would appreciate my going to New York as promptly as possible to see his friend in consultation. He then gave me the telephone number of the Philippine Consulate in New York City and asked me to call the Consul General to arrange with him my transportation and accommodations during the trip. I replied, "Thank you, Mr. President, I will take care of the matter as promptly as possible," and hung up. Dr. Bulger and the others present all thought that it was President Jimmy Carter and were duly impressed. I excused myself from the meeting, returned to my office, and proceeded to make arrangements for the emergency trip.

When I arrived at the hospital in New York, I found the patient in a coma, receiving artificial life support. His wife informed me that their children were already on their way from Manila. With the concurrence of his physicians, it was agreed that we would keep the respirator going until the other family members had gathered in New York. I remained there until the family members were all together and a decision was made to turn off the respirator.

Soon after my return to Houston, I received another overseas telephone call in my office from Mrs. Imelda Marcos, thanking me very much for taking time to make the trip to New York to be with her friend, Ofelia Recto, and the family. I wrote to Mrs. Recto and in due course received a letter stating, "We were very fortunate and grateful that you found time to be with us during the last remaining days of Vincente's hospital stay in New York, for which we cannot find words enough. Your presence gave us hope and confidence and later resignation because we knew that Vincente was in excellent hands. We know that what happened was the will of God."

My plane fare, hotel bill, and expenses were taken care of by the Philippine National Bank in New York, but I never received payment for my consultation. This was not surprising, considering what everyone else eventually learned of President Marcos' way of conducting business.

Not long after the arrival of Roger Bulger in Houston, Charles Franklin, vice-president for business affairs, was promoted to a position in the System Administration in Austin. Dr. Bulger arranged an afternoon farewell reception for Charles in his administrative offices, which at that time were still in the Freeman Building at the medical school. I was invited to this social affair and planned to attend. However, the day before it was to take place, I received a call requesting my presence in Monterrey, Mexico, to see in consultation a wealthy woman whose family I had known previously.

A private plane was dispatched for me and I left from Hobby Airport early in the morning. Although we already had daylight savings time in Houston, Mexico remained on standard time, permitting me to arrive an hour earlier. While there, I was asked by the same physician to see another of his wealthy patients who had requested a consultation. Payment for each visit was made in U.S. dollars by a personal check drawn on a Houston bank.

Because of the time difference, I was still able to attend the reception not too long after it had gotten under way. I apologized for arriving late, and Roger Bulger, whom I met at the door, asked me where I had been. After telling him that I had gone to Mexico that morning to see two patients in consultation, I showed him the checks which I had received and intended to turn over to the medical practice plan. Charles Franklin then told him that, although this was not something done with regularity, I had made similar substantial deposits in the past during his tenure in the business office.

Soon after taking over as president of The University of Texas Health Science Center at Houston, Roger Bulger decided that he was going to drastically reorganize the leadership in the medical school to fit his own agenda. He met with the dean, Robert Tuttle, and asked him to prepare a detailed statement indicating the need for reorganization of various medical school departments. The dean then wrote a rather lengthy letter describing what he perceived as the deficiencies and the needs of each department. It appeared to have been done by him only after repeated urging by Bulger. This all came to my attention when I received in the mail at home a photocopy of the letter from the dean to the president. It came anonymously and to this day I have no knowledge of the identity of the sender, only a suspicion. At about the same time, I had had a telephone conversation with Bulger regarding his proposal that I step down from my position as chairman of the Department of Neurology at the medical school and take on the responsibility for development of a program in geriatric medicine. My title, according to the president, was to be professor of geriatric medicine. I told Dr. Bulger that I would not turn down his offer out of hand but would prefer to take it under advisement and get back with him shortly. Within two days after this telephone conversation and before I could respond, I received a handwritten letter from Bulger in which he said that he was at 23,000 feet over Tennessee on his way to the East Coast. In this communication he stated that I would continue to be what he called part-time chairman of neurology and take on the responsibility of developing a program in geriatric medicine. Moreover, he indicated that he would ask my associate, Ian Butler, to take over the responsibility for administration of the Department of Neurology on an *interim* basis. To me this was an inexcusable breach of good faith. It was obvious that this was his method of informing me that I would be removed from my responsibilities at the medical school while avoiding having to confront me with his decision. However, as president this action was clearly his prerogative.

Shortly after I received the aforementioned letter from Dr. Bulger, he left to go on his annual August vacation in New England. He had hardly departed when all hell broke loose. It was announced from his office that Stanley Dudrick, professor and chairman of surgery, and Donald Cannon, professor and chairman of the Department of Pathology, were both being removed from their chairmanships. I was also targeted for replacement. Needless to say, the manner in which this was done was an affront to both Dudrick and Cannon, and they went public with their feelings. This became a cause celèbre throughout the Medical Center community and made headlines in both Houston newspapers. It was clear that the manner in which Bulger had undertaken to do this was going to produce a storm, and he found himself at the center of it. He interrupted his vacation and returned to Houston, where he called an urgent meeting of the Academic Council in the conference room adjacent to his office in the Main Building of the university. He tried to explain the reasons for the steps he had taken and asked for support from those in attendance. Following the meeting and before his return to New England for continuation of his vacation, he wrote a three-page, single-spaced letter, which was circulated to every faculty member in The University of Texas Health Science Center. Needless to say, it immediately became public. This was an appalling document that clearly could not possibly have been understood by persons in other administrative units of the Health Science Center who were not party to all of the circumstances surrounding the removal of two medical school professors from their administrative posts. The document caused considerable consternation among the various faculties, and very soon members of the medical school faculty began to choose sides. Within both the Departments of Surgery and Pathology, there were many supporters of the respective chairmen who had been removed. In Pathology, in particular, the members of the department made an attempt to form a solid front and formally requested the reinstatement of Cannon as chairman.

All of this maneuvering would have gotten nowhere and would have quickly died down, possibly with the removal of Roger Bulger, for the manner in which he had conducted the entire affair. However, Donald Cannon, who was incensed at what had been done and the manner of its implementation, hired an outside attorney, whose recommendation, unfortunately, was to sue the president and the university. This was obviously a tactical error and rather poor advice, but the attorney, the same Larry Watts who had been involved in a number of lawsuits against the university on civil rights issues, was delighted to have another opportunity to take a crack at the university under what he saw as such favorable circumstances. So with a lawsuit pending, continuing publicity in the newspapers, and Roger Bulger in a precarious position, it became evident that the university was going to have to defend him. Considering the foregoing chain of events, there was really no alternative.

When the events in this affair had reached a crescendo, the medical school faculty members were notified that E. Don Walker, chancellor of the university, would come from Austin to address them. A meeting was convened and Walker, in a brief address to the convocation, and without discussion, stated that the removal of Cannon and Dudrick had the approval of his administration and that no further unrest would be tolerated. Moreover, if there was more newspaper publicity, those responsible for it would be dismissed from the university as well. This should have terminated the entire affair, but there remained an undercurrent of unrest among the faculty.

In retrospect, I felt almost certain that if Cannon had not been so hasty and so foolhardy as to take on The University of Texas, as well as the president of the Health Science Center at Houston, by initiating a lawsuit which he could not possibly win, Bulger would have not survived long in his position. My suspicion about his survival was confirmed by Don Walker when he became my neighbor about ten years later, after his retirement from the university. Roger Bulger, however, continued in his administrative post for nearly ten years and then resigned to go to Washington to take on new responsibilities at the Institute of Medicine.

It seemed that The University of Texas Health Science Center at Houston was destined to continue on its tumultuous course.

Dean Tuttle resigned his post shortly after these disturbing events occurred and moved to El Paso, where he became dean of clinical programs for Texas Tech University School of Medicine. He remained in that post for only a short while before retiring completely to his home in New England. In my opinion, Bob Tuttle is a fine gentleman who would have been quite successful in Houston had he been able to remain in the position for which he had been recruited, namely, associate dean for academic affairs. He was forced into a position that he certainly had not sought following the dismissal of Cheves Smythe by President Berry. I will never forget, in the midst of all of the upheaval, Tuttle's comment to me that I would have been a great success in Renaissance Italy. No doubt, he, too, was familiar with the writings of Nicolo Machiavelli.

Ernst Knobil, who had been professor and chairman of the department of physiology at the University of Pittsburgh, replaced Bob Tuttle as dean. Knobil, a basic scientist, was internationally recognized for his outstanding work in physiology of the endocrine system. He had been a visitor to the medical school as a member of the Accreditation Committee in the early seventies and had more than a passing acquaintance with its history. He had chosen to take on this challenge and worked hard at trying to make his administration a success. The tragedy for him was that The University of Texas Medical School at Houston did not have any serious problems in the basic science departments. The most troublesome issues were all in the clinical arena, particularly with respect to the interface between the medical school and the Hermann Hospital. Knobil, who had little background or experience to relate to the pressing clinical problems, found himself in an extremely difficult position. He made a valiant attempt to bring the parties on both sides together and made some progress in this respect while constantly being plagued by interference from President Bulger. Eventually, Knobil was obliged to resign from his administrative position. Even his removal was accomplished in a manner calculated once again to produce considerable unhappiness among the faculty. Unfortunately, this appeared to be Roger Bulger's preferred method of conducting business. Ernst Knobil, a fine gentleman and outstanding academician, much to his credit, has continued to serve on the faculty at the medical school and has successfully maintained his international reputation for scholarly achievement.

Once again the medical school was confronted with the need to have an acting dean. President Bulger appointed Dr. Louis Faillace, professor and chairman of psychiatry to serve in that capacity. He served admirably for about one year and had many of the clinical departmental problems well in hand. It is my understanding that Bulger subsequently offered the deanship to him on a permanent basis. Faillace agreed to take the appointment but with certain conditions, which apparently were unacceptable to Bulger. After that, Faillace returned to his departmental duties and subsequently to a very successful private practice.

The position of dean was then offered to Dr. C. Frank Webber, chairman of the Department of Family Practice. The choice of Frank Webber, who had been president of the Harris County Medical Society in 1980, was well received by both the medical school faculty and the physicians of the Houston community. Tragically, Webber, who was a diabetic, died of a massive heart attack not long after assuming his new responsibilities. President Bulger then appointed John Ribble, who had been serving as associate dean for clinical affairs and professor of pediatrics, as acting dean. Ribble eventually was appointed dean and has continued to serve in that position up to the present time. After Bulger resigned to take his new post in Washington, Ribble also assumed the title and the responsibilities of interim president of the Health Science Center, a position in which he served for about two years before returning full time to the dean's office.

The clinical program has had its rough spots largely because there was an inadequate number of beds for teaching medical students. The faculty was forced by the legislature and by The University of Texas Board of Regents into a Catch 22. We were told that we had to expand our classes up to 200 students a year within a specified period of time and, if we did not, we would lose capitation of $25,000 for each student. Unfortunately, no one in Austin ever bothered to ascertain whether we really had a sufficient number of beds or patients anywhere in Houston to provide clinical teaching for those in the final two years of their medical school education.

The fact remains that we have been training too many physicians nationally, and the state of Texas is no exception. Virtually every study, either by government or by private foundations, has indicated a need to reduce enrollment, but the Texas Legislature has been reluctant to reduce the number of entrants into Texas medical schools. Moreover, the legislators have funded three additional medical schools in the last twenty years: one at Texas Tech University in Lubbock and El Paso, another at Texas A&M in College Station and Temple, and an Osteopathic School in Fort Worth.

The federal government, really in two guises, has done a great deal of harm to academic medicine. The first, which not too many laypersons appreciate, is the creation of a great flood of grant support provided by the National Institutes of Health and the U.S. Public Health Service beginning soon after World War II. This was largely the work of two or three influential people in the Congress, prodded by medical school deans and some professors, who kept pushing to have more and more money appropriated for medical research each year. What happened was that medical schools changed considerably in the 1950s from what they had been prior to that time, namely, institutions for training physicians, with the teaching done primarily by physicians. In a lot of the medical schools the basic science teaching, in particular, was taken over completely by Ph.D.s, who previously would have been on undergraduate campuses at institutes of biology, physiology, genetics, and so on. However, they found themselves in medical schools and they attracted a lot of grant money. The institutions got the spin-off from indirect costs, and these basic scientists kept getting more and more grant money and recruiting a larger number of graduate students. That was the goal, to obtain grants and attract graduate students. The medical schools were nurtured by those indirect costs and the prime beneficiaries were the Ph.D. programs and, to a lesser extent, the M.D. programs. The Ph.D. faculty members devoted far more time to their graduate students than to the stated objective, which was the training of physicians, much to the detriment of both the postgraduate trainees and/or the medical students. By the late 1980s, much of the financial support from federal government grants had dried up. The schools still had the big buildings and the big overhead, and the presidents and deans found themselves having to turn more and more to the private sector for support and to consider, as well, the reduction of the number of students enrolled.

I can recall a pronouncement made by Wilbur Cohen when he was secretary of the Department of Health, Education, and Welfare during the Kennedy administration. He was an academician who had come from Ann Arbor, Michigan, to take over that government post. Soon after arriving in Washington, he said, "If we are ever going to achieve government controlled medicine in the United States, it will not come about until we have unemployed physicians." We are not all that far away from government control of medical practice now, and yet we continue to train more and more doctors. If one stops to do a head count, he will find that in the state of Texas in 1992 we had 200 medical students graduating from each of the four University of Texas schools, 185 from Baylor College of Medicine in Houston, about 100 from Texas Tech in Lubbock, and another forty or fifty each at Texas A&M in College Station and the Osteopathic School in Fort Worth, which was the last to come on line. That makes a total of between 1,100 and 1,200 students graduating in medicine every year. There are not enough positions available in the hospitals in Texas to provide residency training for all of them, so many of them go out of state. Much of their education was paid for with tax revenues from Texans on the faulty premise and promise that the taxpayers were putting the money into training of doctors who would take care of Texans. In that way our elected representatives could tell voters in their respective constituencies that they were going to have a doctor in every hamlet. It is common knowledge that one cannot easily persuade a medical school graduate who has spent eight years going into debt while getting his education, and another one to four years of postgraduate work, to go to some remote location which has little or no hospital facilities. Even if one could find doctors to go to small communities, one doctor alone cannot survive in most of those areas since he or she needs to have some relief. The doctor not only needs to maintain the health and well being of the patients but should have time to keep current with the rapid changes in the profession by attending postgraduate refresher courses, meeting with other doctors, and taking some vacation. That cannot be done unless there is someone to substitute while he or she is absent.

The urbanization of the United States has been accompanied by urbanization of medicine as well — bringing more and more people into large medical centers or suburban hospitals. In this respect, the Texas Medical Center still is unique in this country, and maybe in the world. However, over the last two decades the population of Houston has continued to gravitate more and more from the center of the city out into the periphery. There are a lot of excellent, recently developed hospital facilities and well-trained doctors out there taking good care of people. Considering all the time and effort involved in trying to get from some of the outlying areas to the city center, more and more people are receiving their health care in the suburbs. Parking is a problem in the congested inner city, and the patient seldom makes just one trip to the doctor but rather needs to return for follow-up visits. Furthermore, as the average age of the population increases, it will be more difficult for those older persons to get to the Medical Center for treatment and the situation will probably worsen with time. Even though we may have improved public transportation, it has been too long a time in coming to Houston and traffic congestion will predictably get worse.

When Roger Bulger asked me to chair the Steering Committee of the Program on Aging of The University of Texas Health Science Center, one of the first projects we looked into was the possibility of having a day care center for elderly persons in the southwestern part of the city. It was to be in conjunction with the Memorial Hospital System, particularly Southwest Memorial. This whole idea remained on the back burner for a long time but was later revived under the auspices of The University of Texas Family Practice Program. It is clear that such facilities need to be replicated many times to even make a dent in the problem.

It is interesting how the place of origin of the majority of patients in the Texas Medical Center has shifted from the local populace to people from out of town, out of state, and even out of the country. This is probably less true at Hermann Hospital than it has been at St. Luke's, The Methodist, Texas Children's, and M. D. Anderson Cancer Center. This trend is not inappropriate, and every effort should be made to encourage people from elsewhere to come to this great Medical Center.

Hermann Hospital also has changed considerably since I first knew it. Now it has a Trauma Center, a Burn Center, a Kidney Center, and is essentially a tertiary-care hospital. Even the Pediatrics Service is, for the most part, taking care of high-risk patients. The Neonatal Intensive Care Unit is doing an excellent job in taking care of premature babies. The Helicopter Service, which was developed first in Houston at that hospital, has become one of the busiest in the nation.

Chapter 15

Travel to the Soviet Union, 1971–1972

IN EARLY 1970, I RECEIVED A LETTER, written in Russian, from the Academy of Medical Sciences in Moscow inviting me to lecture in Moscow, Leningrad, and Kiev during a two-week period. This invitation was initiated by academician Evgeny Vladimirovich Shmidt, who had been my guest in Houston about seven months earlier, and it was the official manner of saying "thank you." The letter stated that my expenses would be paid while in the Soviet Union if I could obtain elsewhere the funds for my round-trip fare from Houston to Moscow. Since I had no way of doing this through the university, I communicated with the United States-Soviet Health Exchange Program in the Department of Health, Education and Welfare. I was informed that they would support my travel expenses only if the length of my stay was four weeks or more. After ten months of negotiations between the two great bureaucracies, it was finally arranged, with the United States government covering my expenses for the trip across the Atlantic and the Soviet Ministry of Health paying all expenses incurred within the U.S.S.R.

My departure from Houston was scheduled for May 22, 1971. My passport, which I had sent to Washington, was returned with the required Soviet visa only twenty-four hours before my scheduled departure. It was a real cliffhanger, as I had been cautioned that it might be.

I traveled first to London and then on to Moscow on a British Airways flight to Tokyo. When we flew over the Baltic, we were informed that no photographs were allowed while passing over Soviet territory. This was my initiation to the kind of control to be expected during the remainder of the visit. There were six other passengers who disembarked in Moscow and were quickly spirited away. I was left standing there looking for a friendly face and wondering what I was going to do. I had been given no information about my hotel reservations or the itinerary that the Soviets had planned for me.

I located the Intourist Office at the end of the disembarkation lounge, where a young woman, sitting at a table, had a large ledger book with lists of names written in longhand. She responded to my inquiry by saying abruptly, "You are not on our list for today." I told her that I was coming as a guest of the Soviet Ministry of Health. Fortunately, I had kept close at hand the letter of invitation originally received from the Academy of Medical Sciences, U.S.S.R. This promptly got her attention. She then announced my name over the loudspeaker system but this failed to produce any response. As the time was drawing close to 5:00 P.M., I said to her, "Perhaps you should call the Academy of Medical Sciences." The young woman telephoned the Academy and upon her return, she merely said, "Follow me." In front of the terminal she hailed a taxi. We proceeded into town and arrived at the Academy offices just prior to closing time. The taxi driver waited with my luggage while I crossed the street and went into the building to announce myself. After about ten minutes, a young blond gentleman came down the main staircase, approached me and in perfect English without a trace of an accent, said, "Professor Fields, I am Dr. Yuri Puchkov. We have been wondering when you would arrive and had contacted your Embassy to find out. No one there seemed to have any information about the time of your arrival or the number of your flight." When I spoke with officials at the Embassy the next day, this was confirmed. This, of course, did not provide me with any great feeling of security.

Dr. Puchkov accompanied me in the cab to the Hotel Rossiya. After settling me in my room, he departed, telling me that Dr. Aleksandr Nikolaevich Konovalov would pick me up the following morning.

With the evening to myself, I went to the lobby to find a place for dinner. I had a fairly simple meal which I later learned was from the standard Intourist menu used in almost every large hotel in the Soviet Union.

The next morning I breakfasted in the buffet, which was very neat and clean. There was a waiting line but that was not unexpected since in the Soviet Union one queued up for everything. When I sat at a vacant table, I was told that one did not sit by himself at a table but rather was expected to take an empty seat at an occupied table until all the places were filled. In this manner I encountered some fascinating people. It got rather interesting on occasion to sit down to a meal with one Bulgarian and two Uzbeks, or perhaps three Mongolians, and try to have some kind of communication. Amazingly enough, people manage to communicate if they make the effort. I found that most of those I met in this manner were extremely interested in what was going on in the United States. This seemed to be universal, even though some of the listeners appeared skeptical.

Konovalov met me at the Hotel Rossiya at 9:00 A.M. and took me in his own car directly to the Burdenko Institute of Neurosurgery. We had previously met in October 1969, when he visited Houston and was a guest one evening in my home. At the Institute, he escorted me to the office of the director, Professor Alex I. Arutiunov, who was very gracious and said, "Please feel at home here. In medicine we have no secrets." One wall of his office was covered with autographed pictures of neurosurgeons from various parts of the world whom he referred to jokingly as "my residents." Following this introduction, I was taken by Dr. Konovalov for an overview of the Institute in order to meet the various senior staff members and decide in which of the departments I would prefer to spend more time during the next several days.

On my second morning at the breakfast buffet there was a man in line who was unmistakably an American and he was having a terrible time making himself understood. I moved up a couple of places in the queue and tried to help him. I learned that he was Edward Hutchinson, an attorney in the Washington office of the Houston law firm of Fulbright, Crooker, Bates and Jaworski. He was tremendously relieved to find somebody with whom he could communicate. I learned from him that there was to be a World Petroleum Congress in Moscow the following week.

Konovalov came for me again with his car and took me to the Ministry of Health for a discussion concerning my itinerary for the remainder of the visit in the Soviet Union. After formal signing of several official documents, I was presented with an air ticket to Leningrad, a letter from the Ministry, and 465 rubles for travel expense and incidentals. How they arrived at this figure was not at all clear to me.

From the Ministry we proceeded to the Institute, where I was introduced to Feodor A. Serbinenko, a staff doctor who was utilizing a technique he had developed for opacification of the intracranial branches of the internal carotid artery. He had specially prepared filiform catheters of various lengths with small rubber balloons affixed by means of adhesive material at the end, which he could pass upward into the head and block off a branch artery by inflating the rubber balloon. The procedure was carried out with x-ray image amplification and a television monitor. This balloon technique had been pioneered by Serbinenko and used by him in over 120 cases of arteriovenous fistula in the cavernous sinus. Because of the high degree of specialization within the institutional organization, Serbinenko had been able to see a large number of such cases, many referred to him from a great distance.

Konovalov also arranged for me to watch Nikolai Vasin operate on an anterior communicating artery aneurysm. I was particularly interested in the operating table, which was on tracks so that it could be moved from the operating room to the radiographic suite without disturbing the patient. I was shown some cases with unusual vascular problems, the likes of which I had never encountered before.

Next I visited the Electroencephalography Laboratory, which was housed in cramped quarters. All of the people working there were women. Work was being conducted using evoked potentials in humans and, in some cases, with very primitive frequency analysis techniques.

Following this I spent more than an hour with Dr. A. Shaknovich, chief of the Cerebral Blood Flow Laboratory. This laboratory was outfitted primarily with imported equipment. They were also beginning some interesting work with implanted electrodes for cerebral blood flow measurements during neuropsychological testing. No data were available for my examination.

At the end of the day, I returned to the Hotel Rossiya. This hotel, with 5,000 rooms, was not run in a very efficient manner. It soon became obvious that certain categories of persons were placed in certain parts of the hotel. For example, Americans were placed on certain floors in a specific area of the hotel. One day when I was coming up in the elevator, I got off on the wrong floor. To my left there was a door that was partly open. When I looked in, I saw men and women with earphones seated at separate booths. These people were listening to whatever went on all over the hotel. I had heard that there were microphones in the rooms, and this tended to confirm my suspicions. Also, there was always someone, usually an elderly woman, seated at a desk close to the elevator on each floor. When one wanted to enter his room for the first time, the card obtained at the front desk upon registration was presented to the person at the desk on that floor, and that person would release the key to the room. Each time one left the room, he returned the key and picked up the card. This was done to prevent any Soviet citizens from making unauthorized visits to persons in the hotel.

The next morning Konovalov came to the hotel to drive me to the apartment of Professor Aleksandr Romanovich Luria. This charming, brilliant gentleman was well known outside the Soviet Union for his work in neuropsychology. During our conversation, Professor Luria told me, in an almost pleading manner, that he would be delighted if I would find some young neurologist in the United States who would be willing to learn enough Russian to come to the Soviet Union and observe his techniques during a period of six to twelve months. We had some coffee and cakes served with the inevitable offer of a small glass of cognac.

Konovalov returned with the car and drove me back to the Burdenko Institute. In the director's office I was given a white coat, a cap, and a mask. I wore these during the next several days *without a fresh change*. There seemed to be a general lack of concern with asepsis away from the immediate vicinity of the operating table, and there was a good deal of traffic in and out of all of the operating suites.

During the weekend, and actually during my entire stay in Moscow, I had no trouble moving around on my own, particularly in the central part of the city. I visited the Art Museum to see a Van Gogh exhibition on loan from France. From there I went to the swimming stadium, and then to the Moscow Circus. The show, which is world-renowned, was absolutely fabulous. I walked at my leisure, took photographs, and had no problems except on one memorable occasion. I went into the large department store known by the initials G.U.M. (Glavny Universalny Magazin). The windows of this store faced Red Square and contained some rather attractive items. However, inside the store, I found very little worth purchasing and nothing that resembled the display in the windows. I started to take a picture inside when somebody came up and took me by the arm and would have taken my camera if I had not covered the lens. It was very evident to me that I could take pictures of buildings, churches, and other architectural features, but the moment I tried to take pictures of store fronts or anything that would reflect on the poor quality of the goods or the lack of them, I would be in trouble.

On Sunday, Sasha Konovalov came with his small car to take me to the Economic Achievement Park, which I found very impressive. There was one pavilion after another, just like one would find at a World Fair. This was truly a world-class exhibition which was open all year round. I was very impressed with the Space Exhibit, which I thought was much more instructive and better assembled than that which I had seen at the NASA Museum at Clear Lake outside of Houston. After leaving the park, Konovalov invited me to accompany him to his home. We walked through the lobby and up four flights of stairs. I had already learned that in every apartment building there was someone, usually an elderly man or woman, observing who was coming and who was leaving. Consequently, I said nothing until we got inside the door of his apartment. The rooms were rather crowded and cluttered, furnished mostly with antique overstuffed chairs and a couch that had obviously been in the family for a long time. I learned that Sasha, his wife, his mother (who was a retired general surgeon with whom I conversed in French), his brother (who was a civil engineer), and the brother's wife all shared that apartment. The family offered me some food and drink, of which there was obviously a limited amount. They were very polite, generous, and interested in what I had to say regarding my observations about Moscow.

That evening I walked from the hotel to the Bolshoi Theater and purchased a ticket for the performance of *Swan Lake*. The entire production was extremely beautiful and done to perfection.

The next day at the Burdenko Institute I spent the entire morning with Professor Luria, observing his application of the neuropsychological techniques that he had developed for examination of his patients. His principal interest was in post-traumatic aphasia (language dysfunction) and in alterations of other brain functions created by intracranial tumors.

Luria handled several languages fluently and had no difficulty in communicating with the patient or with me. We examined two patients in great detail, one with a bilateral internal carotid artery occlusion and the second with a pure frontal lobe memory defect following brain tumor resection. The demonstration was most impressive.

That afternoon I presented my first lecture, with Konovalov translating. Much to the surprise and pleasure of the audience, I made my introductory remarks in Russian. The room was full and the question period afterward was very lively.

It was fortunate that Konovalov could serve as my guide through the Institute and also during visits to other parts of the city. When he was unable to make the trip himself, he would arrange with other members of the staff who handled English sufficiently well to accompany me. One afternoon they took me on a tour of the Kremlin museums. The Kremlin is very old, beautiful, and fascinating, but the Soviet government blemished it by putting inside its walls a monstrosity called the "Kremlin Palace of Congresses," which seats 6,000 in the main hall.

Within the Kremlin I visited several multiple-domed churches. Another large building housed the National Museum and in it were many artifacts of the Romanov czars and their predecessors, including the imperial jewels. The museum is a remarkable landmark which the Soviet government preserved as a national treasure.

Outside of the Kremlin in Red Square is the Lenin Mausoleum, where two soldiers continuously stand guard. The guard was changed every hour and a security guard from the KGB sat just inside the door. It was a spectacular sight to see them change the guard on the hour at precisely the moment that the clock in the tower over the Kremlin gate chimed. I told one of the Russian doctors that I would like to come and get in the queue some morning to go through the tomb so that I could see Lenin. I asked him if he had visited the tomb and he replied, "Twice. I went back a second time to make sure that Lenin was still there. In Moscow we speak about this often and we want to keep him in there. We believe that is why they have the security guard because if he ever got out, he would want to change things."

At the same time that I was staying at the Hotel Rossiya, it was the headquarters hotel for Russian Orthodox priests from all over the world who were coming to the town of Zagorsk for the election of a new Patriarch of the Eastern Church. I was fascinated by the groups of people and their various colorful indigenous costumes.

In the early afternoon, I presented my second lecture on "The role of arterial reconstructive surgery in the management of extracranial vascular disease." I also reviewed the recent studies which we had been doing to determine the effect of oral aspirin on platelet aggregation. After the lecture, time was arranged for me to visit Professor Gabib Gabibov, a specialist in the surgery of meningiomas (benign intracranial tumors). He had operated on more than 500 parasagittal meningiomas and had developed procedures for plastic repair of the sagittal sinus. His two-volume doctoral thesis and others were housed in a small library on the top floor of the Institute. Most of the material there consisted of bound doctoral theses. I asked where they kept the more current material for reference and bibliographic search and was told that one would have to go to the central library of the Academy of Medical Sciences, which was located elsewhere in Moscow.

That evening I was invited to go to a soccer game at the Central Lenin Stadium in the company of Oleg Chikovani, one of the young staff neurosurgeons. There was not a vacant seat to be found anywhere in the stadium. I was very impressed by Dr. Chikovani's command of English and had a very enjoyable evening with him. Afterward we met Professor Edvard Israelovich Kandel of the Neurological Institute and Galina Volchek, one of the directors of the Moscow Repertory Theater. I never dreamed that I would encounter her again five years later in Houston, where she came to direct a Russian play at the Alley Theater. She was very surprised when I recalled our first meeting.

The next morning at 9:15, Akademik Evgeny Vladimirovich Shmidt, whom I had met in New York and later in Houston, arrived in a car to take me to the Institute of Neurology. I was taken immediately to the director's office in order to discuss my itinerary for the remainder of the trip in the Soviet Union for which Professor Shmidt was largely responsible.

The Institute of Neurology, I was informed, was divided into six departments. In the clinical sector, there were about 200 beds: 68 for acute stroke; 30 for rehabilitation; 30 for neurosurgery, with 10 more in the intensive care unit; 30 for amyotrophic lateral sclerosis (Lou Gehrig's disease); and 30 for the neurogenetic diseases.

Because of my interest in cerebrovascular diseases, Professor Shmidt reviewed in greater detail the research and clinical programs directed toward those conditions. After that, Professor Kandel, chief of neurosurgery, took me to see the operating room, an exceedingly well-equipped new facility screened for both x-ray and the recording of physiological data. The equipment was principally of Japanese and East German manufacture with a few instruments for recording or stimulation made in the Soviet Union.

That evening I went by taxi to the apartment shared by two young German friends. He was the local correspondent for the West German newspaper *Neue Presse*, and she, the daughter of longtime friends in Frankfurt. The taxi took me directly to the entrance of their block of apartments. I was let out near the door since the taxi was not allowed into the courtyard. Just inside the only entrance, which opened into a large, attractively landscaped area, stood a kiosk with two uniformed policemen who monitored everyone coming in or going out. I soon learned that people who lived in such a complex, which they referred to as a "ghetto," seldom talked about anything that was of any great importance since they knew that their conversations were being monitored. This was a frightfully uncomfortable way in which to live one's life, but most of them had adapted reasonably well to such circumstances.

Vladimir Smirnov, a neurologist, and his wife, Natalia Innekentyevna Perevodchikova, a well-known oncologist at the Cancer Institute, came with their car at 9:30 the next morning to take me directly to the Neurological Institute. It was planned for me to visit various departments with Professor Shmidt. We went first to the department for the management of acute emergencies, which was referred to as the "Reanimation Department." This was run by a most efficient woman physician. From there we went to the acute stroke unit to talk with the chief. I did not visit any of the patients who occupied the sixty beds there since my hosts suggested to me that an acute stroke patient is the same no matter where he or she is being cared for. This was a very odd approach to acute stroke management.

At the end of our morning meeting, Kandel indicated to me that he would like for me to come with him briefly to his office. He showed me a letter which he had received from the American Association of Neurological Surgeons indicating that during the meeting of the Society the previous year in Houston, Texas, he had been elected an honorary corresponding member. The letter requested that he submit $5 to the office of the secretary so that his certificate could be forwarded to him. He made it clear to me that he had about as much chance of getting $5 to send for the certificate as he would of having a handful of lunar dust and begged me to intercede for him. Upon my return to Houston, I called the secretary of the association, whom I knew personally. Professor Kandel's dilemma was explained to him and I offered to pay the $5 so that the certificate could be forwarded. I told him that he should make certain that in the accompanying letter there was no comment thanking Kandel for submitting $5 for the certificate. Any such suggestion might result in Kandel being taken for a visit to KGB Headquarters to be interrogated.

After lunch, I gave a lecture in a large room where it was almost impossible to obtain a satisfactory degree of darkness to show my slides. In spite of this problem, the room was full. The audience, including fifteen to twenty in military uniform, was very attentive. One could not fail to be impressed by the number of people throughout the Soviet Union who were in one form of uniform or another. They seemed to be a very disciplined group who took great pride in the military establishment. Also, the women one saw with Soviet military or naval personnel were the best dressed and seemed to have the best of everything. I understand that this changed drastically after the war in Afghanistan.

My second lecture the next day was in the same room but with a smaller audience. Professor Kandel provided an excellent translation and afterward I conversed directly with several vascular surgeons who had come from other institutions in Moscow.

That evening I met my German friend in the basement restaurant at the Hotel National. This was a place which catered to Westerners, and only hard currency was accepted there in payment for a meal. While we were eating, two young men in rather ill-fitting clothes came in and sat at a nearby table. They were speaking German and, when the waiter asked them to pay for their drinks, the only money which they had consisted of rubles and *Ost* marks (East German marks). The waiter was furious and was about to have them thrown out when my friend and I came to their rescue. We not only paid for their drinks in *Deutsche* marks (West marks) but said that they would be our guests for dinner. The two were astounded and remarked that everywhere they had been, their "Socialist brothers" had treated them in similar shabby manner. Clearly, this kind of courtesy from the "enemy" was contrary to everything they had been taught. We felt that one small blow had been struck for western democracy.

While driving through the streets of Moscow, my friend

pointed out that as we passed each uniformed policeman, he would take a radio transmitter from his lapel and announce us to the next one about 100-150 meters further down the street. I asked him how the policemen could tell anything about the car or its occupants and he showed me how easy this was to achieve. All cars belonging to foreigners had white license plates with black letters while those of the indigenous population had black plates with white letters. Moreover, diplomats had a "D" in front of the numbers on the plate, correspondents had a "K," and so forth. In this manner the movements of foreigners in cars could be monitored readily anywhere in the city. This was unpleasant for the person under scrutiny and was also an expensive exercise for the government since it cost a great deal to maintain the apparatus required for control.

On June 5, I was driven to the Venukovo Airport, which was used for domestic flights, and put on an Aeroflot plane bound for Leningrad. Only a few passengers bothered to attach their seatbelts. Either they did not know how or no one bothered to explain. When I assisted the woman sitting next to me in attaching her belt, she was very appreciative but also astonished. Overhead there was no shelf on which to put carry-on baggage so everything went into a fishnet arrangement above the seats. The plane was towed to the end of the runway before the engines were "revved up" in order to save fuel. I had the impression that if there was a problem, the pilot would not be aware of it until he got to the other end of the runway. This certainly did not provide much comfort with regard to safety. However, every flight that I took was uneventful and the service was passable.

At the Leningrad airport I was met by the scientific secretary of the Polenov Institute of Neurosurgery and taken to the Hotel Oktiabrskaya on Ploschad Vosstanya, the square adjacent to the Moscow railway station. After the representatives of the Institute departed and left me on my own, I spent the evening walking the streets using a small tourist map as a guide. Leningrad was so far north that the sun never went down completely at that time of the year, and even at 2:00 A.M. one could read the newspaper while on the street.

The next day was Sunday and the vice-director of the Polenov Institute of Neurosurgery, Professor Nikolai Andreevich Shustin, took me on a sightseeing tour around the city of Leningrad. It was a beautiful, sunny day and I found the city to be very attractive, with many architectural gems, most of which had been reconstructed since World War II (The Great Patriotic War) as near as possible to their prewar condition.

On Monday, Dr. Ludmila Astakhova from the Department of Information of the Polenov Institute came to accompany me on foot from the hotel to the Institute only three blocks away. The director, Professor Veniamin Mikhailovich Ugrumov, who had also been my guest in Houston, was away on official business and so Professor Shustin took me on a general tour of the Institute through the various wards and the Intensive Care Unit. From there we went to the Clinical Physiology Laboratory, where several doctors were recording from the patients before, during, and after surgery. There was only one piece of Soviet-built equipment which was partially hidden on top of a Swedish multi-channel polygraph. I could never understand why the United States government had placed an embargo on our export to the Soviet Union of American-manufactured radiologic and electronic equipment while our competitors in Germany and Japan had no such restrictions. It seemed to me to be self-defeating.

My lecture on Tuesday was scheduled for 10:00 A.M. The auditorium was packed and there was standing room only. It was a much better room for projection than either one provided in Moscow. A young man, Dr. Aleksandr Trohatchev, was dispatched from the Institute of Experimental Medicine to translate for me. I felt that my words were being translated more accurately on this occasion than they had been at the Institute of Neurology in Moscow. Later that day, Sasha Trohatchev asked me to accompany him to the Moscow railway station to see his young lady friend off on the train to Moscow. He then invited me to accompany him that evening to the home of a friend who was a pianist and composer. I said that I would be delighted.

Sasha came to my hotel that evening and we took the trolley bus across the river to visit his friend, Sergei Benyevich, who lived in small, cramped quarters on the fourth floor of an apartment building. We could barely squeeze into the room where he had his piano, bed, desk, and all of his books. We sat on the bed while Sergei played, and it was immediately obvious that he was an accomplished musician. At 10:00 P.M. it began to get a little darker outside but he was still playing. I thought of what might happen if someone played a piano at that hour in an apartment dwelling in Houston. His mother brought us some cake, which undoubtedly had been sitting on the shelf for several days since it was quite dried out. However, they behaved as though it was a special feast and I responded accordingly.

At 1:00 A.M., as I was about to leave the apartment, Sasha announced that he was planning to spend the night there with Sergei Benyevich and assured me that I would have no difficulty traveling across the city by myself once I got on the trolley bus. It took me about thirty-five minutes to reach the square near the hotel. There was no one else on the street and I was the last person to get off the bus. On arrival at the hotel, I found the front door locked; however, when I rang the bell, a man came to let me in. He was rather indignant about my disturbing him at that hour, but when I showed him the card with which I could obtain my room key, there were no further questions.

On June 9, Dr. Astakhova and another young female doctor from the Institute of Neurosurgery accompanied me by car to the Pavlov Institute of Physiology located in a forest on the edge of the city. I was taken straight away to the office of the director, Professor Konrady. Although Konrady understood English, he preferred to speak in French, and the remainder of the visit was conducted in that language. The laboratories had the usual mixed bag of equipment, but more pieces of Soviet manufacture were being used there than in the laboratories of the other institutes I had visited previously.

One of the senior researchers, Dr. Tetlov, took me on a tour of the adjacent museum in which the Institute took special pride. This had been the summer house and personal laboratory of Professor Ivan Petrovich Pavlov, the world-famous experimental psychophysiologist. I was very surprised to see on the wall a picture of Pavlov in his laboratory with a man I immediately recognized as Boris Babkin, former professor of physiology at McGill University Medical School in Montreal. Professor Tetlov obviously knew nothing of Professor Babkin, who had left the Soviet Union and immigrated to Canada many years earlier. It may very well have been that, as a result of his leaving, he became a "non-person."

Early next morning, Trohatchev came by car with a driver to escort me to the Neurological Clinic of the Institute of Experimental Medicine. This clinic was a part of the Department of Applied Neurophysiology founded in 1963 by Professor N. P. Bekhtereva and had as its main task the study of neurophysiology, neuropsychology, and the structural-functional organization of the brain, as well as problems of causation and treatment of various brain diseases. There was special emphasis being placed, I was told, on the treatment of epilepsy, parkinsonism, and related movement disorders such as chorea and Wilson's disease.

We drove back into the city to the Institute of Experimental Medicine itself, where I presented a lecture in two parts, the first describing our experience with new drugs in the management of parkinsonism and the second concerned with intra-arterial microembolism. Professor Bekhtereva, who was on vacation, honored me by coming to attend my lecture. I found her to be a very imposing personality and regretted that I did not have an opportunity to spend more time with her.

The Bekhterev Leningrad Psychoneurological Research Institute was located across the Neva River and beyond a workers' district on the edge of town. It was founded in 1908 by V. M. Bekhterev (father of the aforementioned Bekhtereva), a prominent Russian neurologist and psychologist, after whom it was named in 1925. It was directly subordinated to the Ministry of Health of the Russian Federated Soviet Socialist Republics (RFSSR). This Institute provided both clinical and basic science training in psychiatry and neurology. The clinical departments of the Institute comprised approximately 450 beds and there were just over 2,000 admissions per year for clinical examination and definitive treatment. This was certainly not a very large turnover of patients.

In the main building I presented a lecture which, with translation, took approximately two hours. The translation was done by Professor I. P. Lapin, chief of the Psychopharmacology Laboratory, who spoke excellent English and German.

Since my obligation at that Institute was finished early in the afternoon, Professor Lapin offered to accompany me personally on a tour of Impressionist paintings at the Hermitage Museum, where he said he was a frequent visitor. I found him to be a delightful and knowledgeable companion who was surprisingly open in his criticism of many things in the Soviet Union. He asked me an innumerable number of questions about how certain specific things were done in the United States.

A sightseeing trip had been planned for the Sunday before my departure from Leningrad. Professor Shustin, Dr. Astakhova, and another gentleman from the Polenov Institute's Department of Information came to take me by car to Pushkin (Tsarkoye Selo) for a visit to the palace of Catherine the Great. This palace, on the northern outskirts of the city, is an immense structure which was largely rebuilt after World War II. Most of the artifacts contained therein had been hidden underground during the long siege of the city by the Germans. I was astonished to see prominently displayed at the end of one large room a map of the Soviet Union made from various kinds of inlaid stone and brilliants. I had seen this masterpiece in the Soviet Pavilion at the New York World's Fair in 1939. After leaving that locale, we visited the palace of Czar Paul I at Pavlovsk. At one point during the tour we had to wait for a large group of British tourists to crowd their way past us. I remembered later having been jostled a bit at that moment. After a full day they delivered me to my hotel at about 6:00 P.M. I was very tired and lay down on the bed to watch a performance of the Bolshoi Ballet in Moscow on the black and white television set in my room. I fell asleep and did not awaken until about two and a half hours later.

I needed to get my bags packed for departure to the airport soon after breakfast. It was only then that I realized that my passport was missing. It was nowhere to be found. Although shaken by my discovery, I immediately went to the lobby and in English told the woman behind the counter that my passport was missing. I was concerned that it had been lost or stolen. She replied in Russian that she could not understand me, although I had heard her speak English earlier that day. I returned to my room to make a telephone call to Moscow. The code number for Moscow was on a list under the glass covering the bedside table. I dialed 9, and then the code number for Moscow, but before I could continue with the number of the American Embassy which I had memorized, I was interrupted by the operator. I told her in Russian that I wanted to speak with the American Embassy in Moscow and gave her the number. She told me to hang up and wait. In exactly thirty minutes, which undoubtedly provided sufficient time to make arrangements for monitoring my conversation, the phone rang. At the other end I heard what sounded to me at the time like the sweetest voice I had ever heard — that of the U.S. Marine sergeant on duty at the Embassy. He told me that I should call the Astoria Hotel the next day and ask for Culver Glysteen, the consul designate of the United States in Leningrad.

In the morning I went immediately to the Intourist Office. Sitting behind a large desk facing the double doors was an attractive young brunette. I had seen her previously and had heard her speak

English, but when I spoke to her about the problem with my passport, she replied in French. She seemed surprised when I responded in French and this left her no alternative but to continue conversing with me. When I told her about my situation, she said that she would find someone who spoke English. I had been instructed by the Embassy to insist on reporting to the District Security Police and not dealing with any "hotel police." At that time I also called Mr. Glysteen at the Astoria Hotel and told him the nature of my concern. He said, "Doctor, I'm in no position to help you. Please do not bother me, get on the train, and go back to Moscow." I subsequently learned that he had been relieved of his duties in Leningrad and therefore was not at all surprised considering his lack of concern.

About fifteen minutes later, two men arrived at the door of the Intourist Office. We went over to the corner of the room and the three of us sat down around a folding card table with a young woman from the Aeroflot office as our interpreter. The larger and more officious man began to interrogate me. He asked a lot of irrelevant, inane questions while his smaller assistant frantically recorded my responses on his notepad. The larger man then said that he would make a few telephone calls and be back shortly. Upon his return he gave me a document, handwritten on a piece of beige-colored stationery and said, "Do not worry, Professor, this will serve as a substitute for your passport during the remainder of your travels. However, we will endeavor to find your passport here." I told him that I had already spoken with the gentleman at the U.S. Consulate in Leningrad and with the first secretary of the U.S. Embassy in Moscow about my problem. He seemed both surprised and perturbed by this piece of information.

In midmorning, Dr. Astakhova and I went downstairs to the front of the hotel, where a car was waiting. We were standing there while the driver was putting my luggage in the trunk of the car when I saw the large plainclothes policeman hurrying down the street waving something in his hand. When he arrived, he handed me what clearly was my passport and said (in Russian), "Is this your passport?" I asked him where he found it and he inquired again, "Is this your passport?" I asked him once more what happened and where the passport had been. He asked a third time, "Is this your passport?" So I took it, put it in my pocket, and said no more.

I got into the waiting car and headed for the airport with Dr. Astakhova, who left me there and promptly disappeared. I had the distinct impression that she wanted to divest herself of further responsibility for my welfare.

I decided that it was indeed very fortunate that folded inside my passport I had left a letter of introduction provided me by Professor Boris Mikhailovich Petrovsky, minister of health and member of the Politburo. This must have made the person or persons who had removed the document from my pocket more than a little uneasy. Throughout the remainder of my stay in the Soviet Union, I left my passport with the hotel administration and never carried it again on my person except while in travel status.

The plane for Kiev was five hours late in departing. I had to remain in the airport building in a room separated from the other passengers during that entire period. On arrival in Kiev, Konstantin Rudyak, an interpreter from the Department of Information (Public Relations) of the Scientific Research Institute of Neurosurgery, met me at the airport and took me to the Hotel Ukraine. After delivering me to the hotel, he promptly disappeared, leaving me to my own devices.

The next morning Professor Andrei Petrovich Romodanov, director, and Rudyak took me by car to the Scientific Research Institute of Neurosurgery on Manuilsky Street. The organizational structure was similar to that of both the Leningrad and Moscow neurosurgical institutes.

The primary concern of this institute was brain tumor investigation. Romodanov had a very interesting philosophy about how to deal with brain tumor cases. He felt that their own therapeutic results had been vastly improved by admitting the patients to the intensive care department for work-up prior to surgery and then returning them there following radical resection. They were, in this manner, seen both pre- and post-operatively in the same department by the same physicians.

The Vascular Department was concerned primarily with surgery of aneurysms and arteriovenous malformations, but only from the practical clinical point of view since scientific investigation of such lesions was a problem assigned to the Moscow Institute. This fragmentation of effort was in my opinion a serious impediment to both high quality research and patient management.

A visit to the director's office was followed by a general tour of the hospital with Rudyak and introduction to the department chiefs. Then in another brief visit to the office of the director, along with the interpreter, I was informed that my lecture was not scheduled to be delivered until the following day and arrangements had been made for me to take a tour of the city that afternoon. They also told me that the driver could speak English and asked me to sit in the front seat alongside him. At the same time two young men got in the back of the car without introduction. I had no idea who they were or why they were there. I turned to the driver as we were leaving the Institute and asked in English, "Where are you going to take me?" He looked rather blank and said, "I beg your pardon?" I repeated the question and once again he said, "I beg your pardon?" I made no further attempt to engage him in conversation.

I was partially turned toward the back seat and could hear the two men in back talking. I thought that out of all their conversation I heard two words in Spanish, *"Muy bien."* Much to my surprise and delight, when I spoke to the one whom I thought had used Spanish words, he responded in Spanish and asked where I had learned the language. They were both neurosurgeons and had worked in a Russian military hospital in Cuba near the town of Orguin. I knew that this town was close to Santiago, Cuba, and approximately equidistant from the U.S. Naval Base at Guantanamo Bay. They were both so pleased that they could converse with me that they took me to their swimming club on the Dnieper River and then later to a restaurant at an old mill in the suburbs of Kiev. We had a very interesting evening and after several drinks, they opened up and told me a great deal about what was going on in Cuba with respect to Soviet military activity. The driver of the car, who did not take a drink, was extremely upset since he spoke only Russian and a few words of English. He knew not one word of Spanish and, consequently, was left out of our conversation completely. I was certain that he had been assigned to be my driver by Intourist, which I knew to be an arm of the secret police. I had the distinct impression that the two neurosurgeons were delighted they could converse with me and at the same time embarrass the young KGB agent. I learned that one of them was Yuri Kopiakovsky, but the other remained anonymous.

The next day, a car came to take me to the Institute and I went directly to the radiology department. There I saw serial angiograms of excellent quality produced with Swedish Elema-Schonander rapid film changers. Unfortunately, the quality of interpretation was not up to the quality of the films, a situation which was just the reverse of what I had encountered in Moscow.

Rudyak took me to the Department of Pathomorphology, where I visited with the chief, Professor Khominsky, conversing in French with him. He was an elderly gentleman who had devoted most of his life to the classification of brain tumors and was still very much concerned with the details of this work. The electronmicroscope being used there was the first one of Russian manufacture that I had seen. The fidelity of the electronphotomicrographs and work in general in this department appeared to be of high caliber.

The following day I waited at the hotel for Rudyak to take me to the Institute of Gerontology. The difference in attitude and behavior of the people in Kiev, Moscow, and Leningrad impressed me very much. In the latter two cities, when someone made an appointment at a specific time, he was always punctual. In Kiev everything seemed to be more casual and relaxed. I suspected that this apparent cultural trend was not too different from what one might find when comparing New York and New Orleans.

The Institute of Gerontology was close to a forest on the periphery of the city and surrounded by gardens where the patients could walk or sit and relax. The building was relatively new, and two additions were under construction. Both were expected to be completed in six to eight months, in time for the 9th International Congress of Gerontology to be held in Kiev in July 1972. I was given a briefing in the office of the vice-director, Professor Mankovsky, a neurologist, prior to being taken on a tour.

A large-scale experiment was under way with comparisons between two groups of residential patients: one group of twenty- to thirty-year-olds and another group of sixty-five to seventy-year-old individuals. Each group was put on the same special regimen with restriction of movement. The older patients developed severe functional changes beginning with the cardiovascular system. These were far more severe than similar changes developed in the younger patients. This was certainly not surprising. The ethics of this kind of human experimentation would, in my opinion, have been seriously questioned in the United States.

In the early afternoon, I was scheduled to present an illustrated lecture to the staff in the conference room adjacent to the director's office at the Institute of Neurosurgery. Rudyak, my interpreter, suddenly became ill during lunch and had to leave for home. Professor Romadanov was frantically trying to find someone else fluent in English but time would not permit this. I suggested that I give my one-hour lecture in Spanish with the aforementioned Dr. Kopiakovsky translating to Russian. Approximately thirty persons attended and the discussion, which lasted another hour, was very animated and the younger physicians asked many searching questions. The translation worked out just fine.

The next day Kopiakovsky took me on another tour of Kiev during which he told me a lot about the hospital and the activities in which the neurosurgeons were engaged. Since we conversed in Spanish throughout the entire day, the visit was quite relaxed and I had an opportunity to learn from him a good deal of what he had observed during his time in Cuba. Later in the day he took me to the Pioneer Palace, where I could observe some young people working in various activities, including science training, drama, journalism, and many other things for children between the ages of five and sixteen. I was rather surprised at the completeness of the program. Although Kopiakovsky's daughter had spent time there, this was his first visit and he was delighted with what he saw.

The following morning, Kopiakovsky came with a car and driver to take me to the Borispol Airport. It was a wild ride and I was relieved when it was over. The plane was full, as usual, but I was given a window seat toward the front, which provided me with a splendid view of the southern Ukraine, the Crimea and Caucasus Mountains on my way to Tbilisi. This was my first flight in the USSR during which I could see the ground.

In Tbilisi, Dr. Alexander Kakauridze and Professor Sigua, chief of neurosurgery at the Institute of Experimental and Clinical Neurology, met me at the airport. They took me directly to the Hotel Iveria, where I had excellent accommodations on the eleventh floor. My balcony overlooked the Kura River, which flows through the heart of the city. From there one could also see a tall aluminum statue, called "Mother Georgia," on a hilltop overlooking the surrounding area. At night this figure was quite spectacular in floodlights. The Georgians were very philosophical about their status at that time. They had been invaded forty times in their recorded history and had been under Russian domination for about 150 years. They prefer to be thought of as "Georgians" and not "Russians." They may have been Soviets, but they were Georgians first.

Around midmorning the next day, which was Sunday, I was met by Kakauridze, Sigua, and Professor Gabashvili, chief of neurology. Arrangements had been made for an Armenian driver from the Institute to take us on a trip into the countryside in his new car.

In the town of Mtskheta, we visited a beautiful garden owned by a lively elderly man named Michael Manulashvili, an amateur horticulturist, who was said to be 110 years old. This was his own private plot of ground where he engaged in his well-known hobby. I asked the guide for an introduction to the old gentleman so that I could tell him how pleased I was to see his place and that I had come all the way from America. Tears came to his eyes and he rose up, threw his arms around me, and kissed me on both cheeks. It was really an unforgettable scene. A large number of people living in the Republic of Georgia are said to be 100 or more years old. This has become of great interest to gerontologists worldwide and there have been several scientific studies made. It is said that the answer might be in the genetic background of these individuals; however, I wondered how accurately their birth dates had been recorded.

We drove along the rapids of the Aragvi River to the foothills of the Shenpovari Mountains. About a half hour down the road, we came to a place that had been washed out by a flash flood. A convoy of armored military vehicles had been halted by a small car obstructing their path. A senior officer arrived in his jeep, jumped out, and in an officious manner began screaming about getting that "damned car" out of the way so that he could get his vehicles through. He ordered his men down from their trucks and they literally lifted the small car and put it up on the bank. Then the convoy continued on its way. Later at the American Embassy in Moscow, I was told that the Soviets had been conducting military maneuvers all along the Turkish and Armenian border and that the region was out of bounds for foreigners. Our embassy officials were surprised to know that I had been there and were keenly interested in what I had observed.

We drove approximately sixty kilometers northwest of Tbilisi along the river to the town of Pasanauri. A delightful luncheon had been arranged for us there at a well-known restaurant with tables built in the trees. That was another novel experience for me.

The next morning, Kakauridze came to take me to the Institute. The director, Professor Seradjishvili, was a charming, seventy-seven-year-old gentleman. I had been told beforehand that he did not speak English and that he had a rather severe "logoneurosis." I tried to be polite and not ask what this meant, but when I was introduced to the professor and we began to converse in French, it was quite obvious that he was a stutterer. A tour of the Institute was arranged by Seradjishvili and the vice-director, Professor Zedginidze, with whom I also spoke in French. In the x-ray department I was introduced to another doctor who had spent two years in Cuba. Later an opportunity occurred for me to converse with him in Spanish and ask the same questions about his experience that I had put to Kopiakovsky in Kiev. His answers served to confirm much of the information given to me previously.

That evening the lecture I gave on the "Role of Vascular Surgery in the Management of Extracranial Vascular Lesions" was held in a large, comfortable hall at the Academy of Sciences. In attendance were guests invited from other institutes and polyclinics. A young neurophysiologist, Professor Okujawa, who had spent six months at the National Institutes of Health in Bethesda, Maryland, did a superb job of translating.

Upon my return to the hotel, I got stuck in the elevator with a group of clinical psychologists. I had wondered what the large gathering in the hotel represented and found out that they were psychologists from all over the Soviet Union and the other socialist countries. I had been quite surprised to find that there were no westerners in the Iveria Hotel during my entire stay. This, too, was related to the military maneuvers near the Turkish frontier. For some reason or other my presence was either condoned or overlooked.

The following day in the early afternoon, I presented a lecture on "Collateral Circulation of the Brain" at the Institute. After the lecture, the director and the senior members of his staff took me to a restaurant on the Tbilisi Sea for a "stag" dinner. It was a typical Georgian affair, with plenty of singing and many raucous stories after a few drinks. Some of us went out on the terrace to sing and dance to a balalaika. I found myself dancing with our Armenian driver, much to the delight of the others present. Having survived, with some difficulty, the almost overwhelming Georgian hospitality, with plenty of good food and drink, I was glad to return to the hotel in reasonably good condition.

Next morning I departed for the airport in the company of Kakauridze and Sigua, the same two gentlemen who had picked me up there on my arrival. I had presented to each of them a small American flag lapel pin, which they wore very proudly during the last day of my visit.

The day after my return to Moscow, I reported to the American

Embassy to retrieve my mail which had accumulated during the three weeks I had spent in other parts of the country. A debriefing session lasting nearly three hours was arranged, during which I described my observations during the trip.

The next day, Dr. Sakarova, my interpreter from the Neurological Institute, came to pick me up and deliver me to the airport for my departure to Copenhagen. I gave her several American coins from my change purse to take to her young son. She was very appreciative but quickly secreted them somewhere on her person. Then I passed quickly through a gate into the departure lounge and surrendered my exit visa. About thirty minutes later I boarded the Scandinavian Airlines plane and took my seat. A uniformed customs officer who had followed me on board began arguing loudly with the steward about some problem with the manifest. Outside on the tarmac the plane was ringed by armed guards. This made me very uneasy and gave me concern about a possible long delay. However, after a lengthy and heated discussion the customs officer seemed satisfied and left, the door was closed, and we were on our way.

The time aloft provided me with an opportunity to reflect on my impressions of my first visit to the Soviet Union. In spite of the friendly reception with which I was received and the gracious hospitality everywhere, I was relieved to be on my way to the West. When I disembarked in Copenhagen, I was tempted to get down on my knees and kiss the ground.

Return Trip: September 19-23, 1972

After my return to the United States in the summer of 1971, I sent to Professor Shmidt, director of the Institute of Neurology in Moscow, a copy of my new book *Aspirin, Platelets, and Stroke — Background for a Clinical Trial*, which I had edited with Dr. William K. Hass of New York University. In April 1972 a letter arrived from Shmidt thanking me for the book and expressing his interest in further study of antiplatelet agents for the prevention of stroke.

During the first week of September, another letter arrived from Shmidt inviting me to come to Moscow prior to the Salzburg Conference on Cerebral Circulation, to be held in Austria later that month. He and his colleagues wanted to discuss with me the possibility of cooperation in research.

In view of the fact that the ongoing cooperative study of aspirin in cerebral ischemia, of which I was the coordinator, was being supported by the National Heart and Lung Institute, it seemed appropriate to contact Dr. Theodore Cooper, director of that institute, about these overtures from the Soviet Union. A very encouraging letter came back promptly from Cooper urging me to accept the invitation and undertake these exploratory discussions. He made it quite clear, however, that no commitment for financial support could be made at that time but he expressed hope that something would come of this proposal after the implementation of the new Health Exchange Treaty early in 1973.

I waited for my visa to arrive, but by the date of my departure I still did not have it in hand. I proceeded to London anyway and the day following my arrival went to the Soviet Consulate in Hyde Park. Much to my surprise they were able to confirm that I was expected in Moscow, and the visa was approved on the spot.

From London I sent a cable to Shmidt and, upon my arrival in Moscow, the vice-director, Kanareikin, and Vladimir Smirnov from the Institute of Neurology were at Sheremetyevo Airport to meet me in the reception hall.

The following morning, Smirnov came to the hotel with his car and we drove to the Institute to meet with Shmidt. The latter arranged for several of his colleagues, including Kandel, Maxudov, and Smirnov, to meet with us in his office. They were presented with two copies of the "Manual of Procedure" for the collaborative study. These had been prepared during the previous six months. It was agreed that it would be to our mutual benefit to work out a method of collecting data employing the same source documents for purposes of comparative study. After that morning session, I took Kandel aside and asked him if he had ever received his certificate as an honorary corresponding member of the American Association of Neurological Surgeons (Harvey Cushing Society). He asked me to follow him into his office, where he showed me with great pride the framed document prominently displayed on the wall. It was obvious that he was tremendously pleased to have this honor. (In 1991, Kandel accepted an invitation to be the annual George Ehni Lecturer at Baylor, but much to our regret he succumbed to lung cancer before being able to fulfill the commitment. He had been an inveterate chain smoker for many years.)

The atmosphere during the entire session was relaxed and friendly and all of those present appeared to be intensely interested in the material which I had brought with me. Their position seemed to be, at least in part, a reflection of the fact that they knew me better as a result of my weeklong stay in Moscow the previous year. Since there would be one intervening day between the two sessions in Shmidt's office, I requested that he arrange another visit for me to the Burdenko Institute of Neurosurgery. This was confirmed with Konovalov, who had recently become director of the Burdenko Institute. The previous director, Arutiunov, had died suddenly of a heart attack during the year since my first visit.

Upon my arrival, Sasha Konovalov met me in his office and, in deference to my request, asked Feodor Serbinenko to meet with us. Serbinenko, the neurosurgeon I visited on my previous trip, had developed a new technique for insertion of latex balloons into the intracranial arteries and also into the communicating aperture of arteriovenous fistulas.

Professor Luria, unfortunately, was available for only a thirty-minute visit during that morning at the Burdenko Institute. He apologized profusely for not being able to spend more time with me, and have me once again at his home, but indicated that his wife was still recuperating from recent surgery. He was particularly pleased that one of my students would be coming to work with him during the following year.

Konovalov suggested that we go to lunch and asked Professor Samuel Blinkov and Dr. Oleg Chikovani to accompany us. Chikovani, a young neurosurgeon from Soviet Georgia, whom I had met on my previous visit and who had accompanied me one evening to the Central Lenin Stadium for a soccer match, was surprised that I still recognized him. He arranged for us to go to Aragvi, a very popular Georgian restaurant on Gorky Street. The meal and wine were excellent and we stayed there for nearly two hours discussing both medical and non-medical matters. It was my impression that they were looking forward to the implementation of the new Health Exchange Treaty which was being arranged with the Nixon administration in Washington.

(In 1973 I received a letter, mailed from West Germany, with no return address. Inside there was a note from Oleg Chikovani expressing hope that I would remember him from our brief encounters in Moscow. He stated that he was intent on leaving the Soviet Union and would arrive in Vienna on a specific date. He indicated that he would appreciate any help that I could provide him in getting to the United States. I promptly called Dick Coombs, whom I had met at the American Embassy in Moscow in 1971 and who later served as an assistant to Ambassador George Bush at the United Nations in New York. In 1972 he was in charge of the Soviet Desk at the State Department in Washington. I asked him to have someone meet Chikovani when he arrived in Austria. He agreed to do so and also arranged for the International Refugee Committee to bring him to New York. Several months later he went to the University of California at Davis to work with John Youmans and then to the Los Angeles area, where he completed residency training in neurosurgery. He is now in private practice in Newport Beach, California, married to an American and has two children. It pleases me to know that I had a small part in getting him launched on a successful career in the United States.)

Konovalov had only recently acquired a new Russian-built Fiat station wagon. He was most anxious for me to ride in his car, which was quite comfortable and mechanically well constructed. During our drive downtown I informed him that one of my former students might be coming shortly to work with Professor Luria at the Burdenko Institute. At that time this man and his wife were attending language school in California so that both could become proficient in Russian.

During a meeting at the Institute of Neurology, Shmidt surprised me by telling me that the following week he would be in Tashkent, in the Uzbek Soviet Republic in middle Asia, attending a conference of the All-Union Commission on Neurology, of which he was then the chairman. He said that at that meeting he intended to bring up the matter of international cooperative research and discuss in detail the proposal we had reviewed during my visit. This seemed to me to be most encouraging and indicative of the fact that some Soviet physicians were definitely interested in pursuing this matter for our mutual benefit.

On the day of my departure from Moscow, there was still ample time for a visit to the environs of the city. During my previous visit, I had made several requests to be taken to Gorky-Leninskye, where Lenin had lived during the last two years after his disabling stroke. On each occasion it was suggested that we go to some other place. This time they were most agreeable, so I jumped at the opportunity, and, in fact, Vladimir Smirnov said that he would like to take me personally since he had never been there himself.

Gorky-Leninskye is approximately forty-five kilometers from the center of Moscow and not one of the usual tourist attractions. Lenin's residence, which in czarist times had been the residence of a nobleman, turned out to be intensely interesting. There was even a telephone on the wall in the hallway with a direct line to the Kremlin. It had been installed explicitly for the purpose of a call to the Central Committee in the event that Lenin recovered his speech, which had been lost as a result of a stroke some months earlier.

On the wall of one room in the house was a large mural of Lenin's funeral. Members of the Central Committee of the Communist Party were standing around the head of the bier. Many years earlier, I had seen a copy of this picture in the United States and had noted that one of the persons near the head of the bed was Leon Trotsky. His head had been completely removed from the version which was on the wall in this house and replaced with the head of someone whom I did not recognize. Lenin's electric wheelchair was also there for inspection. Outside, in the garage adjacent to the main house, there was a large Rolls Royce touring car of early 1920 vintage. It had rear caterpillar treads and front skis so that Lenin could use it to take him back and forth from Gorky-Leninskye to Moscow during the winter months.

At the end of the day my hosts took me to Sheremetyevo Airport. The visit seemed to have been a most successful one in all aspects, leaving me with the feeling that important developments might be derived from this exploratory visit.

When I departed Moscow, it was my sincere hope that this would be just one small, but important, step toward a much wider range of cooperative projects. Sadly, however, that never happened. I have suspected that it was the result of bureaucratic inertia or interference.

One year later a second Baylor medical graduate, J. Thomas Hutton, who had started neurology residency training at the University of Minnesota, asked me to assist him in obtaining a fellowship with Professor Luria. This eventually came to fruition and Tom and his wife spent a year in Moscow. He was very successful in developing a close relationship with Luria and they ultimately produced several joint publications. He also became fairly proficient in Russian and found that skill to be invaluable in dealing with patients. This pleased me very much since Luria had begged me to send him a young American to learn his techniques and bring them back to this side of the Atlantic.

Although what is written in these pages took place more than twenty years ago, it would appear to be applicable in almost every aspect to what one might find traveling in the same part of the world today. The overall situation, however, is quite unstable and the world is watching anxiously to make sure that the internal affairs of that great country and its more than 250 million people can avoid the devastating consequences of internal strife. There is no doubt that civil war in the former Soviet Union would have catastrophic consequences which would reverberate throughout the world.

On the day before my departure, Professor Shmidt asked me if I would accompany him and a man from the Ministry of Health to see a patient of his who lived in a dacha outside of Moscow. We drove into the countryside and into a forest before arriving at a very imposing house. Up to that point, I had only been told the nature of the clinical problem but not the patient's name. When we arrived, the three of us were ushered into the presence of an emaciated elderly male seated in a wheelchair. It was only then that I was introduced to Maestro Dimitri Shostakovich. He expressed his appreciation for my visit and said that he wished to cooperate with my examination. We remained at the house for the best part of an hour. In the car, during the return trip, Professor Shmidt asked for my opinion and, when I said that the patient was suffering from progressive muscular atrophy, he agreed. It soon became evident that the Ministry had arranged for this consultation because the judgment and opinion of their own neurologists was not trusted. I subsequently learned that a well-known American neurologist and also a neurosurgeon had previously seen Shostakovich and had expressed the same opinion as I.

At the time of my departure from Moscow, a man from the Ministry came to the airport and presented me with a brown envelope. I put it in my pocket without opening it. On the plane when I decided to look, I found twenty one-hundred-dollar bills.

Chapter 16

Medico-Legal Matters

MY FIRST EXCURSION INTO MEDICO-LEGAL activity occurred soon after my arrival in Houston in the 1950s. I was asked by Douglas McGregor, U.S. attorney for the Southern District of Texas, to be an expert witness in a federal narcotics trial case which involved several prominent Houston citizens and was, therefore, front-page material for the newspapers. So much so, in fact, that it was deemed by the court to be impossible to provide the accused with a fair trial in Harris County.

A well-known Houston osteopathic physician, who was a graduate of Rice Institute (now Rice University), was accused of conspiring to provide excessive amounts of codeine for the then Houston chief of police, L. D. Morrison, who had been suffering considerable pain from arthritis in his neck. This physician's management of the problem might not have received much attention had it not been for the fact that many of the prescriptions that he issued for large numbers of tablets were written in the name of one of his cancer patients, a black man who was already deceased.

The trial was moved to Corpus Christi, with U.S. District Judge Alan Hannay of Houston presiding. I flew there with two other medical witnesses, James Greene, chairman of the Department of Medicine at Baylor, and Claude Pollard, Jr., a neurosurgeon who had been requested to see the police chief as a patient. The prosecuting U.S. attorney was Malcomb Wilkey, also from Houston. The doctor was found guilty on all counts and sentenced to a jail term. One must remember that this was in the 1950s and when compared with the level of illegal drug activity in Houston in the early 1990s, the issues in that case, although clearly illegal, seem ridiculously inconsequential. I was astonished to meet Wilkey again in 1991, at the home of mutual friends in Montevideo, Uruguay, where he was serving as U.S. ambassador. We both recalled that landmark case from nearly forty years earlier.

The next time that I was asked to serve as an expert witness in a lawsuit was in the late 1950s. I received a call from William Keith of the law firm of Cecil, Keith, and Mahaffey in Beaumont, Texas, and subsequently met with him in the doctors' library at The Methodist Hospital in Houston to discuss the case in which he was defense counsel. Keith presented me with records for review related to a lawsuit filed in behalf of an oilfield worker who had succumbed to brain hemorrhage from a ruptured intracranial aneurysm while working on an oil rig in the vicinity of High Island, Texas. The deceased had gone to the Port-a-Can to relieve himself. On the way back to the job site, he had suddenly cried out that he had a severe headache and lost consciousness. An ambulance was summoned but he was dead on arrival at John Sealy Hospital in Galveston, where an autopsy revealed the cause of his death.

The trial in this case was held at Anahuac, in Chambers County, on the east side of Galveston Bay. Before appearing in court for the defendant, McCarthy Oil & Gas Company, I reviewed what was in those days the most authoritative text on intracranial aneurysms, written by Dr. Wallace Hamby of Buffalo, New York, and published in 1951. I was convinced that the plaintiff's attorney would use that book as a reference source during the trial, so I memorized the numbers of key pages on which there was material related to the specific issues which were almost certain to be raised.

After being qualified to the jury by the defense attorney, Bill Keith, and stating my opinions about the manner of the plaintiff's death, I was cross-examined by the plaintiff's counsel, Russell Marquard, a prominent Galveston attorney, whom I knew to be well versed in trying personal injury lawsuits. Just as I had anticipated, I noted a copy of Dr. Hamby's book lying on the table in front of him. After a few preliminary questions, he picked up the book, which he had already earmarked for reference purposes. He asked me if I accepted Dr. Hamby as an authority in these matters and I conceded that I did. Then he proceeded to read from the book to me and the jury. He wanted to know if I had any disagreement with what he had just read and I said, "No," but I hastened to point out that he had taken the quotation completely out of context. I requested that he read to the jury the paragraph preceding and the one following the quotation he just read, and the judge instructed him to do so. I pointed out that this material was on page 167 in the book and that if he would please turn to page 211 and read the middle paragraph to the jury, they would see that the latter statement completely refuted his position with regard to the causation of the man's death. Needless to say, this totally destroyed the argument which he was following and he did not have anywhere to go after that. Consequently, he could not get me off the witness stand and away from the jury quickly enough.

The most interesting aspect of this case, as far as I was concerned, took place about six weeks later when I received a telephone call from Marquard inquiring as to my availability to review a case for him and to appear in court in Galveston. I consented to do so and reviewed the material forwarded to me, following which I reported to him by telephone. To my regret, the matter was settled out of court and I did not go to Galveston after all to testify in behalf of Marquard's client.

One day in 1960, a Houston attorney, whom I had never heard of before, brought to my office at Baylor an elderly woman who, he informed me, lived in a house close to downtown. He was anxious to have me speak with her and examine her to determine if she was mentally competent and could execute some legal papers. The woman was clean, well dressed and spoke quite convincingly about her home, her current activities, and the fact that she had no living relatives. Nevertheless, simple verbal testing and the urgency apparent in the demeanor of the lawyer accompanying her suggested to me that the information provided by both of them was not completely reliable and perhaps a downright fabrication.

The attorney appeared to be too eager to have me provide him with a letter attesting to the lady's mental competence so I put him off by saying that I would need more time and an opportunity to obtain more facts. However, I saw no harm in providing him with a letter merely stating that she had been seen and examined in my office.

He then took my noncommittal letter and tried to use it as a means of acquiring certification of a legal instrument which he had prepared. This document had been signed by his "client," and appropriately witnessed. It made him in effect the woman's guardian and gave him control of her assets. I knew nothing about this until Joyce Cox, a prominent Houston attorney, called and informed me that he was representing the woman's niece who lived in Philadelphia. She had become aware that something was awry after receiving several telephone calls from her aunt. I told Cox, whom I had met on one previous occasion, that I was not at liberty to discuss the matter on the phone but would be pleased to meet with him and the niece in my office. They came several days later and presented me with a letter on what appeared to be my letterhead and had what purported to be my signature. I had never seen it before and told them that it was a cleverly devised forgery.

As a result of this criminal activity, the attorney who had brought the woman to my attention in the first place was brought to trial and I was subpoenaed to testify against him. He was convicted, disbarred, and sent to the state penitentiary. Although I saw his name again years later, our paths never crossed. It was a great relief to me since I could easily have been duped into playing a more significant role in the case.

In the early 1960s, I was contacted by Richard Roberts, an attorney who was one of my friends and a neighbor in Bunker Hill Village. He requested that I review a file for him and, if necessary, testify in court. The lawsuit in question concerned several prominent Houstonians and received a considerable amount of publicity in the local press. It involved the estate of Mrs. W. D. Haden, the wife of "Cap" Haden, who had built a substantial tugboat and barge business in the Galveston-Houston area. The Hadens also had a large commercial operation making building material from cement and oyster shell dredged from the Galveston Bay. Mrs. Haden, an elderly woman, had been enticed into signing a new will by her son, Edgar, with the connivance of a well-known Houston lawyer, John Crooker, Sr. One weekend these two men took her to a ranch in the country in order to have this legal instrument, prepared by Crooker, signed and witnessed. It, in effect, deeded all of her sizable estate to her son, Edgar, and cut out her other son, Cecil.

Shortly after her death, when the new will was probated, the disposition of her assets was revealed. Cecil Haden protested and sought redress in a lawsuit claiming that his mother was incompetent at the time she signed the legal document in question. I was asked to address the issue of her mental capacity.

Mrs. Haden, despite inheriting a large estate from her husband, had for many years been a recluse living on such a restricted diet that she developed pellagra, a condition resulting from a deficiency of niacin, an integral part of the vitamin B complex. As a consequence, she had the classical symptoms referred to by medical students as the three D's, namely, dermatitis (skin rash), diarrhea, and dementia. Review of the records from Memorial Baptist Hospital left no doubt regarding the nature and severity of her symptoms. There was no question in my mind that she was incompetent to execute a last will and testament.

The case was tried in the district court of Judge Thomas Stovall, with Dick Roberts and his co-counsel, Dow Heard, representing Cecil Haden, and John Crooker, representing Edgar Haden and his father. I was on the witness stand from midmorning of one day to midmorning of the next, while the opposing counsel tried to break down my testimony and put words in my mouth. He eventually ran out of questions. I was glad to be dismissed because the need to concentrate on each question had left me with a severe headache which lasted well into the following day. Ultimately, the jury found in favor of the opponent, Cecil Haden, and the new will was declared null and void. I was pleased to learn from Dick Roberts that Judge Stovall thought I had performed in an exemplary fashion on the witness stand.

That case taught me an important lesson: When I go on the witness stand, I should be well prepared and assume that I know more about the medical aspects of the case than anyone else in the courtroom. Such an attitude prevents one from being verbally abused by the opposing attorney during cross-examinations. It has kept me out of difficulty in court on several occasions since that landmark case.

About two years before I left Baylor and moved to Dallas, my secretary informed me that I had received a telephone call from Leon Jaworski requesting an appointment to discuss an important legal matter. Jaworski, a member of the board of trustees of Baylor College of Medicine and a powerful figure in Houston legal circles, made it clear that it concerned one of his wealthy clients and that the matter was urgent.

He came to my office accompanied by an attractive woman in

her late fifties, who was the widow of one of Houston's wealthiest citizens. I had not met her before but her husband had been my patient for more than three years. Although this woman had lived with the man for many years, she had not married him until about eighteen months before his death. After their marriage, he had executed a new will providing her with a lifetime income. However, the bulk of his substantial estate was designated to go to a foundation which he had established with his brother.

Jaworski wanted me to attest that the deceased had been mentally competent at the time he had signed that legal instrument. This was something that I could not and would not, in good conscience, do. I preferred not to discuss the situation further in front of his client and asked him to give me a little time to review the matter and get back to him. I called the next day and told him that I valued my reputation for integrity too much to be persuaded. He thanked me, and I thought that the matter ended there.

Four years later, after I had moved back to Houston from my brief sojourn in Dallas, I sent a written request to the M. D. Anderson Foundation for support of a scientific symposium which I planned for the following spring. The letter was sent to John Freeman, chairman of the Foundation's board of trustees, of which Leon Jaworski was a member. Much to my satisfaction, the Foundation made an award of $15,000, a sizable sum in 1972. Leon Jaworski called me and said that he would like to deliver the check personally. I was flattered that he wished to do so, but was even more surprised when he told me, during his visit to my office, that he wanted to compliment me on my honesty and integrity.

In the spring of 1969, only a few days after my return from Dallas, I read in the *Houston Post* about the unexpected death of Joan Robinson Hill, the wife of plastic surgeon John Hill. The circumstances surrounding her death were unusual, to say the least, and engendered a lot of speculation with regard to the cause.

Several weeks later, Dr. and Mrs. Howard Siegler, whom we had met in Dallas, invited Bette and me to visit them at Chatsworth Farm on what is now South Gessner Road. They were renting the property from Mr. and Mrs. Ash Robinson, parents of Joan. The Robinsons, Ash and Rhea, whom we had never met before, proceeded to tell us, with considerable emotion, what they believed had happened to their daughter. Ash in particular was very bitter and left no doubt that he was convinced his daughter had been murdered by

John Hill. Not knowing anything about the matter, I made no comment, although it was obvious that Ash was trying to enlist my help in bashing John Hill. I had known John only as one student among many at Baylor College of Medicine and had no opinion of him one way or the other.

Ash Robinson, determined to see John Hill brought to trial for murder, soon began a crusade to see that this was accomplished. Finally, the Harris County district attorney, Carol Vance, was pressured into empaneling a grand jury to investigate the matter. The aforementioned Cecil Haden, a friend of Ash Robinson, was named foreman. This hardly seemed likely, in my opinion, to result in an unbiased assessment of the evidence. For reasons known best to them, Cecil and Ash would frequently come to my office in the basement of St. Anthony Center on Almeda Road to discuss the details of the grand jury proceedings. I refused to be a party to these discussions since I knew that what went on in the jury room was supposed to be privileged information. I finally had to tell them that they were no longer welcome.

An autopsy had been performed by the pathologist at Sharpstown Hospital, where Mrs. Hill had died. Because of his suspicions about the manner in which she died, Ash Robinson obtained a court order to have his daughter's body exhumed for another private autopsy by Milton Halpern, former chief medical examiner of New York City, whom Ash had hired to come to Houston. I was invited to attend the procedure at the medical examiner's office but declined. That evening I was invited by Ash to have dinner at Ye Olde College Inn on South Main Street with Dr. Halpern and a local physician friend of Ash. Several weeks after that, I received a phone call from Joseph Jachimczyk, the Harris County medical examiner, requesting that I come to his office to examine the spinal cord removed at the exhumation autopsy and the brain delivered to him by the pathologist who had removed it at the original postmortem examination. The latter gentleman reported that the brain, after being placed in formaldehyde, had been in the trunk of his car for an extended period of time.

My review in the medical examiner's office of tissue sections from both the brainstem and the spinal cord, prepared for microscopic examination, was very revealing. The former had been part of the material delivered by the hospital pathologist to the Harris County medical examiner and clearly showed evidence of purulent meningitis. The latter, which was removed by Halpern at the exhumation autopsy, showed no evidence whatsoever of infection. It was, therefore, my conclusion that the brain had to be that of another person since it would have been impossible to have evidence of a severe infection in one area and not see any in a location less than a quarter of an inch away, particularly when both parts were contained within the same fluid-filled space of the spinal canal. The part of the foregoing regarding the autopsy and my written report is included in Thomas Thompson's best-selling book entitled *Blood and Money*, but I was never interviewed by the author. I was delighted that he never saw fit to call on me.

When my report became public, the hospital pathologist was incensed and referred to me in very uncomplimentary terms in the local newspapers. I did not make at that time, and have never made since, any comment other than the fact that in my opinion the specimens had to have come from two different individuals.

Later, Ash Robinson had me subpoenaed for a deposition in the offices of his attorney. He evidently had told the lawyer that I must have had information about the case which I had withheld, but since I knew nothing more, this tactic got him nowhere.

Another case I will never forget involved a man in his early forties who had just been promoted to vice-president of a large Houston company. His wife was an ardent long-distance runner and had competed in several important races in various parts of the country. They decided to drive to Boston, where she was to compete in the April 18th Patriot's Day Marathon, and they took along their teenaged son and daughter. Eastbound on the interstate highway across New York state, they were involved in a head-on collision with a large trailer truck. The driver had been observed by other motorists to be in a race with another truck. The trucks sideswiped, causing one to veer across the median directly into the path of the oncoming vehicle. The wife and daughter were killed while the son escaped with only minor injuries. The husband survived although he had sustained multiple severe injuries, including a blow to the head. After a long period in a coma, it was evident that he had devastating permanent brain injury.

I was requested by one of the plaintiff's attorneys, Richard Mithoff, to examine the man and testify regarding the extent of his injury and provide an estimation of long-term disability. I accompanied Mithoff to the home of the plaintiff's parents, where he was being cared for by his mother. At the bedside, I noted a book, entitled *Coping with Stroke: Communication Breakdown of Brain Injured Adults,* by Helen Broida, Ph.D. I had written the foreword for this book and both the man's mother and Mithoff were surprised by this revelation.

I sent a written report to the leading attorney for the plaintiff, none other than the now famous Joseph Jamail. The case was to be tried in federal court in Beaumont, Texas, but was settled on the courthouse steps, so to speak. Joe Jamail called me from there to tell me that I would not be needed in court. He also made a point of informing me that the settlement was the largest ever in Texas for a personal injury case. How much my report had to do with settling the matter, I will never know, but my fee as I recall was far too modest.

Richard Mithoff, who was no longer associated with Jamail, called me in 1989 and requested that I examine a three-year-old child who had suffered brain injury during a traumatic childbirth. I agreed to do so with the understanding that I would limit my opinion to the extent of the injury and the long-term outlook. It has always been my position not to testify against a fellow physician in my own community no matter what the opinion might be.

I went with a registered nurse, employed by Mithoff, to examine the child at home. The following month, in deposition at Mithoff's office, when I said that I had taken a clinical history from the mother, the defendant's attorney asked how I managed to do this when she spoke no English. I hastened to point out that our conversation had been in Spanish. Later in court, while on the witness stand, I took note of the fact that three of the jurors were Hispanic. Mithoff asked me to examine the child and point out to the jury the extent of her handicap. I approached the mother, who was on the other side of the courtroom holding the child, and asked her in Spanish to assist me with my demonstration. There was no doubt that this maneuver scored "brownie points" with those jurors. During the recess immediately following my testimony and just before I left the courthouse, the defendant's leading attorney, whom I knew personally, remarked to me as an aside, "Fields, you absolutely destroyed us in this case." Under the circumstances, I considered that comment to be grudgingly complimentary.

As previously mentioned, during the two years while Truman Blocker was acting president of The University of Texas Health Science Center, I chaired the Professional Liability Committee to review cases in which a faculty member had been sued. Almost all of those cases were malpractice issues, which was not surprising in view of the escalation in the number of such lawsuits in Harris County, Texas, beginning in the late 1970s.

One case of note at Hermann Hospital involved a patient scheduled to have orthopedic surgery for a ruptured lumbar disk. During the induction of anesthesia, the endotracheal tube was improperly placed in the patient's esophagus (throat) rather than in the trachea (windpipe) and then he was turned face down on the table. It was several minutes before the mistake was recognized. The patient had stopped breathing and required resuscitation. The operation was canceled and the patient transferred to the medical intensive care unit. He died several days later. Consequently, it was no surprise when a lawsuit was brought several months afterward by the patient's widow.

I personally undertook a thorough review of the medical chart. The anesthesia record was very neat and complete but made no mention of the circumstances surrounding the patient's failure to breathe normally during the induction of anesthesia. Then I noticed that on that record the name of the patient stamped at the top of the page was correct but the imprint had the name of the pulmonary medicine specialist to whose service the patient had been transferred from the operating room. The imprint was from a plate that would normally not have been available for at least two days after the patient was transferred to the medical service. It was immediately evident that the original page had been removed and another record substituted. When confronted with this scenario several months after the procedure, the anesthesiologist said that he had rewritten the record following the operation because coffee had been spilled on the original and it was illegible. He had then destroyed the original instead of leaving it in the chart along with the new record which he had substituted. He stated that he had informed the chairman of his department. The latter had apparently chosen to ignore the incident. When it was pointed out that the record in the chart had to have been written three or four days after the operation, he vehemently denied this and accused me of harassing him. However, after this information surfaced, a meeting was arranged with the anesthesiologist and his chairman in the office of the chief of surgery. The culprit was asked to tender his resignation from the faculty or be dismissed. He was advised to look elsewhere as promptly as possible.

Assuming that what had been done would sooner or later be discovered by the plaintiff's attorney, who was also a physician, I invited the latter to meet with our Professional Liability Committee and the hospital's general counsel to avoid possible adverse publicity directed at our university group practice, the hospital, or both. The attorney was satisfied when a substantial out-of-court settlement was reached.

Chapter 17

M. D. Anderson Cancer Center and Retirement (Perhaps)

THE M. D. ANDERSON HOSPITAL for Cancer Research, at the time of my arrival in Houston in July 1949, was located on the former estate of James Addison Baker, known as "The Oaks," at Baldwin and McIlhenny streets. Shortly before I came, several Quonset huts, originally used by the U.S. Army, had been purchased from the War Assets Administration for $55,000. These buildings had been transported from Camp Wallace to the hospital's temporary site, where they were remodeled and furnished. Three of them became inpatient wards, one became the location for laboratories, while another provided additional office space. Patients requiring major surgery or intensive care were admitted to Hermann Hospital across town on what was referred to as the "Anderson Floor" (twenty-two beds) or to the Houston Negro Hospital (ten beds). At these locations the diagnostic and treatment procedures, except for pathology and radiology, but including nursing, were conducted by members of the M. D. Anderson Hospital staff. In the event of an emergency, residents and interns at Hermann Hospital were available for immediate assistance. This arrangement continued until the new Anderson Hospital in the Texas Medical Center was officially opened on February 28, 1954. I recall visiting there that day with some colleagues from Baylor College of Medicine. The dedication ceremonies, however, did not take place until October 21-23 of that year.

The hospital grew rapidly and very soon the space provided by the initial construction was found to be inadequate. In September 1964 work was begun on the Research and Gimbel Building additions, which were completed in June 1969.

The Mayfair Apartment Hotel, located directly across Holcombe Boulevard from the hospital, had been taken over by the Cancer Center administration shortly before I returned to Houston in February 1969. Dr. R. Lee Clark had lived in one of the two penthouses there, while the other was occupied by the man who originally owned the hotel and had a large lien against it. In the evenings the owner and Clark would sit out on the balcony and talk. It wasn't long before Clark talked the man into selling the Mayfair to The University of Texas. The vice-president for business affairs was against the idea at first since he did not think that the State of Texas should be involved in the hotel business. However, in the long run the deal turned out to be a very successful one. The building, constructed during the late 1950s, was deemed a suitable structure for housing the families of patients in the hospital or being treated as outpatients. That building was demolished in 1990 and replaced by a new hotel.

Lee Clark was the one who promoted the institution and essentially kept it afloat. He was responsible for the structural additions, hiring more people, and getting additional appropriations. However, others who stand out in my mind who have not gotten the credit which they deserve are State Senator Aiken, at one time chairman of the Senate Appropriations Committee, whose sister had been treated for cancer at the hospital, and Frank Irwin, chairman of the Board of Regents of The University of Texas. When Lee Clark said that he needed some money to support his program, another million dollars would be forthcoming. He was exceedingly persuasive.

My first contact with M. D. Anderson Hospital came about in a rather unusual manner. Early in 1951, some psychiatrists who had come to Houston to establish themselves in private practice after World War II contacted me and said that they wanted instruction in neurology and neuropathology so that they would be sufficiently knowledgeable in those disciplines to obtain specialty board certification. The American Board of Psychiatry and Neurology from its inception has been a dual specialty board, largely because in the early days of its existence there were not enough neurologists to financially support a separate accrediting agency. All candidates then seeking certification had to take an examination in both disciplines, but with emphasis on one or the other. Today the examinations are quite separate although still administered by a single board.

In order to accommodate these doctors, I spoke with William O. Russell, then chief of pathology at M. D. Anderson Hospital, to work out a teaching schedule. Bill and I had been engaged in postgraduate work at Washington University in St. Louis — he in pathology and I in neurology — and came to Houston at about the same time. I was aware that he had an excellent background in neuropathology and would be the ideal person to collaborate with me in developing a course. Together we arranged some sessions to be conducted on two nights a week for six weeks in one of the Quonset huts at the Baker Estate. The curriculum included both clinical and pathological subject material. As a consequence of that inauspicious beginning, my association with M. D. Anderson Hospital as a consultant or part-time staff member (and later full-time) goes back to several years before that institution moved into permanent quarters in the Texas Medical Center.

Beginning in the late 1950s, after I had become chairman of the newly created Department of Neurology at Baylor, I frequently received requests for either me or one of my associates to see patients in consultation at M. D. Anderson Hospital. The neurosurgery and most of the neurology at that time was being done by George Ehni, and to a lesser extent by Marshall Henry, both of whom had clinical appointments at Baylor College of Medicine and were on the staff at The Methodist Hospital. I continued to serve in the capacity of consultant until 1962. At that time I recommended that Israel H. Schuleman, whom I had brought back to Texas from Michigan to be chief of neurology at the Veterans Administration Hospital, assume the responsibilities of consultant in neurology at M. D. Anderson. He was then in private practice but still had a clinical appointment in the Department of Neurology at Baylor. I agreed, however, to continue to assist Ehni and Schuleman in the outpatient clinic when requested.

By the late 1960s, while I was still at Baylor, George Ehni devoted less time to M. D. Anderson Hospital and many of his responsibilities there were assumed by his associate, Milam Leavens, who had been in the private practice of neurosurgery with him for several

M. D. Anderson Cancer Center and Retirement (Perhaps)

years. Schuleman continued to serve as a part-time consultant until he suffered a heart attack and died rather suddenly and unexpectedly in 1972, at the age of fifty-two. Following Israel's death, Milam requested that I come back and assist him in the outpatient clinic, which I did one day each week for many years. By that time I was at The University of Texas Medical School and Hermann Hospital.

As a consequence of my association with M. D. Anderson Hospital on a part-time basis for almost two decades, I was brought in contact with many of the staff and faculty members. The ones with whom I had the closest relationship at that time, apart from the neurosurgeons, were Gerald Dodd in diagnostic radiology and Gilbert Fletcher in radiotherapy. They were both very helpful in the early development of The University of Texas Medical School.

In 1966, when my situation at Baylor had begun to unravel, Lee Clark contacted me and asked me to consider joining his staff. He took me to lunch on two occasions and tried to convince me to do so. I told him at the time that it would be ill advised for me to accept his invitation and perhaps might be embarrassing as well in view of the difficulties which I had been having with Michael DeBakey. He agreed rather reluctantly, and I went on to Dallas to accept the academic position.

When I returned to Houston in March 1969, the Graduate School of Biomedical Sciences of The University of Texas was being administered by the M. D. Anderson Hospital and Tumor Institute and it was from there that I received my monthly paycheck. The dean was an old friend, H. Grant Taylor, and I was appointed as his special assistant, although it was never made clear to me what that meant. My office was at St. Anthony Center on Almeda Road and my professional activities and funds were administered by Elmer Gilley, business manager at Anderson. My job was not on the state budget, so I earned my own income from clinical activities in which I was involved at other hospitals in the Medical Center. It was a rough two years because I had rather substantial research responsibilities and little financial support for myself.

In January 1971, a group of staff members of the Cancer Center, led by William Derrick, chief of anesthesiology, requested permission from the administration to start a faculty club at the Anderson-Mayfair Hotel across the street from the hospital. The Physicians Referral Service put up some money for remodeling space on the second floor, which was subsequently used for the club. This included a faculty dining area with an adjacent lounge and bar. Across the hall there was another large room which was set aside for meetings and could also be used for table tennis. Bill Derrick was elected president of the club and I was asked to serve on the house committee. Lee Clark was very supportive of the plan, and the facility was used regularly by the Anderson faculty and others from the School of Public Health during the midday lunch break.

I was elected president of the club in 1972 during the second year of its existence and was, to my knowledge, the only person not on the Anderson full-time faculty to ever serve in that capacity. This provided me with an excellent opportunity to become more closely acquainted with a large number of members of that faculty.

One evening during my tenure as president, I had called a meeting of the house committee to discuss the hiring of a new manager. What I did not know was that a dinner meeting of the Board of Regents of The University of Texas was to take place in the main dining room immediately after the adjournment of ours. When I came out of our small meeting room into the dining area, I was surprised to find Regent A. G. McNeese of Houston visiting with Charles Sprague, president of the Health Science Center at Dallas; William Levin, president of the Medical Branch in Galveston; and Frank Harrison, president of the Health Science Center at San Antonio. I had known each of these doctors on a first-name basis for several years, but the reception which I received was surprisingly cool. While I was speaking with them, Lee Clark came into the room with John Victor Olsen, dean of the Dental Branch and acting president of the Health Science Center at Houston. They were accompanied by regent Joseph Nelson, M.D., of Weatherford, Texas. When Joe Nelson greeted me effusively and expressed his pleasure at seeing me, the demeanor of the gentlemen with whom I was speaking changed abruptly. Charlie Sprague asked Joe Nelson, "How do you know this man?" He replied, "Bill was one of my favorite teachers in medical school and we have been friends ever since." The atmosphere changed immediately, almost as though someone had thrown a switch and everything was sweetness and light. I thoroughly enjoyed the moment and then excused myself.

The Faculty Club served as a regular meeting place at noon for a small group, including Ed White, Cliff Howe, Felix Haas, Stuart Zimmerman, occasionally C. C. Shullenberger, and myself. These informal gatherings were very revealing and provided me with considerable insight into the functioning of M. D. Anderson Hospital and Tumor Institute.

One day I had occasion to talk at the club with Cliff Howe, chief of medicine, and told him, "I have known you a lot longer than you are aware. We met when you and I were residents at the Royal Victoria Hospital in Montreal, Canada. I was in internal medicine and you were at the Maternity Hospital doing obstetrics and gynecology with Newell Philpot." Cliff was astonished and said, "How did you know that?" I replied, "Well, we were on the house staff there at the same time. You left to join the British army and a year later I left to join the Canadian navy."

I continued to frequent the club and maintain contact with many of its members as long as I remained at St. Anthony Center and had a clinical faculty appointment at Anderson. After I moved my department, in 1976, from St. Anthony Center to the medical school building next to Hermann Hospital on the north side of the Medical Center, it became less convenient to frequent the Faculty Club and I no longer participated in the day-to-day activities. However, my association with these men and others had provided me with contacts that served me well later while at The University of Texas Medical School and then at M. D. Anderson Hospital after I joined the full-time staff in 1982.

I was still chairing the Department of Neurology at The University of Texas Medical School thirteen years later when Charles "Mickey" LeMaistre became president of the M. D. Anderson Hospital and Tumor Institute. Even before LeMaistre's arrival in Houston, neurology consultation was being provided there by members of our medical school department. Although Milam Leavens had been the full-time neurosurgeon on the Anderson Hospital staff for many years, with a resident rotating from the Baylor neurosurgery program, there was no full-time neurologist or neurology service. When J. Peter Glass (who had trained in neuro-oncology with Jerome Posner at Memorial Sloan-Kettering Cancer Center in New York) was recruited to our medical school department in August 1978, I arranged for him to work more than half-time at M. D. Anderson Hospital. A neurology resident from our medical school training program was also assigned. This latter person was expected to divide his or her time between Anderson and St. Anthony Center. After 1978, when the neurology department of the medical school had moved from St. Anthony Center to the new U.T. Medical School building in the medical center, each resident spent three months full-time at M. D. Anderson Hospital.

When Peter Glass arrived at the cancer hospital, there was no office which could be provided for him and so he operated out of a conference room at Station 60 in the Clinic Building. Consultation requests came in slowly at first, at the rate of approximately twenty per month. There was only one half-day of neurology clinic activity per week. There was no full-time neurologist, no neuropathologist, and no scheduled conferences. Only one computed tomography (CT) scanner was available, and this was being used primarily for examination of organ systems other than the brain and spinal cord.

During his first two years, Peter Glass worked alone at Anderson, at times conferring with Milam Leavens in neurosurgery and at other times by telephone with me and with those who had been responsible for his training at Memorial Sloan-Kettering in New York. These consultations by phone were related principally to difficult clinical problems. He also endeavored to acquaint staff doctors and fellows with neuro-oncology through lectures and case presentations, but most importantly, by providing a constant visible presence, thorough evaluations, appropriate answers to diagnostic questions, and an underlying commitment to the best possible patient care.

In late February 1980, soon after his arrival in Houston as president of M. D. Anderson Hospital and Tumor Institute, Mickey LeMaistre expressed to me an interest for further development of neurology at the Cancer Center.

In March 1980, at my suggestion, Milam Leavens, chief of neurosurgery, wrote to Robert C. Hickey, director of M. D. Anderson Hospital, recommending the recruitment of two more medical neurologists. These physicians would be responsible for neurology consultations and chemotherapy of primary malignant brain tumors. A copy of this memorandum was sent to Dr. LeMaistre. The latter immediately wrote to Hickey as follows:

> I like the concept of a joint neurology and neurosurgery program, including both inpatient and outpatient programs. In the outpatient program, I would like to see a first class pain clinic developed with a strong commitment to inpatient consultation. The pain clinic should be developed in conjunction with the excellent pain clinic at Hermann Hospital. Would you please discuss this with

Fred Conrad. Dr. Conrad should recommend the final program and plan after discussion with Drs. Leavens, Fields, Glass and others.

This resulted in a meeting the following month, attended by Fred Conrad, vice-president for patient care, Robert Hickey, Milam Leavens, Peter Glass, and myself, to discuss the establishment of a neuro-oncology program and a pain clinic. The concept of a combined neurosurgery and neurology program was discussed. The issues were directed toward an amalgamation of the neuroscience disciplines and the allocation of approximately ten dedicated beds. It was recognized that both disciplines were understaffed and active recruitment should be initiated. In addition, there was agreement that the pain clinic should be multidisciplinary but have its base in neuro-oncology. There was unanimity of opinion that additional input should be sought from anesthesiology, psychiatry, physical medicine, and nursing. It amazed me that in a major facility for treatment of cancer such as M. D. Anderson, these matters had until then been addressed inadequately.

Robert Hickey kept referring to the planned program as a "brain tumor section," but I pointed out to him in a memo in June 1980 that neuro-oncology encompassed not only the diagnosis and management of primary and metastic brain tumors, but also the neurological complications of radiation therapy and chemotherapy and the remote effects of some cancers on the nervous system. This suggestion seemed to strike a sympathetic cord because, from that time on, the planned program was referred to as one in neuro-oncology. At that point arrangements for Peter Glass to transfer to M. D. Anderson from the medical school were finalized. Since Glass was already spending almost all of his time at Anderson, it seemed reasonable, and acceptable to me, for him to be offered a full-time position there. However, I felt that additional neurologists should be sought, so I initiated the recruitment of two other recent graduates from Posner's program in New York, Eugenie A.M.T. Obbens and W. K. Alfred Yung.

While I was still at the U.T. Medical School, "Mickey" LeMaistre contacted Roger Bulger, president of The University of Texas Health Science Center, and requested that I be permitted to chair a panel to investigate alleged improprieties on the part of several faculty members at M. D. Anderson Cancer Center, in dealing with cancer chemotherapy protocols. These protocols, dealing with experimental antitumor agents, were under the strict supervision of the National Cancer Institute in Bethesda, Maryland. This matter had come to the attention of a committee of the U.S. Congress, chaired by Senator Paula Hawkins of Florida, who threatened to cause serious repercussions in our dealings with the National Cancer Institute. Important government contracts and other major funding were at stake. Our investigation was thorough and the deliberations were recorded and transcribed. Apparently our committee did its job well because the matter was adjudicated promptly and we avoided what might otherwise have been considerable embarrassment for the institution and perhaps the loss of substantial financial support. I was pleased that LeMaistre had expressed his confidence in my ability to handle the matter expeditiously and without further publicity.

This experience helped prepare me in many ways for the administrative relationships that existed in M. D. Anderson Hospital. Being both forewarned and forearmed enabled me to adjust and encounter fewer surprises than might have occurred when I moved to M. D. Anderson from the medical school about a year and a half later.

In the early part of 1981, Philip Gildenberg, professor of neurosurgery at The University of Texas Medical School, engaged in discussions concerning the establishment of a neurosurgery residency training program. Over many years, prior to Gildenberg's coming to Houston and before The University of Texas Medical School appeared on the scene, the neurosurgery program at M. D. Anderson had been closely affiliated with that of Baylor College of Medicine. LeMaistre undertook to discuss this matter with both Gildenberg and Robert Grossman, professor of neurosurgery at Baylor and director of the training program there. He stated that it was his desire to continue the utilization of such beneficial arrangements as feasible with either or both medical schools in the future. He expressed the opinion that Baylor College of Medicine had been an effective collaborator over many years in the development of the neurosurgical-service at M. D. Anderson Hospital.

Late in 1981, I informed Dean Ernst Knobil at The University of Texas Medical School and President Bulger at the Health Science Center once again that I was anxious to be relieved of my duties as department chairman and requested formally that a search committee be appointed to find my successor. LeMaistre learned of this almost immediately. He called me and asked if I would be interested in moving to M. D. Anderson Hospital at the end of the academic year to personally undertake the development of the neuro-oncology program. I assured him that although I had contemplated retiring, I would be interested inasmuch as I considered the project to be a worthy challenge. However, I wanted to be certain that those persons already on board at M. D. Anderson would greet me with enthusiasm and not with suspicion. I did not want to just walk in and risk stepping on the toes of other people, even those whom I had recruited, since they already had a vested interest in what was going to be developed.

I received a letter from LeMaistre informing me that not only had those persons already on board expressed interest in his proposal but had also sent a joint memorandum on the subject of a neuro-oncology center to Fred Conrad. This pleased me very much and allayed any concern that I had. The group included Milam Leavens, the three neurologists — Glass, Obbens, and Yung, and Lynn Fuen, a medical oncologist who was working with them. Fuen had been responsible for the brain tumor chemotherapy program in what was formerly the Department of Developmental Therapeutics and he had been transferred to the neurology section. I was extremely pleased that all of those on the scene supported my recruitment as director of the new unit. Once this was accomplished, I proceeded to make arrangements to join the M. D. Anderson faculty and move across the campus.

While making plans for my move, with September 1982 as the target date, I had been advised by LeMaistre to work out with Fred Conrad a suitable agenda for the development of an independent neuro-oncology service. I recommended that we recruit at least one more neurologist since the number of consultation requests was already escalating and the clinic census had risen dramatically. It appeared as though this was a fulfillment of my prophecy that the demand would increase as soon as an adequate presence could be demonstrated. Moreover, it seemed to me that the pain service should be broadened to include not only the outpatient clinic activities but the inpatient services as well. I also felt that it was imperative to establish our own educational program in neuro-oncology, to begin July 1, 1982, two months before my anticipated move to M. D. Anderson from the medical school. Institutional funds for two fellowships were requested and the funds were provided by Dr. James Bowen, vice-president for academic affairs.

My mission as I saw it was to pull together all the diverse elements of clinical and basic neuroscience already in operation within the institution and establish a cohesive program to study and treat all aspects of neuro-oncology, both medical and surgical. At first glance the administration had thought of neuro-oncology only as the study of brain tumors, but in my opinion, a comprehensive approach to neuro-oncology (cancer neurology) encompassed a considerable number of other medical problems. Management of brain tumors was only a relatively small part of a much broader discipline. Advances in the treatment of primary brain cancers had not progressed as rapidly as treatment of those in other anatomic areas, and, consequently, the outlook for persons suffering from brain tumors was still grim. Few adult patients survived more than six months beyond the time of diagnosis, although the survival of children with brain tumors was considerably more optimistic.

In addition to those patients with primary tumors within the brain, there are far more who suffer brain and spinal spread from other systemic malignancies, most commonly lung and breast cancers and the lymphomas. Another important aspect of neuro-oncology is the frequent occurrence of toxic side effects on the nervous system produced by commonly employed treatment modalities, including chemotherapy and radiation. It had been, from the onset, my conviction that neuro-oncology as a discipline encompassed the central and peripheral nervous system complications of a variety of cancers and the agents used to treat them and not just the treatment of brain tumors.

In any categorical hospital such as a cancer hospital, there are also many individuals who have disorders of the nervous system unrelated to their cancers. I knew, from time spent at M. D. Anderson Hospital before coming on board in a full-time capacity, that there was a sizable number of neurological problems present among the patients seen there and that these were often either untreated or undertreated. Moreover, the medical oncologists, traditionally, had felt little need to have outside assistance in addressing the neurological complications of their patients with system cancers. It was clear to me from the outset that a lot of time and effort would be required to educate the staff physicians in general about the role of neurologists in a cancer hospital.

M. D. Anderson Cancer Center and Retirement (Perhaps)

Since I was not really ready to "hang it up," I enthusiastically launched the new program at M. D. Anderson on September 1, 1982. Before my arrival, however, a section of neurology had been created in the Department of Internal Medicine under the chairmanship of Dr. Thomas P. Haynie. Fortunately, I had known Tom from the days when he was a medical student at Baylor in the mid-1950s. This made the administrative relations go more smoothly than might otherwise have been the case.

Almost immediately after my arrival at M. D. Anderson, I began to reorganize the neurology inpatient consultation service and outpatient clinic. It was evident that a need had existed for several years at least, since from the outset there was an increase in demand for these services. I met with Fred Conrad at least once weekly to discuss plans for the new service and to determine how it was to relate, both in the clinic and the hospital, to other departments, not only internal medicine but also to neurosurgery and the other surgical disciplines. We had put together the framework of a program, but before our plan could be implemented, Fred was suddenly removed from the scene.

It was his habit to come to the hospital at about 6:30 in the morning to start his daily routine. On the morning of his death, he was sitting at his desk as usual with his back toward the office door. Someone, whom he almost certainly never saw, came in through the door behind him, drew a pistol, and shot him in the back of the head. This tragic occurrence caused great consternation throughout the institution and a reshuffling of responsibility in the clinical arena. The murder of Fred Conrad has never been solved. Unfortunately, what we had decided to implement for neuro-oncology was in Fred's "memory bank" and, like many of his discussions with others, never committed to paper, so our carefully designed plan died with him. This immediately put on hold any further discussion about neurology. Regrettably, the arrangements for our team to have any autonomy whatsoever took almost three more years before they were realized.

Four months after my arrival at Anderson and about six weeks after the tragic demise of Fred Conrad, I wrote to Mickey LeMaistre informing him of my attempts to develop a neuro-oncology center in accordance with the assignment given to me by him and Fred. In that letter I described the establishment of an interdisciplinary team which included persons from diagnostic radiology, radiotherapy, and medical oncology, as well as from neurology and neurosurgery. This team was already meeting regularly in several newly established conferences. Office space was being renovated on the seventh floor of the hospital to accommodate the neurologists and neurosurgeons and their support personnel.

I also pointed out in my letter that the concept of a neuro-oncology center was an excellent one, but without a budget identified for that purpose it would be impossible to establish. However, as a practical matter, it appeared that little or no additional money would have to be budgeted for such a center than was already being budgeted for the same individuals who were currently in other departments. It seemed reasonable for those in the other departments to be cross-appointed so that they might maintain their identities within their primary disciplines.

It was suggested that the pain clinic be incorporated into neuro-oncology and include persons from anesthesiology, social service, and nursing. Moreover, Frank Adams in psychiatry had sent a memorandum expressing his concurrence with my idea that psychiatry be a section in the Department of Neuro-oncology. The proposal was accompanied by an offer to have Milam Leavens, Frank Adams and myself meet with LeMaistre and Haynie for further discussion.

All of this came about at a time when a reorganization of the Department of Internal Medicine was being contemplated. LeMaistre shared my letter with Haynie, who called me expressing concern. The following is excerpted from my letter, dated January 27, 1983, to LeMaistre in an attempt to allay any fears about my proposed plan:

> If I have learned anything from the new science of ecology, it is that the mutual adjustments by which creatures coexist are delicate in the extreme. Even when conditions are out of whack, the careful ecologist does not proceed too quickly to institute the obvious remedies. Creatures adapt to, and become dependent on, the damnedest things.
>
> I have no idea, for example, what the bowel habits of pigeons were before the advent of heroic sculpture, but I suspect that if, in the interest of civic improvement, one were to remove all classic friezes and equestrian statues, he might find himself personally providing the service now rendered by General Sam Houston across from the Warwick Hotel. Before one sets about to remedy

a difficult situation, he must be sure that he has a better one to take its place — and, perhaps even more important, be sure that the new balance doesn't have half a dozen unforeseen disasters hidden in its vest pocket.

LeMaistre got a hearty laugh out of my letter, but the plan for administrative reorganization for neuro-oncology was put on the back burner.

Coincident with the expansion of clinical services, there also arose a need to enlist the help of physicians in other departments who had expertise in dealing with tumors of the nervous system. A neuroradiologist, Ya-Yen Lee, was recruited with the cooperation of Gerald Dodd, chief of radiology. I had had the pleasure of working with both of them previously while at The University of Texas Medical School. Within eighteen months a second neuroradiologist, Pamela van Tassel, finished her fellowship and joined the staff.

John Batsakis, chief of pathology, was persuaded that we should bring on board a full-time neuropathologist. The first to be recruited was Adam Borit, a foreign-educated pathologist, who had been at The University of Texas Medical School while I was there. When he decided to leave M. D. Anderson after one year, a recent trainee from the Baylor program, Janet Bruner, joined the staff. My next step was to request from Lester Peters, chief of radiation therapy, that he appoint one of his associates to serve as a liaison person with our prospective brain tumor program. He assigned his colleague, Moshe Maor, to this task. This decision turned out to be a fortuitous one and provided a close working relationship.

In spite of administrative delays in the establishment of a neuro-oncology unit, the cooperation of the chairmen of other departments in the institution in providing personnel and other assistance was exceptional. I cannot recall going to a single service chief and receiving anything other than enthusiastic support. This enabled me to turn my attention to the establishment of a teaching program.

Regular conferences were arranged where problem cases could be reviewed. These were attended by staff, fellows, rotating residents, and medical students. In less than a year, a structured program was well developed and well received by all concerned. Such was real progress that required the participation and cooperation of many people across several disciplines. It pleased me that so much had been accomplished in a relatively short period of time.

Within a year, a fellowship program had received administrative approval and the first two fellows in neuro-oncology were appointed to begin on July 1, 1983. Arrangements were also made with my successor at The University of Texas Medical School, Frank Yatsu, for the continued rotation of residents from his department, as well as continuing the well-established rotation of a resident in neurosurgery from Baylor College of Medicine. The nucleus of this new program included the three neurologists besides myself and two neurosurgeons, Milam Leavens and Richard Moser. The latter had just arrived after completing his training at the University of Minnesota.

Almost from the outset of the new program, it was my desire to establish criteria for determining the effectiveness of what we might be undertaking in the clinical arena. I was already aware of what had been implemented by Jan van Eys, chief of pediatrics, in regard to assessment of treatment in children suffering from brain tumors, and I felt that it was imperative to undertake a similar approach with the adult population.

It soon came to my attention that a well-trained neuropsychologist, Christina Meyers, who was working at The University of Texas Medical Branch in Galveston, might be available and interested. I persuaded her to come on board with the promise that we would work together toward the establishment of a close relationship with the Department of Psychology at the University of Houston. Approval of the plan which she developed was obtained from the M. D. Anderson Cancer Center administration, and an affiliated graduate fellowship program was established. This proved to be a resounding success as a result of Chris Meyers' efforts and the contributions from this pool of talent.

Within the next year, a pediatric neurologist, Tallie Baram, was recruited from Baylor to devote full time to that aspect of the program. This was particularly important since brain tumors are the most common solid tumors in children and the most common of all childhood malignancies apart from leukemia. Jan van Eys received this arrangement with enthusiasm. He was pleased to have a closer relationship with the neurologists and neurosurgeons and participated actively in our conferences.

One day I received a call from a longtime friend, Beng Ho, who had been on the staff of the Texas Research Institute of Mental Sciences as a research pharmacologist. He informed me that the institute was about to be taken over by The University of Texas Health Science Center and that he needed to find other employment. Since his wife, Dah Hsi, worked as a research scientist in the Department of Medical Oncology at M. D. Anderson and had no desire to leave Houston, he was inquiring about a job. I told him that I would arrange for his appointment to the Department of Neuro-oncology but that within a year he would have to find his own support through research grants. It pleased me very much that he was able to accomplish that goal and that he has remained active in the department since my retirement.

About eighteen months after I transferred to M. D. Anderson Hospital, a major administrative reorganization took place and new clinical divisions were created. Because of the new administrative arrangements, any decision regarding neuro-oncology was held in abeyance until Irwin Krakoff, a well-known medical oncologist, took over as head of the Division of Medicine on September 1, 1983. Krakoff was enthusiastic about having a neuro-oncology unit and, after several months of discussion, it was decided to formally establish a Department of Neuro-oncology. Effectively, this only meant that the entity for which I was responsible was changed from a section in internal medicine to a department in the Division of Medicine. The impetus for the creation of such an entity, I believe, came from recognition that an interdisciplinary approach to the involvement of the nervous system by cancer and its treatment would provide the greatest reward.

Interaction among staff members was encouraged in order to address in a timely fashion topics related to cancer causation, prevention, and treatment. To minimize possible divisions along programmatic lines, staff persons in other departments whose training background and professional concerns related to basic and clinical neuroscience were provided with cross appointments in neuro-oncology as adjunct faculty. This approach almost immediately stimulated cooperative ventures and resulted in a rapid expansion of staff, followed by improved funding.

Another of my responsibilities at M. D. Anderson in addition to program development was fundraising. In this respect we had been successful to a modest degree. One day I was talking to a friend about my experience as chairman at Baylor, then at The University of Texas Medical School and finally as director of a new program at M. D. Anderson. He looked at me and said, "I never knew that you were out to win the triple crown." I had never thought about what I had accomplished in those terms, but that seemed to be a reasonable description. I sincerely doubt that anyone else will be foolish enough to attempt to duplicate that feat.

C. Stratton Hill, who was overseeing the pain service of the department, sent me a memorandum in January 1983, proposing that we organize a pain conference with a focus on the clinical setting in which pain occurs and the application of various modalities of treatment, with particular emphasis on a multi-disciplinary approach. He suggested that material be presented on the proper use of narcotic analgesics, discussing the differences between oral and parenteral administration. He also felt that other issues including tolerance, physical dependence, addiction, and the attitudes of physicians and nurses should be addressed. I received the proposal enthusiastically and took it to LeMaistre for his approval. He agreed that by having such a program we could provide more visibility and activity for the pain service. Since support for the conference was to come largely from the pharmaceutical industry rather than from direct university financing, he endorsed the plan.

The meeting entitled "Management and Theory of Pain in Cancer Patients" was held in March 1984 and was attended by nearly 300 people from across the United States and Canada. It was a resounding success. My only disappointment was that almost no physicians or surgeons from our own institution attended, but a substantial number of our nurses and social workers were present. This convinced both Stratton and me that it would not be easy to persuade our own doctors to devote sufficient attention to symptom management.

About four years after this first effort to get the message regarding pain management as widely disseminated as possible, Stratton and I decided to put forth an even greater second effort. We were anxious to see this accomplished before I retired. On this occasion we contacted a pharmaceutical company which had been supporting some of Stratton's clinical research. The vice-president and medical director of that firm was very enthusiastic about the plan and ultimately supported it handsomely.

It was decided to extend this second pain conference over a three-day period. The orientation of the program on this occasion was completely different and we chose for a title "Drug Treatment of Cancer Pain in a Drug Oriented Society: Adequate or Inadequate?" We were able to entice a truly multidisciplinary group of contributors who carefully and thoughtfully addressed the issues surrounding the medical, cultural, and legal barriers to adequate control of cancer pain. A really concerted effort was made to mobilize action for improving pain control and overcoming cultural attitudes, legal restrictions, and misinformation. I was delighted to have participated with Stratton Hill in this conference, particularly in view of my impending retirement from the chairmanship of the department. He has been able since then to push toward better understanding among physicians of the need for adequate pain control.

In early 1987, I was approached by Professor Klaus Joachim Zülch, my friend in Cologne, Germany, with a proposal that I arrange to convene as soon as possible a meeting in Houston, Texas, for the purpose of considering recent research developments that might have an influence on the classification of brain tumors. Klaus and I had thought that it would be particularly appropriate to have this meeting in Houston because of, first, our close friendship over many years and, second, his personal family association with the state of Texas.

Klaus came from a Hessian family and for a long time had known that in the 1830s the then Duke of Hesse had bought from the Indians a large tract of land northeast of San Antonio in the vicinity of what are now the towns of Fredericksburg and New Braunfels. Subsequently, after the Revolution of 1848 in Europe, many Hessians settled in this region. One of them, Julius Zülch, the brother of Klaus Zülch's grandfather, turned out to be an independent sort of fellow, who, after arriving by ship in Galveston, decided to stake out a claim to land further east in Madison County north of Harrisburg (now Houston). There he established a small community, the town of North Zulch. The town still flourishes with two grocery stores, three gasoline stations, a post office, four churches, and a fire station which doubles as a senior citizens' center and domino hall. The railroad station survived until 1986, when it was demolished by a switching engine that jumped the tracks. Of his many descendants who live in that surrounding area, only the widow of Julius' grandson, Jack Zulch, still carries the family name (but without an umlaut).

It was further considered by both Klaus and me that a review such as he proposed might ultimately necessitate revision of the World Health Organization (WHO) "Blue Book" of *Histological*

Typing of Tumours of the Central Nervous System. Among the group which met in Houston in March 1988 were members of the original Collaborating Centre of WHO that were still active and other neuropathologists from around the world who had expertise in these matters. Forty people from fifteen countries were invited, and every one of the invitees attended.

From the outset, it had been the aim of the "Blue Book" to provide a standardized system to facilitate communication between cancer researchers and practitioners worldwide. The classification of brain tumors had been oriented toward defining and naming entities based on images obtained by light microscopy. It was recognized, however, that concepts may have changed more toward histogenetic than descriptive approaches and that they might even be stifled by standards. By separating descriptive terms from conceptual terms, it was deemed possible to avoid controversies that might stand in the way of better comparability of data.

Although the use of conventional light microscopy had been the mainstay of the original classification, in order to achieve general application on a worldwide basis, immunohistochemistry, electron microscopy, and molecular biology had become recognized as important adjuncts, especially when dealing with poorly differentiated tumors.

At the Houston meeting, it became evident that some of those who had originally been involved in the Collaborating Centre felt that time-honored and widely used terms should be retained unless considered misleading or undesirable. For purposes of identification, light microscopy should be used in daily routine diagnosis and more sophisticated methods, which have since become available, should be adopted only when necessary to explain the remaining scientific tumor problems but within the existing classification. Resistance to change on the part of some persons present tended to color the deliberations to a considerable extent. Some felt that the classification had served its purpose extremely well during a period of almost ten years. Still others felt that testing of the current classification should continue for a longer period to determine what impact the newer techniques developed in cytogenetics and immunohistochemistry would have on the classification. However, the majority of those in attendance felt strongly that an upgrade in the classification of some tumor entities was required and that there should be no unnecessary delay in accomplishing such a revision.

Almost all agreed strongly with a remark made by Professor Paul Kleihues of Zürich, Switzerland: "If neuropathologists as a group do not act when they have the opportunity to do so, someone else will take the initiative and then they are not going to like it." Frankly, it was our intention to use the meeting as a springboard for further discussion leading to an early revision of the "Blue Book."

A great deal of time and energy was spent on discussion of the PNET (primitive neuro-ectodermal tumor) concept as proposed by Dr. Lucy Rorke of Philadelphia. She voiced the opinion that the proposed revision of pediatric brain tumors presented on that occasion had been much misunderstood. She pointed out that although the previously published WHO classification had been carefully prepared by neuropathologists and had been used for a number of years, it did not fit very well when dealing with pediatric brain tumors. The other pediatric neuropathologists present appeared to find her recommendations for change acceptable even though her remarks engendered a lot of controversy.

At the end of the meeting, a committee of three persons, under the chairmanship of Paul Kleihues and including Berndt Scheithauer (Rochester, Minnesota) and Peter Burger (Durham, North Carolina), was formed to carry on with the effort which had been given impetus at Houston.

Before the proceedings of the Houston conference were published, my friend and collaborator in this effort, Klaus Zülch, died unexpectedly in Berlin, where he had gone to give an invited lecture. Those of us who knew him well envied his good fortune to have been actively engaged in the pursuit of his chosen work until the very end.

The volume, entitled *Primary Brain Tumors — A Review of Histologic Classification* (Springer Verlag, Berlin, 1989), which I had the privilege of editing, was dedicated to him. All of the discussions from the Houston meeting were recorded, transcribed, and incorporated into the book. It is perhaps those discussions which constitute the most valuable part of the publication rather than the formal presentations.

This volume can be considered a predicate to the deliberations at a subsequent meeting in Zürich. The three-person subcommittee of the Collaborating Centre, chaired by Kleihues, did an admirable job of preparing a framework upon which to build further discussion. Their work proved to be invaluable in enabling the participants in Zürich to achieve several reasonable compromises. As a clinician and not a neuropathologist, it pleased me tremendously to see that there was far less adherence to some of the rigidly held opinions that had been so evident in Houston. It was my distinct impression that all of those in attendance at the March 1990 meeting in Zürich were reasonably satisfied with the end product and were prepared to accept the revised classification in a form suitable for early publication. The success of that project was in large measure attributable to the great effort expended by the three members of the Organizing Committee.

On January 31, 1988, I retired from the chairmanship (ad interim) of the Department of Neuro-oncology at The University of Texas M. D. Anderson Cancer Center. Although relinquishing my administrative responsibilities, I accepted what was nominally a one-third time appointment with the university. In addition, I was appointed professor emeritus of neurology at both The University of Texas Health Science Center Medical School at Houston and the School of Public Health.

Noreen Lemak, whom I had coaxed out of retirement as a hospital volunteer into a productive second career as a research and clinical colleague, collaborated with me during her last years as my associate on the preparation of a book entitled *A History of Stroke*, published by Oxford University Press. We decided from the outset that we could not be so presumptuous as to call it *The History of Stroke*. In 1988, when I retired to part-time employment, Noreen transferred to a different department within the institution. However, I was fortunate to have her continue to share an office with me. She deserves every ounce of my unflagging gratitude. She has had considerable forbearance for my foibles and idiosyncrasies and during the more than twenty years of our association has offered me her support through times of personal tragedy as well as during the trials and triumph along the rocky road of academic medicine.

During this voyage, which began so long ago, interest in cerebrovascular diseases, particularly ischemic stroke, has had a renaissance: an important journal, *STROKE,* has appeared; an annual national stroke conference has achieved international recognition; and most significant of all, a new generation of enthusiastic and dedicated clinical and basic researchers has arrived. It has been a pleasure to have been a part of this scene.

Thanks go to many friends and collaborators in these cooperative ventures, some of whom have toiled in anonymity but whose contributions have been immeasurable. With respect to some of the latter, we have led the way, while in others we have merely been fellow travelers always with the hope that we will have added in some small measure to the burgeoning fund of available scientific and clinical information. In retrospect, these latter years have been splendid years, not without curves, corners, and even bumps along the way but, above all, they have been interesting and, in the final analysis, satisfying.

After having been in the medical profession for more than fifty years, I have learned that there are very few M.D.s who understand how to run a business operation. I believe that those in academia should let their business managers run the business affairs with little or no interference. However, the manager must report regularly to the doctor to keep him or her apprised of what is going on. To put an M.D. in any other position is very shortsighted since he will be wasting his talents, which should be devoted to other important matters. Nevertheless, he should have enough background information and a general idea of what is going on and not turn over all matters to just anybody.

It has always been my view that the chief executive officer in a medical institution, academic or clinical, has two broad areas to which he must devote his attention: professionalism and development. The head of such an institution should know his staff, but this does not have to extend to the technicians and clerks. He does not need to know whether they are paid by the week or the month, but he does need to know whom he is hiring. Moreover, if he wants to construct a new building, he has to determine how and where he is going to find the money.

My odyssey to and through the Texas Medical Center and its component parts drew to a close at the end of 1992. It has been an exciting journey with some regrets but many more rewards. To have seen the center when it consisted of one building surrounded by prairie and then to have been a part of its growth for over forty-five years has been reward enough. However, the opportunities provided me both at home and abroad as a consequence of my association with its people and its institutions have been immeasurable. I can only hope that I have made a worthwhile contribution. Most important of all, it has been my good fortune to have been able to share with many young people, particularly students and residents, the enthusiasm with which I entered a great profession and endeavored to maintain throughout the years. As I wind down now, even the few regrets are tempered by the splendid memories of people, places, and time well spent.

Over these many years I have been privileged to visit more than sixty countries on six continents, traveling on nearly fifty different airlines, many of which exist now only in memory. I trust that I have made the most of, and profited by, the contacts, the friendships, and the experience which I have been provided.

I must go now to other pursuits and try to continue to contribute in some small measure during such time as I may have remaining in which to do so.

Thanks for listening.

M. D. Anderson Cancer Center and Retirement (Perhaps)

The International Society for Cardiovascular Surgery/
The Society for Vascular Surgery

July 26, 1991

William S. Fields, M.D.
Professor of Neurology
University of Texas
M.D. Anderson Cancer Center

Dear Dr. Fields:

With the recent release of the Clinical Alert of the National Institutes of Health on the findings of the North American Symptomatic Carotid Endarterectomy Trial, it has been close to a quarter of a century since your landmark report on the role of surgery in the prevention of stroke due to carotid artery occlusive disease. Your pioneering efforts to demonstrate the safety, the benefits, and the durability of carotid endarterectomy have resulted in a vastly improved quality of life for countless thousands.

You have been a steadfast source of support to vascular surgeons everywhere. The generous gift of your presence on innumerable programs and symposia throughout the world and your sharing of your enormous experience in vascular diseases of the brain have been inspirational to experienced and to neophyte surgeons as well. You have led the way among your neurology colleagues during this critical period and often with substantial criticism. The vindication of your advice and recommendations provided by this Clinical Alert must be a source of great satisfaction. You deserve the sense of relief you undoubtedly feel now that this clinical debate has ended so decidedly in your favor.

In recognition of your enormous contribution, your unstinting zeal in the pursuit of the truth, coupled with desire to provide relief and protection to that segment of mankind suffering from or threatened by cerebrovascular disease, the Joint Council of the North American Chapter of the International Cardiovascular Society and of the Society for Vascular Surgery has caused this expression of recognition and appreciation to be conveyed to you and to be laid upon the minutes of the two Societies.

Signatories: For the North American Chapter of the
International Cardiovascular Society

Robert W. Barnes, M.D.   Jerry Goldstone, M.D.

For the Society for Vascular Surgery

Calvin B. Ernst, M.D.   Norman R. Hertzer, M.D.

On the occasion of the Annual Meeting of the North American Chapter of International Cardiovascular Surgery and the 45th Annual Meeting of the Society for Vascular Surgery, Boston, Massachusetts, June 1, 1991

Index

A

Abbott, Douglas, 71
  Walter, 73, 198
Abercrombie, James, 213
Abergavenny, Wales, 46
Academy of Medical Sciences (Moscow), 281, 282, 288, 302
Acosta, Bert, 12
Adams, Frank, 332
  Kenneth "Bud," 218
  Nancy, 218
  Raymond, 157
Adrian, Lord, 50
Afghanistan, 290
Aiken, Senator, 321
Air Canada, 37, 98
Aizawa, Toyozo, 112, 113
Alameda Naval Air Station, 60
Albany Medical College, 74
Albert Einstein Medical Center, 252
Alexandra Hospital, 37
Alford, Bobby, 199, 218
Allen, Garrett, 31, 32
Allende, Norberto, 236
Alley Theater, 288
All-Union Commission on Neurology, 306
Al-Naaman, Yousef, 147–148
Alvord, Ellsworth C., 110, 118–119, 140
America, 12
America First, 2, 18
American Academy of Neurological Surgery, 109
American Academy of Neurology, 148, 244, 260
American Association of Neurological Surgeons, 79, 110, 165, 289–290, 304

American Board of Neurological Surgery, 107, 108
American Board of Psychiatry and Neurology, 81, 139, 321
American College of Physicians, 30
American College of Surgeons, 30, 228
American Embassy (Moscow), 295, 296, 301, 302–303, 306
American Epilepsy Society, 133
American General Insurance, 257
American Heart Association, 243
American Medical Association, 188
American Museum of Natural History, 17–18
American Neurological Association, 82, 120, 162, 169
American Psychiatric Association, 172
Ames, Charles E., II, 210
  Marian, 210
Amsler, Neil, 247, 255
Anacostia Naval Air Station, 60
Anahuac, Texas, 310
Anderson, A. Burton "Tex," 87
  Leland, 123, 257
  Monroe D., 122, 142
  Thomas, 142, 143
Anderson, Clayton Cotton Company, 85
Anderson-Mayfair Hotel, 323
Andrews, Forrest Lee, 215, 216
Ann Arbor, Michigan, 278
Apollo-Soyuz, 266
Appel, Stanley, 239
Appomattox, 7
Aragvi River, 301
Araki, Professor, 114
Arlington National Cemetery, 37
Armed Forces Medical Library, 191
Armstrong, John, 189, 193

arteriography, 103–104
artificial heart program, 165–169, 234–236
Arutiunov, Alex I., 283, 305
Asenjo, Adolfo, 150
Ashkenasy, Moses, 106
aspirin research, 147, 206, 240–245, 288, 303–304
Aspirin Myocardial Infarction Study, 244
Aspirin, Platelets, and Stroke — Background for a Clinical Trial, 241, 303
Aspirin in Transient Ischemic Attacks Study, 242
Association of American Medical Colleges, 249
Association of British Neurologists, 156
Association for Research in Nervous and Mental Diseases, 82, 151
Astakhova, Ludmila, 292, 293, 294–295, 296–297
Astrodome, 157
Atlanta, Georgia, 60
Aune, Janet, 255
Austin, Texas, 248
Awapara, Amador, 149
   Jorge, 149
Axel Wennergren prize, 5
Azambuja, Nestor, 151

B

Babcock, Lester, 12
Babkin, Boris, 293
Baden, Charles, 4
Baird, William, 87
Baisas, Rogelio, 117
   Roger, 115
Baker, James A., III, 219
   James Addison, 320
Balch, Reverend Frank, 262
Ballantine, H. Thomas, 150
balloon technique, 284, 305
Bangs, Jack, 217–218, 219, 220–221, 222, 255, 216
   Tina, 216, 218, 220–221, 222
Bank of the Southwest, 228

Banting, Frederick, 48
Banting Institute, 48
Baram, Tallie, 334
Baranowski, Taddeus Z., 80–81
Barbeau, Antonio, 43
Barbour, Violet, 13
Bardwil, John, 260
Barker, Halsey, 30
   Lewellys, 30
Barnes Hospital, 29, 76, 78, 132, 158, 209
Barnett, Henry, 244, 245
Barnstone, Howard, 212
Barré, Jean, 102–103
Barrow Neurological Institute, 224
Basingstoke, England, 41
Bates, John, 150
Bates College of Law, 269
Batsakis, John, 333
Baudoin, King, 119
Bauer, Raymond, 243
Baylor College of Medicine, 39, 40, 83, 84, 86–98, 106–110, 123, 126, 128–131, 132, 133, 137, 138–141, 162, 171, 174, 177, 197, 199, 218, 219, 229, 234, 237, 252, 259, 260, 313, 315, 322, 328, 334
Baylor football, 143
Baylor Medical School, 85
Baylor-Methodist Complex, 132
Baylor University, 84, 123, 124, 132, 234, 252
Baylor University Hospital, 229
Baytown, Texas, 134
Beaumont, Texas, 310, 317
Beecher, Henry K., 203
Bekhterev, V. M., 294
Bekhtereva, N. P., 293–294
Bekhterev Leningrad Psychoneurological Research Institute, 294
Bell, Roderic, 226
Bellegie, Philip, 260
Bellevue Hospital, 74
Belmont, Massachusetts, 1
Bennett, Floyd, 12
Ben Taub Hospital, 171
Benyevich, Sergei, 292–293

Berger, Hans, 50
Berger Rhythms, 50
Berlin, Charles, 221
Berry, Charles, 221, 264, 265–269, 276
Bertner, Ernst William, 122–124
Best, Charles, 48
Bielstein, Charles, 134
Bingham, Hiram, 149
Bintliff family, 138
Birmingham Veterans Administration Hospital, 83
Bishop, George, 74, 78
  Jim, 8
Bispebjerg Hospital, 100
Blalock, Alfred, 155
Blattner, Russell, 87, 127–128, 129, 132–133, 134, 136, 138, 197, 209, 211, 213
Blinkov, Samuel, 305
Blocker, Truman, 221–222, 248, 268–271, 317
  Virginia, 268
Blood Bank Committee (HCMS), 186
Blood and Money, 316
Bloodwell, Robert, 155
Bloom, Sol, 23
Blue Bird Circle, 134–138
Blue Bird Clinic for Children's Neurological Disorders, 133–138, 139, 161, 216
"Blue Book," 337–338, 339
Bobcaygeon, Ontario, 21
Bolshoi Ballet, 295
Bolshoi Theater, 286
Bonaparte, Napoleon, 101
Boniuk, Milton, 237
Booth's Gin, 50
Booz, Allen and Hamilton, 175
Bordeaux, France, 105
Borispol Airport, 300
Borit, Adam, 333
Borreca, Frank, 211–215
Boston Bruins, 78
Boston Children's Hospital, 130
Boston City Hospital, 74, 75, 102
Boston Globe, 19
Boston Marathon, 15, 19

Bottoms, Lemuel, 186
Bowen, James, 330
  Ted, 132, 134, 166, 167, 237
Bowman Gray School of Medicine, 252
Boyd, Howard, 257
Boynton, Ben, 86
Bradford, F. Keith, 106, 108–109, 131, 195, 197
Bradley, Frank, 132
BRAIN, 197, 198
Brain, Sir Russell, 105, 156
Brain Research Institute, 83
brain tumor program, 333
brain tumors, 297, 326, 327, 329, 330, 334, 337–340
Bramlett, Henry, 79
Breggin, Peter Roger, 202, 203, 204, 205
Brew, Joseph, 16
British Army, 66
British Military Intelligence, 81
Brochstein Library, 111
Brochstein, Mr. and Mrs. Isaac, 111
  Raymond, 111, 261
Brochsteins, Inc., 111
Brockman, Henry, 55
Brödel, Max, 4
Broida, Helen, 317
Bromo-Seltzer, 6
Brooke Army Medical Center, 106, 129
Brooklyn Naval Hospital, 55
Brooklyn, New York, 169
Brooks, Max, 248
Brown, James Albert, 195
  Warren, 83, 86, 126, 138–139, 142, 143
Broyles, George, Jr., 55
  George, Sr., 131
Bruetman, Martin, 156
Bruner, Janet, 333
Brussels, Belgium, 118, 119
Buckingham Palace, 98, 99
Buenos Aires, Argentina, 159, 235, 263
Bulge, Battle of the, 64
Bulger, Roger, 222, 271, 272, 273–275, 280, 327, 328

Burdenko Institute of Neurosurgery, 283, 285, 286, 305, 306
Burger, Peter, 339
Burgess, Inspector, 35
Burke, Adrian, 143
Bush, George, 306
Butcher, R. William, 222
Butler, Ian John, 260–261, 274
  Patricia, 260–261
Byrd, Richard, 11, 12

C
Cady, Lee, 88, 89, 90
California Institute of Technology, 56
Calvert, Charles, 3
Cambridge, Massachusetts, 16
Cameron Fairchild and Associates, 179
Camp Moosilauke, 13
Campos, Guillermo, 150
Camp Pendleton, 57
Camp Wallace, 320
Camp Zakelo, 13, 14
Canada Steamship Lines, 25
Canadian National Railway, 62
Canadian Neurological Hospital, 41
Canadian Neurological Society, 155, 156
Canadian Pacific Railway, 61
Canadian stroke study, 244, 245
Cancer Institute, 289
Cannon, Donald, 274–275
cardiovascular surgery, 146
Carlin, Walter, 221–222
Carlos Paz, Argentina, 236
Carmichael, E. A., 68, 98
carotid artery surgery, 147–149, 151–152, 153–154, 228–229, 236, 287
Carpenter, Scott, 266
Carpentier, Georges, 1
Carrea, Raul, 236
Carter, Jimmy, 272
Carton, Charles, 106–107, 108, 147–148
Casey, Bob, 177
Castaigne, Agrégé Paul, 101
Cataratas Hotel, 262
Catherine the Great, 295

Catholic University, 236
Catonsville, Maryland, 3
Cavendish, Spencer, 46
Cavendish Hotel, 46
Cecil, Keith, and Mahaffey, 310
Center Pavilion, 238, 253, 261
Central Lenin Stadium, 288, 305
Central Neuropsychiatric Society, 145–146
Cerebral Blood Flow Laboratory, 284
Cerebrovascular Clinical Research Center, 228
cerebrovascular research, 167, 171, 225, 239, 250, 288–289, 340
Cerebrovascular Research Program, 164, 171
Chamberlin, Clarence, 11
Chambers, Joan, 225
Chambers County, Texas, 310
Chandy, Jacob, 120–121
Chao, Dora, 134, 135–136
  Mei-Su, 135
Charcot, Jean, 101
Charring Cross railway station, 53
Charles and Herschel Duncan Laboratory of Neuropathology, 110
Chateau Frontenac, 48
chemotherapy, 326, 327–328, 329, 330
Cherry, Glenn, 230
Chikovani, Oleg, 288, 305–306
Childe, Arthur, 38
Children's Medical Center (Johns Hopkins), 247
Children's Memorial Hospital (Montreal), 30, 36
Childs Restaurants, 24
Churchill, Edward (Pete), 31
Circle of Willis, 156
Clark, Miss, 40
  R. Lee, 169, 189, 190, 219, 232, 248, 255, 321, 323–324
Clarke, Jared E., 185
Clayton Fund, 131
Clinical Physiology Laboratory, 292
Clinic Building, 247, 248
Coco Beach, 267

Index

Cody, Claude C., Jr., 178, 185, 188
Coffey, John, 246, 254, 255
Coggerhall, Howard, 227, 228
Cohane, Patrick, 65, 66
Cohen, Mandel, 75
  Wilbur, 278–279
Cole, Sarah, 230
Collaborating Centre of WHO, 338, 339
Collateral Circulation of the Brain, 156
Collins, Vincent, 96
Colonial Daughters of the 17th Century, 36
Columbia-Presbyterian Medical Center, 31
Columbia University, 17, 102, 110, 169, 171
Columbia University College of Physicians and Surgeons, 241
Community Council, 215
Concepcion, Peru, 149
Cone, William, 41
Congressional Record, 205
Connally, John B., 200
Conrad, Fred, 327, 329, 331
Cooley, Denton, 145, 146, 147, 155, 235
Coombs, Dick, 306
Cooper, Jack, 86
  Theodore, 304
Cooperative Study of Extracranial Vascular Disease, 163
Copenhagen, 100
Coping with Stroke: Communication Breakdown of Brain Injured Adults, 317
Coramine, 181
Cora and Webb Mading Foundation, 131
Cordoba, Argentina, 236
Cornell University Medical School, 141
Coronado Beach, 55, 58, 131
Corpus Christi, Texas, 309
Corregidor, 116
Coughlin, Father, 2
Countway Library, 191

Cox, Joyce, 312
Craft, Christopher, 266–267
Craig Rehabilitation Center, 129
Craik, Bernard, 68
Craven, Lawrence L., 241–242
Crawford, E. Stanley, 146, 147, 148–149, 229
Crawley, James W., 91, 140
Creech, Oscar, 146
Critchley, Macdonald, 103
Cromwell, Walter, 59
Crook, William, 8–9
Crooker, John, Sr., 312–313
Crow, Trammell, 226
Crown Cork and Seal Corporation, 6
Croyden Airport, 99
Crozier, Lee, 124, 125, 246
Cuban "missile crisis," 158–159
Cullen Building, 86, 95, 179
Cullen Pavilion, 234
Cullen Residence Hall, 214
Cullinan, Joseph S., III, 219–220
  Nina, 216
Cummings, Hatch, 178
Curb, Dolph, 145
Cushing, Harvey, 4
Cutrer, Lewis, 177
Cuzco, Peru, 149
cytogenetics, 338
Czechoslovak Medical Association, 157–158

D

D'Agostino, Anthony, 225
Dallas Apparel Mart, 230
Dallas Neurological Society, 230–231
Dallas Neurological Symposium, 230–231
Dallas, Texas, 86, 87
Daly, David, 224, 225, 226, 231–232, 233
  Harriet, 225
Dandy, Walter, 30
Daughaday, Jewel, 124
Davis, Admiral, 58
  Gene, 166
  Theo, 34
Day Lincoln Was Shot, The, 8

Dean's Committee, 125
DeBakey, Michael, 87, 96, 106, 117,
    125–126, 132, 146–149, 151–155,
    158, 161, 162, 166–170, 175, 218,
    219, 234–236, 237, 238, 239, 251,
    323
  Mickey (Michael, Jr.), 126
DeBakey Building for Medical
    Education and Research, 169
DeBakey Surgical Foundation, 153
de Castro, Professor, 105
Declaration of Independence, 7
DeGaulle, General, 67
DeJong, Russell, 90
Delta Zetas, 217
DeLucchi, Milton, 266
DeMar, Clarence, 15
DeMonbreun, William, 32, 33
DeMoss, John, 259
Dempsey, Gerald, 37
  Jack, 1
Denny-Brown, Derek, 75, 150
Denver, Colorado, 129
Department of Health, Education and
    Welfare, 116, 278, 281
DePelchin Faith Home, 126–127
Derrick, William, 323–324
Detroit Lions, 143
de Wolf, Professor, 105
Diagnostic Clinic and Hospital, 250
Dickson, Charles, 136, 215, 216
Digby, Nova Scotia, 45
Dilantin, 27, 39
Dippel, Louis, 247, 248
Directory of Medical Specialists, 172
Doctors' Club, 196
Dodd, Gerald, 251, 323, 333
Donoso, Manuel, 150
Dorchester Hotel, 51
Dorsey, Fred, 211, 215
Doyle, Sir Arthur Conan, 64
Dramamine, 49
Druckman, Ralph, 135–136, 140
Dublin, Ireland, 46
Dudley, Sir Sheldon, 66
Dudrick, Stanley, 259, 274–275
Dukakis, Michael, 160

Duke, Herbert, Sr., 174
  James "Red," 254
Duke University, 74
Duke University Medical School, 41
Duncan, Charles, Jr., 110
  Charles W., Sr., 110
  Herschel, 110
  Joe, 61
  John, 110
  Lillian, 110
Duncan Coffee Company, 110
Duncan Laboratory, 111
Dunedin, New Zealand, 70
Dunham, Reginald, 49, 51
Dunn, John, 246, 255
Dunn Chapel, 248
Dunnington, Florence, 25
DuPont, Henry, 24
Dyken, Mark, 229, 243

E
Earickson, Mrs., 24
Eastern Church, 287
Eastwood, Richard, 189–190
Economic Achievement Park, 286
Edwards, Sterling, 229
Edward VII, 47
Eggers, Harold, 48, 262
Ehlers, H. J., 185
Ehni, George, 109, 195, 197, 207, 322
Eisenberg, Stephen, 203–204
Elder, Robert, 36
electrodes (implanted), 284
electroshock therapy, 242
Elema-Schonander rapid film chang-
    ers, 298
Elliott, Frederick, 124, 177, 180
Ellis, William, 59
El Paso Natural Gas Company, 257
Elvidge, Arthur, 41
Emerson, Isaac, 6
encephalitis, 197
encephalitis lethargica, 92–93
Eniwetok, 57
Enna, Sam, 261
Ensenada, Baja California, 57
epilepsy, 82, 89, 92, 116, 117, 134, 226,
    294

Index

Epstein, Harold, 55
  Sadie, 130
Erickson, Theodore, 41
Erlanger, 74
Ervin, Frank, 202–203
Estoril, Portugal, 102, 104
Euston Hotel, 64
Euston Station, 63, 64
Evans, Dennis, 46
  Howard, 90, 125, 195
Exeter Academy, 25
experimental neurosurgery, 201–205
expert witness, 309–319

F

Faculty Club, 323–325
Fahlberg, Wilson, 189
Faillace, Louis, 259, 277
Fairchild, Cameron, 179, 186
Fairmont School, 24
Fannin Bank Building, 264
Farmers Branch, 232
Faulkner, William, 258
Faust, 258
Federal Bureau of Investigation, 80–81, 96–97
Feindel, William, 156
Fellows, Kenneth, 219
Fernandez, Fabio, 138
Fields, Alma, 9, 13, 132, 262–263, 267
  Anna, 2
  Anne, 13, 17, 127, 157, 224, 262
  Arthur, Jr., 6, 11, 13, 15–16, 23, 36–37, 55
  Arthur Mortimer, 1, 2, 7, 10–11, 15, 59
  Ben, 2
  Bette, 54, 61–63, 69, 70, 71, 76, 83, 84–85, 98–99, 100, 101, 120, 126–127, 145, 157, 159, 224–225, 232, 233, 244, 260, 262, 314
  Esther, 2
  Henry, 1
  Janet, 2
  Lenore Gutmann Straus, 1, 4–5, 6, 13–14
  Susan, 127, 157, 224, 262
  W. C., 62

Findlay, Prentice, 129
First Methodist Church Ladies Auxiliary, 134
Fisher, C. Miller, 39–40, 147
Fishman, Marvin, 138
Flanagan, Eileen, 151
  Ralph, 61
Flanz, Bernard, 262
  Ruth, 262
Fleming, Durward, 265
  Jon H., 265–266, 271
  Lamar, 128, 131
  Mrs. Lamar, 128
Fleming Department of Rehabilitation Medicine, 131
Fletcher, Gilbert, 323
Floyd Bennett Field, 60
Flushing, Long Island, 50, 57, 59, 60
Fog, Mogens, 100
Foley, Joseph, 229
Fondren, Mrs., 210
  Walter, 210
Fondren home, 210
Food and Drug Administration, 245
Forbes, Gilbert, 82
Ford Motor Company, 76, 97
Fort Sill, Oklahoma, 56
Foulks, Alma Sicard, 262
  Cathy, 262
  Jay, 262
Fourquean, Tom, 167
Franklin, Charles, 265, 272, 273
Frankowski, Ralph, 244
Fraser, Ian, 47, 55
  N. D., 115
Frazier, Bill, 35
  Shervert, 141, 160–161, 164, 171–172
Fredericksburg, Texas, 337
Free French, 67
Freeman, John, 314
French, John, 83
Friedman, David, 164
Friends School, 6
Frykholm, Dr., 99
Fuchs, Henry, 79
Fuen, Lynn, 329
Fulbright, Crooker, Bates and Jaworski, 283

Fulbright, Worth, 56
Fulton, John, 105
Furlow, Leonard, 107, 108
Futcher, Palmer, 30

G

G.U.M. (Glavny Universalny Magazin), 285
Gabashvili, Professor, 300–301
Gabibov, Gabib, 288
Gaitz, Charles, 260
Galbraith, J. Garber, 154
Galveston, Texas, 87, 194, 195
Gamble, Jess, 89
Gamez, Gilberto, 116, 117
Garrett, Ross, 175–176, 177
Garrott, Helen Holt, 182–183, 184
Gasser, 74
George Ehni Memorial Lecture, 207, 304
George VI, 64, 71, 120
Georgians (U.S.S.R.), 300–301, 302, 305
geriatrics, 211, 215, 239, 273
Ghent, Belgium, 156
Gibbs, Erna, 73
  Frederick, 73, 133
Giddings, Phil, 30
Giddings Studio, 193
Gildea, Edwin, 73
Gildenberg, Philip, 206, 328
Gilley, Elmer, 323
Gilliatt, Roger, 231
Gillies, Wayne, 254
Gilruth, Dr., 267
Girard, Louis, 236–238
Glass, J. Peter, 325, 326, 327, 329
Glen, John, 174
Glenbrook Laboratories Division (Sterling), 245
Glendale, California, 241
Glenn, Annie, 159
  John, 159–160, 267
Globe Insurance, 10
Glysteen, Culver, 295
Gneisenau, 67
Goar, Everett L., 178, 237
Goethe, 258

Goldstein, Murray, 164
Goldstone, Sanford, 152
Gomez, Manuel, 223
Goodpasture, William, 32
Good Samaritan Hospital (Boston), 130
Gordon, Albert, 10–11, 12
  Bessie, 10
  Lynne, 11
  Mack, 10–11
  Mack, Jr., 10
  Paula, 10
  Therése, 10
Gorky-Leninskye, 306–307
Gottschalk, Louis, 29
Gould, Franklin, 2
Graff, James, 65
Grand Hotel (Stockholm), 99
Graves, Robert, 74
Green College, 40
Greene, James, 87, 125, 128, 309
Greenridge, Nancy, 211
Greenwood, James, Jr., 106, 107, 108–109, 131, 136, 137, 142, 143, 194–195, 197
Greer, David, 127
Gregory, William King, 17
Groff, A. Edward, 87
Grossman, Robert, 328
G-suit, 78
Guantanamo Bay, 298
Guerry, Joe, 17
Gurdjian, E. S., 154
Gustilo, Romeo, 116
Gutmann, Joel, 3–4
Guzenko, Igor, 69–70

H

Haas, Felix, 324
Hackerman, Norman, 267
Hackley School, 13
Haden, "Cap," 312
  Cecil, 312–313, 315
  Edgar, 312–313
  Mrs. W. D., 312–313
Halpern, Milton, 315
Halpert, Bela, 195
Hamby, Wallace, 310–311

Index

Hamilton, James, 175
Hamrick, Wendell H., 173–174
Hankamer, Earl, 93
Hannah, David, 218
    Katherine, 218
Hannay, Alan, 309
Hannon, Theodore R., 87, 178
Hardy, George, 269
    Robert, 244
Harriet Lane Pavilion, 247
Harris, Sir Frederick, 99
    Herbert H., 216
Harris County Hospital District, 126, 174
Harris County Medical Society, 173–194, 212, 237, 277
Harris County, Texas, 88, 173, 269, 309, 315–316, 318
Harrison, Frank, 324
Harrower, David, 13
Harvard College, 2, 14, 15, 16, 21, 23, 78
Harvard Divinity School, 203
Harvard Medical School, 21, 22, 28, 39, 55, 78, 87, 110, 147, 150, 171, 172, 191, 202, 203, 229, 248
Harvard Yard, 15
Harvey Cushing Society, 79, 109–110, 165, 304
Harvin, Marie, 190, 191
Hashimoto, Professor, 114
Hass, William K., 240–241, 242, 303
Hauser, Abe, 145–146, 195, 197
Hawkins, Paula, 328
Hayes, Helen, 130
Hay Ling Chau, 115
Haynie, Campbell, 32
    Thomas P., 331, 332
Health Exchange Treaty, 304, 305
Heard, Dow, 313
Heard, J. Griffin, 185
Heights Hospital, 97
Heine, Mr. and Mrs. Fred, 181
Held, Berel, 259
Helsingor, 100
Hendricks, Richard, 262
Henke-Pillot Grocers, 215

Henry, Marshall, 109, 156, 322
Hermann Estate, 124, 128, 246–264
Hermann Eye Center, 251, 254
Hermann Hospital, 84, 87, 89, 90, 91, 92, 93, 109, 124, 125, 128, 174, 177, 192, 234, 237, 246–264, 276, 280, 318, 320, 323, 325, 326
Hermann Park, 122
Hermann Professional Building, 144, 254
Hermitage Museum, 294
Hesse, Duke of, 337
Hesser, Frederick, 74
Hickam, John, 248–249
Hickey, Robert C., 189, 326–327
Hickox, James, 188
High Island, Texas, 310
Hill, C. Stratton, 336–337
    Joan Robinson, 314–316
    John, 314–316
Hill-Burton construction funds, 212, 217
Hiroshima, 71
Histological Typing of Tumours of the Central Nervous System, 337–338
History of Stroke, A, 340
Hitler, Adolf, 18, 38
Hitt, Sam, 191
Ho, Beng, 334
Hodges, Alton, 255
    J. Edward, 178
Hoff, Hebbel, 40, 87, 95, 133, 134, 195
Hogle, George H., 202
Holcombe, Oscar, 84
Holmes, John, 246, 255
Holt, Helen, 179, 182, 183, 187
Hong Kong, 115
Honolulu, Hawaii, 118
Hood, Sir Alexander, 66
Hooks, Charles, 246, 255
Hooten, Ernest A., 16
Hôpital de la Salpétrière, 101
Horace Mann School, 13
Hospital Italiano, 235
Hotel Del Coronado, 55, 58, 62
Hotel National, 290
Hotel Oktiabrskaya, 291

Hotel Rossiya, 282, 283, 284–285, 287
Hotel Ukraine, 297
Houston Academy of Medicine, 111, 177–193
Houston Academy of Medicine-Texas Medical Center Library, 32, 75
Houston Chronicle, 177, 181
Houston Community Chest, 210
Houston Council for Mentally Retarded Children, 208–214
Houston Endowment, 184, 190
Houston-Galveston Neuropsychiatric Society, 195
Houston Independent School District, 208, 211, 218
Houston Lighting and Power Company, 209, 267
Houston Museum of Natural History, 178
Houston Negro Hospital, 320
Houston Neurological Society, 157, 195–207, 230
Houston Neurological Symposium, 73, 157
Houston Police, 203
Houston Speech and Hearing Center, 187, 215–222, 257, see also Speech and Hearing Institute
Houston State Psychiatric Institute, 141
Houston, Texas, 83, 84–85, 86, 88, 146, 172, 195, 233, 279–280
Howe, Cliff, 324, 325
Howell, R. Rodney, 259, 260
Sarah, 214
Hradec Kralóvé, 158
Hsi, Dah, 335
Hubbard, John R., 257
Hudson, Don, 267
Hughes, Barney, 115
Marnie, 115
Hull House, 2
Humble Oil Company, 188
Huntsville, Alabama, 68
Hurricane Carla, 157
Hutchinson, Edward, 283
Hutton, J. Thomas, 307–308
Hyde Park Corner, 98

I
Iannucci, Christopher A., 90, 195
Ibor, Lopez, 105
Idlewild Airport, 159
Iguaçu Falls, 262
Ile de France, 47
Illinois Neuropsychiatric Institute, 72
immunohistochemistry, 338
Imperial Castle, 114
Imperial Valley, California, 61
Indiana University, 225, 229, 243, 248
Information Storage and Neural Control, 73
Institute of Experimental and Clinical Neurology, 300
Institute of Experimental Medicine, 292, 293–294
Institute of Geographical Exploration, 23
Institute of Gerontology, 299
Institute for Interprofessional Study of Health Law, 270
Institute of Medicine, 275
Institute of Neurology (Uruguay), 159
Institute of Neurology (Moscow), 288, 292, 303, 304, 306
Institute of Neurosurgery (Leningrad), 293, 299
Institute for Scientific Investigations, 104–105
Instituto Barraquer, 236
International Conference on Cerebral Circulation, 231
International Congress of Gerontology, 299
International Congress of Neurology, 97, 101, 156, 157
International Congress of Neuropathology, 156
international cooperative research, 303–304, 306–307
International House, 112
International Panel for Multiple Sclerosis, 102–103
International Refugee Committee, 306
intracranial tumors, 198

Index

Irvine, Russell, 66
Irving, Colin, 25
   John, 25
Irwin, Frank, 265, 321
Ithaca College, 221
Iveria Hotel, 300, 302
Iwata, Kinjiro, 114
   Mitsunori, 112, 114
   Zenjuro, 112, 113–114

J

Jachimczyk, Joseph, 315
Jackson, Ira, 194
   Robert, 129
Jacobson, Eugene, 259
Jamail, Joseph, 317
Janeway, Richard, 244
Jasper, Herbert, 42, 43, 51
Java Sea, Battle of the, 36
Javier, Melchor, 115
Jaworski, Leon, 313–314
Jefferson Davis Hospital, 86, 89, 90, 91, 96, 108, 125, 126, 128, 129, 131, 139, 171, 176, 177
Jeffs, James, 63, 64, 98
Jenner, Albert E., Jr., 203
Jerger, James, 218
Jesse H. Jones Library Building, 84, 97, 180–185, 186, 189–190, 192–193, 196, 198, 249, 251
Jex, Harold, 76–77
John F. Kennedy International Airport, 159
John H. Freeman Building, 261, 268
John Sealy Hospital, 310
Johns Hopkins Hospital, 30, 74, 78
Johns Hopkins Medical School, 4, 5, 17, 129, 150, 162, 260
Johns Hopkins University, 5
Johnson, Alfus, 238
   George, 35
   Lady Bird, 9
   Lyndon B., 8, 9, 162, 213
Johnson Space Center, 266–267
Joint Study of Extracranial Arterial Occlusion, 32, 159, 171, 225, 239–240
Jones, Andrew B., 81
   J. Randolph, 92, 131, 195
   Jesse, 181–185
   John, 109
   John T., Jr., 181
   Mrs., 182
   Randy, 109
   T. Duckett, 130
"Jones Essentials," 130
Jones Pavilion, 248
Jordan, Barbara, 214
   Paul, 188
Jorns, C. Forrest, 175
   Cecil, 185, 186
Josey, Jack, 246, 254, 255
Journal of Diseases of the Nervous System, 196
Journal of Neurosurgery, 199
Junior League Children's Clinic, 128
Junior League of Houston, 217

K

Kadrovach, Dan, 192, 246, 247–250, 253–255, 263
   Nancy, 263
Kahn, Eugen, 138–139, 171
Kaiser, Irene, 110
Kakauridze, Alexander, 300–301, 302
Kameyama, Minoru, 112
Kanareikin, Director, 304
Kandel, Edvard Israelovich, 288–290, 304
Kantonsspital, 157
Kantrowitz, Adrian, 169
Kappa Alpha Theta Sorority, 217
Karolinska Institute, 99
Karp, Haskell, 235
Kayton, Bertha, 3
   Caroline Elder, 3
Kegon Falls, 113
Keio University, 112
Keith, William, 310
Kellaway, Peter, 40, 95–96, 133, 134, 135–136, 161, 168, 195
Kelly, Thomas, 71
Kelsey, Mavis, 144, 145
Kelsey-Leary Clinic, 144
Kelsey-Seybold Clinic, 144
Kennedy, Foster, 74–75

Jacqueline, 213
John F., 213
Katherine, 74
Kennedy Foundation Awards, 213
Kennerly, Thomas, 96, 184–185
Kershman, Jack, 43
KGB, 287, 290, 298
Khominsky, Professor, 299
Kiev, 299, 300
Kilgore, Bassett, 225, 229
Kilpatrick, J. Walter, 252–253
King, Robert, 79
Kinkaid School, 131
Kinross-Wright, Vernon John, 87
Kirkendall, Walter, 259
Klanke, Charles W., 178
Kleihues, Paul, 339
Knapp, Rev. Arthur S., 208, 209
  Betty, 209
Knobil, Ernst, 193, 276, 328
Knox, Grace, 126–127
Knudsen, Alfred, 220
Konovalov, Aleksandr Nikolaevich, 282, 283–284, 285, 286, 287, 305, 306
Konrady, Professor, 293
Kopiakovsky, Yuri, 298, 300
Kori, Carl, 80
  Gerti, 80
Krakoff, Irwin, 335
Krayenbühl, Hugo, 157
Kremlin, 287, 307
Kremlin Palace of Congresses, 287
Krieg, Wendell, 92
Kroger Grocery Stores, 215
Kura River, 300
Kyoto, Japan, 114

L

Lac des Deux Montagnes, 26
Lac St. Jean, 26
Lake Chuzenji, 113
Lake Garda, 120
Landau, William, 79
Landry, James, 265
Lapin, I. P., 294
Lassman, Al, 14–15
Latin-American Congress of Neurosurgery, 149–150, 159

Lavadia, Pedro, 117
Law, Tom, 271
Leahy, Frank, 30–31
Leary, William, 144, 145
Leavens, Milam, 322, 325, 326–327, 329, 332, 334
Leavitt, Lewis A., 206
Le Bourget Airport, 100
Le Bourget Field, 12
Ledbetter, Paul, 122
Lee, Robert E., 7
  Ya-Yen, 333
LeMaistre, Charles "Mickey," 9, 219, 226, 228, 232, 233, 251, 256, 325, 326–329, 331–333, 336
Lemak, Leslie, 239
  Noreen A., 239–240, 242, 244, 340
Lenin, Vladimir, 287, 306–307
Leningrad, 291–296, 299
Lenin Mausoleum, 287
Lennox, William, 73, 133
Leopold II, 120
Les Invalides, 101
Leverett House, 15
Levin, William, 324
  Charles, 11
Levy, Irwin "Bud," 81–82, 182
  Moise D., Sr., 111, 179, 183–184, 185, 187–188
  Sarah, 187–188, 218
Lewis, Everett, 174–176, 247
  Kay, 214
  Rosa, 46–47
Lhamon, William, 138–139, 140, 141, 152
Life magazine, 166
light microscopy, 338
Lima, Peru, 258
Lincoln, Abraham, 7–8
Lindbergh, Anne Morrow, 18
  Charles, 11–12, 18
  Charles, Jr., 18
Ling, Thomas, 99, 126, 127
  Mrs. Thomas, 99, 127
Liotta, Domingo, 234–236
Lipscomb, Harry, 260
Lisbon, 101–102

Liske, Edward, 223
Lombardo, Guy, 26
London, England, 46, 51, 52–53, 54, 63–65
London, Ontario, 246
Long, Huey P., 25
Long Beach, California, 55, 59, 60
Lota, Chile, 150
Lou Gehrig's disease, 111, 117, 288
Louisiana State University School of Medicine, 221
Lovett, Malcolm, 127
Lowry, Oliver, 80
Loyola University, 87
Lucas, William, 157
Lucchini, Carlo, 120
Lummis, Frederick R., 185
Lumsden, Bruce, 99
Luria, Aleksandr Romanovich, 285, 286–287, 305, 306, 307–308
Luzon, Philippines, 116
Lynch, Joan, 222
Lyndon B. Johnson Library, 9
Lyons, Champ, 32
   William, 265–266, 269

M

M. D. Anderson Cancer Center, 280, 320–323
M. D. Anderson Foundation, 122, 123, 128, 131, 179, 184, 190, 314
M. D. Anderson Hospital, 89, 144, 169, 174, 187, 218, 232, 238, 248, 251, 323–342
MacArthur, Douglas, 89–90
McArthur, Mary, 130
Macashan Research and Education Trust, 131
McCall, Charles, 226
McCallum, Archie, 68, 70, 72
McCampbell, Paul, 59
McCarthy, Joseph, 96
McCarthy Oil & Gas Company, 310
McCollum, L. F., 219
McCulloch, Warren, 72, 73
Macdonald, Mary, 225
McDowell, Fletcher, 244

McGill University, 48, 69
McGill University Medical School, 40, 87, 124, 133, 293
McGinty, Milton, 142, 143
McGregor, Douglas, 309
McGuire, Thomas H., 91
Machiavelli, Nicolo, 258, 276
Machu Picchu, 149
McLaughlin, Edward, 266
MacLean Hospital, 172
McMaster, Robert, 223
McMillan Hospital, 76
McMillian, Earl, 97, 98
McNaughton, Francis, 38, 41
McNeese, A. G., 324
Macon, Don, 166
Madison County, Texas, 337
Madrid, Spain, 104–105
Magellan, Ferdinand, 118
Magoun, Horace, 83
Magsaysay, Ramon, 115–116
Maimonides, 75
Main Building, 247, 248
Malacañan Palace, 115
Mal de Mer, 48
Mallinckrodt Institute of Radiology, 29
Mallory Institute of Pathology, 75
malpractice, 14, 201
Management of Epileptic Seizures in Children, The, 136
Mankovsky, Professor, 299
Manly, Dixon, 247, 255
Manoir Richelieu, 26
Manulashvili, Michael, 301
Maor, Moshe, 333
March Field, 59
Marcos, Ferdinand, 271–272
   Imelda, 272
Markand, Omkar, 225
Mark IV LSTs, 65–67
Marmell, Howard, 261
Marquard, Russell, 310–311
Mary McArthur Polio Respiratory Center, 130
Massachusetts General Hospital, 18–19, 29, 31, 39, 137, 147, 150

Massachusetts Institute of Technology, 73
Masterson, Harris, 211
Matthews, R., 50
Maulsby, Robert, 225
Maxudov, 304
Mayfair Apartment Hotel, 321
Mayfield, Jack, 185
Mayo Clinic, 80, 138, 141, 144, 145, 172, 175, 223, 224, 225, 231, 243
Meakins, Jonathan, 39
Medical Arts Building, 94, 95
Medical Committee for Human Rights, 202
Medical and Dental Service Bureau, 179
medical ethics, 299
medical lawsuits, 309–319
Medical Towers, 144
Medical University of South Carolina, 249
medico-legal matters, 309–319
Meduna, Ladislas, 73
Melnick, Joseph, 189
Memorial Baptist Hospital, 181, 313
Memorial Hospital System, 280
Memorial Park, 85
Memorial Sloan-Kettering Cancer Center, 325, 326
mental retardation, 208–215
Merchants Development Corporation, 271
Merizo, 118
Merritt, H. Houston, 74, 102, 103, 169
Methodist Hospital, 91, 95, 97, 106–107, 109, 124, 125–126, 131–132, 132–138, 139, 142–143, 146, 152, 161, 165–167, 171, 177, 194, 215, 216, 217, 234, 237, 252, 280, 322
Meyer, John Stirling, 162, 239
  Leopold L., 127, 210–211, 212, 213
Meyers, Christina, 334
  Lewis, 30
Middleton, Harry, 9
Milburn, Charlotte, 9
  Devereux, 9–10
  Grace, 9

Miller, Henry, 197, 205
Ministry of Health, 283–284, 308
Minkowski, Ladislao, 102
Mischer, Walter, Sr., 246, 255
Mississippi Valley Medical Journal, 241
Mithoff, Richard, 316–317
Miyako Hotel, 114
Molins, Mahels, 236
Monaco, Theresa, 211
Moncton, Nova Scotia, 45
Moniz, Antonio Egas, 103–104
Monrad-Krohn, Professor, 102
Montefiore Hospital, 74
Monterrey, Mexico, 272
Montevideo, Uruguay, 159, 227, 263, 310
Montreal General Hospital, 48
Montreal Neurological Institute, 38, 39, 41, 47, 48, 51, 71, 72, 82, 92, 116, 120, 135, 142, 151, 156, 198
Monumental Brewing Company, 6
Moody, Irving, 97
Moore, Conard, 236–237
  Floy J., 91
  John T., 178
Moore-Jones, Dominic, 260
Morente, Lorenzo, 117
Moreton, Robert, 255
Morrison, L. D., 309
Moscow, 290–291, 299
Moscow Art Museum, 285
Moscow Circus, 285
Moscow Institute, 297
Moscow Repertory Theater, 288
Moscow, Russia, 285–286
Moseley, Fred, 48, 70
Moser, Richard, 334
Mother Georgia, 300
motion sickness research, 48–49, 50, 56, 57
Mount Nantai, 113
Moursund, Liz, 98, 99
Moursund, Walter, 90, 97, 98, 143, 174, 178, 191
Moursund, Walter, Jr., 98–99, 191
Mtskheta, Georgia (U.S.S.R.), 301

Index

multiple sclerosis, 88, 102–103, 112
Münchausen syndrome, 30
Murphey, Francis, 154
Murray Bay (La Malbaie), 26
Musée du Louvre, 101

N

Nagoya, Japan, 114
NASA Museum, 286
Nashville General Hospital, 32
Nasser, Abdel Gamal, 111
National Advisory Committee for Psychiatry and Neurology (VA), 171
National Aeronautics and Space Administration, 68, 264, 266
National Archives, 8, 9
National Cancer Institute, 328
National Commission on Causes and Prevention of Violence, 203
National Foundation for Infantile Paralysis, 128, 129
National Garden (Shinjuku Goyen), 112
National Heart Institute, 32, 159, 228, 239, 240
National Heart and Lung Institute, 304
National Hospital (London), 68, 98, 99, 231
National Institute for Neurological Diseases, 164
National Institute of Neurological Diseases and Blindness, 139, 140
National Institute of Neurological Diseases and Stroke, 228
National Institutes of Health, 164, 191, 192, 232, 242, 278, 302
National Library of Medicine, 191
National Museum (Moscow), 287
National Preservation Society, 8
National Science Council of Japan, 112
Nazis, 18
NBC, 166
Neilsen, Johannes, 83
Nelson, Joseph, 324

Neue Presse, 289
Neuman, Alfred, 267
Neural Bases of Violence and Aggression, 205
Neurological Institute, 288, 289
Neurological Institute of The Methodist Hospital, 143
NEUROLOGY, 148
neuro–oncology programs, 329–333, 335
neuropsychopharmacology, 197
Neurosensory Center, 138
New Braunfels, Texas, 337
Newcastle, England, 197
Newport Beach, California, 306
Newton, Berne L., 83, 195
Newton, Kay, 83
New York Neurological Institute, 81, 90, 106, 120, 169
New York Times, The, 148
New York University, 14, 237, 261, 303
New York University Medical School, 240
Nicolay, John, 7
Nieuw Amsterdam, 63
night vision research, 50
Nikko, Japan, 113
Nixon, Richard, 192, 305
Norsworthy Hospital, 131
North, Richard, 225
North Island Naval Air Station, 59, 60
Northwestern University Medical School, 92, 106
North Zulch, Texas, 337

O

Oakland, California, 60
"Oaks, The," 320
Obbens, Eugenie A.M.T., 327, 329
O'Brien, George, 59
Ocean Limited, 47, 70
Odom, Guy, 41
Office of Scientific Naval Research, 56
Ogura, Joseph, 77
Okinaka, Professor, 112, 113
Oklahoma City, Oklahoma, 134
Okujawa, Professor, 302

O'Leary, James, 73, 78, 79, 82, 167–168
Olivecrona, Herbert, 99, 104
Olsen, John Victor, 255, 264, 324
Olson, Stanley W., 138, 139, 141, 163, 174–175, 176, 197
Opton, Edward M., Jr., 202
Order of the British Empire (M.B.E.), 71
Orguin, Cuba, 298
Osler, Lady, 40–41
  William, 4, 5
Osler Society, 40
Osteopathic School, 278
Ottawa, Canada, 54
Oxford University Press, 340

P
pain clinic, 326–327, 329, 332
pain conference, 336–337
Painters' Union, 209
Palace Hatters, 35
Palace Hotel (Copenhagen), 100
Palais de Justice, 120
Panama Canal, 149
PanAmerican Congress of Neurology, 161
Pannill, F. Carter, 89
Pardo, Leopoldo, Jr., 115
Paris, France, 12
Paris Match, 169
Parish, Frank, 247
Park, James, 128
Parkinsonism, 197, 294
Parkland Hospital, 225, 228, 232
Park Plaza Hospital, 250
Parsons, A. M., 185
Pasanauri, Georgia (U.S.S.R.), 301
Paton, David, 237–238
Paul I, 295
Pavlov, Ivan Petrovich, 293
Pavlov Institute of Physiology (Leningrad), 293
Pavlovsk, 295
Peabody Museum, 16
Pearson, Lester, 213
Peck, Anna Fields, 2
  Col. Luke, 2

pediatric neurology, 132–138, 339
Peking Union Medical College, 134
Pendergrass, Mrs., 179
Penfield, Wilder, 41–42, 47, 48, 71, 72, 142, 198
Perevodchikova, Natalia Innekentyevna, 289
Peribonka River, 26
Peron, Juan, 235
Perry, John H., 91, 195
  Malcolm, 229
Persantine, 245
personal injury lawsuits, 310
Peters, Lester, 333
Peterson, John, 43
  Lysle, 265
Petr, Rudolf, 119, 158
Petrovsky, Boris Mikhailovich, 297
phantom limb pain, 171
Phi Beta Kappa, 23
Philippine National Bank, 272
Philpot, Newell, 325
Phoenix, Arizona, 224
Physicians Referral Service, 323
Pieper, Sam, 117–118
Pierson, Earl, 214
  Wendell, 214
Pioneer Palace, 300
Pittman, James, 175–176
Pitts, Walter, 73
Poblete, Reinaldo, 150
Pointe St. Charles, 37
Polenov Institute of Neurosurgery, 291, 292, 294
polio, 128–130
Politburo, 297
Pollard, Claude, Jr., 195, 309
Ponce, Juan Franco, 258
Poppen, James, 198
Porter, Helen, 80, 81, 98, 99
Posner, Jerome, 325
Poyner, Herbert, 87
Prague, Czechoslovakia, 158
Presbyterian Hospital of Dallas, 226–227, 232
Price Brothers Lumber Company, 26

Index 361

Primary Brain Tumors — A Review of Histologic Classification, 339
Prince Eugen, 67
Prince, The, 258
Princeton, New Jersey, 243
prisoners, 201–205
Prison Health Committee, Medical Committee for Human Rights, 201–202
Proceedings of the Mayo Clinic, 80
Professional Liability Committee, 317–319
Program on Aging, U.T., 280
Progressive Labor Party, 204
Provencher, Jimmy, 117
Pruitt, Raymond D., 162–163, 164
Psychiatric Institute, 141
Puchkov, Yuri, 282
Pudenz, Robert, 38
Pudenz valve, 38
Punta del Este, Uruguay, 263
Purkinje, Jan, 158
Pushkin, 294–295

Q
Quebec City, Quebec, 25, 48
Queen Victoria, 46, 47
Quin, Bishop Clinton S., 209–210
  Mrs. Clinton S., 209–210

R
radiation therapy, 327, 330
Radziwill, Lee, 213
Ramon y Cajal, Santiago, 104
Raney, Aidan, 83
Rasmussen, Theodore, 41
Raven, Harry, 17
Reader's Digest, 152
Reconstruction Finance Corporation, 181
Recto, Ofelia, 272
  Vincente, 271–272
Redburn, Dianna, 206
Red Rose, 47
Red Square, 287
Reece, Charles, 174
Regional Medical Program of Texas, 226, 227, 228, 232

rehabilitation, 205–206
Resettlement Administration, 24, 25
Reyes, Victor, 116
rheumatic fever, 130
Rhind, John A., 55–56, 63, 70–71
Ribble, John, 277
Rice, Alexander Hamilton, 22–23
  Eleanor Widener, 22–23
Rice Institute, 234, 309
Rice University, 84, 143, 149, 234, 246, 267
Richardson, C. R. "Bob," 251–252
Richelieu River, 25
Rich Farm, 130
Richmond (Texas) State School, 214
Riley, William, 214
Rindge Technical High School, 2
Riskin, Leonard, 269
Ritchie, Bette, 48
  W. Lloyd, 48, 124
Riverdale School, 12
River Oaks Country Club, 257
Robb, J. Preston, 72, 155
Roberts, Josie, 131–132, 142–143
  Richard, 312–313
Robertson, Corbin, 246–247, 250, 255
  Robert C. L., 106, 108–109, 131, 195, 197
Robertson Pavilion, 124, 247, 248
Robinson, Ash, 314–316
  Hampton C., 186, 187, 212
  Rhea, 314–316
  William, 3
Robison, Alan, 259
Rochester, Minnesota, 141
Rockefeller Foundation, 112
Rockwell, James W., 215
Rockwell International, 267
Rodgers, Rodney, 247, 248
Rogers, Frank, 99, 191–192
Rome, Italy, 157
Romodanov, Andrei Petrovich, 297, 299
Roosevelt, Franklin D., 18, 23, 44, 62
  Franklin Delano, Jr., 23
  Theodore, 8, 11
Roosevelt Field, 11, 18

Roosevelt Hospital, 241, 271
Roosevelt Hotel, 26
Rorke, Lucy, 339
Ross, Dudley, 38
Rote, Tobin, 143
Rourke, Anthony, 175
Rouse's Point, New York, 25
Royal Air Force, 66
Royal Air Force Club, 63, 64
Royal Air Force Experimental Station, 50
Royal Army Medical College, 65
Royal Army Medical Corps, 49, 51, 66
Royal Canadian Air Force, 83
Royal Canadian Army Medical Corps, 52
Royal Canadian Army Volunteer Reserve, 38
Royal Canadian Navy, 39, 43, 44, 47, 51, 56, 72, 155
Royal Commonwealth Society, 53
Royal Empire Society, 53, 55
Royal Marines, 55
Royal Navy, 44, 47, 51, 66, 67, 68
Royal New Zealand Navy, 55, 63
Royal Society, 50
Royal Victoria Hospital, 38, 39, 48, 262, 325
Royal York Hotel, 69
Royce, Thomas, 188
Roy and Lillie Cullen Building, 86, 95, 179
Rudnick, Andrew, 269
Rudyak, Konstantin, 297, 299
Ruiz, Richard, 193, 237, 247, 251, 254
Russell, William O., 322
Russian Federated Soviet Socialist Republics, 294
Rutgers University, 191
Ryan, Bill, 247
    Frank, 55, 56–57, 58

S
Sahs, Adolph L., 199
St. Albans, New York, 73
St. Anthony Center, 132, 238–240, 253, 260, 261, 323, 325
St. Francis Episcopal Church, 96, 252

St. John's, New Brunswick, 45
St. Joseph Hospital, 238, 239
St. Joseph's Infirmary, 92
St. Lawrence River, 25, 68
St. Lawrence waterway, 68
St. Louis Children's Hospital, 82, 128, 209
St. Louis, Missouri, 77, 80, 82, 167, 225
St. Louis Post Dispatch, 168
St. Luke's Episcopal Hospital, 111, 144, 252–253, 264
St. Luke's Hospital, 155, 235, 280
St. Luke's Methodist Church, 265
St. Luke's Presbyterian Medical Center, 259
St. Philip's Anglican Church, 48
St. Thomas' Hospital (London), 205
Sakarova, Dr., 303
Salazar, Antonio, 103
Salmon, George, 127, 128
    Harold, 24
Salzburg, Austria, 231
Salzburg Conference on Cerebral Circulation, 303
Sammons, James, 188
Sampson, Whitney, 237
San Angelo, Texas, 141, 172
Sandburg, Carl, 8
San Diego, California, 55–56
Santa Fe Chief, 62
Santiago, Chile, 149
Santiago, Cuba, 298
Santo Tomas University, 116
Sargent, William, 205
Saslow, George, 81
Saucier, Jean, 43
Savoy Hotel, 156
Scandinavian Airlines, 303
Schachtel, Hyman Judah, 203, 204
Schaltenbrand, Georg, 102
Scheinberg, Peritz, 223
Scheithauer, Berndt, 339
Schmidt, Richard, 161–162
Schofield, James R., 162–163
Schroeder, Henry, 78
Schuleman, Israel H., 90, 322–323

Schwab, Robert, 133
Scientific Research Institute of Neurosurgery, 297
Scott, John S., 140
Sears-Roebuck, 86, 123, 175
Seizure Clinic, 128
Seradjishvili, Professor, 301–302
Serafimerlasserettet, 99
Serbinenko, Feodor A., 284, 305
Severinghaus, Ara, 110
Seybold, Frances, 145
  William, 144–145
Shaknovich, A., 284
Shamrock Hilton Hotel, 77, 84, 268
Shapiro, Philip, 201–203
Sharkey, Paul C., 140
Sharpstown Hospital, 315
Shaw, Margery, 269, 270
Shenpovari Mountains, 301
Sheremetyevo Airport, 307
Sherry, Sol, 240
Shmidt, Evgeny Vladimirovich, 281, 288, 289, 303, 304, 305, 308
shock therapy, 73
Shostakovich, Dimitri, 308
Shriner's Hospital for Crippled Children, 91, 124, 134
Shullenberger, C. C., 324
Shustin, Nikolai Andreevich, 291, 292, 294–295
Siegler, Howard M., 228, 314
  Mrs. Howard, 314
Sigua, Professor, 300–301, 302
Sisters of Charity of the Incarnate Word, 238
Sisters of the Sacred Heart of the Incarnate Word, 260
Skewes, Eduardo, 150
Skogland, John, 87, 180, 195
Smirnov, Vladimir, 289, 304, 306
Smith, Benjamin F., 178
  Burt B., 180
  Camille, 127
  Gerald L. K., 2
  Jackson, 86–87
  Kline and French Laboratories, 49
  Preston, 233, 247
  R. E. "Bob," 137
  Vivian, 137
Smolik, Edmund, 158
Smythe, Cheves, 189, 190–191, 192, 201, 202, 205, 249–261, 263–264, 276
  Polly, 263
Snedeker, Bob, 17
Snodgrass, Sam, 194
Snow, Robbie, 261
Society of Neurology and Psychiatry, 116
Soller, William, 245
Sorel, Quebec, 25
South Baltimore General Hospital, 14
Southern Neurosurgical Society, 196
Southwestern University, 265
Southwest Memorial, 280
Southwest Polio Respiratory Center, 129
Soviet Consulate (England), 304
Soviet Ministry of Health, 281, 282
Soviet Pavilion, 295
Spanish Neurological Society, 105
speech and hearing, 215–222
Speech and Hearing Institute, 215–222, 255, 270
Spellman, Cardinal, 116
Spencer, Walter, 94
  William, 129, 130, 165
Spirit of St. Louis, 11
Sprague, Charles, 224, 228, 230, 231, 232, 233, 324
Stallones, Reuel, 255
Stanford University, 202
Stanley Cobb Laboratories for Psychiatric Research, 202
Stansbury, Bill, 77
  Rosemary, 77
State Board of Health, 212–213
State Department, 306
State University of New York, 89
State University of New York Medical School, 79, 191
Steinberger, Anna, 252
  Emil, 252
Stendahl, Krister, 203

Stephens, Winston B., 24
Sterling, Walter, 246–247, 255
Sterling Drug Incorporated, 243, 245
Stevens, James, 136
Stevenson, Adlai, 213
Stewart, Ross, 219
Stockholm, Sweden, 99
Stonybrook, 191
Stovall, Thomas, 313
Straus, Ada, 41
  Louis, 5, 7
Straus, Pauline Gutmann, 3
Straus, Philip, 7, 9
Straus, William L., Jr., 5, 17
Straus, William Levi, 5–6
Stritch School of Medicine, 87
STROKE, 244, 245, 340
stroke conference, 340
Stroke Registry, 226, 227–228
stroke research, 147–149, 154–155, 162, 206, 226–233, 236, 239, 240–245, 258, 289, 303
Stroke Treatment Demonstration Unit, 227
Students for a Democratic Society, 203–204
Suez Canal, 111
Sul Ross University, 252
Surratt, John, 7
  Mary, 7
Sutherland, W. D., 215, 216
Sweet, William H., 200, 202, 203

T

Tarague Beach, 117
Tarkington, R. L. (Bob), 34–35
Tarrytown, New York, 13
Tashkent, Uzbek Soviet Republic, 306
Taub, Ben, 126, 127, 130
Taylor, Fred, 211, 214
Taylor, H. Grant, 180, 238, 248, 255, 323
Tbilisi, Georgia, U.S.S.R., 300
Terry, Francisco Belaunde, 258
Tetlov, Dr., 293
Texas A&M University, 227, 278
Texas Children's Foundation, 127
Texas Children's Hospital, 127, 138, 210, 213, 280

Texas Institute for Rehabilitation and Research, 131, 165, 218
Texas Legislature, 277–278
Texas Medical Association (TMA), 222–223
Texas Medical Center, 83–84, 86: access to, 279–280; concept of, 137; development of, 89, 341; former layout of, 143–144; patients of, 280; proposed, 122–124; rehabilitation unit of, 131
Texas Medical Center, Inc., 179
Texas Medicine, 227
Texas Neurological Society, 223
Texas Research Institute of Mental Sciences, 139, 334
Texas Southern University, 203
Texas Tech University, 278
Texas Tech University School of Medicine, 276
Texas Wesleyan College, 271
Texas Woman's University-Houston Center, 255
Textbook of Neurology, 156
Textbook of Physiology, 48
Thompson, Jesse, 228–229
  Thomas, 316
Thorndike Memorial Clinic, 102
Thurston, Don, 82
  Jean, 82
Tijuana, Mexico, 56
Tilden, William (Bill), 59
TIME magazine, 169
Titanic, 22
Tivoli Garden, 100
Tokyo, Japan, 112–113
Tosteson, Dan, 172
Trans Canada Airline, 37, 98
Transderm Scop, 49
Trauma Center, 248
Trelles, Oscar, 105
Trinity Episcopal Church, 208
Trohatchev, Aleksandr, 292–293
Trotsky, Leon, 307
Truman, Harry, 89
Tulane University, 146
Tulane University School of Medicine, 109

Index

Tunney, Gene, 14
Turkel, Stanley, 76, 77
Turner, Roscoe, 57, 66
Tuttle, L.L.D. "Dewey," 132, 178
  Robert, 252, 265, 269, 273, 276
21st Field Ambulance, 52
22nd Field Ambulance Unit, 38
Tyler, David, 56–57

U

U.S. Public Health Service, 227, 278
Ugrumov, Veniamin Mikhailovich, 292
Umatac, 118
Union Memorial Hospital, 1
United Automobile Workers, 55
United Fund, 210, 217, 220
United Nations, 306
United States-Soviet Health Exchange Program, 281
U.S. Amphibious Forces, 54, 55–56, 57, 131
U.S. Naval Academy, 23, 36
U.S. Naval Hospital, 36–37, 88, 106
U.S. Naval Institute, 36
U.S. Navy, 44
U.S. Public Health Service, 111, 117
United Way, 210, 217
University of Alabama, 32, 189, 229
University of Baghdad, 148
University of California, 236
University of California at Davis, 306
University of California at Los Angeles, 83
University of California Medical School, 202
University of Cambridge, 68
University of Cincinnati, 220
University City, 77
University of Colorado Medical School, 136, 140, 191
University of Concepcion, 150
University of the Far East, 116
University of Florida Health Sciences Center, 161
University of Houston, 203, 211, 218, 269, 334
University of Houston at Clear Lake, 267
University of Illinois College of Medicine, 138
University of Iowa, 164, 199
University of London School of Agriculture, 80
University of Miami, Florida, 223
University of Michigan, 90
University of Minnesota, 307, 334
University of Mississippi, 91
University of Montevideo, 159
University of Newcastle-upon-Tyne, 205
University of Oklahoma School of Medicine, 86
University of the Philippines, 116
University of Pittsburgh, 259, 276
University of Puerto Rico, 56
University of Southern California, 257
University of Tennessee, 168
University of Texas at Austin, 200
University of Texas Board of Regents, 265, 271, 277, 321, 324
University of Texas Dental Branch, 125, 187, 255, 324
University of Texas Family Practice Program, 280
University of Texas Graduate School of Biomedical Sciences, 219–222, 232, 238, 255, 269, 270, 323
University of Texas Health Science Center (Dallas), 224, 324
University of Texas Health Science Center (Houston), 215, 221, 222, 264, 269–280, 317, 324, 327, 335, 340
University of Texas Health Science Center (San Antonio), 324
University of Texas Medical Branch, 87, 90, 144, 191, 251, 268, 324, 334
University of Texas Medical School, 40, 55, 129, 189, 192, 193, 201, 206, 233–234, 238, 239, 246–280, 323, 325, 328, 333, 334
University of Texas Medical School at San Antonio, 89, 251

University of Texas Mental Science Institute, 139
University of Texas Police, 202, 205
University of Texas School of Allied Health Sciences, 255
University of Texas School of Public Health, 242, 255, 340
University of Texas Southwestern Medical School, 199, 214, 224, 227, 229, 230
University of Texas System, 256
University of Texas System Cancer Center, 189
University of Tokyo Hospital, 112
University of Toronto, 124
University of Washington, 139
University of Washington Medical School, 82
University of Western Ontario, 244, 246
University of Wisconsin, 168
University of Zürich, 157
Up from the Ape, 16
USS *Concord*, 36
Utterback, Robert, 168

V
V. Luna General Hospital (Army), 117
V-1 rockets, 67
V-2 rockets, 67
Vallee, Rudy, 19
Vance, Carol, 315
Vanderbilt Hall, 22
Vanderbilt Hospital, 32
Vanderbilt University Medical School, 31–32
van der Eecken, Henri, 156
van Eys, Jan, 334
van Haareveld, Dr., 56
Van Horn, Gage, 259–260, 261
van Tassel, Pamela, 333
vascular surgery, 153–155, 302
Vasin, Nikolai, 284
Venukovo Airport, 291
Veterans Administration Hospital (Brockton, Massachusetts), 2
Veterans Administration Hospital (Houston), 29, 86, 88, 89–90, 91, 106, 125, 139, 146, 171, 177, 270, 322
Veterans Administration Medical Center in New Orleans, 192
Victoria Hospital, 246
Victoria Pier, 25
Vineberg, Arthur, 38
violence, studies on, 200–205
Volchek, Galina, 288
von Braun, Werner, 67
von Storch, Theodore, 74

W
Waikiki Beach, 118
Waites, Lucius, 91
Wakesaka, Dr., 114
Waldron, George, 125, 181
Walker, A. Earl, 150, 162
  E. Don, 275
  Jimmy, 12
Wall, John, 145
Walsh, Senator, 37
Walshe, Francis, 99, 103
Walter, Paul J., 90, 125, 195
Walton, John, 40
War Assets Administration, 320
Ward, Arthur, 82
Warren Commission, 203
Warwick Hotel, 179
Washington Redskins, 143
Washington University, 75, 77, 88, 110, 164, 322
Washington University Affiliated Hospitals, 132
Washington University School of Medicine, 73, 78, 79–80, 81
Watts, Larry, 270, 275
Wayne State University, 162, 239, 243
Wayne State University Medical School, 240
Weatherford, Texas, 324
Webber, C. Frank, 277
Webster, A. Ross, 56
Webster, Margaret, 56
Weibel, Jorge, 149, 156
Weiss, Harvey, 240, 241
Welch, Louie, 267
Werlein, Presley, 257

Index

Westminster Abbey, 52
Westminster School, 52
West University, 84
Whalen, Grover, 12
Wheeler, Jack, 211
White, Ed, 324
    Elizabeth, 32
Whitman, Charles Joseph, 200
Whittington, Horace, 85
    Horace, Jr., 85
Widener, Eleanor Elkins, 22–23
    Harry, 22–23
Widener Library, 19, 22–23
Wilford Hall Air Force Hospital, 137, 159
Wilkerson, Edward (Ted), 89
Wilkey, Malcomb, 310
Williams, Denis, 198
William S. Fields Lecture in Neurology, 207
William S. Fields Neurosciences Library, 193
Williford, Louis E., 185
Willimack, Mrs. Dale, 223
Willis, Sir Thomas, 156
    William, 230
Williston, C. Lincoln, 222
Wilmer Eye Institute at Johns Hopkins Hospital, 237
Wilson, Woodrow, 9
Wilson's disease, 294
Wimpee, James, 141, 172
Windsor, Duke and Duchess of, 64
Windsor, Ontario, 56, 76
Winn, Toddie Lee, 226–227
Wittingham, Sir Harold, 66
Wolf, Pauline Sterne, 129
Wolf Estate, 129
Wolf Home, 129–131
Women's Auxiliary, 217
Women's Royal Naval Service, 63
Wood, Joe G., 193, 206, 251

Wood, W. Barry, 30, 78
Woodmere Academy, 9, 10, 12, 24
Woodmere, Long Island, 9
Woolsey, Clinton, 167–168
Wootters, John H., 185
Workers Action Movement, 204
World According to Garp, The, 25
World Congress of Neurological Sciences, 118–120, 158
World Health Organization, 337–338, 339
World Petroleum Congress, 283
World's Fair, 295
Wortham, Gus, 257
    Mrs. Gus, 216, 257
Wright Institute, 202
Wylie, E. J. "Jack," 229, 236

Y
Yasargil, Gazi, 157
Yale University, 105, 138
Yale University Medical School, 83
Yates, Charles, Jr., 260
Yatsu, Frank, 334
York, Byron P., 173
Youmans, John, 306
Young, Arthur, 43
Yung, W. K. Alfred, 327, 329

Z
Zabotin, Nikolai Nikolayevich, 69–70
Zagorsk, Russia, 287
Zale, Donald, 227
Zarakov, Isadore "Izzy," 14
Zedginidze, Professor, 302
Zeller, Robert, 138
Zimmerman, Stuart, 324
Zion, Thomas, 137
Zulch, Jack, 337
Zülch, Julius, 337
    Klaus Joachim, 156, 337–338, 339
Zürich, Switzerland, 156–157, 339–340